Robert Geffner, PhD
Susan B. Sorenson, PhD
Paula K. Lundberg-Love, PhD
Editors

Violence and Sexual Abuse at Home: Current Issues in Spousal Battering and Child Maltreatment

Pre-publication REVIEWS, COMMENTARIES, EVALUATIONS . . .

This state-of-the-art collection will more than meet the needs of clinicians, researchers, educators, and advocates alike. The Editors have distilled the important questions at the cutting edge of the field of violence studies, and have brought rigor, balance and moral fortitude to the search for answers.

Virginia Goldner, PhD
Co-Director
Gender and Violence Project
Senior Faculty
Ackerman Institute for Family Therapy

More pre-publication
REVIEWS, COMMENTARIES, EVALUATIONS . . .

This is an exciting new addition to the field of family violence. This important compilation of chapters would be especially critically important to any therapist. All therapists today need to be aware of the social, psychological and health effects of all kinds of family violence, and this volume combines it all under one cover.

This important new volume addresses some of the therapeutic controversies related to family violence head-on, and the authors are not afraid to take a stand on the issues. What is noteworthy and laudable is that these stands are taken based on careful reviews and critiques of existing research rather than only ideology.

The editors have brought together an important compilation of writings of many of the leaders across the breadth of family violence. The contributions by such authors as Pagelow and Courtois are sure to become classics. There are also articles by relative newcomers such as Sorenson and Rossman and Rosenberg who are rapidly adding important original research insights to the field.

The insights offered by this new book on family violence for both therapists and researchers are exciting. One especially important addition to the field is the overview and integration of the new neuro-physiological research into a biopsychosocial model of relationship aggression that should be used by both clinicians and scientists if they are to conduct the complex research and treatment needed in family violence today.

The specific treatment models, overviews and detailed modality descriptions provided by this volume are extremely valuable, especially in the area of sexual abuse and the children of battered women. What is unusual and particularly valuable is that the treatment guidelines are based on careful research reviews in addition to intervention models.

Clinicians in several fields will find this book invaluable. It combines research reviews with discussions of critical clinical issues such as ethical imperatives and specific treatment guidelines and models across all forms of spouse and child abuse.

Jacquelyn Campbell, PhD, RN, FAAN
Anna D. Wolf Endowed Professor
Johns Hopkins University
School of Nursing

HMTP

Haworth Maltreatment and Trauma Press
An Imprint of The Haworth Press, Inc.

Violence and Sexual Abuse at Home: Current Issues in Spousal Battering and Child Maltreatment

The *Aggression, Maltreatment & Trauma* Series:

Senior Editor: Robert Geffner, PhD, Founder/President, Family Violence & Sexual Assault Institute, Tyler, Texas

Violence and Sexual Abuse at Home: Current Issues in Spousal Battering and Child Maltreatment, edited by Robert Geffner, PhD, Susan B. Sorenson, PhD, and Paula K. Lundberg-Love, PhD

These books were published simultaneously as special thematic issues of the *Journal of Aggression, Maltreatment & Trauma* and are available bound separately. For further information, call 1-800-HAWORTH (outside US/Canada: 607-722-5857), Fax 1-800-895-0582 (outside US/Canada: 607-771-0012) or e-mail getinfo@haworth.com

Violence and Sexual Abuse at Home: Current Issues in Spousal Battering and Child Maltreatment

Robert Geffner, PhD
Susan B. Sorenson, PhD
Paula K. Lundberg-Love, PhD
Editors

Haworth Maltreatment & Trauma Press
An Imprint of
The Haworth Press, Inc.
New York • London

Published by

Haworth Maltreatment & Trauma Press, 10 Alice Street, Binghamton, NY 13904-1580 USA

Haworth Maltreatment & Trauma Press is an imprint of The Haworth Press, Inc., 10 Alice Street, Binghamton, NY 13904-1580 USA.

Violence and Sexual Abuse at Home: Current Issues in Spousal Battering and Child Maltreatment has also been published as *Journal of Aggression, Maltreatment & Trauma,* Volume 1, Number 1 (#1) 1997.

The development, preparation, and publication of this work has been undertaken with great care. However, the publisher, employees, editors, and agents of The Haworth Press and all imprints of The Haworth Press, Inc., including The Haworth Medical Press and Pharmaceutical Products Press, are not responsible for any errors contained herein or for consequences that may ensue from use of materials or information contained in this work. Opinions expressed by the author(s) are not necessarily those of The Haworth Press, Inc.

Cover design by Thomas J. Mayshock Jr.

Library of Congress Cataloging-in-Publication Data

Violence and sexual abuse at home : current issues in spousal battering and child maltreatment / Robert Geffner, Susan B. Sorenson, Paula K. Lundberg-Love, editors.
    p. cm.
    Includes bibliographical references and index.
    ISBN 0-7890-0329-5 (alk. paper).–ISBN 1-56024-681-2 (alk. paper)
    1. Family violence. 2. Family violence–Treatment. 3. Victims of family violence–Rehabilitation. I. Geffner, Robert. II. Sorenson, Susan B. III. Lundberg-Love, Paula K.
RC569.5.F3V564 1997
616.85'822–dc21   97-2798
                                                             CIP

INDEXING & ABSTRACTING

Contributions to this publication are selectively indexed or abstracted in print, electronic, online, or CD-ROM version(s) of the reference tools and information services listed below. This list is current as of the copyright date of this publication. See the end of this section for additional notes.

- *Cambridge Scientific Abstracts, Risk Abstracts*, 7200 Wisconsin Avenue #601, Bethesda, MD 20814

- *CNPIEC Reference Guide: Chinese National Directory of Foreign Periodicals*, P.O. Box 88, Beijing, People's Republic of China

- *Criminal Justice Abstracts,* Willow Tree Press, 15 Washington Street, 4th Floor, Newark, NJ 07102

- *Criminology, Penology and Police Science Abstracts,* Kugler Publications, P. O. Box 11188, 1001 GD Amsterdam, The Netherlands

- *Digest of Neurology and Psychiatry,* The Institute of Living, 400 Washington Street, Hartford, CT 06106

- *Family Studies Database (online and CD/ROM),* National Information Services Corporation, 306 East Baltimore Pike, 2nd Floor, Media, PA 19063

- *Index to Periodical Articles Related to Law,* University of Texas, 727 East 26th Street, Austin, TX 78705

- *Mental Health Abstracts (online through DIALOG),* IFI/Plenum Data Company, 3202 Kirkwood Highway, Wilmington, DE 19808

- *Psychiatric Rehabilitation Journal,* 930 Commonwealth Avenue, Boston, MA 02215

- *Published International Literature on Traumatic Stress (The PILOTS Database),* National Center for Post-Traumatic Stress Disorder (116D), VA Medical Center, White River Junction, VT 05009

(continued)

SPECIAL BIBLIOGRAPHIC NOTES

related to special journal issues (separates)
and indexing/abstracting

- ☐ indexing/abstracting services in this list will also cover material in any "separate" that is co-published simultaneously with Haworth's special thematic journal issue or DocuSerial. Indexing/abstracting usually covers material at the article/chapter level.

- ☐ monographic co-editions are intended for either non-subscribers or libraries which intend to purchase a second copy for their circulating collections.

- ☐ monographic co-editions are reported to all jobbers/wholesalers/approval plans. The source journal is listed as the "series" to assist the prevention of duplicate purchasing in the same manner utilized for books-in-series.

- ☐ to facilitate user/access services all indexing/abstracting services are encouraged to utilize the co-indexing entry note indicated at the bottom of the first page of each article/chapter/contribution.

- ☐ this is intended to assist a library user of any reference tool (whether print, electronic, online, or CD-ROM) to locate the monographic version if the library has purchased this version but not a subscription to the source journal.

- ☐ individual articles/chapters in any Haworth publication are also available through the Haworth Document Delivery Services (HDDS).

Violence and Sexual Abuse at Home: Current Issues in Spousal Battering and Child Maltreatment

CONTENTS

SEXUALLY MALTREATED CHILDREN, INCEST
SURVIVORS, AND INCEST OFFENDERS:
ISSUES, INTERVENTIONS, AND RESEARCH

ABOUT THE EDITORS

Robert Geffner, PhD, is Founder and President of the Family Violence and Sexual Assault Institute in Tyler, and former Professor of Psychology at the University of Texas at Tyler. A licensed psychologist and marriage, family, and child counselor, he is Clinical Director of Counseling, Testing, and Psychiatric Services in Tyler, Texas. He is a founding member and former President of the Board of the East Texas Crisis Center and Shelter for Battered Women & Their Children. Dr. Geffner is a member of the American Psychological Association, the American Association for Marriage and Family Therapy, the American Professional Society on Abuse of Children, the International Society for Traumatic Stress Studies, the National Academy of Neuropsychologists, the American Family Therapy Academy, and several other related organizations. He is an adjunct faculty member of the National Judicial College. In addition to editing several international journals, he is Editor-in-Chief for Haworth Maltreatment & Trauma Press. He has authored numerous books, chapters, and articles. He has also served as a consultant to several national and state agencies, and has served on numerous national and state committees concerning family violence and child abuse.

Susan B. Sorenson, PhD, is Professor in Residence at the UCLA School of Public Health. A specialist in violence and injury prevention, she has taught a graduate-level course on family and sexual violence since 1986. She has published numerous articles on homicide, suicide, sexual assault, battering, and child abuse, as well as research on psychiatric epidemiology. In 1991, Dr. Sorenson co-founded the Violence Prevention Coalition of Greater Los Angeles. She was a member of the National Research Council panel on Research on Violence Against Women and serves on the advisory boards of several local organizations.

Paula Lundberg-Love, PhD, is Professor of Psychology at the University of Texas at Tyler and an adjunct faculty member of the Family Practice Residency Program at the University of Texas Health Center at Tyler. She is a licensed psychological associate and licensed chemical dependency counselor at Counseling, Testing and Psychiatric Services. Also a research consultant for the Family Violence and Sexual Assault Institute in Tyler, she is a member of the editorial board for the *Journal of Child Sexual Abuse*. Recently, she created a children's group treatment program for recovery from sexual abuse called "Tall Trees" to provide services for children from indigent families in Tyler.

ABOUT THE CONTRIBUTORS

Judith L. Alpert, PhD, is Professor in the Doctoral Programs in School Psychology and Child/School Psychology at New York University, and faculty member and supervisor at NYU Postdoctoral Program in Psychoanalysis and Psychotherapy. She is the author of numerous articles and the editor of four books, including her recent edited book, *Sexual Abuse Recalled: Treating Trauma in the Era of the Recovered Memory Debate*, published by Jason Aronson Publishers. Dr. Alpert was Co-Chair of the American Psychological Association's Working Group on Evaluation of Memories of Childhood Abuse. She has a private practice in psychoanalysis and psychotherapy in New York City.

Robert T. Ammerman, PhD, is Director, Mental Health Programs in Childhood Disabilities, Allegheny General Hospital, and Associate Professor of Psychiatry and Neurosurgery at MCP◆Hahnemann School of Medicine, Allegheny University of the Health Sciences. He has published extensively in the area of child abuse and neglect, in general, and in the maltreatment of children with disabilities, in particular. He is the recipient of grants from the National Institute on Disabilities and Rehabilitation Research and the Vira I. Heinz Endowment for research on the causes, treatment, and prevention of abuse and neglect in children with disabilities. He is co-editor of four books on family violence: *Children at Risk* (1990), *Treatment of Family Violence* (1990), *Case Studies in Family Violence* (1991), and *Assessment of Family Violence* (1992). He serves on the editorial boards of the *Journal of Family Violence* (for which he is also Book Review Editor), *Behavior Modification*, and *Aggression and Violent Behavior.*

Sheldon Benjamin, MD, is Associate Professor of Psychiatry and Neurology at the University of Massachusetts Medical School in Worcester, Director of Neuropsychiatry and Neurology, and Director of Psychiatric Education and Training. He is board certified in Psychiatry and Neurology. Dr. Benjamin's clinical and research interests include behavioral and psychiatric manifestations of neurologic disease, functional imaging, and movement disorders.

George S. Brown, PhD, received his doctorate in Counseling Psychology from Duke University. His areas of expertise include chronic patients, substance abuse, mood disorders, and impulse disorders. Since 1993, he has been Director of Clinical Programs for Human Affairs International. Presently, he heads their project to develop a Clinical Information System to link practitioners and facilities with advanced information and communications technology.

Joanne L. Brown, PhD, received her doctorate in Counseling Psychology from the University of Utah. Currently, she is a licensed psychologist and maintains a private psychotherapy practice for children, adults, couples, and families, specializing in family violence and mood disorders. She also provides consultation and training to a community agency that treats family violence. Prior work includes appointments at the University of Utah and 10 years with an agency dedicated to the prevention and treatment of child sexual abuse, and the treatment of sexual abuse victims, survivors, and offenders.

Nancyann N. Cervantes, PhD, JD, is a clinical psychologist who received her PhD from Emory University and her JD from the University of Arizona School of Law. She has a specialty in child and family psychology. Dr. Cervantes has served on several psychological ethics committees and has taught ethics and therapist responsibility at the university level. Currently, she is in private practice in Reno, Nevada. She is Co-Chair of the Education and Training Committee for Washoe County Missing and Exploited Children Comprehensive Action Program (M-CAP). Her presentations and publications have been in the areas of ethics, mental health services and children and families.

Christine A. Courtois, PhD, is a psychologist in private practice in Washington, D.C., and Clinical Director, The CENTER: Post-traumatic & Dissociative Disorder Program, The Psychiatric Institute of Washington, Washington, D.C. She conducts workshops nationally and internationally on the treatment of incest and other forms of sexual assault. She is the author of *Healing the Incest Wound: Adult Survivors in Therapy* (1988) and *Adult Survivors of Child Sexual Abuse*, a workshop model (1993), and has published numerous articles and chapters. She is currently under contract with W. W. Norton for a new book on treatment guidelines with attention to delayed memory issues. Dr. Courtois recently served as an appointed member to the American Psychological Association (APA) Working Group on the Investigation of Memories of Childhood Abuse and on the APA Presidential Task Force on Family Violence.

Robert Geffner, PhD, is Founder and President of the Family Violence and Sexual Assault Institute located in Tyler, TX, a Licensed Psychologist and a Licensed Marriage, Family & Child Counselor who is the clinical director of a large private practice mental health clinic in Tyler (Counseling, Testing & Psychiatric Services). He is an adjunct faculty member for the National Judicial College, and a former Professor of Psychology at the University of Texas at Tyler. He is Editor-in-Chief of Haworth Maltreatment & Trauma Press, which includes being the Editor of the *Journal of Child Sexual Abuse, Journal of Aggression, Maltreatment & Trauma,* and Co-Editor of *Journal of Emotional Abuse.* He is also the Executive Editor of the *Family Violence & Sexual Assault Bulletin.* Dr. Geffner has a Diplomate in Clinical Neuropsychology from the American Board of Professional Neuropsychology. Publications include treatment manuals and books concerning spouse abuse (based upon the treatment programs he and his colleagues have developed, and their research), and numerous book chapters, journal articles and research papers concerning family violence, sexual abuse, family and child psychology, neuropsychology and psychological assessment.

Kevin Hamberger, PhD, is Professor of family and community medicine in the Department of Family and Community Medicine, Medical College of Wisconsin. For over a decade, he has conducted a program of treatment and research for domestically violent men. For the past several years, Dr. Hamberger's research has focused on characteristics and treatment outcome with domestically violent offenders, and the interface of these variables with policy making. More recently, he has begun exploring different gender-related contexts and motivations for the use of violence against partners. He has published numerous articles and chapters, and has edited three books. In addition to his clinical and research work in domestic violence, Dr. Hamberger has chaired the Kenosha Domestic Abuse Intervention Project, a coordinated community response to woman abuse. He has also chaired the Society of Teachers of Family Medicine Group on Violence Education, and serves on the Wisconsin Governor's Council on Domestic Abuse.

Marsali Hansen, PhD, received her doctorate in psychology from Peabody College at Vanderbilt University. She is currently the curriculum development specialist for the Pennsylvania CASSP Training and Technical Assistance Institute, the training arm of the Bureau of Children's Mental Health Services. Dr. Hansen specializes in developing and providing training in the delivery of children's and family mental health services. She has written extensively in the area of spousal abuse, and has co-edited books on this topic.

Michele Harway, PhD, received her doctorate in psychology from the University of Maryland. She is Core Faculty and Director of Research at the Phillips Graduate Institute (formerly the California Family Study Center), an accredited independent graduate program in Marriage and Family Therapy. She is editor of *Treating the Changing Family: Handling Normative and Unusual Events,* co-editor (with Marsali Hansen) of *Battering and Family Therapy: A Feminist Perspective,* and co-author (also with Marsali Hansen) of *Spouse Abuse: Assessing and Treating Battered Women, Batterers and their Children.*

Honore M. Hughes, PhD, specializes in clinical child psychology, and is Professor of Psychology at Saint Louis University. Her teaching and research interests lie in the area of family violence, including the psychological functioning of women and children in shelters for battered women. For ten years she was associated with the children's program at a shelter for battered women in Fayetteville, Arkansas while at the University of Arkansas; she now consults with several shelters in St. Louis. She has published a number of journal articles and book chapters related to the adjustment of children of battered women. Clinically, she provides treatment for children who have experienced different forms of violence and their families, as well as supervision for graduate students in the Clinical Psychology Training Program at Saint Louis University in their work with families.

Anthony Kubicki, MS EdPsy, is Coordinator of the "Beyond Abuse" program for Sojourner Truth House in Milwaukee, WI, and has his private practice in psychotherapy at ICF Consultants. He has been a member of the Milwaukee's Common Council Task Force on Sexual Assault and Family Violence since 1986, and is a founder of the Milwaukee Men's Center. Since 1985, he has been recognized for successful relationship abuse programs for men, women, teens and children.

Eve Lipchik, MSW, has been a psychotherapist for over 20 years. Her experiences as a psychodynamic play therapist early in her career led to her decision to seek further training in marriage and family therapy to help parents as well as children. She was a full-time member of the Brief Family Therapy Center where she contributed to the development of the solution-focused brief therapy model. She also began her association with battered women's shelters and programs at that time. In 1988, she founded ICF Consultants, Inc. with Marilyn Bonjean, and she is in private practice there. Ms. Lipchik is a Clinical Member and Approved Supervisor of the American Association for Marriage and Family Therapy and a member of the American Family Therapy Academy. Her clinical and theoretical ideas have been widely published in professional books and journals.

Paula Lundberg-Love, PhD, is Professor of Psychology at the University of Texas at Tyler and the Behavioral Science Preceptor for the Family Practice Residency program at the University of Texas Health Center at Tyler. She also is a licensed psychological associate and licensed chemical dependency counselor at Counseling, Testing & Psychiatry Services in Tyler, a consultant for the Family Violence and Sexual Assault Institute in Tyler, and a member of the editorial board for the *Journal of Child Sexual Abuse*. In addition to having published many research articles and chapters, she recently created a children's group treatment program for recovery from sexual abuse which provides services for children from indigent families.

Mildred Daley Pagelow, PhD, clinical sociologist, is Adjunct Research Professor of Sociology at California State University, Fullerton, and Director of Educational Consulting Services. She has conducted extensive research on family violence; her latest research centers on adolescents as victims and abusers, interfamily sexual abuse of children, and elder abuse. She has written two books for professionals, *Family Violence* and *Woman-battering: Victims and their Experiences*. Her next book, *Understanding Family Violence*, is being written for the general public. Other publications include numerous book chapters and articles in journals.

Julie G. Peterson, MA, has a masters degree in public policy and is completing her doctorate in social psychology at the Claremont Graduate School. She has published on the topics of child homicide, juror sentencing in death penalty cases, child pornography and sexual abuse. Current research interests include murder and attempted murder in domestic violence cases.

Barbra Richardson, PhD, received her doctorate in Biostatistics from the University of California, Los Angeles. Her research interests include statistical methods for missing data and statistical analysis of longitudinal data. Dr. Richardson is a NIH post-doctoral fellow in AIDS/STD research at the University of Washington in Seattle.

Alan Rosenbaum, PhD, is Professor in the Department of Psychiatry at the University of Massachusetts Medical School in Worcester, and the Director of the Marital Research and Treatment Program. He has been operating a program for batterers since 1980. He has published numerous journal articles and papers in the field of relationship aggression, several of which have helped define the standards for research in this area. Current research includes the impact of biological factors, especially neurological and neuropsychological ones, on relationship aggression, outcome of batterers' treatment, and prevention of dating aggression. His research has been supported by grants from NIMH.

Mindy Rosenberg, PhD, is in private practice as a clinical psychologist and forensic consultant in the area of violence and its effects on child, adolescent, and young adult development. After receiving her doctorate from the University of Virginia in clinical/community psychology, she joined the faculties of the University of Denver and Yale University to pursue her research interests in child maltreatment. She is currently Assistant Clinical Professor at the University of California, Berkeley. Dr. Rosenberg's professional contributions include numerous journal articles, book chapters, papers, national and international lectures and workshops on various issues involving child maltreatment. She has co-edited two books, *Prevention of Child Maltreatment: Developmental and Ecological Perspectives* with Diane Willis and E. Wayne Holden and the forthcoming *Multiple Victimization of Children: Conceptual, Research and Treatment Issues* with Dr. Rossman.

Robbie Rossman, PhD, is Senior Clinical Professor in the Psychology Department at the University of Denver. She has worked on projects regarding the well-being of children who experience abuse and/or parental violence. Dr. Rossman is particularly interested in forging an understanding of the impact of family violence on children which brings together the literatures on trauma, abuse, domestic violence, and child development. Dr. Rossman contributes to and reviews for professional journals, is on the editorial boards of the *Journal of Child Sexual Abuse* and the *Family Violence and Sexual Assault Bulletin*, and is co-editor for the *Journal of Emotional Abuse* and of an upcoming book, *Multiple Victimization of Children: Conceptual, Developmental, Research, and Treatment Issues*.

Andrea J. Sedlak, PhD, is a social psychologist and Associate Director of the Human Services Area at Westat, Inc. Westat is an employee-owned company headquartered in the Washington, D.C. metropolitan area and one of the nation's largest social science research organizations, primarily conducting large surveys under contract to the federal government. Dr. Sedlak has been project director on nine major research studies ·which involved abused or neglected children, including the second and third national incidence studies (the NIS-2 and NIS-3) on child abuse and neglect.

Elizabeth A. Sirles, PhD, is Associate Professor in the Social Work Department at the University of Alaska, Anchorage. She has 15 years of experience in the fields of child sexual abuse and domestic violence. She has published extensively on topics such as risk factors for victims, disclosure of abuse, and family variables associated with family violence and incest.

Susan B. Sorenson, PhD, Professor in Residence at the UCLA School of Public Health, specializes in violence and injury prevention. She teaches a graduate-level course on family and sexual violence, and has published numerous articles on homicide, suicide, sexual assault, battering, and child abuse along with research on psychiatric epidemiology. In 1991, she co-founded the Violence Prevention Coalition of Greater Los Angeles. Dr. Sorenson was a member of the 1995-96 National Research Council panel on Research on Violence Against Women and is on the advisory boards of several local organizations.

Carolyn Ivens Tyndall, PhD, a licensed clinical psychologist in the state of Texas, received her doctorate in psychology from the University of Houston. Dr. Tyndall has published and presented nationally on topics of sexual trauma, child and adult depression, and clinical hypnosis. She also serves on the editorial board of the *Journal of Child Sexual Abuse*. In her clinical practice, Dr. Tyndall provides psychotherapy for children (from preschool through adolescence) and adults, and conducts professional supervision and training.

We extend our appreciation to **Evalon Witt**, who edited and formatted the manuscripts with care and good cheer. We also appreciate the dedication and efforts of **Christi Lloyd**, Editorial Assistant of *Journal of Aggression, Maltreatment & Trauma*, who helped with the compilation and proofing of this book.

INTRODUCTION

Family Violence:
Current Issues, Interventions, and Research

Robert Geffner

SUMMARY. Family violence has been recognized as an international epidemic for over a decade, and our knowledge base has increased dramatically during this time. We now have more information and research to help us in understanding the issues, the characteristics of the victims and offenders, and the etiologies of many aspects of the problem. However, we still do not have adequate research concerning the interrelationship of physical violence and psychological maltreatment within the family, and the reasons why some children and adults are resilient to the long-term consequences. We also do not have sufficient data regarding the effectiveness of intervention programs. The purpose of this article is to discuss some

Address correspondence to: Robert Geffner, PhD, Family Violence & Sexual Assault Institute, 1121 E. South East Loop 323, Suite 130, Tyler, TX 75701.

[Haworth co-indexing entry note]: "Family Violence: Current Issues, Interventions, and Research." Geffner, Robert. Co-published simultaneously in *Journal of Aggression, Maltreatment & Trauma* (Haworth Maltreatment & Trauma Press, an imprint of The Haworth Press, Inc.) Vol. 1, No. 1 (#1), 1997, pp. 1-25; and: *Violence and Sexual Abuse at Home: Current Issues in Spousal Battering and Child Maltreatment* (ed: Robert Geffner, Susan B. Sorenson, and Paula K. Lundberg-Love) Haworth Maltreatment & Trauma Press, an imprint of The Haworth Press, Inc., 1997, pp. 1-25. Single or multiple copies of this article are available for a fee from The Haworth Document Delivery Service [1-800-342-9678, 9:00 a.m. - 5:00 p.m. (EST). E-mail address: getinfo@haworth.com].

1

of the major issues, interventions, and research questions facing us, and some of the approaches that various professionals in the domestic violence field have taken in an attempt to address these concerns. Additionally, some of the innovative approaches, programs, theories, and research described in this volume are introduced and described. *[Article copies available for a fee from The Haworth Document Delivery Service: 1-800-342-9678. E-mail address: getinfo@haworth.com]*

KEYWORDS. Domestic violence, child abuse, wife abuse, maltreatment, custody, false allegations

Family violence has gained increased attention in the media and in public policy circles over the past several years. For over a decade, it has been recognized as an international epidemic, and a major mental health, social service, health care, and criminal problem. However, it is important to first define what we mean when we refer to family violence, and to describe the associated terms.

DEFINITION OF TERMS

Family violence refers to those acts of physical, sexual, or psychological maltreatment, aggression, and violence that occur in a family unit whereby one family member with more power or authority attempts to gain control over another family member (American Psychological Association Presidential Task Force on Violence and the Family, 1996). The family unit can be broadly defined, and may include those who occupy a family role but may not legally be a family member. Victims may be adults or children, and the perpetrators are usually adults but may also be older children. Family violence generally includes spouse/partner maltreatment, child maltreatment, and elder/parent maltreatment. These categories can be further subdivided into physical, sexual, and psychological maltreatment/neglect. Thus, all combinations of these acts make up the field of family violence.

The use of some of the terms above is somewhat different from those that have been utilized in the past. As the family violence field has matured and developed a larger research and theoretical foundation, precision in our operational definitions is important. For example, the terms abuse and violence are somewhat vague, have different connotations for various professionals and the public, and do not adequately appear to represent the direction of future research and theory. However, the term maltreatment seems better to delineate the types of behaviors included in family violence, and the type of aggression involved. The effects of victimization via maltreatment is generally traumatic for children and adults. Thus, the body of research, theory, and interventions that have been in existence for some time concerning maltreatment, aggression, and trauma should be utilized and integrated into the field of family violence. If we can use common terms, incorporate our existing knowledge base concerning the fields of human aggression, maltreatment, and trauma, then this will help advance the integration of the field of family violence. The first step has been taken with the recent publication of an integrated textbook concerning family violence (Barnett, Miller-Perrin, & Perrin, 1997).

CURRENT ISSUES, RESEARCH, AND INTERVENTIONS

The purpose of this volume is to present some of the current issues, interventions, and research concerning spouse/partner and child maltreatment. Some areas that are not addressed in this volume due to space limitations, but are nevertheless quite important in the family violence field, include elder/parent maltreatment, multicultural/ethnic issues, forensic issues, and prevention programs. Because these areas have limited data, and have not been sufficiently emphasized in the research, they will be discussed briefly at the end of this article.

This volume is the initial issue of the new *Journal of Aggression, Maltreatment & Trauma* that is devoted to the presentation and integration of new research, theory, and interventions concerning human maltreatment and trauma. It is fitting that we begin this endeavor with a problem that often goes undetected in many homes (i.e., family maltreatment), but can cause such tragic and devastating effects for all who are directly involved or even exposed to such conditions. Thus, the goal of this volume is to review what we know about some of these problems and to present innovative theories and approaches to understanding and reducing these epidemics. Viewing family violence as a public health and criminal issue will help bring these problems out from behind closed doors (Straus, Gelles, & Steinmetz, 1980; Gelles, 1997). Being open to new ways of conceptualizing family violence will enable us to understand the dynamics better which should, in turn, lead to more effective intervention and prevention programs. Thus, this volume focuses on issues, interventions and research concerning aspects of spouse/partner maltreatment, child physical maltreatment, exposure to family maltreatment, and sexual maltreatment (with respect to children, adult survivors, and incest offenders). Each of these topics is discussed below.

Spouse/Partner Maltreatment

As noted in the recent report on violence against women by the National Research Council (1996), there are numerous issues regarding spouse/partner maltreatment that still require resolution. One is the terminology. It is not yet clear whether we should refer to such adult maltreatment as "spouse abuse or maltreatment," "partner abuse or maltreatment," or "wife abuse or maltreatment." There have been numerous arguments for each of these terms during the past decade, but due to the varying philosophies of those in this field, the issue has not yet been resolved. The use of the term battering also has been common, but some have argued that several types of maltreatment often co-occur that might not be defined as battering. Also, there has been substantial disagreement about some of the terms within this area of family violence. For example, as pointed out by Hamberger (1997a) and Pagelow (1997) in this volume, the issues of who is the offender and what defines mutual combat have caused considerable controversy with respect to research, data interpretation, clinical interventions, and public policy. Some of these terms recently have been defined by Geffner and Mantooth (1995). It appears that a distinction should be made among spouse/partner maltreatment and mutual abuse/maltreatment, mutual combat/aggression, and self-defense. To be maltreated, abused or battered implies that one person in the relationship utilizes physical or psychological coercion against the other person in order to gain control. This process usually involves a pattern of attempts at intimidation by the perpetrator and often produces fear in the victims. If these components are present in a situation, then we could state that maltreatment or abuse has occurred. Thus, mutual abuse would indicate that both partners are attempting to utilize coercive, intimidating and/or physical methods to control the other, and both are producing elements of fear in their respective partner. Utilizing such a definition, the amount of mutual abuse in relationships is probably small. However, from various national studies and clinical reports (e.g., Straus & Gelles, 1986), the level of mutual combat and aggression in relationships may be higher than some would like to believe. In many of these cases of mutual combat, there are probably incidents of "pure" self-defense wherein a battered woman hits her batterer while trying to protect herself. There also may be situations where a battered woman initiates aggressive acts for a variety of reasons, including times when the tension has reached very high levels and she knows she is going to be battered, but does not know when. At these times, she may initiate aggression "to get the violence over with." However, in most of these situations, this is not mutual abuse and she is not the primary perpetrator since she is not attempting to control her partner, does not intimidate him, and does not produce fear. In some relationships there is definitely mutual aggression. The distinctions in these situations are important for the determination of policy (e.g., mandatory arrest and treatment), intervention programs, and the more accurate assessment of prevalence rates. Intervention programs need to vary depending upon the particular type and severity of aggression, and the frequency, duration, motivation, and level of intimidation, fear and harm.

Another important issue concerns the theories and models of spouse/ partner abuse. Until recently, the main models proposed for spouse/partner maltreatment were a social learning perspective, feminist patriarchal views, cultural transmission, and other psychosocial models. Unfortunately, none of the proposed models of this type of family violence account for sufficient amounts of the variance in studies. In each case there are too many exceptions that do not fit the model. For example, while it is clear that alcohol is a significant associated factor in spouse/partner maltreatment, reviews of the research indicate that this is not the reason for such maltreatment (e.g., Geffner & Rosenbaum, 1990).

Another body of research has focused on typologies of batterers (e.g., Hamberger, Lohr, Bonge, & Tolin, 1995; Holtzworth-Munroe & Stuart, 1994; Saunders, 1995). Again, none of the typologies, usually developed with factor analyses, seems to fit all batterers. This is not surprising, given that none of these models includes any biological components. In all forms of aggression, whether animal or human, biological issues are also involved. However, this has generally been overlooked when dealing with family violence, as discussed by Rosenbaum (e.g., Geffner & Rosenbaum, 1992; Rosenbaum & Hoge, 1989). Therefore, in this volume, Rosenbaum, Geffner, and Benjamin (1997) attempt to rectify this situation, by proposing a biopsychosocial model of relationship aggression, based in part on the innovative research of Rosenbaum and his colleagues. Such a model has important ramifications for intervention and prevention programs. Since this model includes a variety of psychological, sociological/cultural, and biological/physiological factors, then a comprehensive assessment of an offender is necessary to determine the relevant factors or variables that may be involved in his aggressive behavior. Intervention would then be tailored toward dealing with all problem areas. While this is standard practice for all other mental health or medical problems, it is often not the case in the field of family violence.

Thus, the first step is to recognize and identify likely perpetrators and victims of spouse/partner maltreatment. Unfortunately, many clinicians do not conduct such assessments. Intervention should then be based upon this assessment, and matched to the offender's needs to ensure safety for the victims and to eliminate the perpetrator's aggression (Geffner & Mantooth, 1995; Geffner & Rosenbaum, 1990; Saunders, 1993, 1995). For the treatment of batterers, "one size" does not fit all. Such practice may be one significant reason for the relatively low success rates in the outcome studies of batterer intervention (e.g., Edleson, 1996).

In order to conduct treatment, the clinician, social service worker, or health care provider must be aware of the ethical responsibilities and the potential danger in these situations, as pointed out in this volume by Harway, Hansen and Cervantes (1997), and Cervantes and Hansen (1997), and by others (e.g., American Psychological Association Ad Hoc Committee on Legal and Ethical Issues in the Treatment of Interpersonal Violence, 1996a, 1996b; American Psychological Association Task Force, 1996). Harway et al. discuss the lack of awareness of many clinicians concerning the dynamics of family maltreatment and the subsequent problems that can occur. Cervantes and Hansen go further and discuss the ethical issues and legal mandates involved in reporting family maltreatment. They note that mandatory reporting of child and elder maltreatment has been in existence for several years, but such reporting of spousal maltreatment is new, and is only mandated for certain providers in California. The issue of mandatory reporting has been quite controversial in general and will probably continue to be so in the future.

As suggested by the work of Harway et al. (1997), research concerning risk and lethality assessment of spouse/partner maltreatment is still in its infancy. Some strides have been made recently, by researchers who have developed measures to focus on this issue (e.g., Campbell, 1995; Elliott & Shepard, 1995). However, predicting the potential level of danger always has been a complex issue. The first step in the process is the training of professionals to recognize the signs and symptoms of maltreatment, and to understand the dynamics. In this volume, Hamberger (1997b) addresses this issue with respect to physician training. Also in this volume, Pagelow (1997), in reviewing the research over the past two decades, focuses on the various myths that many professionals and the public tend to believe concerning spouse/partner maltreatment. Others also have pointed out the need for better training and understanding of the dynamics of family violence (e.g., APA Presidential Task Force, 1996). The National Research Council's report concerning family violence prevention and treatment, to be released this year, should also provide information in this area.

Once an assessment has been conducted by trained professionals in various disciplines, then the appropriate interventions can be conducted. The most typical treatment for batterers has been gender specific group therapy with a cognitive-behavioral emphasis (Edleson & Tolman, 1992; Geffner, & Rosenbaum, 1990). Some have argued that an educational model of group intervention should be the recommended course of action, and others have indicated that a complex problem such as human aggression directed toward a spouse or partner requires therapy by a trained clinician. This controversy is still being debated. Some clinicians and researchers have advocated the use of additional treatment alternatives depending upon the results of the assessment and situation. One such approach that has generated significant controversy due to ideological criticisms is couples or family treatment. In fact, some jurisdictions (e.g., California, Colorado, Florida, Massachusetts, etc.) have mandated that this approach cannot be used initially with batterers (and their partners) who have been court ordered into treatment. At the present time, no research data exist that indicate such an approach, given that it is provided by trained professionals and modified to focus on the violence reduction, is inherently more dangerous than gender-specific group therapy (Geffner & Mantooth, 1995; O'Leary, 1996). Thus, it appears premature to establish standards and statutes based upon ideology rather than on research and/or clinical data (Geffner, 1995). In fact, more clinicians and researchers are beginning to realize that this may be a viable approach for certain batterers in certain situations, and that we need as many alternatives as possible to deal with this complex problem (Geffner & Mantooth, 1995; Hansen & Goldenberg, 1993; Shamai, 1996; Sonkin, 1995).

Some have argued that batterers need to complete an educational program and be violence-free for six months prior to entering couples therapy (e.g., Edleson & Tolman, 1992). However, research is beginning to show that a conjoint approach may indeed be effective in eliminating violence for certain couples who have decided to remain in the relationship (Brown & O'Leary, 1995). In this volume, one type of program for working with couples when spouse abuse has occurred, a solutions-focused approach, is presented by Lipchik, Sirles, and Kubicki (1997). They present an alternative approach that they have used successfully for several years with certain couples with whom violence has been an issue.

Child Physical Maltreatment and Exposure to Family Violence

The prevalence of child maltreatment, including neglect, has been a focus of national surveys and research for many years. A few years ago, the National Research Council (1993) summarized the research and made recommendations for future priorities in this area. They recommended a

broad ecological perspective to attempt to understand this complex problem. In the present volume, Sedlak (1997) discusses some of the results of
a national incidence study of child maltreatment with respect to the risk
factors. This statistical information helps refine our understanding of the
causes of child physical maltreatment, which will therefore help direct
future research and intervention programs. Then Sorenson, Peterson, and
Richardson (1997) present an examination of child homicide in a large city
in order to understand the dynamics of the problem facing us. They focus
on the relationship between alleged perpetrators and victims as well as on
ethnic issues. Their research yields important data on this increasing area
of violence directed at children. In order to develop better intervention and
prevention programs, recent books and articles also have focused on
understanding child maltreatment (e.g., American Psychological Association Committee on Professional Practice and Standards, 1995; Melton &
Barry, 1994; Wiehe, 1996). It appears that child maltreatment is yet
another symptom of the general increase in aggression and violence in
society, and there does not appear to be an end in sight (e.g., Goldstein,
1996; Tedeschi & Felson, 1994).

One aspect of child physical abuse that often is overlooked is the
maltreatment of children with disabilities. According to recent research,
these children are at higher risk for maltreatment. Ammerman (1997), in
this volume, discusses the risk factors, assessment issues, and treatment of
such children. Unfortunately, many of these children "fall between the
cracks" of our social service, medical, and mental health programs.

Another aspect of maltreatment that has not received adequate attention
until recently is the trauma experienced by children who are exposed to
violence in their homes. At first these children were referred to as child
witnesses, but then Geffner recommended that this be changed to child
observers due to the confusion with children who testify in court as witnesses (Geffner & Pagelow, 1990). We now realize that actually children do
not have to observe abuse between their parents to be affected, but to merely
be exposed to such violence can often produce posttraumatic stress disorder
(e.g., Graham-Bermann & Levendosky, In Press; Holden, Geffner, & Jouriles, 1997; Peled, 1996). Research findings concerning the effects on children of battered women are described by Hughes (1997) in this volume.
Identification of these children is quite important in the family violence
field, and treatment programs need to be established to help resolve some of
the trauma. It has now been recommended that the battering of one parent
by a child's other parent be viewed as psychological maltreatment (APA
Presidential Task Force, 1996). In their article in the present volume, Rossman and Rosenberg (1997) focus on this type of psychological maltreat-

ment from a developmental perspective. In recent years, others have also focused on these hidden victims of family violence (e.g., Cummings & Davies, 1994; Peled, Jaffe, & Edleson, 1995). The articles by Hughes and by Rossman and Rosenberg suggest conceptual models for this type of maltreatment, provide suggestions for clinical intervention to reduce the trauma, and make recommendations for future research.

Child Custody Issues in Family Violence

Related to the effects of exposure to family violence are the issues of custody, visitation and mediation when the relationship between abusive partners dissolves. Geffner and Pagelow (1990) warned several years ago about the dangers of awarding custody to a batterer, and the effects that the attitudes and behaviors of a batterer have on child rearing. Also, both of these authors also have focused on the problems of mandated mediation with cases of family violence (e.g., Geffner, 1992a; Geffner & Pagelow, 1990). Some of these issues are reviewed by Pagelow (1997) in her article in this volume. The American Medical Association, the Committee on Children and the Law of the American Bar Association (Davidson, 1994), and the American Psychological Association Task Force (1996) all have recommended that if battering and maltreatment have occurred in a relationship, then the perpetrator should not be awarded sole or joint custody, and that visitation must be monitored until the batterer successfully completes treatment for the aggressive behaviors. The suggestion of many researchers and clinicians in this field is that spouse/partner maltreatment presumes poor parenting because battering a child's other parent ignores the needs of the child, creates and promotes substantial fear and tension, and models poor communication, anger management, and conflict resolution. Recently, this view has been put incorporated into some family law statutes, the first being in Louisiana.

What has complicated this issue is that sometimes women who have been maltreated for several years develop post traumatic stress disorder, depression, and other emotional problems as a result of the battering (e.g, Dutton, 1992). This may affect their parenting ability unless they receive treatment for the psychological symptoms. While treatment for these consequences of maltreatment is definitely needed (e.g., Schlee & O'Leary, 1995), this does not mean that a battered woman is at fault for her subsequent problems. Since the perpetrator may appear more emotionally stable, more financially responsible, and perhaps more capable, some judges have awarded the accused batterer custody of his children (e.g., Jaffe & Austin, 1995; Jaffe & Geffner, In Press). This situation often becomes a self-fulfilling prophecy because many battered women have been threatened that if they ever left the relationship, they would lose their children, and indeed they do. Such issues will need further research in the future.

Child Sexual Maltreatment

Numerous books have been written and substantial research has been conducted in the past several years concerning child sexual maltreatment. In fact, several years ago, Geffner (1992b) stated that additional studies and techniques were needed concerning interviewing children in alleged sexual abuse cases, the use of anatomically detailed dolls, the effects of suggestibility on children, and the need for more intervention programs to reduce the effects of the trauma. Some of these needs have been addressed in recent years while others are still in process. For example, research has indicated that anatomically detailed dolls do not produce sexualized behaviors nor lead to specific stories or descriptions of sexual behaviors when appropriate procedures are followed (Boat & Everson, 1993; Simkins & Renier, 1996). Better techniques which minimize suggestibility have been developed for the objective interviewing of children who have alleged sexual abuse (Faller, 1995; Morgan, 1995; Saywitz & Goodman, 1996; Walker & Warren, 1995). Additionally, we have a better understanding of the treatment needs for sexually maltreated children (for a review, see Finkelhor & Berliner, 1995). However, we are still in the early stages of having adequate knowledge concerning all aspects of sexual maltreatment.

In this volume, for example, Alpert (1997) discusses a type of sexual abuse that has not received adequate attention in the literature: sibling child sexual abuse. She reviews the little research that does exist, and recommends additional focus on this area of child maltreatment. Also, she discusses the need for a greater emphasis on the identification of these situations in clinical practice, and she provides some suggestions for doing so. Treating the victims of child sexual maltreatment in general has received more attention in the past few years.

New books have been published describing programs and techniques for helping children and adolescents recover from the trauma (e.g., Deblinger & Heflin, 1996; Gil, 1996; Karp & Butler, 1996; Wieland, 1997). In this volume, Tyndall (1997) describes some strategies, incorporating a multimodal approach, for treating sexually abused children and adolescents. She provides practical information about various interventions, from the initial evaluation and treatment to termination. She discusses different types of individual therapy, including clinical hypnosis, as well as group therapy. Some clinical techniques have been criticized because they supposedly lead to false allegations of maltreatment, but her focus is on treatment after the abuse has been confirmed so that the victim can heal and recover from the trauma.

False Allegations, Suggestibility, "False Memories," Divorce, and a Backlash Concerning Child Sexual Maltreatment

There has been a substantial backlash movement which has proposed that many of the allegations of child abuse are false, due to the programming or leading questioning of clinicians and investigators (see Myers, 1994, for a discussion of this backlash movement). This backlash has been extended to adults who recall memories of childhood sexual abuse years later, with the perspective again that most of these delayed recollections are "false memories." It is clear that people sometimes have distorted memories of past events, and some people confabulate reports for various reasons, but there is no evidence that there is such a phenomenon as a "false memory syndrome" as has been promoted by an advocacy organization. Even though we do not yet understand the mechanisms of the repression, dissociation, and delayed recall of traumatic events, substantial information has been published or presented recently concerning these issues (e.g., Alpert, 1995; Elliott & Briere, 1995; Ney, 1995; Pope & Brown, 1996; van der Kolk & Fisler, 1995; Whitfield, 1995; L. Williams, 1995). As Brown (1995) pointed out, the suggestibility of children that has been exhibited in laboratory studies has not been shown to be generalizable in the same manner to sexual abuse cases. Others have argued similarly (e.g., Pope & Brown, 1996; Whitfield, 1995), and in fact there is substantial research that children are generally resistant to suggestibility for events of particular personal salience unless repeated and extremely coercive techniques are used (e.g., Saywitz & Snyder, 1993).

Does this mean that false allegations of sexual abuse do not exist? Of course not. In fact, there definitely are false allegations, but exactly what percentage is unknown. Research generally indicates that between 5-12 % of allegations of sexual abuse may be false (e.g., Everson & Boat, 1989; Jones & McGraw, 1987). There has been even more controversy about allegations of abuse in divorce cases. In fact, some have argued that there is an epidemic of false abuse allegations in divorce cases due to a so called "parent alienation syndrome" (Gardner, 1992). However, this appears to be a myth because the percentage of false allegations, according to several research studies on large samples of divorce cases (e.g., Faller & DeVoe, 1995; Thoennes & Tjaden, 1990) appears to be small. In addition, there appears to be no systematic research to support any parent alienation syndrome. Some have argued that this was merely a coined phrase by its author and that it has been overgeneralized and overutilized without any scientific evidence. Indeed, the book discussing and promoting this "syndrome" was published by the author himself, and no peer reviewed research or data have yet been published. Some have argued that this label has been used to pathologize women (APA Task Force, 1996; Faller, Olafson, & Corwin, 1993).

Unfortunately, many women who may have been in abusive relationships appear to be in a "no win" situation if their children allege some type of maltreatment by their fathers before, during, or subsequent to a divorce proceeding. When a child makes such an allegation, it should be reported to local child protective services agencies for investigation, as is customary practice. The "nonoffending parent" must be able and willing to believe and to protect the child. If not, she risks removal of her child for "failure to protect." However, if she does indeed report and attempt to protect her child from the alleged perpetrator, she is at risk for being labeled as a "programmer" of the child and as "alienating" the child from the other parent. In some of these situations, the alleged abusive parent (who also may have maltreated the woman during the relationship), files in court for sole custody on the basis of this so-called "alienation syndrome." Too often, judges and juries have removed a child from the mother's custody with no evidence of poor parenting other than the circular argument of alienation because of the allegations by the child against the father.

Does this mean parents never attempt to alienate children against their current or former partners? Of course not. Clinicians long have been aware of such situations, but to date no evidence exists for such a syndrome. Thus, each case must be investigated thoroughly by someone with expertise, knowledge of the research, and training in the dynamics of maltreatment and family violence, custody, and child development, utilizing accepted techniques and procedures (APA Ad Hoc Committee, 1996b; APA Task Force, 1996; Briere, Berliner, Bulkley, Jenny, & Reid, 1996; Faller, 1996; Kuehnle, 1996; Ney, 1995). Preconceived perceptions or biases in this area must be avoided since they can influence the evaluation (Everson, Boat, Bourg, & Robertson, 1996; Jackson & Nuttall, 1997).

Adult Sexual Abuse Survivors

In recent years, there has been an increase in research, theory, and treatment concerning the survivors of childhood sexual maltreatment (e.g., Briere, 1996; Freyd, 1996). Specific areas of focus have included group treatment of adult survivors (e.g., Donaldson & Cordes-Green; 1994; Webb & Leehan, 1996), treatment of male survivors (e.g., Mendel, 1995), treatment of dual issues of recovery from abuse and from addiction (Evans & Sullivan,

1995), and systemic treatment of the families (Gil, 1996). In this volume, two specific areas of treatment of adult sexual abuse survivors are emphasized. The first issue involves the treatment of the sexual concerns of adult survivors and their partners. Courtois (1997) discusses the impact of child sexual maltreatment on the survivor's sexuality and sexual functioning, and then provides recommendations for treating these issues. Also, recommended are strategies for including the partner in the treatment.

The second issue concerns discussion of dissociative disorders in adult survivors of sexual maltreatment. Severe post traumatic stress disorder in young children as a result of trauma can produce a dissociative disorder (see van der Kolk, McFarlane, & Weisaeth, 1996, for a review). In this volume, Lundberg-Love (1997) discusses the different types of dissociative disorders that may result from severe child sexual maltreatment, and various strategies for treating these in adult survivors. Her discussion takes into consideration some of the criticisms of the existence of dissociative identity disorder in these clients. Additionally, she provides practical techniques for working with adult survivors who exhibit the symptoms of dissociative disorders, and she makes recommendations for the use of specific techniques as part of a careful process of assessment and intervention in these cases.

Incest Offenders

The final topic included in this volume focuses on the offenders of child sexual maltreatment within the family. Brown and Brown (1997) first present some of the characteristics of incest offenders and discuss the difficulties in diagnoses, since there is no "profile" of such an offender (for a further discussion of the issues of assessment and diagnosis of these offenders, see APA Task Force, 1996; Murphy & Smith, 1996; Quinsey & Lalumiere, 1996). They then present some of the different techniques for treatment of these offenders, as well as their effectiveness in reducing recidivism. Since there is more information available regarding male offenders, they focus on this group (for further information concerning female sex offenders, see Elliott, 1993; Faller, 1995).

AREAS THAT REQUIRE ADDITIONAL RESEARCH OR INTERVENTION

One of the main areas of research still needed in the family violence field concerns methodology, particularly instruments and measures. About nine years ago, Geffner, Rosenbaum, and Hughes (1988) presented some important methodological problems in family violence research methodology, and recommendations were made for improvement. Some of the main issues involved terminology, operational definitions, and instrumentation. Some researchers are addressing the need for reliable, valid, and standardized measures of child maltreatment (e.g., Milner, 1990), trauma (e.g., Briere, 1995; Carlson, 1996), child sexual behavior (e.g., Friedrich et al., 1992), spouse/partner maltreatment (e.g., Straus, Hamby, Boney-McCoy, & Sugarman, 1995; Tolman, 1995), and risk assessment for adults (e.g., Campbell, 1995) and for children (Gelles, 1995). Unfortunately, there are still significant problems in the research (Schafer, 1996). Risk and lethality assessment techniques are difficult to design, validate, and standardize. As a result, more emphasis is required in this area to improve our capabilities in recognizing dangerous situations for all types of family maltreatment so that intervention and prevention strategies can be improved and implemented.

Also, it is hoped that a better understanding of the dynamics of family maltreatment will be forthcoming as more integration of the research and theories of trauma, aggression, and maltreatment occurs. Unfortunately, clinicians, researchers, advocates, and other professionals still tend to focus on their own perspectives in their specific area of family maltreatment. A broadening of perspectives in all types of family maltreatment to include developmental, social, psychological, cultural, and biological issues, theory and research will be beneficial in the long term, and should enhance our ability to develop intervention and prevention programs. Indeed, some researchers are currently developing or expanding upon such theories and perspectives (e.g., Briere, 1996; Pearlman, In Press; van der Kolk, 1995). Based upon many years of research, we now know that there is substantial overlap among the prevalence of all forms of family maltreatment, and that if one type exists in the home, it is likely that other types also may be present. It is therefore important for those focusing on one particular aspect of family maltreatment to learn about other types of family violence so that we can work together to eliminate these epidemics.

Another weakness in the field is the lack of sufficient outcome research for the various treatment and prevention programs in existence. Some notable efforts have been undertaken to evaluate the effectiveness of treatment for victims of child sexual abuse (e.g., Berliner & Saunders, 1995), for child sexual offenders (e.g., Marshall, Jones, Ward, Johnson, & Barbaree, 1991), for adult incest survivors (e.g., Follette, Alexander, & Follette, 1991), for victims of child physical maltreatment (e.g., Wolfe & Wekerle, 1993), for child physical maltreatment offenders (e.g., Oates & Bross, 1995), for batterers (e.g., Edleson & Tolman, 1992), for battered victims (e.g., Jouriles et al., In Press), and for children exposed to marital violence (e.g., Jaffe, Wolfe, & Wilson, 1990). However, additional research in all areas of family maltreatment is still needed to determine the efficacy of various treatment programs in comparison to control groups. For treatment of offenders, it is important to look closely at the characteristics of drop outs (for example with batterers, see Edleson & Tolman, 1992; Heyman, Brown, & O'Leary, 1995). Differences between those who complete treatment and those who do not must be considered before reaching conclusions that may not be generalizable.

Another group with respect to victimization that requires further study are those who appear to be resilient regarding the negative effects of trauma. It is not yet clear why some children and adults do appear to suffer less from the traumatic consequences of their victimization. This issue is just beginning to be studied with respect to abused children (e.g., Kinnard, 1995) and to adult survivors (e.g., Hyman & Williams, 1995). Information from future research in this area should help us better understand the dynamics of victimization and resiliency. Similarly, it is not yet clear why some victimized individuals later become offenders and some do not. The issues of vulnerability, risk factors for victimization and offending, are important areas for future research.

Finally, more research, intervention, and prevention data also are needed in other aspects of family maltreatment not discussed in this volume. One such area is elder maltreatment (e.g., Aitken & Griffin, 1997; APA Task Force, 1996; T. F. Johnson, 1995; Marin et al., 1995). Another area is that of cultural and ethnic issues. For example, Williams has pointed out the need for cultural competence when treating batterers and when conducting spouse/partner maltreatment research (e.g., O. Williams, 1995; Williams & Becker, 1995). This needs to occur much more often in all aspects of family maltreatment so that we all are better informed and sensitized. Prevention programs also were not emphasized in this volume. This area needs more research, although a few excellent examples of prevention based upon research results exist (Wolfe et al., 1996 for prevention of relationship aggression, and Wurtele & Miller-Perrin, 1993 for sexual abuse prevention). Viewing some of these issues from cross cultural perspectives also is important (e.g., Bottoms & Goodman, 1996; Kosberg & Garcia, 1995).

Similarly, other specific populations need to be emphasized more. For example, children who sexually act out against other children have been clinically studied for many years, but only recently has this been addressed in some depth (e.g., English, 1995; Friedrich, Berliner, & Cohen, 1995; T. C. Johnson, 1995). Another population that increasingly has been recognized as needing more information and intervention involves gay and lesbian relationships. All aspects of family maltreatment occur in gay and lesbian relationships, but these must be studied in more depth to determine whether the theories and interventions being proposed in heterosexual populations are applicable for this population as well (see Renzetti & Miley, 1996, for various articles dealing with this topic). In addition, more research and intervention emphasis are needed to focus on male victims of family maltreatment and female offenders, as stated above. Our knowledge in these areas is still quite superficial (for recent reviews of some of these issues and innovative programs, see Chesney-Lind, 1997; Friedrich, 1995; Gonsiorek, Bera, & LeTourneau, 1994).

Research, public exposure, and scrutiny concerning family violence has increased in part due to the large numbers of people affected as well as to the increase in the numbers of these cases which have entered the legal arena. Various professional organizations have addressed this issue due to the numerous controversies involving court testimony (e.g., APA Ad Hoc Committee, 1996a; APA Task Force, 1996; Davidson, 1994). New books have been published, mostly focusing on this topic regarding child maltreatment or adult survivors of sexual abuse (e.g., Goodman & Bottoms, 1993; Myers, 1994; Pope & Brown, 1996; Zaragoza, Graham, Hall, Hirschman, & Ben-Porath, 1995). Nevertheless, we must not allow forensic issues to determine the themes for research, assessment, and the treatment of victims and offenders of family maltreatment because legal agendas often are different from mental health, health care, and social service agendas. These differences should be acknowledged and integrated without losing the benefits of each field. What this does mean, though, is that professionals working in the various arenas (including the forensic one) must be well trained specifically in family maltreatment issues and dynamics (for a recent example of such training for health care providers, see Hamberger, Burge, Graham, & Costa, In Press). Hence, training for all graduate students and residents in mental health, health care, and social service fields has been recommended by various national advisory boards, interdisciplinary task forces, and professional organizations. Indeed we hope that this volume will be a valuable resource for such training. As more professionals become involved in working regularly with trauma victims and survivors, it also will be important for them to be aware of secondary or vicarious traumatization, and to focus on self-care and countertransference issues (e.g., Pearlman & Saakvitne, 1995; Stamm, 1995).

CONCLUSION

Spouse and child maltreatment have occurred at epidemic rates for over a decade. The costs to individuals, families, businesses, and society have been overwhelming. It is therefore time to allocate more resources to the funding of research and intervention programs, and to the training of professionals in the area of family violence. Until this occurs, the substantial funds needed for dealing with the symptoms rather than the problems themselves, the aftermath of the violence, the loss of productivity for society, and the loss of human lives will not be diminished. It is time for all those working in the areas of family maltreatment, whether advocate or researcher, policy maker or clinician, professional or lay person, to work together for the common goals of eliminating family violence.

REFERENCES

Aitken, L., & Griffin, G. (1997). *Gender issues in elder abuse*. Thousand Oaks, CA: Sage.

Alpert, J. L. (1997). Sibling child sexual abuse: research review and clinical implications. *Journal of Aggression, Maltreatment & Trauma, 1*, 263-275.

Alpert, J. L. (Ed.). (1995). *Sexual abuse recalled: Treating trauma in the era of the recovered memory debate*. Northvale, NJ: Jason Aronson.

American Psychological Association Ad Hoc Committee on Legal and Ethical Issues in the Treatment of Interpersonal Violence. (1996a). *Professional, ethical, and legal issues concerning interpersonal violence, maltreatment and related trauma*. Washington, DC: American Psychological Association.

American Psychological Association Ad Hoc Committee on Legal and Ethical Issues in the Treatment of Interpersonal Violence. (1996b). *Potential problems for psychologists working with the area of interpersonal violence*. Washington, DC: American Psychological Association.

American Psychological Association Committee on Professional Practice and Standards. (1995). Twenty-four questions (and answers) about professional practice in the area of child abuse. *Professional Psychology: Research and Practice, 26(4)*, 377-385.

American Psychological Association Presidential Task Force on Violence and the Family. (1996). *Violence and the family: Report of the APA Presidential Task Force*. Washington, DC: American Psychological Association.

Ammerman, R. T. (1997). Physical abuse and childhood disability: Risk and treatment factors. *Journal of Aggression, Maltreatment & Trauma, 1*, 207-224.

Barnett, O. W., Miller-Perrin, C. L., & Perrin, R. D. (1997). *Violence across the lifespan: An introduction*. Thousand Oaks, CA: Sage.

Berliner, L., & Saunders, B. (1995, July). *Variables associated with outcome in sexually abused children at two years post treatment*. Paper presented at 4th International Family Violence Research Conference, Durham, NH.

Boat, B. W., & Everson, M. D. (1993). The uses of anatomical dolls in sexual abuse evaluations: Current research and practice. In G. S. Goodman & B. L. Bottoms (Eds.), *Child victims, child witnesses: Understanding and improving testimony* (pp. 47-69). New York: Guilford Press.

Bottoms, B. L., & Goodman, G. S. (1996). *International perspectives on child abuse and children's testimony: Psychological research and law.* Thousand Oaks, CA: Sage.

Briere, J. (1996). A self-trauma model for treating adult survivors of severe child abuse. In J. Briere, L. Berliner, J. A. Bulkley, C. Jenny, & T. Reid (Eds.), *The APSAC handbook on child maltreatment* (pp. 140-157). Thousand Oaks, CA: Sage.

Briere, J. (1995). *The Trauma Symptom Inventory professional manual.* Odessa, FL: Psychological Assessment Resources.

Briere, J., Berliner, L., Bulkley, J. A., Jenny, C., & Reid, T. (1996). *The APSAC handbook on child maltreatment.* Thousand Oaks, CA: Sage.

Brown, D. (1995). Sources of suggestion and their applicability to psychotherapy. In J. L. Alpert (Ed.), *Sexual abuse recalled: Treating trauma in the era of the recovered memory debate* (pp. 61-100). Northvale, NJ: Jason Aronson.

Brown, J. L., & Brown, G. S. (1997). Characteristics and treatment of incest offenders: A review. *Journal of Aggression, Maltreatment & Trauma, 1,* 335-354.

Brown, P. D., & O'Leary, K. D. (1995, July). *Marital treatment for wife abuse: A review and evaluation.* Paper presented at 4th International Family Violence Research Conference, Durham, NH.

Campbell, J. C. (Ed.). (1995). *Assessing dangerousness: Violence by sexual offenders, batterers, and child abusers.* Thousand Oaks, CA: Sage.

Carlson, E. B. (Ed.). (1996). *Trauma research methodology.* Lutherville, MD: Sidran.

Cervantes, N. N., & Hansen, M. (1997). Therapist ethical responsibilities for spousal abuse cases. *Journal of Aggression, Maltreatment & Trauma, 1,* 41-56.

Chesney-Lind, M. (1997). *The female offender: Girls, women, and crime.* Thousand Oaks, CA: Sage.

Courtois, C. A. (1997). Treating the sexual concerns of adult incest survivors and their partners. *Journal of Aggression, Maltreatment & Trauma, 1,* 293-310.

Cummings, E. M., & Davies, P. (1994). *Children and marital conflict: The impact of family dispute and resolution.* New York: Guilford.

Davidson, H. (1994). *The impact of domestic violence on children: A report to the president of the American Bar Association (2nd rev. ed.).* Chicago, IL: American Bar Association.

Deblinger, E., & Heflin, A. H. (1996). *Treating sexually abused children and their nonoffending parents: A cognitive behavioral approach.* Thousand Oaks, CA: Sage.

Donaldson, M. A., & Cordes-Green, S. (1994). *Group treatment of adult incest survivors.* Thousand Oaks, CA: Sage.

Dutton, M. A. (1992). *Empowering and healing the battered woman: A model for assessment & intervention*. New York: Springer Publishing.

Edleson, J. L. (1996). Controversy and change in batterers' programs. In J. L. Edleson & Z. C. Eisikovits (Eds.), *Future interventions with battered women and their families* (pp. 154-169). Thousand Oaks, CA: Sage.

Edleson, J. L., & Tolman, R. M. (1992). *Intervention for men who batter: An ecological approach*. Newbury Park, CA: Sage.

Elliott, B. E., & Shepard, M. (1995, July). *Domestic violence: Assessing dangerousness*. Paper presented at 4th International Family Violence Research Conference, Durham, NH.

Elliott, D. M., & Briere, J. (1995). Posttraumatic stress associated with delayed recall of sexual abuse: A general population study. *Journal of Traumatic Stress, 8(4)*, 629-647.

Elliott, M. (1993). *Female sexual abuse of children*. New York: Guilford.

English, D. J. (1995, July). *Children who sexually abuse other children: Findings from three studies*. Paper presented at 4th International Family Violence Research Conference, Durham, NH.

Evans, K., & Sullivan, J. M. (1995). *Treating addicted survivors of trauma*. New York: Guilford.

Everson, M. D., & Boat, B. (1989). False allegations of sexual abuse by children and adolescents. *American Academy of Child and Adolescent Psychiatry, 28*, 230-235.

Everson, M. D., Boat, B. W., Bourg, S., & Robertson, K. R. (1996). Beliefs among professionals about rates of false allegations of child sexual abuse. *Journal of Interpersonal Violence, 11(4)*, 541-553.

Faller, K. C. (1996). *Evaluating children suspected of having been sexually abused: The APSAC study guides 2*. Thousand Oaks, CA: Sage.

Faller, K. C. (1995). A clinical sample of women who have sexually abused children. *Journal of Child Sexual Abuse, 4(3)*, 13-30.

Faller, K. C., & DeVoe, E. (1995). Allegations of sexual abuse in divorce. *Journal of Child Sexual Abuse, 4(4)*, 1-25.

Faller, K. C., Olafson, E., & Corwin, D. (1993). Research on false allegations of sexual abuse in divorce. *The APSAC Advisor, 6(3)*, 1, 7-10.

Finkelhor, D., & Berliner, L. (1995). Research on the treatment of sexually abused children: A review and recommendations. *Journal of the American Academy of Child and Adolescent Psychiatry, 34*, 1408-1423.

Follette, V. M., Alexander, P. C., & Follette, W. C. (1991). Individual predictors of outcome in group treatment for incest survivors. *Journal of Consulting & Clinical Psychology, 59*, 150-155.

Freyd, J. J. (1996). *Betrayal trauma: The logic of forgetting and childhood abuse*. Cambridge, MA: Harvard University Press.

Friedrich, W. N. (1995). *Psychotherapy with sexually abused boys: An integrated approach*. Thousand Oaks, CA: Sage.

Friedrich, W. N., Berliner, L., & Cohen, J. (1995, July). *Sexual behavior in sexually abused children.* Paper presented at 4th International Family Violence Research Conference, Durham, NH.

Friedrich, W. N., Grambsch, P., Damon, L., Koverola, C., Hewitt, S. K., Lang, R. A., & Broughton, D. (1992). Child sexual behavior inventory: Normative and clinical comparisons. *Psychological Assessment, 4,* 303-311.

Gardner, R. (1992). *The parental alienation syndrome.* Cresskill, NJ: Creative Therapeutics.

Geffner, R. (1995). Standards for batterer intervention: Editor's response. *Family Violence & Sexual Assault Bulletin, 11 (3-4),* 29-32.

Geffner, R. (1992a). Guidelines for using mediation with abusive couples. *Psychotherapy in Private Practice, 10,* 77-92.

Geffner, R. (1992b). Current issues and future directions in child sexual abuse. *Journal of Child Sexual Abuse, 1,* 1-13.

Geffner, R., with Mantooth, C. (1995). *A psychoeducational approach for ending wife/partner abuse: A program manual for treating individuals and couples.* Tyler, TX: Family Violence and Sexual Assault Institute.

Geffner, R., & Pagelow, M. D. (1990). Mediation and child custody issues in abusive relationships. *Behavioral Sciences & The Law, 8,* 151-159.

Geffner, R., & Rosenbaum, A. (1992). *Brain impairment and family violence.* In D. Templer, L. Hartlage, & W. G. Cannon (Eds.), *Preventable brain damage: Brain vulnerability and brain health* (pp. 58-71). New York: Springer.

Geffner, R., & Rosenbaum, A. (1990). Characteristics and treatment of batterers. *Behavioral Sciences & The Law, 8,* 131-140.

Geffner, R., Rosenbaum, A., & Hughes, H. (1988). Research issues concerning family violence. In V. B. Van Hasselt, R. L. Morrison, A. S. Bellack, & M. Hersen (Eds.), *Handbook of family violence* (pp. 457-481). New York: Plenum.

Gelles, R. J. (1997). *Intimate violence in families (3rd edition).* Thousand Oaks, CA: Sage.

Gelles, R. (1995, July). *Using the transtheoretical model of change to improve risk assessment in cases of child abuse & neglect.* Paper presented at 4th International Family Violence Research Conference, Durham, NH.

Gil, E. (1996). *Systemic treatment of families who abuse.* San Francisco, CA: Jossey-Bass Publishers.

Goldstein, A. P. (1996). *Violence in America: Lessons on understanding the aggression in our lives.* Palo Alto, CA: Davies-Black Publishing.

Gonsiorek, J. C., Bera, W. H., & LeTourneau, D. (1994). *Male sexual abuse: A trilogy of intervention strategies.* Thousand Oaks, CA: Sage.

Goodman, G. S., & Bottoms, B. L. (1993). *Child victims, child witnesses: Understanding and improving testimony.* New York: Guilford Press.

Graham-Bermann, S., & Levendosky, A. (In Press). The social functioning of preschool-age children whose mothers are emotionally and physically abused. *Journal of Aggression, Maltreatment & Trauma.*

Hamberger, L. K. (1997a). Female offenders in domestic violence: A look at actions in their context. *Journal of Aggression, Maltreatment & Trauma, 1,* 117-129.

Hamberger, L. K. (1997b). Research concerning wife abuse: Implications for physician training. *Journal of Aggression, Maltreatment & Trauma, 1,* 81-96.

Hamberger, L. K., Burge, S. K., Graham, A. V., & Costa, A. (In Press). *Violence issues for health care educators and providers.* Binghamton, NY: Haworth Maltreatment & Trauma Press.

Hamberger, L. K., Lohr, J. M., Bonge, D., & Tolin, D. (1995, July). *A typology of men who batter: Relationship to violence severity.* Paper presented at 4th International Family Violence Research Conference, Durham, NH.

Hansen, M., & Goldenberg, I. (1993). Conjoint therapy with violent couples: Some valid considerations. In M. Hansen & M. Harway (Eds.), *Battering and family therapy: A feminist perspective* (82-92). Newbury Park, CA: Sage.

Harway, M., Hansen, M., & Cervantes, N. N. (1997). Therapist awareness of appropriate intervention in treatment of domestic violence: A review. *Journal of Aggression, Maltreatment & Trauma, 1,* 27-40.

Heyman, R., Brown, P. D., & O'Leary, K. D. (1995, July). *Drop-out in spouse abuse treatment: Role of couples' communication.* Paper presented at 4th International Family Violence Research Conference, Durham, NH.

Holden, G., Geffner, R., & Jouriles, E. (Eds.). (1997). *Children exposed to marital violence: Theory, research, and intervention.* Washington, DC: American Psychological Association.

Holtzworth-Munroe, A., & Stuart, G. L. (1994). Typologies of male batterers: Three subtypes and the differences among them. *Psychological Bulletin, 116,* 476-497.

Hughes, H. M. (1997). Research concerning children of battered women: clinical implications. *Journal of Aggression, Maltreatment & Trauma, 1,* 225-244.

Hyman, B., & Williams, L. (1995, July). *Resilience in adult women survivors of child sexual abuse.* Paper presented at 4th International Family Violence Research Conference, Durham, NH.

Jackson, H., & Nuttall, R. (1997). *Childhood abuse: Effects on clinicians' personal and professional lives.* Thousand Oaks, CA: Sage.

Jaffe, P. G., & Austin, G. W. (1995, July). *The impact of witnessing violence on children in custody & visitation disputes: Current clinical and legal dilemmas.* Paper presented at 4th International Family Violence Research Conference, Durham, NH.

Jaffe, P. G., & Geffner, R. (In Press). Child custody disputes and domestic violence: Critical issues for mental health, social service, and legal professionals. In G. Holden, R. Geffner, & E. Jouriles (Eds.), *Children exposed to marital violence: Theory, research, and intervention.* Washington, DC: American Psychological Association.

Jaffe, P. G., Wolfe, D. A., & Wilson, S. K. (1990). *Children of battered women.* Newbury Park, CA: Sage.

Johnson, T. C. (1995). *Treatment exercises for child abuse victims & children with sexual behavior problems.* Pasadena, CA: T. C. Johnson Publications.

Johnson, T. F. (Ed.). (1995). *Elder mistreatment: Ethical issues, dilemmas, and decisions.* New York: The Haworth Press, Inc.

Jones D., & McGraw, M. (1987). Reliable and fictitious accounts of sexual abuse to children. *Journal of Interpersonal Violence, 2(1)*, 27-45.

Jouriles, E. N., McDonald, R., Stephens, N., Norwood, W., Spiller, L. C., & Ware, H. S. (In Press). Breaking the cycle of violence: helping children departing from battered women's shelters. In G. Holden, R. Geffner, & E. Jouriles (Eds.), *Children exposed to marital violence: Theory, research, and intervention.* Washington, DC: American Psychological Association.

Karp, C. L., & Butler, T. L. (1996). *Treatment strategies for abused children: From victim to survivor.* Thousand Oaks, CA: Sage.

Kinnard, E. M. (1995, July). *Resilience in abused children.* Paper presented at 4th International Family Violence Research Conference, Durham, NH.

Kosberg, J. I., & Garcia, J. L. (1995). *Elder abuse: International and cross-cultural perspectives.* New York: The Haworth Press, Inc.

Kuehnle, K. (1996). *Assessing allegations of child sexual abuse.* Sarasota, FL: Professional Resource Press.

Lipchik, E., Sirles, E. A., & Kubicki, A. D. (1997). Multifaceted approaches in spouse abuse treatment. *Journal of Aggression, Maltreatment & Trauma, 1,* 131-148.

Lundberg-Love, P. K. (1997). Current treatment strategies for dissociative identity disorders in adult sexual abuse survivors. *Journal of Aggression, Maltreatment & Trauma, 1,* 311-333.

Marin, R. S., Booth, B. K., Lidz, C. W., Morycz, R. K., Wettstein, R. M. (1995). In T. F. Johnson (Ed.), *Elder mistreatment: Ethical issues, dilemmas, and decisions* (pp. 49-68). New York: The Haworth Press, Inc.

Marshall, W. L., Jones, R., Ward, T., Johnson, P., & Barbaree, H. E. (1991). Treatment outcome with sex offenders. *Psychology Review, 11,* 465-485.

Melton, G. B., & Barry, F. D. (1994). *Protecting children from abuse and neglect: Foundations for a new national strategy.* New York: Guilford Press.

Mendel, M. P. (1995). *The male survivor: The impact of sexual abuse.* Thousand Oaks, CA: Sage.

Milner, J. S. (1990). *An interpretive manual for the Child Abuse Potential Inventory.* DeKalb, IL: Psytec.

Morgan, M. (1995). *How to interview sexual abuse victims: Including the use of anatomical dolls.* Thousand Oaks, CA: Sage.

Murphy, W. D., & Smith, T. A. (1996). Sex offenders against children: Empirical and clinical issues. In J. Briere, L. Berliner, J. A. Bulkley, C. Jenny, & T. Reid (Eds.), *The APSAC handbook on child maltreatment* (pp. 175-191). Thousand Oaks, CA: Sage.

Myers, J. B. (1994). *The backlash: Child protection under fire.* Thousand Oaks, CA: Sage.

National Research Council. (1996). *Violence against women.* Washington, DC: National Academy Press.

National Research Council. (1993). *Understanding child abuse and neglect.* Washington, DC: National Academy Press.

Ney, T. (Ed.). (1995). *Allegations of child sexual abuse: Assessment and case management*. New York: Brunner/Mazel.

Oates, R. K., & Bross, D. C. (1995). What have we learned about treating child physical abuse? A literature review of the last decade. *Child Abuse & Neglect, 19*, 463-474.

O'Leary, K. D. (1996). Physical aggression in intimate relationships can be treated within a marital context under certain circumstances. *Journal of Interpersonal Violence, 11(3)*, 450-452.

Pagelow, M. D. (1997). Battered women: A historical research review and some common myths. *Journal of Aggression, Maltreatment & Trauma, 1*, 97-116.

Pearlman, L. A. (In Press). Trauma and the self: A theoretical/clinical framework. *Journal of Aggression, Maltreatment & Trauma*.

Pearlman, L. A., & Saakvitne, K. W. (1995). *Trauma and the therapist: Countertransference and vicarious traumatization in psychotherapy with incest survivors*. New York: W.W. Norton.

Peled, E. (1996). "Secondary" victims no more: refocusing intervention with children. In J. L. Edleson & Z. C. Eisikovits (Eds.), *Future interventions with battered women and their families* (pp. 125-153). Thousand Oaks, CA: Sage.

Peled, E., Jaffe, P. J., & Edleson, J. L. (1995). *Ending the cycle of violence: Community response to children of battered women*. Thousand Oaks, CA: Sage.

Pope, K. S., & Brown, L. S. (1996). *Recovered memories of abuse: Assessment, therapy, forensics*. Washington, DC: American Psychological Association.

Quinsey, V. L., & Lalumiere, M. L. (1996). *Assessment of sexual offenders against children: The APSAC study guides 1*. Thousand Oaks, CA: Sage.

Renzetti, C. M., & Miley, C. H. (1996). *Violence in gay and lesbian domestic partnerships*. New York: The Haworth Press, Inc.

Rosenbaum, A., Geffner, R., & Benjamin, S. (1997). A biopsychosocial model for understanding relationship aggression. *Journal of Aggression, Maltreatment & Trauma, 1*, 57-79.

Rosenbaum, A., & Hoge, S. K. (1989). Head injury and marital aggression. *American Journal of Psychiatry, 146*, 1048-1051.

Rossman, B. B. R., & Rosenberg, M. S. (1997). Psychological maltreatment: A needs analysis and application for children in violent families. *Journal of Aggression, Maltreatment & Trauma, 1*, 245-262.

Saunders, D. G. (1995, July). *Matching domestic violence offenders to treatment methods: Evidence from an experimental comparison of two treatments*. Paper presented at 4th International Family Violence Research Conference, Durham, NH.

Saunders, D.G. (1993). Husbands who assault: Multiple profiles requiring multiple responses. In N. Z. Hilton (Ed.), *Legal responses to wife assault: Current trends and evaluation* (pp. 9-34). Newbury Park, CA: Sage.

Saywitz, K. J., & Goodman, G. S. (1996). Interviewing children in and out of court: Current research and practice implications. In J. Briere, L. Berliner, J. A. Bulkley, C. Jenny, & T. Reid (Eds.), *The APSAC handbook on child maltreatment* (pp. 297-318). Thousand Oaks, CA: Sage.

Saywitz, K. J., & Snyder, L. (1993). Improving children's testimony with preparation. In G. S. Goodman & B. L. Bottoms (Eds.), *Child victims, child witnesses: Understanding and improving testimony* (pp. 117-146). New York: Guilford Press.

Schafer, J. (1996). Measuring spousal violence with the Conflict Tactics Scale: Notes on reliability and validity issues. *Journal of Interpersonal Violence, 11(4)*, 572-585.

Schlee, K. A., & O'Leary, K. D. (1995, July). *Treatment for abused women: Are there different effects for women with PTSD?* Paper presented at 4th International Family Violence Research Conference, Durham, NH.

Sedlak, A. J. (1997). Risk factors for the occurrence of child abuse and neglect. *Journal of aggression, maltreatment & trauma, 1*, 149-187.

Shamai, M. (1996). Couple therapy with battered women and abusive men: Does it have a future? In J. L. Edleson & Z. C. Eisikovits (Eds.), *Future interventions with battered women and their families* (pp. 201-215). Thousand Oaks, CA: Sage.

Simkins, L., & Renier, A. (1996). An analytical review of empirical literature on children's play with anatomically detailed dolls. *Journal of Child Sexual Abuse, 5(1)*, 21-45.

Sonkin, D. J. (1995). *The counselor's guide to learning to live without violence.* Volcano, CA: Volcano Press.

Sorenson, S. B., Peterson, J. G., & Richardson, B. A. (1997). Child homocide in the city of Los Angeles: An epidemiologic examination of a decade of deaths. *Journal of Aggression, Maltreatment & Trauma, 1*, 189-205.

Stamm, B. H. (Ed.). (1995). *Secondary traumatic stress: Self-care issues for clinicians, researchers, and educators.* Lutherville, MD: Sidran Press.

Straus, M. A., & Gelles, R. J. (1986). Societal change and change in family violence from 1975 to 1985 revealed by two national surveys. *Journal of Marriage & the Family, 48*, 465-479.

Straus, M. A., Gelles, R. J., & Steinmetz, S. K. (1980). *Behind closed doors: Violence in the American family.* Garden City, NJ: Doubleday.

Straus, M. A., Hamby, S. L., Boney-McCoy, S., & Sugarman, D. B. (1995, July). *The partner and relationship profile: A package of instruments for research and clinical screening.* Paper presented at 4th International Family Violence Research Conference, Durham, NH.

Tedeschi, J. T., & Felson, R. B. (1994). *Violence, aggression, and coercive actions.* Washington, DC: American Psychological Association.

Thoennes, N., & Tjaden, P. (1990). The extent, nature, and validity of sexual abuse allegations in custody/visitation disputes. *Child Abuse & Neglect, 14*, 151-163.

Tolman, R. M. (1995). *The validation of the Psychological Maltreatment of Women Inventory.* Paper presented at 4th International Family Violence Research Conference, Durham, NH.

Tyndall, C. I. (1997). Current treatment strategies for sexually abused children. *Journal of Aggression, Maltreatment & Trauma, 1*, 277-291.

Van der Kolk, B. (1995). The body, memory, and the psychobiology of trauma. In J. L. Alpert (Ed.)., *Sexual abuse recalled: Treating trauma in the era of the recovered memory debate* (pp. 29-60). Northvale, NJ: Jason Aronson.

Van der Kolk, B. A., & Fisler, R. (1995). Dissociation and the fragmentary nature of traumatic memories: Overview and exploratory study. *Journal of Traumatic Stress, 8(4),* 505-525.

Van der Kolk, B. A., McFarlane, A. C., & Weisaeth, L. (Eds.) (1996). *Traumatic stress: The effects of overwhelming experience on mind, body, and society.* New York: Guilford Press.

Walker, A. G., & Warren, A. R. (1995). The language of the child abuse interview: Asking the questions, understanding the answers. In T. Ney (Ed.), *True and false allegations of child sexual abuse: Assessment and case management* (pp. 153-162). New York: Brunner/Mazel.

Webb, L. P., & Leehan, J. (1996). *Group treatment for adult survivors of abuse: A manual for practitioners.* Thousand Oaks, CA: Sage.

Whitfield, C. L. (1995). *Memory and abuse: Remembering and healing the effects of trauma.* Deerfield Beach, FL: Health Communications.

Wiehe, V. R. (1996). *Working with child abuse and neglect: A primer.* Thousand Oaks, CA: Sage.

Wieland, S. (1997). *Hearing the internal trauma: Working with children and adolescents who have been sexually abused.* Thousand Oaks, CA: Sage.

Williams, L. M. (1995). Recovered memories of abuse in women with documented child sexual victimization histories. *Journal of Traumatic Stress, 8(4),* 649-673.

Williams, O. (1995, July). *What do African American men who batter think of partner abuse treatment?* Paper presented at 4th International Family Violence Research Conference, Durham, NH.

Williams, O., & Becker, R. L. (1995, July). *Partner abuse treatment programs and cultural competence: The results of a national survey.* Paper presented at 4th International Family Violence Research Conference, Durham, NH.

Wolfe, D., & Wekerle, C. (1993). Treatment strategies for child physical abuse and neglect: A critical progress report. *Clinical Psychology Review, 13,* 473-500.

Wolfe, D. A., Wekerle, C., Gough, R. et al. (1996). *The youth relationships manual: A group approach with adolescents for the prevention of woman abuse and the promotion of healthy relationships.* Thousand Oaks, CA: Sage.

Wurtele, S. K., & Miller-Perrin, C. L. (1993). *Preventing child sexual abuse: Sharing the responsibility.* Lincoln, NB: University of Nebraska Press.

Zaragoza, M. S., Graham, J. R., Hall, G. C., Hirschman, R., & Ben-Porath, Y. S. (1995). *Memory and testimony in the child witness.* Thousand Oaks, CA: Sage.

Therapist Awareness
of Appropriate Intervention
in Treatment of Domestic Violence:
A Review

Michele Harway
Marsali Hansen
Nancyann N. Cervantes

SUMMARY. Given the widespread nature of relationship violence, psychotherapists must recognize the probability that at some point they will treat a violent couple or someone involved in a violent relationship, even if they do not specialize in the treatment of family violence. Two analogue studies reported in this chapter were designed to investigate how therapists conceptualize cases involving domestic violence families and the types of interventions they indicate they would make. The first study surveyed 362 members of the American Association for Marriage and Family Therapy (AAMFT). Respondents were asked to conceptualize and provide interventions for one of two actual cases that involved family violence. The second study surveyed 402 members of the American Psychological Association (APA). Respondents were asked to give a diagnosis based on a case presentation. After being informed the case resulted in a homicide, respondents were asked what interventions they would have made

---

Address correspondence to: Michelle Harway, Phillips Graduate Institute, 5445 Balboa Boulevard, Encino, CA 91316-1509.

[Haworth co-indexing entry note]: "Therapist Awareness of Appropriate Intervention in Treatment of Domestic Violence: A Review." Harway, Michele, Marsali Hansen, and Nancyann N. Cervantes. Co-published simultaneously in *Journal of Aggression, Maltreatment & Trauma* (Haworth Maltreatment & Trauma Press, an imprint of The Haworth Press, Inc.) Vol. 1, No. 1 (#1), 1997, pp. 27-40; and: *Violence and Sexual Abuse at Home: Current Issues in Spousal Battering and Child Maltreatment* (ed: Robert Geffner, Susan B. Sorenson, and Paula K. Lundberg-Love) Haworth Maltreatment & Trauma Press, an imprint of The Haworth Press, Inc., 1997, pp. 27-40. Single or multiple copies of this article are available for a fee from The Haworth Document Delivery Service [1-800-342-9678, 9:00 a.m. - 5:00 p.m. (EST). E-mail address: getinfo@haworth.com].

27

prior to the outcome, had they been given the opportunity to provide counseling. Results from both analogue studies indicate that a large number of respondents were unable to properly assess the danger inherent in cases of domestic violence, and many more would not have intervened in a timely and appropriate manner. *[Article copies available for a fee from The Haworth Document Delivery Service: 1-800-342-9678. E-mail address: getinfo@haworth.com]*

KEYWORDS. Spouse abuse, ethics, treatment, risk assessment, lethality, battering

Recent domestic violence statistics in the United States are alarming. Koss (1990) reports that as many as 25-33% of married couples engage in some form of domestic violence at some point in their relationship. Every year, at least 16% of couples experience violence at home (Straus & Gelles, 1989). In many instances, the violence may be so extreme as to result in murder, with lethality in cases of wife battering most likely to occur when the woman tries to leave (Browne, 1987). Moreover, more than twice as many women are killed by their husbands or boyfriends as are murdered by strangers (Kellerman, 1992).

These data indicate that family violence is widespread and that it can result in serious consequences. Psychotherapists must recognize the probability that at some point during their practice they will treat a violent couple, or someone involved in a violent relationship, even if they do not specialize in the treatment of violent families. Thus, it is particularly important that psychotherapists be skilled in both the recognition of violence and the use of appropriate interventions.

Recently, the role that therapists play in the identification and treatment of violent families has come under scrutiny (Cervantes, 1993). Family therapists, in particular, have been criticized because they may address family violence only within the theoretical context of systemic patterns, which may obscure the seriousness of the act and the perpetrator's responsibility for the violence (Bograd, 1984; Pressman, 1989). Cook and Cook (1984) warned that working within the context of couples therapy could obscure the recognition of violence. They indicated that this is likely to happen because in such a context the husband will understate the events and the wife will be fearful of the consequences of addressing them. Moreover, traditional couples' therapy by its very nature assumes that if the wife changes her behavior then her husband will be better able to control his acts of violence. He does not, therefore, have sole responsibility for his own behavior. The perspective of shared responsibility common in the family therapy literature is advocated by well known family therapists, such as Minuchin (1984) who indicated that in cases of violence, "only when you remove the violence from a family member, and locate it in the interactions among members, can you determine the appropriate distance for defusing destructiveness" (p. 170). Moreover, Harway (1992) and Goodwin (1993) have argued that training programs do not sufficiently prepare clinicians to work with domestic violence and suggest that such training be focused on directly in graduate programs and internships.

If criticisms of such therapeutic interventions are valid, therapists may be harming the very people they intend to help. Until recently, little research has looked directly at therapists' conceptualizations in cases of abuse. Cook and Cook (1984) expressed concern that therapists were failing to detect abuse. However, evidence for the concern was a case report. The two studies which follow were designed to investigate therapists' conceptualization of cases involving violent families using an analogue design. The purpose of the first study was to examine how therapists assess and intervene in cases involving domestic violence.

STUDY 1

Method

Participants. Participants consisted of 362 members of the American Association for Marriage and Family Therapy (AAMFT) who responded to a mail questionnaire sent to a randomly selected sample of the total AAMFT membership. The 20% response rate obtained here is typical of mail surveys with one follow-up. A higher return rate would not necessarily guarantee generalizability (Berdie & Anderson, 1974); only in the hypothetical instance where all those who received the questionnaire returned it, would it be possible to ascertain the representativeness of the sample. Thus, the 362 respondents in this study may or may not be representative of AAMFT membership.

Procedure. Respondents received a mail questionnaire presenting an actual case in which family violence was implicated. Two parallel versions of the questionnaire were developed to ascertain whether demographic differences or differences in the abuse described resulted in different responses. Half the sample received Version A of the questionnaire while the other half received Version B (about equal numbers of respondents responded to each version). The two questionnaire versions were identical except for the case that was presented to respondents: One case (Case A) was obtained from court records where, unbeknownst to study participants, the woman was later killed by her spouse. The second case (Case B) involved a violent couple who had presented for therapy as part of a diversion program from the courts. Respondents were asked to give a conceptualization of the case and state what interventions they might make. Comparisons were later made of responses to the two separate questionnaire versions and no significant differences emerged. Thus, the two subgroups were combined for data analysis.

Case A

Tony, age 20, and Beth, age 19, have been married a total of three years. They have been separated for the last year. They have a 3 year old daughter and a 1 year old son and Beth is 2 months pregnant. Both Tony and Beth are living with their respective parents although they see each other frequently and have continued sexual relations. Tony states that he had to quit school to support his wife and children. He hopes to finish school and to apply to the local police department academy. He wants Beth to terminate the pregnancy. Beth states that Tony gets mad easily and she suspects that he has another girlfriend. Recently, she followed him to the liquor store and found him in a phone booth talking to an old girlfriend. They argued about this phone call. She claims he punched her in the back and stomach and caused her to miscarry. He claims that she tried to hit him and then punched herself in the back.

Case B

Carol and James have been married 10 years. They have two children, Dana, 9, and Tracy, 7. James is employed as a foreman in a concrete manufacturing plant. Carol also is employed. James is upset because on several occasions Carol did not return home from work until two or three in the morning and did not explain her whereabouts to him. He acknowledges privately to the therapist that the afternoon prior to the session he had seen her in a bar with a man. Carol tells the therapist privately that she has made efforts to dissolve the marriage and to seek a protection order against her husband because he has repeatedly been physically violent with her and the kids, and on the day prior, he grabbed her and threw her on the floor in a violent manner and then struck her. The family had made plans to go shopping, roller skating and out to dinner after the session.

Respondents were then asked:

1. What is going on in this family?
2. How would you intervene?
3. What outcome would you expect from this intervention?
4. What outcome would you expect without any intervention at all?
5. What legal/ethical issues does this case raise?

Data Processing. Open-ended responses were coded through the following process: Categories for responses to the question "What is going on?" were developed through key word analysis. Based on this analysis, five categories were developed: (1) violence addressed, (2) family-of-origin issues addressed, (3) other specific problems, (4) further assessment needed, (5) not able to answer. For each of these categories, two raters independently ascertained whether the category was addressed and, if it was, what specific words were used to describe that category. If violence was addressed in any fashion, then the severity was assessed, again by the two raters acting independently. The ratings were consistent across the board with the exception of one questionnaire where the lowest of the two severity ratings was retained.

Results

When asked to describe what was going on in the clinical case, 40% of the practitioners in this sample failed to address the issue of violence (N = 141). The remaining 60% gave a response which focused on the violence. Any answer was coded in this category if it addressed the violence, regardless of the words the respondents used to describe it and the order in which they presented their perceptions. When the descriptions of the conflict were coded in a way that took into account the language and level of severity used by the respondents, 91% of those who addressed the conflict considered it mild or moderate.

Recognition of family violence is an important first step, but no less important are the therapists' descriptions of how they would intervene. Fully 55% of respondents did not suggest interventions focusing on the crisis nature of the violence. Only 11% said they would obtain protection for the wife; responses suggesting that protection would be obtained included either helping her develop a safety plan, getting her to a shelter, or helping her get a restraining order. In contrast, 14% indicated they would work on the couple's communication style.

An analysis of the interventions recommended by clinicians who initially did identify the violence compared to those who did not reveals a significant difference between groups. Clinicians who did not initially identify the violence were significantly less likely to address the violence in their interventions ($\chi^2 = 51.1$, p < .01, df = 1). Similarly, in a stepwise multiple regression examining which variables predicted the identification of violence as a primary problem, the single best predictor (accounting for 52% of the variance) was recognizing the seriousness of the conflict.

A number of analyses comparing respondents by sex, theoretical orientation and training were conducted. There were no differences between male and female therapists in terms of whether they addressed the conflict, how serious they saw the conflict to be, nor how they would intervene. Theoretical orientation was inconsistently related to whether the conflict was addressed in the conceptualizations (see Hansen, Harway, & Cervantes (1991) for a more detailed description of these results). Finally, clinicians self-identifying as psychologists (only 14% of the sample) were significantly less likely to address the conflict than other clinicians ($\chi^2 = 17.4$, p < .001, df = 1), and less likely to describe the family conflict as violence or battering than other mental health professionals ($\chi^2 = 15.58$, p < .001, df = 1).

Discussion

Results suggest that a substantial number of AAMFT clinician members do not identify violent behavior as a primary treatment concern and, thus, would be unable to intervene appropriately in cases of domestic violence. Unclear from these results is whether those therapists are missing the indicators for violence and therefore are generating inappropriate interventions, or whether they were able to identify violence as a cause for concern but cannot intervene appropriately. A majority of the sample was comprised of marriage and family therapists, thus, the results may be limited to those studied. Consequently, a second study was undertaken to address this question.

STUDY 2

Method

Participants. Participants consisted of 405 members of the American Psychological Association's (APA) Divisions of Clinical Psychology, Psychotherapy, and Independent Practice (Divisions 12, 29, and 42, respectively) who responded to a mail questionnaire (a response rate of about 30% from a randomly selected sample of the total membership of the above-listed divisions). The limits on the generalization of the results as described above also apply here.

A random numbers table was used to select respondents from membership rosters of the above-listed divisions, lists which were obtained from the Central APA office. These divisions were selected because their memberships were likely to include a large proportion of clinicians and the survey indicated that this was the case: only 4% of the respondents indicated that they spent no time delivering clinical services whereas 70% of the respondents spent more than 50% of their time in clinical service delivery. The sample thus generated was a stratified random sample, representing each division proportionately to the size of its membership. Because no question was included in the questionnaire about divisional membership, it was not possible to compare respondent rates by division membership.

Procedure. A mail questionnaire was sent to the randomly selected sample. The questionnaire requested demographic data and information about professional affiliation, theoretical orientation and the impact of feminism on their therapeutic approach. As in Study 1, the questionnaire included a case (Case B) in which family violence was implicated. Respondents were asked to apply a DSM III-R diagnosis, and then were informed that the husband murdered his wife:

> James came home prior to the roller skating date. Carol was in the shower getting ready to go out with the family. He and Carol had an argument as she came out of the shower and he strangled her to death.

Respondents then were asked:

1. Given that an opportunity for counseling existed prior to the outcome, describe an intervention you might have used.
2. What do you perceive to have been the underlying dynamics of this case?
3. What would your goals have been for your intervention?
4. What outcome would you have expected?
5. What ethical/legal issues does this case raise?

Informing respondents of the lethal outcome was a deliberate change in procedure. Its purpose was to follow-up on the findings of Study 1, in particular to ascertain whether therapists do not know the appropriate interventions to make in the case of domestic violence or whether an inability to identify violence resulted in inappropriate interventions. Telling respondents that the outcome was lethal allowed an examination of the interventions clinicians would implement when the presenting problem of

TABLE 1. What DSM-III-R Diagnosis Would You Make in This Case?

	%
Diagnosis of the couple's marital problems (usually V61.10)	23
Both the husband and the wife diagnosed as having pathology (e.g., the husband: intermittent explosive disorder or conduct disorder; the wife: self-defeating personality or dependent personality)	20
Diagnosis only of the husband (e.g., intermittent explosive disorder)	16
The husband diagnosed as having pathology (e.g., intermittent explosive disorder), the wife as reacting (e.g., adjustment reaction)	2
Diagnosis only of the wife (e.g., passive-aggressive)	2
Other diagnoses	2
Not enough information to make a diagnosis	36

violence was clearly identified and the crisis nature of the case was underlined.

Results

Diagnosis. The single most common diagnosis made by 23% of the respondents was one that focused on the couple's marital problems (DSM III-R code V61.10). (See Table 1.) Next most common (20%) was a diagnosis indicating that both the husband and the wife were suffering from some form of pathology. Typically, the husband was found to be suffering from intermittent explosive disorder or a conduct disorder, and the wife a self-defeating or dependent personality. An additional 16% diagnosed the husband only. Over one third (36%) of respondents claimed that they did not have enough information to make a diagnosis. The case consisted of only a one paragraph description which may account for the unwillingness of this group to offer a diagnosis. Two percent diagnosed the husband as having pathology and the wife an adjustment reaction, and 2% restricted their diagnosis to the wife who was seen as passive-aggressive. Miscellaneous other diagnoses were reported by 2% of the respondents.

Dynamics. Almost one third of the sample (31%) reported that the dynamics of the case were couples dynamics (see Table 2). Only 19% pointed to the husband's dynamics, while another 16% were vague about whose dynamics were implicated. Eight percent gave responses which described the wife's behavior as responsible for the violent outcome and

TABLE 2. What Do You Perceive to Have Been the Underlying Dynamics of This Case?

	%
Couple's dynamics: specification of dynamics of both	31
The husband's dynamics	19
Dynamics generally mentioned without specifying to whom they referred	16
Wife's dynamics, seeming to "blame the victim"	8
Couple's dynamics but focused on the husband	3
Other	2
Not enough information to make a diagnosis	21

another 3% referred to the couple's dynamics but focused on the husband. Twenty-one percent stated that they did not have enough information to describe the underlying dynamics of the case even though they had been told that the wife had been killed by the husband. Finally, two percent gave other miscellaneous explanations about the underlying dynamics of the case.

Intervention. After being informed about the lethal outcome of the case, 50% indicated that, if they had an opportunity to provide counseling prior to the final outcome, the intervention of choice would have been to seek protection for the wife. Another 27% indicated that they wanted to assess the couple further to ascertain the seriousness of the violence, and 11% stated they would have focused entirely on the problem as a couple's problem, with interventions focused on getting the couple to communicate or to ventilate their feelings. Five percent gave miscellaneous other responses, and 5% stated that they did not have enough information to describe an intervention. Finally, two respondents (1%) blamed the victim, intervening in such a way as to suggest that the wife was responsible for the husband's violent behavior.

Three major response tendencies characterized respondents' intervention goals: contextual, communication, and noncommittal (see Table 3). The first group included those who said they intervened through crisis intervention because the context of the case suggested that the wife was in grave danger. Thus, the goals of intervention were to remove the wife from the situation of danger through an immediate legal separation or the development of a safety plan. We labeled this group the *Contextualists* (54% of sample). The second group focused on the dynamics of the case to the exclusion of external cues. This resulted in their applying interventions in

TABLE 3. What Would Your Goals Have Been for Your Intervention?

	%
Contextualists	54
Crisis intervention because of the focus on the context: removal of the woman through divorce or a safety plan	
Communication interventionists	34
Focus on the dynamics to the exclusion of external cues; leading to focus on interventions in therapy without recognition of practical context of the case (e.g., communication interventions, self-esteem strategies, empowerment)	
Noncommittal	11
Hesitant to make a decision without further information; no formulations of dynamics or interventions appropriate	
Miscellaneous	2

therapy without recognizing the practical context of the case and thereby missing the need to intervene in an immediate and practical way. They appeared to believe they must do therapy no matter what. We have called them the *Communication Interventionists* (34% of the sample).

The final group includes therapists who were hesitant to make decisions without further information. For this group, there was virtually no formulation of dynamics or description of appropriate interventions. This group we have called *Noncommittal* (11%). The noncommittal group reflects only those who indicated they did not have enough information to formulate intervention goals. The respondents in the noncommittal group represent a sizable subgroup of those respondents who were unable to describe the underlying dynamics, but not the entire group. Likewise, these individuals represented a proportion, but not a totality, of those who reported they could not make a diagnosis without more information. In addition to the three groups named above, 2% of the respondents gave various miscellaneous responses about the thinking behind their interventions.

Discussion

This study was designed to answer some questions which our previous research had left unclear. To recapitulate, we wanted to ascertain whether:

1. findings of our previous study were spurious or idiosyncratic to the sample of Marriage and Family Therapists studied, or
2. therapists were missing indicators of violence and, therefore, were generating inappropriate interventions, or
3. psychotherapists were able to identify violence as a cause for concern but were unable to intervene appropriately.

Spurious Findings. Results of Study 2 support those of Study 1, in that a substantial proportion of the psychologist respondents (50%) did not generate appropriate interventions even when told outright that the case was one of domestic violence with a lethal outcome. The consistency of the results suggest that the findings may apply to psychotherapists of different disciplines and professional affiliations.

Identification of Violence. The relatively consistent findings across both studies suggest that many psychotherapists are unable to formulate appropriate intervention plans even when explicitly told that a case is a violent one. Given the obvious danger to the wife in the case, results suggest that therapists are unprepared to assess for dangerousness in violent families. Diagnoses (made prior to knowing about the homicide) and assessment of dynamics (made after being told of the murder) were very similar: A substantial proportion of respondents used a V-code for marital problems (V61.10) as a diagnosis and speculated that the underlying dynamics of the case were heavily dependent on the couple's issues. In fact, we could anticipate that even those clinicians giving a V-code prior to knowing about the homicide would have changed their diagnosis to one focusing on the pathology of the perpetrator. Only a handful of respondents either before or after learning of the homicide gave an individual pathology diagnosis to the husband. Certainly any number of diagnoses might be given to an individual who expresses anger by being physically abusive (e.g., conduct disorder or intermittent explosive disorder). Knowledge of the ultimate lethality of the violence could have served to underscore the idea that system diagnoses are not useful in preventing damage in violent families.

In addition, an important percentage of the sample was willing neither to give a diagnosis or to outline the underlying dynamics of the case. This was an unexpected outcome especially because the instructions did not appear to encourage a response of this nature. Many other respondents believed that they had insufficient information even after they were told that the wife had been murdered. It appears that an important cross-section of the therapeutic community was unable to assess properly the danger inherent in this case of domestic violence. These findings are cause for concern about the ability and readiness of psychotherapists to identify violence.

Appropriateness of Interventions. Even after being informed that the outcome of the case was homicide, fully one half of the sample stated that they would not have invoked any form of crisis intervention. Crisis intervention might involve a variety of therapist instigated behaviors, including, but not limited to, ways of obtaining protection for the wife or of ensuring her safety. Instead, 27% wanted to assess further the violence inherent in this family, another 11% proposed intervening through couple's communication exercises or the venting of feelings. Finally, a few respondents suggested interventions with the wife to change her behavior (e.g., not to provoke the husband's anger), thereby implying that the wife was responsible for the husband's behavior. Working with a battered woman to help her change her behavior so as not to provoke the batterer's rage suggests that when the violence does explode it is a consequence of her inability to control herself and him, rather than due to his inability to control himself.

Differences Between Therapeutic Groups. In our sample, we found three major conceptual approaches to a domestic violence case:

1. therapists who focused on crisis intervention because of their focus on the context,
2. therapists who focused on the dynamics of the case to the exclusion of external cues, causing them to focus on interventions (such as communication strategies) without recognition of the urgent context of the case, and
3. therapists who were hesitant to make any decision without more information and therefore did not formulate appropriate interventions.

Study Limitations. The validity of these response tendencies must be tempered by the analogue nature of the study and the fact that only a brief vignette was presented to the respondents in a written questionnaire. In working with actual violent families, some of the above-grouped therapists may intervene in very different ways. Thus, other than the responses to our questionnaire, we do not know whether this typology would replicate therapists' actual behavior. Of course, social scientists have known for some time now that analogue research does not always yield results similar to real life situations (Kazdin, 1986).

The hesitance of a sizeable proportion of psychotherapists to operate within a crisis framework may indicate a frank admission that they would have missed the danger signals in a case of domestic violence. Clinicians must routinely make decisions based on incomplete information and, if provided the benefit of hindsight, may be able to identify ways in which they would have changed their work with a client. Thus, rather than chastising this group as potentially not taking appropriate protective measures, their responses may indicate an admirable unwillingness to "second guess" their conceptualizations and interventions based on after-the-fact information.

SUMMARY OF FINDINGS

A large number of respondents were unable to assess properly the danger inherent in cases of domestic violence and many more did not intervene in a timely and appropriate manner. Study 1 indicated that 91% of therapists failed to recognize the seriousness of violence in altercations between couples and that 40% failed to address the issue of violence at all. Because even those who addressed the violence appeared to underestimate its seriousness, the interventions they subsequently recommended were inappropriate. Study 2 reported that a substantial proportion of psychotherapists, from a variety of theoretical orientations, were unable to formulate appropriate intervention plans even when explicitly told that a case was a violent one. Many of these therapists were unprepared to assess for dangerousness in violent families and indicated they would not be able to protect their clients from harm.

Therapists need to increase their awareness of violence within families and to intervene appropriately. The provision of effective treatment in these cases is dependent upon graduate training programs providing adequate training regarding battering and violence toward women in general, accrediting bodies requiring such training and licensing boards requiring continuing education for licensed practitioners.

REFERENCES

Berdie, D. R., & Anderson, J. F. (1974). *Questionnaires: Design and use*. Metuchen, NJ: The Scarecrow Press.

Bograd, M. (1984). Family systems approaches to wife battering: A feminist critique. *American Journal of Orthopsychiatry, 54*, 558-568.

Browne, A. (1987). *When battered women kill*. New York: Free Press.

Cervantes, N. (1993) Therapist duty in domestic violence cases: Ethical considerations. In M. Hansen & M. Harway (Eds.), *Battering and Family Therapy: A Feminist Perspective* (pp. 147-155). Newbury Park, CA: Sage.

Cook, D. R., & Cook, A. R. (1984). A systematic treatment approach to wife battering. *Journal of Marital and Family Therapy, 10*, 83-93.

Goodwin, B. J. (1993). Psychotherapy supervision: Training therapists to recognize family violence. In M. Hansen & M. Harway (Eds.), *Battering and family therapy: A feminist perspective* (pp. 119-133). Newbury Park, CA: Sage.

Hansen, M., Harway, M., & Cervantes, N. (1991). Therapists' perceptions of severity in cases of family violence. *Violence and Victims, 6*, 225-235.

Harway, M. (1992). Training issues in working with violent families. *Family Violence and Sexual Assault Bulletin, 8*, 18-20.

Kazdin, A. E. (1986). The evaluation of psychotherapy: Research design and methodology. In S. L. Garfield, & A. E. Bergin (Eds.), *Handbook of psychotherapy and behavior change (Third Edition)*, (pp. 23-68). New York: John Wiley.

Kellerman, A. L., & Mercy, J. A. (1992). Men, women and murder. *Journal of Trauma, 33*, 1-5.

Koss, M. P. (1990). The women's mental health research agenda: Violence against women. *American Psychologist, 45*, 374-380.

Minuchin, S. (1984). *Family kaleidoscope.* Cambridge, MA: Harvard University Press.

Pressman, B. (1989). Wife-abused couples: The need for comprehensive theoretical perspectives and integrated treatment models. *Journal of Feminist Family Therapy, 1*, 23-43.

Straus, M. A., & Gelles, R. J. (1989). How violent are American families? Estimates from the National Family Violence Resurvey and other studies. In M. A. Strauss and R. J. Gelles (Eds.), *Physical violence in American families* (pp. 95-132). New Brunswick, NJ: Transaction Publishers.

SPOUSE/PARTNER MALTREATMENT: ISSUES, INTERVENTIONS, AND RESEARCH

Therapist Ethical Responsibilities for Spousal Abuse Cases

Nancyann N. Cervantes
Marsali Hansen

SUMMARY. The purpose of this article is to review and delineate the ethical responsibilities owed by clinicians to clients who are involved in abusive relationships. Ethical responsibilities are distinct from legal mandates. There is only one legal mandate that relates to spousal abuse. This mandate is the one recently imposed on individuals working in specific settings in California to report victims who are suffering from a wound or other physical injury as a result of assaultive or abusive behavior due to criminal acts, including batter-

---

Address correspondence to: Marsali Hansen, PhD, PA CASSP Training Institute, Suite 316, Building 1, Harrisburg, PA 17102.

[Haworth co-indexing entry note]: "Therapist Ethical Responsibilities for Spousal Abuse Cases." Cervantes, Nancyann N., and Marsali Hansen. Co-published simultaneously in *Journal of Aggression, Maltreatment & Trauma* (Haworth Maltreatment & Trauma Press, an imprint of The Haworth Press, Inc.) Vol. 1, No. 1 (#1), 1997, pp. 41-56; and: *Violence and Sexual Abuse at Home: Current Issues in Spousal Battering and Child Maltreatment* (ed: Robert Geffner, Susan B. Sorenson, and Paula K. Lundberg-Love) Haworth Maltreatment & Trauma Press, an imprint of The Haworth Press, Inc., 1997, pp. 41-56. Single or multiple copies of this article are available for a fee from The Haworth Document Delivery Service [1-800-342-9678, 9:00 a.m. - 5:00 p.m. (EST). E-mail address: getinfo@haworth.com].

41

ing. The ethical responsibilities are discussed under the categories of the responsibility to provide effective treatment and the duty to warn/protect. Specific recommendations are made to help clinicians make ethical decisions regarding spousal abuse cases. *[Article copies available for a fee from The Haworth Document Delivery Service: 1-800-342-9678. E-mail address: getinfo@haworth.com]*

KEYWORDS. Domestic violence, ethics, duty to warn, legal mandates, victims, battering

Domestic violence and its negative impact on individuals and families has gained national prominence in the last few years, culminating in the passage at the federal level of the Violence Against Women Act (1994). Although the number of arrests has increased 70%, domestic violence is still under reported (Schmidt & Sherman, 1993; Waits, 1995). Fifty percent of all women will likely experience violence in an intimate relationship at some point in their lives (National Clearinghouse for the Defense of Battered Women, 1994). Koss (1990) cites statistics indicating that 31% of couples engage in some form of violence toward each other. Studies conducted to specifically determine the incidence rates have also demonstrated the seriousness of the problem. These studies have been conducted in emergency medical facilities (Abbott, Johnson, Koziol-McLain, & Lowenstein, 1995), psychiatric facilities (Tham, Ford, & Wilkerson, 1995), and military counseling centers (Bohannon, Dosser, & Lindley, 1995). Of the population studied, the percentages range from 40% with a history of violence to 57% reporting violence in their current relationship. An overall summary is that approximately 2 to 4 million women are abused in their homes each year (Novello, 1992). Perhaps more compelling in this time of health care reform and managed care concern are the statistics that domestic violence causes almost 100,000 days of hospitalization, 30,000 emergency room visits, and 40,000 trips to the doctor each year (Jacobs, cited in Jones, 1994). These numbers represent the medical care required for the physical injuries, and are probably a low estimate because many of the women are prevented from receiving medical attention at the time of assault by their batterer (Okun, 1986).

In addition to the physical injuries, the psychological impact is well documented. Walker (1984) found that battered women are twice as likely to be depressed than the general population of women. Carmen, Ricker, and Mills (1984) report that 43% of psychiatric inpatients have a confirmed history of physical and/or sexual abuse either by a current or a former spouse. Stark (1984) estimated that 26% of the women who attempted suicide and 30% of the female alcoholics are the victims of spousal abuse. These data indicate that most, if not all, mental health and health care providers will come into contact with clients involved in a violent relationship at some point in their career regardless of whether they choose to specialize in family violence cases.

Therapist awareness and interest in spousal abuse was initially related to the rise of the feminist movement in this country. Since the mid 1970s, legal reforms have been adopted in every state in an effort to provide greater protection for victims of spousal abuse (Caringella-MacDonald, 1988; Hart, 1993; Keilitz, 1994). The legal reforms have included civil protection orders, warrantless arrests for misdemeanor crimes involving domestic violence, and victimless prosecution. Victimless prosecution allows the case to be prosecuted based upon evidence from medical records, witness reports, physical evidence from the scene, photographs and 911 tapes (i.e., recorded calls to police). Also, this legal reform recognizes the severe stress the victim experiences by allowing the woman's "excited utterances" heard by the police and other witnesses. In San Diego, California, one of the first jurisdictions to utilize victimless prosecution, almost 60% of the 400-500 domestic violence cases prosecuted each month are victimless prosecutions (Jensen, 1994).

A detailed analysis of the legal reforms is beyond the scope of this article. A well documented history of the legal reforms is provided by Burstein (1995). Despite the legal advances, Hart (1993) points out that "Legal strategies collapse if the consciousness of the community is not aligned against violence, if emergency services and housing are not available to the battered woman and her children, if human services institutions are not cognizant of domestic violence and are not employing strategies to safeguard victims and to hold batterers accountable, and if the family and friends of the battered woman and the batterer do not reject violence as an option in intimate relationships and offer support for safety and change" (p. 27).

Mental health providers are not the only profession grappling with the ethical responsibility they owe to clients involved in abusive relationships. Both the medical profession (American Medical Association, 1992) and the legal profession (Waits, 1995) have either adopted guidelines or strongly advocate for the adoption of guidelines for identifying victims of domestic violence. Waits (1995), advocating for the legal profession, delineates several hypotheses for the failure of family lawyers, as well as other attorneys involved with family matters, to identify battered women. These hypotheses include the acceptance of the myths regarding the woman's complicity in the abuse, denial and ignorance about the prevalence of domestic violence, fear of the batterer, and fear of false reports. These hypotheses can also apply to clinicians and health care providers, and their reluctance to identify domestic violence. Hansen and Harway (1993) offer an additional salient possibility. Once domestic violence is identified, then it necessitates that the therapist intervene. Therefore, the purpose of this article is to help clinicians and others realize the ethical responsibilities when working with victims of domestic violence.

The first question usually asked is whether there is a legal mandate to identify domestic violence. Spousal abuse has not, to date, been covered by mandatory reporting requirements. California has come close with AB 1652, which mandates that certain health care professionals must report injuries that result from criminal acts. This law (California Penal Code sec. 11160-11163) covers other acts of violence as well as spousal abuse. At this time, therapists not employed by health care facilities, clinics or physician's offices are exempt from reporting. Thus, a significant number of therapists in California are not covered by this legal mandate. In the absence of legal mandates to report spousal abuse, the ethical issues can be divided into two categories: responsibility to provide effective treatment and the duty to warn/protect.

EFFECTIVE TREATMENT

Psychotherapy has as its primary goal the helping of people in distress. An additional goal is helping distressed individuals without exacerbating the hurt. Pope and Vasquez (1991) assert that by enhancing ethical awareness "helping without hurting" becomes a reality. In spousal abuse cases, the potential for harm is high when the psychological damage that can result from a poorly conceived psychotherapeutic intervention is considered. As therapists become sensitized to the presence of violence in the family, their awareness of the need to address the psychological and physical safety issues should also increase. When clients clearly state that they are being abused, therapists should identify their responsibility to promote the welfare of the client (American Association for Marriage and Family Therapy, 1985; American Psychiatric Association, 1986; American Psychological Association, 1992; National Federation of Societies for Clinical Social Work, 1985) as advising the woman to remove herself from the dangerous situation. Pittman (1987) details a treatment approach that advises the woman of the necessity to remove herself physically from the violent situation. Pittman's approach represents the treatment approaches that emphasize a "problem solving" stance with the problem of violence needing to be eliminated before the productive work of therapy can begin

(Rosenbaum & O'Leary, 1986). Currently, therapists and researchers have shown that the woman's risk of serious bodily harm and even death increases significantly if the woman actually leaves the relationship with the abusive spouse (Bernard, Vera, Vera, & Newman, 1982; Harway, 1993; Walker, 1989; Wilson & Daly, 1993).

As stated above, therapists, unless they are actively involved in the treatment of spouse abuse cases, have not assumed a proactive role in identifying victims of spousal abuse among their therapy clients. Hansen and Harway (1993) offer several possible explanations for the under-assessment of the violence. One possible explanation is the "just world" hypothesis which postulates that bad things happen only to bad people. Thus, if the woman is abused at home then she must be doing something to cause the abuse. Waits (1995) expands on this possibility when she addresses similar issues for attorneys. She postulates that attorneys are hesitant to identify abuse, especially if the client is from higher socioeconomic strata of society, because the attorney cannot envision such a situation happening to someone who is intelligent, educated, and financially secure. This may also apply to clinicians. A second possibility is that the accurate detection of the violence requires the therapist to intervene. Many therapists do not know the appropriate intervention for violence and, therefore, do not acknowledge the violence. A third possible explanation is that the provision of psychotherapy requires a diagnosis, and domestic violence is not a diagnostic category. The therapist must place the abused woman's complaints and symptoms into a diagnostic category according to the Diagnostic and Statistical Manual (DSM IV; APA, 1994), which then forms the basis for the treatment plan. The usual diagnosis utilized is post traumatic stress disorder (Walker, 1991). With these possible explanations in mind, the ethical responsibility to provide effective treatment must be analyzed for both assessment and treatment.

ASSESSMENT FOR THE PRESENCE OF VIOLENCE

Victims of spousal abuse frequently present with problems of anxiety, depression and somatic complaints (Gayford, 1975; Walker, 1991). Since the majority of women seeking psychotherapeutic treatment have these complaints, it would be prudent for therapists to inquire about current and past abusive relationships in all cases. Surveys of police reports have found that 65% of abused women have received psychiatric care, but the majority of therapists failed to inquire about abuse (Goodstein & Page, 1981). Tham et al. (1995) found in a survey for abuse and violence (not only spousal abuse) in a psychiatric sample that 25% felt that the abuse related to their current mental status. Abbott et al. (1995) found similar results in an emergency department where 54% of the women reported being threatened, assaulted, or experiencing intense fear for their lives due to the behavior of a partner or spouse. Research also points to therapist difficulty in recognizing the seriousness of battering along with a tendency to minimize the violence as contributing factor to mental disorders (Hansen, Harway, & Cervantes, 1991). Since the abused woman also is likely to minimize the violence, the tendency is for the therapist and the client to formulate a treatment plan that does not address the issue of violence.

Psychology has a specific section of the Code of Ethics devoted to assessment, and this professional code will be used to illustrate the principles involved. The Code of Ethics states that the assessment is performed within the context of a professional relationship and that the "assessments, recommendations, reports, and psychological diagnostic and evaluative statements are based on information and techniques (including personal interview of the individual when appropriate) sufficient to provide substantiation for their findings" (Standard 2.01; APA Ethical Standards, 1992). This ethical standard requires the therapist to inquire about and attempt to obtain all the relevant information prior to making a clinical formulation. A clinical formulation is based not only on factual information but also on the theoretical orientation of the therapist. Thus, the explanation for why violence occurs within a relationship is embedded within the therapist's own theoretical orientation. Pittman (1987) articulated the shared responsibility hypothesis well. In this formulation, domestic violence is an exaggerated courtship ritual between two individuals who are incapable of expressing love and affection for each other without the violence. Utilizing this model to formulate a treatment plan, the woman often is held responsible for the violence, and treatment focuses on her contribution to and provocation of the violence. Others (Hansen & Goldenberg, 1993; Hansen & Harway, 1993; Walker 1991, 1993) criticized the shared responsibility formulation because the responsibility for the violence still falls on the woman. Holding the woman responsible for the violence is viewed as ineffective treatment. Effective treatment is defined as the cessation of the violence and the prevention of future violence which is accomplished by having the man take full responsibility for the physical violence.

From this latter perspective, the therapist must view the woman as a victim of abuse regardless of her apparent participation in the violence cycle. When the woman is viewed as the victim, the ethical responsibility of the therapist comes sharply into focus. The cessation of the violence as an ethical rather than solely a treatment issue transcends theoretical orientations. The logic is similar to the arguments justifying interventions to stop child abuse. The child is the victim of abuse regardless of the adult's attempts to justify his/her behavior as provoked by the child. While some readers may object to this apparent characterization of the woman as "childlike," it is important to understand that, similar to a child who is being abused, the woman actually has no ability to stop the violence. For ethical considerations, then, we do advocate that the woman be viewed as a victim.

There is little debate that therapists have an ethical obligation to their clients if the clients are victims because, by definition, victims are individuals who are unable to prevent the actions against them. The assessment for the presence of spousal violence is a positive ethical responsibility directly related to the acceptance of the premise that the woman is the victim of the violence.

ASSESSMENT ONCE VIOLENCE IS IDENTIFIED

Assessment, once the violence is identified, requires a different focus. A careful assessment for safety is primary. The therapist needs to ascertain the client's coping skills in order to develop an adequate safety plan. Other pertinent information includes a developmental history (emphasis on the presence or absence of abuse as a child), assessment for the presence or absence of drug or alcohol abuse, and eating disorders (Hansen & Harway, 1993). Once the therapist has been able to assess the client for both the presenting problem (e.g., depression, anxiety, mood disorders) and the violence risk, he/she is then in a position to formulate a treatment plan that provides for the cessation and prevention of the violence while addressing the mental health needs (American Psychological Association, 1996). One needs to always be mindful of the client's "strategic silence" (Waits, 1995). The client may hope that by being silent, the abuse will stop. The health care provider must always be open to reassessing for violence at any point in the treatment process because of the woman's fear of the batterer.

TREATMENT

In order to discharge the ethical responsibility, a standard of care must be articulated. Minimally, the therapist is required to have knowledge of the state laws pertaining to domestic violence and an awareness of the local resources available to assist the client and her family (Hart, 1993;

Jordan & Walker, 1994; Madanes, 1990; Pittman, 1987; Walker, 1991,1993). The domestic violence laws in many states provide for treatment of the victims as well as the perpetrators through court diversion programs. Shelters for battered women usually have some short-term therapy available in addition to other services designed to help the woman become self supporting. Thus, there are two distinct pathways for spousal abuse victims to enter therapy. The first has spousal abuse as the primary presenting problem. The referral is either from the criminal justice system or from a shelter for battered women. The women recognize themselves as "victims" although they may be resistant to the characterization of themselves as victims. The second is with the primary presenting problems of somatic complaints, depression or anxiety symptomatology. The therapist must assess the violence despite the client's resistance to viewing the violence as serious.

Once the spousal abuse has been identified either through careful assessment by the therapist or via direct referral for spousal abuse, the ethical responsibility is to provide effective treatment. Even among therapists knowledgeable about spousal abuse, there is disagreement about the criteria for successful treatment. If successful treatment is defined as the woman leaving the abusive situation, the success rate is usually 50% (Goodman, 1990). Women sometimes refuse to leave the relationship due to psychological issues (fear, shame, love) or financial security (children, lack of employment skills, and unwillingness to give up a certain standard of living) or concern about the welfare of children. Cahn (1991) found that batterers are frequently awarded liberal visitation, joint custody, and even sole residential custody. Within these constraints, effective treatment requires the therapist to assist the woman to achieve her goal of remaining within the relationship and being free from abuse. The ethical responsibility requires a treatment plan that does not continue to hold the woman responsible for the violence. An additional concern is the growing evidence that when the woman does leave the abusive relationship, her chances for further abuse, sometimes with fatal consequences, increase significantly (Wilson & Daly, 1993).

MALPRACTICE LIABILITY

Would the therapist be liable if he/she did not provide an initial assessment for violence and, if violence was present, failed to formulate a treatment plan for the cessation of the violence? Currently, no case law addresses this question. The assessment phase for spousal abuse cases is deceptively simple. The therapist need only inquire about the presence of violence in the home. However, the consequences of implementing routine inquiries regarding violence are worrisome to therapists. One immediate consequence is that the therapist is ethically obligated to provide effective treatment or refer the client to a therapist who can provide effective treatment once the abusive relationship is recognized.

Non-medical therapists have been held legally liable for failing to refer clients to physicians for medical problems that ultimately proved fatal (Woody, 1988). The therapists had not asked the appropriate questions and were held liable for their omission. Extrapolating, therapists who do not inquire or assess for possible violence may be held liable if such abuse occurs and if the client is injured or dies as a result of the abuse. Under the law, there is very little a mental health professional can do to justify a failure to make an appropriate assessment. Thus, liability can result from an inadequate assessment process.

The second source of possible liability is the formulation of the treatment plan. Pope and Vasquez (1991) reviewed closed cases of malpractice against psychologists occurring between 1976 and 1988. They found that incorrect treatment (incompetence in the choice or implementation of the treatment plan) accounted for 8.4% of the total costs and 13.2% of the total claims. While these cases do not address directly the issue of liability raised in this article, therapist exposure to liability increases as abuse victims become more aware of their right to be free from violence in the home.

The third source of liability is the implementation of the treatment plan. The clinical literature has attempted to define appropriate, effective treatment for spousal abuse clients (Jordan & Walker, 1994; Register, 1993; Walker, 1991) and their families (Hansen & Goldenberg, 1993; Hansen & Harway, 1993; Willbach, 1989). Therapy has become the crucial element in breaking the pattern of violence within families.

The following guidelines represent a compilation of the recommendations from the literature:

1. Thorough assessment for violence
2. Assessment for and reporting of child abuse (if children are present in the home)
3. Development of a safety plan which requires the therapist to have knowledge of community resources and possible legal resources
4. Development of a treatment plan with client input
5. Therapist rationale for the choice of modality (individual, couple, family, group) which addresses potential for future violence
6. Documentation that addresses all of the above.

Because both abused spouses and the abusing spouse tend to minimize the presence of violence and the severity of the abuse, the therapist must guard against a tendency to accept the client's disclaimers of danger too readily. The result of this minimization is the formulation of a treatment plan with a focus on the symptoms of anxiety, depression, and somatization rather than the core issue of violence. The treatment plan should address potential for future violence, feelings of shame and guilt, isolation, low self-esteem, anger, and problem solving. Failure to address the core issue of the violence can be tantamount to providing ineffective treatment.

DUTY TO WARN/PROTECT

We have discussed the sources of potential liability for therapists for failure to assess for spousal abuse. Ramifications of holding a therapist liable for this initial assessment include the necessity of providing a course of action once the domestic violence has been identified. Legal reform has been the primary focus for activist efforts to end domestic violence. Hart (1993) notes that the law historically protected perpetrators and that only recently has the law become a tool to provide safety and freedom from abuse. Stark (1995) argued that the law and mental health together must ensure that the women involved in abusive relationships receive effective help from both professions.

There is increased recognition of the potential liability of providing therapeutic services to dangerous clients. Due to the prevalence of spousal abuse, domestic violence is the most likely context for therapists to come into contact with potentially dangerous individuals and situations. Data from the National Crime Victims Survey indicate that 75% of abuse victims are single, separated or divorced (Stark, 1995). According to the U. S. Department of Justice Bureau of Justice Statistics (1988), 16.5% of murders occur within the family, 75% of women who are killed are murdered by domestic partners, 75% of spousal assaults result in visible physical injuries, and 75% of spousal assaults occur at the point of separation or divorce. Wilson and Daly (1993) analyzed spousal homicide statistics from Canada (1974-1990), New South Wales, Australia (1965-1989) and Chicago (1965-1990). They found that spousal homicide victimization increased significantly when the couple was estranged in contrast to when the couple was residing together. The woman's chances of being murdered increase significantly at the point of separation or divorce. Since it is usually at the point of separation that mental health counseling is sought, therapists need to be aware of the potential danger to the client and/or other members of the family.

Despite the fact that spousal abuse is the most likely context for clinicians to encounter dangerousness in their practices, the research emphasis on prediction of dangerousness continues to focus on stranger violence (Borum, 1996; Monahan & Steadman, 1996). One exception to this emphasis is the recent book edited by Campbell (1995). In addition, the recent trends in advising clinicians how to successfully manage managed care with brief therapy do not mention spousal abuse (e.g., Hoyt, 1995).

To date only one state (California) has moved forward to impose a legal mandate to report possible spousal abuse, as stated above. Mandatory reporting laws have applied to children and elderly or incapacitated adults, classes of individuals who are easily recognized as being unable to protect themselves in violent situations. Therapists' reactions to these reporting laws have ranged from favorable to tolerant to oppositional. Therapist primary opposition to mandatory reporting laws is the violation of confidentiality that results with compliance. Confidentiality is the cardinal ethical responsibility of therapists. Victims of spousal abuse have not been protected by mandatory reporting requirements because adult women are not perceived as individuals in need of special protection. Despite the perception that spousal abuse victims may not need special protection, therapists may have an ethical responsibility to protect victims of potential violence from harm. The landmark California Supreme Court decision, Tarasoff v. Regents of the University of California (1976) created such a legal mandate. Subsequent case law has attempted to define the boundaries of therapist duty to protect potential victims of violence (Leslie, 1990; Mills, Sullivan, & Eth, 1987; Sonkin, 1986). Sonkin and Ellison (1986), in their review of these case decisions, found that the research on prediction of violence rather than the research on domestic violence was utilized to shape public policy. The distinction, as well as the irony, is crucial in consideration of the ethical and legal responsibilities of the therapist. The research on prediction of violence seeks to understand the unprovoked violence between acquaintances and strangers. The irony is that Tarasoff is a classical case of a man murdering a former girlfriend when she refused to continue to date him. Because Tarasoff relied upon the prediction of violence literature, it is sometimes interpreted to imply that the therapist has the duty to protect the victim from the harm (Jordan & Walker, 1994). This duty clearly arises from the therapist-client relationship which existed in the facts of Tarasoff. The therapist has the duty to try to prevent the threatening client from carrying out the threat of violence by hospitalizing the client and by warning the potential victim who is then responsible for taking the necessary steps to ensure her/his own safety.

California, in an attempt to clarify therapist liability, drafted a law in

1985 that resulted in limiting the therapist's liability for failure to warn of danger. The therapist has the duty to warn when the client makes a serious threat of physical harm to an identifiable victim. If an abusive spouse is the client, the therapist has the duty to warn the victimized spouse of potential harm. Anecdotal information gathered from therapists suggests that therapists find the execution of this duty frustrating since the victimized spouse already "knows" of the danger and because the alternatives available to the therapist for preventing the harm have not been clearly defined. The 1985 California law is not intended to protect victims of spousal abuse; rather, it is intended to protect therapists from liability, especially breach of confidentiality.

Therapists who treat the victims of spousal abuse solely are not mandated by current law to warn their clients of danger from abusing spouses. Theoretically, a therapist would not be liable for failure to warn even if the client is eventually killed by her spouse because the first criterion of the California law requires therapists to respond to threats from clients. Ironically, the therapist treating the victimized spouse would be required to warn the abusive spouse if the victimized spouse (client) made a threat of serious physical harm.

The California law emphasizes the duty to warn of danger not the protection from danger. A duty imposed upon a therapist should always have a course of action the therapist can follow to discharge the duty. In this case, the therapist discharges the duty by warning the potential victim and by notifying the police. The underlying assumption seems to be that once the police are notified, the laws designed to protect the victim will be enforced. The duty to protect the victim shifts to the criminal justice system and to the victim him/herself.

California recently has enacted another law designed to ensure that law enforcement is informed about crimes of physical violence. Currently, the law mandates health care providers, including certain mental health therapists, to report acts of physical violence that result in physical injury. This mandate supersedes client-therapist confidentiality rights. However, the law has limited applicability because its mandate does not apply to therapists in private practice; it applies only to health and mental health providers who are employed in health facilities (hospital, nursing home, board and care facility, or prison health facility), a clinic (primary care medical clinic, nonprofit, community clinic) or a physician's office. The mandate also includes self-inflicted wounds if caused by a firearm, knife, or other deadly weapon. This law has the potential to have a positive impact on the identification and possible prevention of spousal abuse incidents.

CONCLUSION

Therapists have an ethical obligation to clients who are victims of spousal abuse to incorporate the cessation of violence into the treatment plan. This obligation arises from the ethical mandate to provide effective treatment which originates from the premise that therapy's primary goal is to help without doing harm. To discharge this obligation, therapists must assess for violence even if violence is not the presenting problem. When violence is present, the cessation of the violence needs to be the primary goal. Awareness of the legal reforms in each jurisdiction is essential because therapy can provide alternative problem solving strategies but cannot ensure safety. Legal remedies as well as therapeutic interventions are essential in order to avoid potentially harmful and/or fatal results.

The duty to warn and the recently imposed duty to report physical injuries are forms of legal mandates. Therapists must be committed to stopping the cycle of violence with their clients in order to minimize liability. The debate about the effectiveness of legal mandates imposed upon therapists will continue. Legal mandates in the form of continuing education and mandatory reporting laws may be necessary for therapists to recognize the seriousness of the impact of domestic violence and their contribution to stopping the violence.

REFERENCES

Abbott, J., Johnson, R., Koziol-McLain, L., & Lowenstein, S. R. (1995). Domestic violence against women: Incidence and prevalence in an emergency department population. *JAMA: Journal of the American Medical Association, 273(22)*, 1763-1767.

American Association for Marriage and Family Therapy (1985). *Code of ethical principles for marriage and family therapists.* Washington, D.C.: Author.

American Medical Association. (1992). Diagnostic and treatment guidelines on domestic violence. *Archives of Family Medicine, 1*, 39-45.

American Psychiatric Association. (1994). *Diagnostic and Statistical Manual of Mental Disorders, 4th edition.* Washington, D.C.: Author.

American Psychiatric Association. (1986). *Principles of medical ethics, with annotations especially applicable to psychiatry.* Washington, D.C.: Author.

American Psychological Association. (1992). Ethical principles of psychologists and code of conduct. *American Psychologist, 47*, 1597-1611.

American Psychological Association. (1996). *Violence and the family: Report of the American Psychological Association Presidential Task Force on Violence and the Family.* Washington, DC: Author.

Bernard, G. W., Vera, H., Vera, M. I., & Newman, G. (1982). Till death do us part:

A study of spousal murder. *Bulletin of the American Academy of Psychiatry and the Law, 10,* 271-280.

Bohannon, J. R., Dosser, D. A., & Lindley, S. E. (1995). Using couple data to determine domestic violence rates: An attempt to replicate previous work. *Violence and Victims, 10(2),* 133-141.

Borum, R. (1996). Improving the clinical practice of violence risk assessment: Technology, guidelines and training. *American Psychologist, 51(9),* 945-956.

Burstein, K. (1995). Naming the violence: Destroying the myth. *Albany Law Review, 58,* 961-972.

Cahn, M. R. (1991). Civil images of battered women: The impact of domestic violence on child custody decisions. *Vanderbilt Law Review, 44,* 1041-1085.

California Penal Code Secs. 11160, 11161, 11161.9, 11162, 11162.5, 11162.7, 11163, 11163.2.

Campbell, J. C. (Ed.). (1995). *Assessing dangerousness: Violence by sexual offenders, batterers, and child abusers.* Thousand Oaks, CA: Sage Publications.

Caringella-MacDonald, S. (1988). Parallels and pitfalls: The aftermath of legal reform for sexual assault, marital rape, and domestic violence victims. *Journal of Interpersonal Violence, 3,* 174-189.

Carmen, E. H., Ricker, P. P., & Mills, T. (1984). Victims of violence and psychiatric illness. *American Journal of Psychiatry, 141,* 378-383.

Gayford, J. J. (1975). Wife battering: A preliminary survey of 100 cases. *British Medical Journal, 1,* 194-197.

Goodstein, R. K., & Page, A. W. (1981). Battered wife syndrome: An overview of dynamics and treatment. *American Journal of Psychiatry, 138,* 1036-1044.

Hansen, M., & Goldenberg, I. (1993). Conjoint therapy with violent couples: Some valid considerations. In M. Hansen & M. Harway (Eds.), *Battering and family therapy: A feminist perspective* (pp. 82-92). Newbury Park, CA: Sage.

Hansen, M., & Harway, M. (1993). Intervening with violent families: Directions for future generations of therapists. In M. Hansen & M. Harway (Eds.), *Battering and family therapy: A feminist perspective* (pp. 227-251). Newbury Park, CA: Sage.

Hansen, M., Harway, M., & Cervantes, N. N. (1991). Therapists' perceptions of severity in cases of family violence. *Violence and Victims, 6,* 225-235.

Hart, B. J. (1993). The legal road to freedom. In M. Hansen & M. Harway (Eds.), *Battering and family therapy: A feminist perspective* (pp. 13-28). Newbury Park, CA: Sage.

Harway, M. (1993). Battered women: Characteristics and causes. In M. Hansen & M. Harway (Eds.), *Battering and family therapy: A feminist perspective* (pp. 29-41). Newbury Park, CA: Sage.

Hoyt, M. F. (1995). *Brief therapy and managed care: Readings for contemporary practice.* San Francisco, CA: Jossey-Bass Publishers.

Jacobs, G. (1994, September/October). Where do we go from here? An interview with Ann Jones. *Ms., 4,* 56-63.

Jensen, R. H. (1994, September/October). A day in court. *Ms., 4,* 48-49.

Jordan, C. E., & Walker, R. (1994). Guidelines for handling domestic violence cases in community mental health centers. *Hospital and Community Psychiatry, 45,* 147-151.

Keilitz, S. L. (1994). Civil protection orders: A viable justice system tool for deterring domestic violence. *Violence and Victims, 8,* 79-84.

Koss, M. P. (1990). The women's mental health research agenda: Violence against women. *American Psychologist, 45,* 374-380.

Leslie, R. S. (1990, March/April). The dangerous patient: Tarasoff revisited. *California Therapist,* 11-14.

Madanes, C. (1990). *Sex, love and violence.* New York: W.W. Norton.

Mills, M. J., Sullivan, G., & Eth, S. (1987). Protecting third parties: A decade after "Tarasoff." *American Journal of Psychiatry, 144,* 68-74.

Monahan, L., & Steadman, H. J. (1996). Violent storms and violent people: How Meteorology can inform risk communication in mental health law. *American Psychologist, 51(9),* 931-938.

National Clearinghouse for the Defense of Battered Women. (1994). *Statistics packet, 3rd edition.* Philadelphia, PA: Author.

National Federation of Societies for Clinical Social Work. (1985). *Code of ethics.* Silver Spring, MD: Author.

Novello, A. C. (1992). From the surgeon general, U.S. public service. *Journal of the American Medical Association, 267,* 3132.

Okun, L. (1986). *Woman abuse: Facts replacing myths.* Albany: State University of New York Press.

Pittman, F. S. (1987). *Turning points.* New York: W. W. Norton.

Pope, K. S., & Vasquez, M. J. T. (1991). *Ethics in psychotherapy and counseling.* San Francisco: Jossey-Bass.

Register, E. (1993). Feminism and recovering from battering: Working with the individual woman. In M. Hansen & M. Harway (Eds.), *Battering and family therapy: A feminist perspective* (pp. 29-41). Newbury Park, CA: Sage.

Rosenbaum, A., & O'Leary, K. D. (1986). The treatment of martial violence. In N. S. Jacobson & A. Gurman (Eds.), *Clinical handbook of martial therapy.* New York: Guilford Press.

Schmidt, J. D., & Sherman, L. W. (1993). Does arrest deter domestic violence? *American Behavioral Scientist, 36(5),* 601-609.

Sonkin, D. J. (1986). Clairvoyance vs. common sense: Therapist's duty to warn and protect. *Violence and Victims, 1,* 7-21.

Sonkin, D. J., & Ellison, J. E. (1986). The therapist's duty to protect victims of domestic violence: Where we have been and where we are going. *Violence and Victims, 1,* 205-214.

Stark, E. (1984). *The battering syndromes: Societal knowledge, social therapy and the abuse of women.* Dissertation, Department of Social Work, State University of New York, Binghamton, New York.

Stark, E. (1995). Re-Presenting woman battering: From battered woman syndrome to coercive power. *Albany Law Review, 59,* 973-1026.

Tarasoff v. Regents of the University of California, 17 Cal 3rd. 425.

Tham, S. W., Ford, T. J., & Wilkerson, D. G. (1995). A survey of domestic violence and other forms of abuse. *Journal of Mental Health, 4(3)*, 317-321.

U.S. Department of Justice, Bureau of Justice Statistics (1988). *Report to the nation on crime and justice: The data.* Washington, DC: Government Printing Office.

Violence Against Women Act. (1994). Pub. L. No. 103-322, 108 Stat. 1796. To be codified at 42 U.S.C. secs. 3796gg to 3796gg-5.

Waits, K. (1995). Battered women and family lawyers: The need for an identification protocol. *Albany Law Review, 59*, 1027-1062.

Walker, L. E. A. (1984). Battered woman, psychology, and public policy. *American Psychologist, 29*, 1178-1182.

Walker, L. E. A. (1989). *Terrifying love: Why battered women kill and how society responds.* New York: Harper Collins.

Walker, L. E. A. (1991). Post-traumatic stress disorder in women: Diagnosis and treatment of battered woman syndrome. *Psychotherapy, 28*, 21-29.

Walker, L. E. A. (1993). Legal self-defense for the battered woman. In M. Hansen & M. Harway (Eds.), *Battering and family therapy: A feminist perspective* (pp. 29-41). Newbury Park, CA: Sage.

Willbach, D. (1989). Ethics and family therapy: The case management of family violence. *Journal of Marital and Family Therapy, 15*, 43-52.

Wilson, M., & Daly, M. (1993). Spousal homicide risk and estrangement. *Violence and Victims, 8*, 3-16.

Woody, R. H. (1988). *Protecting your mental health practice: How to minimize legal and financial risk.* San Francisco: Jossey-Bass.

A Biopsychosocial Model
for Understanding Relationship Aggression

Alan Rosenbaum
Robert Geffner
Sheldon Benjamin

SUMMARY. Aggression in adult, intimate relationships is a significant problem with far reaching effects on victims, perpetrators, their
families, and society. Recognizing the import of the problem, the U.S.
Department of Justice has established a Violence Against Women
office, and many states have enacted legislation to protect victims
and deal with perpetrators. It is urgent that we understand the
dynamics of relationship aggression so that effective interventions
and preventive programs can be developed. This article reviews the
current status of research on relationship aggression and identifies
several omissions, most notably, ignorance of the potential contributions of biological factors. Recent research regarding the relevance
of biological factors is reviewed and a Biopsychosocial model is

Address correspondence to: Alan Rosenbaum, Department of Psychiatry, University of Massachusetts Medical School, Worcester, MA 01655.

The authors wish to express their appreciation for the detailed and valuable
feedback provided by Paula Lundberg-Love, PhD, concerning earlier versions of
this article.

Preparation of this paper was supported in part by NIMH Grant # MH44812 to
the first author.

[Haworth co-indexing entry note]: "A Biopsychosocial Model for Understanding Relationship
Aggression." Rosenbaum, Alan, Robert Geffner, and Sheldon Benjamin. Co-published simultaneously
in *Journal of Aggression, Maltreatment & Trauma* (Haworth Maltreatment & Trauma Press, an
imprint of The Haworth Press, Inc.) Vol. 1, No. 1 (#1), 1997, pp. 57-79; and: *Violence and Sexual
Abuse at Home: Current Issues in Spousal Battering and Child Maltreatment* (ed: Robert Geffner, Susan B.
Sorenson, and Paula K. Lundberg-Love) Haworth Maltreatment & Trauma Press, an imprint of The
Haworth Press, Inc., 1997, pp. 57-79. Single or multiple copies of this article are available for a fee from
The Haworth Document Delivery Service [1-800-342-9678, 9:00 a.m. - 5:00 p.m. (EST). E-mail address:
getinfo@haworth.com].

presented. Finally, some suggestions are made for future research.
[Article copies available for a fee from The Haworth Document Delivery Service: 1-800-342-9678. E-mail address: getinfo@haworth.com]

KEYWORDS. Spouse abuse, domestic violence, psychobiology, neuropsychological factors, head injury

Although we know domestic violence to be a long standing social problem, our formal knowledge of this phenomenon is quite recent. Less than 20 years ago, spousal violence was the hidden epidemic. A victim of "selective inattention" by the lay population, health professionals, researchers, and the government, husband-wife violence was viewed as a relatively rare type of behavior (Gelles, 1974). Today, the magnitude of the problem is well known. The fact that spouse/partner abuse is more prevalent than automobile accidents, muggings and cancer deaths combined (U.S. Senate Judiciary Committee, 1992), that assault by an intimate is the primary cause of injuries to women (Novello, Rosenberg, Saltzman, & Shosky, 1992), that a woman is significantly more likely to be killed by her current or former partner than by a stranger (Browne, 1993), and that millions of women are or have been beaten in the U.S. (Straus & Gelles, 1986) has become common knowledge.

The picture has changed dramatically since 1971 when O'Brien noted that *The Journal of Marriage and the Family*, from its inception in 1939, through 1969, had not published one article containing the word "violence" in its title (O'Brien, 1971). With increased awareness has come a corresponding increase in research on relationship aggression. As with many nascent areas of inquiry, the desire to know quickly often preempts methodological rigor. This has been especially true of relationship aggression research. Many of the difficulties in researching relationship aggression have been described elsewhere (Geffner, Rosenbaum & Hughes, 1987; Rosenbaum, 1988), and will not be reiterated here. Despite being plagued by a host of methodological problems, this body of research has contributed much to our formal knowledge of this phenomenon.

The initial focus of domestic violence research was epidemiological and demographic. "Who are these people?," a paraphrase of the title of Gondolf's (1988) article, best describes these efforts. The answer to the question was approached initially by studying victims, since they were more accessible. The wife/victim has received a great deal of attention as an informant on the characteristics of the batterer, as a provocateur (as Claes & Rosenthal, 1990, suggest), and as a subject in her own right. Later, with the advent of court mandated treatment and the proliferation of batterer's treatment programs, the batterer became available as a subject for research. The relationship dynamics of aggressive couples also have received considerable attention.

Studies which focused on the possible contributions of the woman, or the couple dynamics, to the production of relationship aggression have been criticized as absolving the batterer of responsibility for his aggressive behavior, and "blaming the victim." Attempts to identify factors differentiating wife/victims from their non-victimized counterparts have yielded little information. There is, however, a large body of research literature differentiating batterers from non-batterers. Although there are many robust findings, for example, batterers often come from violent family backgrounds, there are also many inconsistencies in this literature. For example, there has been difficulty identifying a batterer personality profile. In the present article, we will examine what the research literature has taught us about male batterers. We also will look at the gaps in our knowledge, present a model of relationship aggression, and suggest some future directions for researchers. It should be noted that we will usually refer to batterers as male and victims as female (see review by Geffner & Rosenbaum, 1990).

PSYCHOSOCIAL RESEARCH

If we have learned anything, it is that batterers are a heterogeneous group, and, not surprisingly, that there is a great deal of inconsistency in the literature regarding their characteristics. There is much variability in sampling strategies and consequently different researchers may be looking at very different groups of subjects, all of whom are described as batterers. Hamberger and Hastings (1991), for example, studied batterers in a violence abatement program. Their sample included both court-and self-referred batterers. In recruiting their comparison sample, however, they "serendipitously" uncovered battering in a substantial number of subjects. They referred to this group as community batterers. They further subdivided their batterers' group into "alcohol abusing" (AA) and "alcohol non-abusing" (NA) batterers. In terms of the differences on the Millon Clinical Multiaxial Inventory scores (MCMI) (Millon, 1983), the community batterers were found to be very similar to non-batterers. Differences also were found between alcohol abusing batterers and alcohol non-abusing batterers, with AA-batterers showing the greatest frequency of personality disorder. The "undiscovered batterer" is apparently a substantial group. According to Holtzworth-Munroe et al. (1992), up to one-half of maritally distressed couples and one-third of maritally non-distressed couples recruited for comparison group purposes, report the occurrence of aggression. Whether these batterers are excluded from the research, included in the batterers group, or treated as a separate comparison group varies across researchers. Batterers may be court-referred (mandated), self-referred, or non-agency identified. This latter group comprises the batterers in the Straus, Gelles, and Steinmetz (1980) national probability samples that have contributed so much to our knowledge about wife/partner abuse (see also Straus & Gelles, 1986).

Many studies do not differentiate batterers on the basis of marital status, including both married and unmarried men in the batterers group. Both groups are further complicated by factors such as the degree of commitment to the relationship. Some married batterers are separated from their spouses, others may be co-habitating. Similarly, unmarried batterers may be dating, engaged, and either co-habitating or not. Both married and un-married batterers may, or may not, have children with their victims. The population may be divided on the basis of whether they abuse substances such as drugs and/or alcohol, and, if so, which. Further differentiation may be made on the basis of whether there is aggression toward others in addition to the partner (i.e., is the batterer more generally aggressive?), and/or whether there has been aggression toward previous partners, children, or others.

To complicate matters even further, Sugarman and Hotaling (1989) divided batterers into three different groups based on Conflict Tactics Scale (CTS) responses: verbal aggression only, minor violence, and severe violence. They reported several differences among groups. Most importantly, batterers using severe violence showed a greater frequency of being exposed to violence in their families of origin. There also were differences in socio-economic status (SES), with that of the more severely violent husbands having a lower SES. However, studies employing samples of identified batterers may over-represent lower SES because they come to the attention of public agencies more frequently. Consequently, the data may be biased, and therefore, affect the conclusions. Thus, understanding of the literature requires the knowledge that different researchers may be looking at very different samples and that sampling techniques may influence the conclusions obtained.

Sampling differences notwithstanding, research has identified a number of factors that appear to be associated with battering. Batterers tend to be younger (Straus & Gelles, 1986), to have defective self-concepts (Goldstein & Rosenbaum, 1985; Sonkin, Martin, & Walker, 1985), and low frustration tolerance (Star, 1983). They also tend to have experienced child abuse (Kalmuss, 1984), and to have been exposed to inter-parental aggression while growing up (Caesar, 1988; Hotaling & Sugarman, 1986). Hotaling and Sugarman (1986) reported exposure to violence as a child or adolescent to be one of the most consistent risk markers of husband-to-wife violence, having been reported as a positive finding in 88% of the 16 studies reviewed. Additionally, batterers may be less assertive (especially with their wives) and more likely to abuse drugs and/or alcohol (Gondolf, 1988; Hotaling & Sugarman, 1986; Rosenbaum & O'Leary, 1981).

A number of studies have examined the personality profiles of batterers using either the Minnesota Multiphasic Personality Inventory (MMPI) (Hathaway & McKinley, 1972) or the MCMI (Millon, 1983). Whereas researchers have been unable to identify a unitary batterer personality profile, studies utilizing standardized personality measures suggest that some batterers often display elevations on anti-social, borderline, narcissistic and dependent personality dimensions (Hamberger & Hastings, 1986). Although the relationship between each of these characteristics and battering has adequate empirical support, no particular factor has received unequivocal support. There also are studies in which the relationship between each of these factors and battering has failed to be supported, suggesting that battering is multi-determined. As Hamberger and Hastings (1991) concluded, ". . . as a group batterers are heterogeneous and fail to conform to a unified 'batterer profile'. Not all batterers look alike, and the question of how batterers differ from the non-batterers must be restated to ask how various groups of batterers differ from other groups of batterers and from non-violent men" (pp. 143-144).

TYPOLOGIES OF BATTERERS

Consistent with this sentiment, one approach to reconciling inconsistencies in the research literature has been the development of typologies of batterers. Both personality based (Caesar, 1986) and behavior based (Gondolf, 1988) typologies have been proposed. Caesar (1986) suggested a four-category schema: the "tyrant," the "exposed rescuer," the "non-exposed altruist," and the "psychotic wife assaulter." This was based on interviews with only 26 batterers. Gondolf (1988) offered an empirically derived, behavior-based typology comprised of three subtypes: the "sociopathic batterer," the "antisocial batterer," and the "typical batterer." This study employed a significantly larger sample, but relied on the victims as informants about their batterer's behavior. A third approach, exemplified by Snyder and Fruchtman (1981), included characteristics of perpetrator, victim, and the relationship, producing a five category solution, one of which was "explosive relationships with injurious violence." This typology also relied on victims as informants. Saunders (1992) employed a clustering strategy to derive three types: family only, generalized aggressors, and emotionally volatile aggressors. Generalized aggressors were more likely to have been abused as children and their aggression was usually alcohol related. There is a great deal of shared variance on the factors examined, however, and it is unclear how these three subtypes correlate with the subtypes derived in other studies. Holtzworth-Munroe and Stuart (1994) provided an excellent review of the typology literature and proposed a typology consisting of three subtypes of batterers (family only, dysphoric/borderline, and generally violent/antisocial). Hamberger, Lohr, Bonge and Tolin (1995) attempted to validate the Holtzworth-Munroe and Stuart typology and reported that their results generally supported the model. Whether this, or any other subtyping schema, proves to be valid, clinically meaningful, and stable remains to be seen, however. Holtzworth-Munroe and Stewart are to be commended for attempting to organize and reconcile a rather large number of typologies.

Most recently, Gottman et al. (1995) have distinguished two types of batterers (I and II) on the basis of differences in heart rate and physiological reactivity. Type I batterers were more severely violent, more likely to have witnessed "husband-to-wife" violence in their families of origin, and were more often emotionally abused. They were also more likely to show decreased heart rate during interactions with their partners. The inclusion of a physiological factor in the typology is a unique and commendable development, which reinforces our contention that comprehensive models of relationship aggression should include biological variables.

Summarizing, interpretation of the research regarding batterers has been complicated by several factors. There is a great deal of variability in sample selection (Court referred, self-referred, and undiscovered community samples are the three most common). There are differences in how battering is defined, both in terms of the reporter (self-report, victim report, judicial or police report), and also whether a standardized instrument was utilized for classification, such as a minimum score on the CT Scale (Straus et al., 1980). Other important methodological differences include the appropriateness of any comparison groups, since many studies of batterers have not employed comparison groups. These methodological inconsistencies, in conjunction with the fact that battering is a complex, multi-determined phenomenon, have precluded the identification of a batterer profile. Neither have replicable, stable, meaningful (either etiologically or clinically) subtyping schemas been developed. An alternative strategy, which has not been widely employed, is to develop theories which account for the inconsistencies in the findings. With few exceptions, research on batterers has not been theory driven.

BIOLOGICAL INFLUENCES

Most theories of human behavior incorporate biological, as well as social, cultural, and psychological influences. Voluntary behaviors involve the decision to act, which is based upon: the actor's *perception of the circumstances* and the necessity for action; the *choice of action*, which is influenced by learning history, behavioral repertoire and shaped by social and cultural conventions; and the *ability to act*, determined by neuro-muscular apparati. For example, shaking hands upon introduction to a stranger, therefore, requires the perception that this is a situation where hand shaking is the socially appropriate behavior, the desire to do the socially appropriate thing, and the ability to perform the behavior.

Despite substantial evidence for physiological mechanisms in the etiology of aggressive behavior in animal models and in humans, biological factors have received scant attention in the literature on battering and domestic violence. Various forms of aggression have been identified and labeled. Predatory aggression (Scott, 1958) and agonistic behavior are most often associated with animals; affective and instrumental aggression are most often associated with humans (Geen, 1990). Aggressive behavior occurs across a range of psychiatric/psychological diagnoses. It is commonly a component of personality change due to general medical conditions (organic personality syndrome), post-traumatic stress disorder, intermittent explosive disorder (episodic dyscontrol syndrome), schizophrenia, attention deficit hyperactivity disorder, conduct disorder, and various personality disorders (including antisocial personality disorder). Aggressive behavior occurs in association with a number of neurological conditions as well, including traumatic brain injury, seizure disorders, and dementia. Biological factors that have been linked to aggression include anatomic brain damage as well as abnormalities of brain electrophysiology and neurotransmission. The most frequent etiologies of electrophysiological and neuroanatomical brain abnormalities in young adults are neurodevelopmental factors and/or traumatic brain injury. Both of these etiologies can give rise to seizure disorders, attentional dysfunction, or focal neurobehavioral syndromes, all of which may lead to the development of aggressive behavior (Bear, Blumer, Chetham, & Ryder, 1982; Cantwell, 1985; Elliot, 1992; McAllister, 1992; Price, Daffner, Stowe, & Mesulam, 1990). In addition, it is well known that both neurodevelopmental abnormalities and traumatic brain injury are common antecedents of the episodic dyscontrol syndrome (Elliot, 1982a; 1982b; 1992).

Seizure disorders can be linked to aggression in several ways. The most common association between seizures and aggressive behavior is in the post-ictal period (the interval immediately following the seizure), during which an individual may be confused and react aggressively to well meaning attempts at aid. Another type of aggression has been described during the interictal period (interval during which no seizures are occurring) in individuals who have complex partial seizures of temporo-limbic origin, the temporal lobes and limbic system being important structures underlying emotional behavior. This aggression, in clear consciousness, can be directed or planned, and it may occur in response to what others may see as minimal provocation. The individual, however, may offer what he or she deems to be justification for the aggression. In contrast to the character disordered individual, the individual with interictal aggression is more likely to accept responsibility for his acts, less likely to claim amnesia for the events, and more likely to feel guilty afterwards (Bear et al., 1982). In some epileptic individuals, behavioral problems actually worsen with improved seizure control, regardless of which anticonvulsant medication is employed. Apart from actual epileptic seizures, it is possible that deep limbic discharges may occur during aggressive behavior in some individuals with intermittent explosive disorder. ADHD (attention deficit hyperactivity disorder) is a common antecedent of adult aggressive behavior. From 10-50% of adolescents with ADHD develop antisocial behavior (Cantwell, 1985). In one study (Hechtman & Weiss, 1986), 23% of hyperactive children were diagnosed with antisocial personality disorder in adulthood compared with 2% of normal controls. Although focal brain lesions often produce attentional dysfunction, they seldom produce true ADHD. However, frontal dysfunction, especially right frontal dysfunction, may produce a similar syndrome with similar symptoms.

Individuals with damage to the orbitofrontal cortex, a common sequel of traumatic brain injury, often become impulsive, labile, irritable and socially inappropriate. They may be overly facetious, childlike, lack empathic capacity, and have shallow emotions. They often respond with aggressive behavioral outbursts to trivial stimuli. The aggression is typically unplanned, without regard for long term consequences, and soon forgotten. The orbitofrontal cortex provides higher control over amygdala and hypothalamic centers associated with basic drives. Orbitofrontal damage is thought to remove this level of control, unleashing lower limbic centers of behavior. Damage to the orbitofrontal cortex in early life has been reported to cause abnormal personality development with severe aggressive and sociopathic behavior persisting into adulthood (Price et al., 1990).

Individuals with congenital or acquired right hemisphere dysfunction may have emotional aprosodia (i.e., difficulty producing or understanding the musical quality of speech used to convey emotion) (Ross & Rush, 1981). Such individuals may also have difficulties interpreting affect and may find double entendre, sarcasm and certain types of humor difficult to comprehend. These paralinguistic deficits can lead to aggressive behavior when the affected individual draws incorrect inferences about the speech or behavior of others.

The three principal Central Nervous System (CNS) sites implicated in aggressive behavior, the neocortex, limbic system and hypothalamus, have hierarchical control over one another. Damage to higher centers may disinhibit aggression from lower centers. Unfortunately, traumatic brain injury frequently involves exactly these centers, potentially leading to aggression from multiple levels of the nervous system.

Neurological functioning requires the contributions of neurotransmitter substances, the best known of which are serotonin, dopamine, and GABA. Dysregulation in each of these systems has been implicated in a host of psychiatric conditions, most notably depression (serotonin), schizophrenia (dopamine), and aggression. The psychological and behavioral implications of neurotransmitter function depends on availability, in combination with the number of receptor sites. Whether it is a reduction in the amount of serotonin or a shortage of receptor sites, reduced serotonergic activity in the brain has been implicated in aggression.

SEROTONIN HYPOTHESIS

Serotonin, or 5-hydroxytryptamine (5HT), is a neurotransmitter which has been implicated in a host of psychiatric/psychological conditions, as well as in the etiology of both inwardly and outwardly directed aggressive behavior. Low CSF levels of 5-hydroxyindoleacetic acid (5-HIAA), a metabolite of serotonin, as opposed to blood levels of this chemical, are considered evidence of decreased levels of serotonin in the brain. Decreased 5-HIAA has been found in the cerebrospinal fluid (CSF) of unipolar but not bipolar depressed individuals who have attempted suicide by violent means (Asberg, Traskman & Thoren, 1976). Low CSF 5-HIAA has been demonstrated in individuals prone to externally directed violence, violent crimes and impulsive aggression (Brown, Goodwin, Ballenger, Goyer, & Major, 1979; Golden et al., 1991; Linnoila et al., 1983). Low 5-HIAA has been shown to correlate with high scores on the MMPI psychopathic deviance scale (Brown et al., 1979). Additionally, low platelet serotonin uptake has been associated with aggressive behavior in various populations (Golden et al., 1991).

Prolactin response to a fenfluramine challenge provides a method of indexing serotenergic activity that is less invasive and risky than the lumbar puncture procedure necessary for obtaining CSF levels of 5-HIAA. Reduced prolactin response to fenfluramine challenge has been correlated with impulsive aggression in character disordered males (Coccaro, Siever & Klar, 1989). Although there are methodological issues that complicate the interpretation of CSF metabolite, platelet binding, and neurochemical or psychopharmacological challenge studies, there are now a number of pieces of evidence that point to serotonin's role in the inhibition of aggression (Lundberg-Love, 1993). Linnoila and Virkkunen (1992) have proposed that a low serotonin syndrome exists that includes early onset impulsive violent behavior, early onset alcohol abuse, increased suicide risk, family history of type II alcoholism (strongly genetic, male form), low CSF 5-HIAA, and a tendency toward hypoglycemia. Serotonin reuptake inhibitors and partial serotonin agonists have been useful in the management of aggression, lending further credence to a serotonergic mediation of aggression (Stein, Hollander, & Leibowitz, 1993). An association between low serotonin and a cluster of impulsivity, monotony avoidance, irritability, verbal aggressiveness, and poor socialization also has been described (Virkkunen et al., 1994). Certainly serotonin is not the only neurotransmitter implicated in aggression. Moreover, it remains unclear regarding which serotonin receptors might be involved. Researchers are examining the roles of dopaminergic, noradrenergic, gabaminergic and other neurotransmitter systems.

Thus, there is ample theoretical reason and empirical evidence to expect an association between brain disruptions and aggression. One type of such disruptions is traumatic brain injury. Many of the personality changes and behavioral sequelae of head injury are recognizable characteristics of maritally violent men, supporting conjecture that traumatic brain injury may play a role here as well. If biological factors are implicated in other forms of human aggression, why should they not play a role in domestic aggression, as well?

HEAD INJURY AND RELATIONSHIP AGGRESSION

In her anthology, Roy (1977) included an article by Elliott that discussed the relationship between head injury and dyscontrol syndrome because she felt that "physical disorders of the brain are sometimes responsible for wife battery" (p. 98). Elliott (1987) provided further support for a relationship between head injury and marital aggression when he identified dyscontrol syndrome, a common sequel to traumatic brain injury, in a substantial proportion of the wife batterers he examined. More recently Rosenbaum and Hoge (1989) evaluated the history of head injury in a sample of 31 men referred to a batterers treatment program and found that 61% described a medical history which included a significant head injury, defined as having received the diagnosis of "concussion" from a physician or having sustained an injury which produced a loss of consciousness. This was, however, a pilot investigation in which the investigator making the head injury decision was not blind to the aggression history of the subject. It also lacked an appropriate comparison group of non-batterers.

A more extensive investigation has corroborated the findings of an association between head injury and marital aggression (Rosenbaum, Hoge, Adelman, Warnken, Fletcher & Kane, 1994). This study employed a blind design wherein assessments of violence history and medical history (including head injury) were made independently by different investigators, each blind to the findings of the other. Thus, the physician making the decision of whether the subject had ever sustained a significant head injury was unaware of the group membership of the subject. In addition to the group of batterers (n = 53), two groups of non-violent men [satisfactorily married (n = 45), and maritally discordant (n = 32)] also were assessed. The results indicated that 53% of the batterers had a history of significant head injury, compared to 25% of the discordant men and 16% of the satisfactorily married men. Logistic regressions demonstrated that, of the variables entered (including the demographic variables of age, job, education and race, as well as psychiatric status, history of antisocial behavior in childhood, alcohol use, and history of head injury), head injury was the best predictor of being a batterer and further, that a significant head injury increased the chances of relationship aggression almost sixfold. Additional analyses allowed for the exclusion of competing hypotheses and suggested that this relationship was not attributable to marital discord, age, occupational status, education, or pre-existing antisocial personality disorder. This study also found that in more than 93% of the head injured batterers, the head injury predated the first instance of marital aggression. Further, in the 14 subjects with a history of arrest for assault and battery, the head injury preceded the assault and battery in every case.

The results of this investigation corroborated those of Lewis et al. (1988) and Lewis, Pincus, Feldman, Jackson and Bard (1986), who found a high incidence of head injury in the medical histories of criminals who had committed violent crimes (death row inmates). Clinically, Geffner and colleagues have found this same pattern of neuropsychological impairment in the fronto-temporal regions in neuropsychological evaluations of several capital murder offenders and death row inmates (25 of 32 subjects) (Geffner, 1995). Morphologically, there is evidence that fronto-temporal head injuries (the most common site) produce impairments in impulse control, which has been cited as a problem for batterers.

As with the other characteristics associated with being a batterer, many abusers were never head injured and many head injured males do not abuse their partners. What, then, is the role of head injury in marital aggression? Head injured males may comprise a new subtype, the "neurologically compromised batterer." There may even be some other characteristics that co-vary with head injury, such as generalized aggression or alcohol sensitivity. The mechanisms by which head injury facilitates aggressive behavior are not well understood. One hypothesis is that head injury disrupts the neurotransmitter system. Diffuse blows to the head might affect the production of neurotransmitters, their re-uptake, or the availability and functioning of receptor sites. Our preference, at this point, is to attempt to reconcile the many differences between batterers, not by adding to the growing list of subtypes, but by developing theoretical models which incorporate the various findings, including biological ones, and account for the variability and inconsistencies. A proposal for such a model is therefore presented.

RELATIONSHIP AGGRESSION: A PROPOSED BIOPSYCHOSOCIAL MODEL

Aggression, in both human and sub-human species, has been the subject of extensive research, theorizing and debate. Curiously, the explanatory potential of this knowledge base for understanding relationship aggression has not been utilized in the domestic violence field. One popular contemporary model of aggression views it as developing out of a context of arousal. Zillman (1983), and more recently, Fogel and Stone (1992) have focused on the importance of arousal in the etiology of aggression and impulsivity, which may include aggressive behavior. According to Fogel and Stone (1992), arousal is a precondition for impulsive action, along with a motive, and a plan. In both of these models, cognition also plays a central role. The term "arousal" is used to describe the individual's net perception of the physiological processes evoked by stimuli in the environment. These processes may actually involve cortical disinhibition of lower arousal centers rather than actual physiological arousal (Lundberg-Love, 1993). A graphical depiction of our proposed model regarding relationship aggression is presented in Figure 1.

Many of the factors that have been associated with relationship aggression can be conceptualized as producing arousal. These enter the model at Point A. Critical masses of stressors can overwhelm inhibitory processes and certain limbic areas can, therefore, become disinhibited. When cortical centers disinhibit lower centers, aggression can occur. Marital discord, work stress, financial problems, and partner behaviors (such as criticism, verbal and physical aggression) may serve as potential arousers. Low self-esteem also may serve to exacerbate the disinhibition potential of many of these events. Financial problems, for example, may be even more troubling to an individual who already feels he is an inadequate provider, inferior in intellect and abilities as compared to his neighbors and peers. Status incompatibility and status inconsistency, which have been identified with relationship aggression (Hornung, McCullough & Sujimoto, 1981) may likewise be exacerbated by low self-esteem. Additionally, physiological variables, such as illness, hunger, or stimulants, might affect one's level of arousal.

As arousal increases, a threshold is reached at which point the individual shifts from cognitive control of behavior, to more automatic responding, or what Zillman (1983) refers to as behaviors of high habit strength. This occurs at Point B in Figure 1 and may be perceived by the actor as a "loss of control" when in fact it is not. Loss of control is a common attribution of batterers for relationship aggression. Batterer's treatment programs frequently argue that violence doesn't result from losing control, but rather represents a way for the batterer to control his partner. The "shift" from cognitive control to more automatic responding suggested here represents an additional way of disputing the "loss of control" excuse, without discounting the batterer's perception of some sort of transition. Alternatively, the batterer's perception of a "snapping point" supports this notion of a transition of some sort.

The behaviors of high habit strength, which occur at Point C in Figure 1, are not necessarily aggressive ones, which explains why everyone doesn't respond aggressively to high levels of arousal. However, if an individual has grown up in a violent environment, has used aggression in the past, or is aggressed against, there is an increased probability that these "automatic" behaviors will be aggressive ones. This may also be influenced by the consequences, or the lack thereof, for violent behavior.

The level of arousal required to reach the threshold for the transition is also variable. First, the threshold level is subject to individual differences, some people having more tolerance for arousal than others. People with

FIGURE 1. The Proposed Biopsychosocial Model of Relationship Aggression

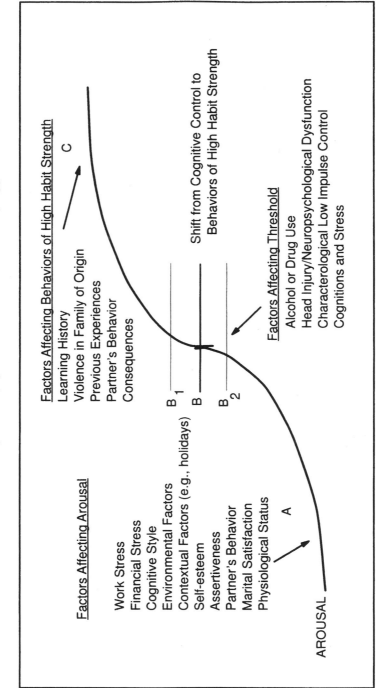

lower thresholds [Point B_2] are often characterized as having "short fuses," while those with higher thresholds [Point B_1] are often labeled "patient" or "tolerant." Neurochemically, the former group may have less effective cortical inhibitory processes and/or a serotonergic "dysfunction." Second, alcohol and other substances, known to have disinhibiting effects on behavior, further reduce the threshold. There is some disagreement regarding the role of alcohol and other substances in promoting relationship aggression. Kantor and Straus (1986) reviewed the research literature in this area and concluded that although alcohol was often implicated in episodes of relationship aggression, it was neither necessary nor sufficient to produce such behavior. The present model is consistent with that conceptualization in viewing alcohol and drugs as capable of reducing inhibitory processes, while allowing that individual differences in threshold, learning history, and contextual (situational) variables may modulate the expression of aggression. In the same vein, head injury, especially to frontotemporal areas, is seen as another factor which anatomically and neurochemically may compromise inhibitory processes, thereby increasing the probability of an aggressive response. According to Fogel and Stone (1992), damage to the frontal lobes promotes aggression by decreasing an individual's ability to develop complex plans. Damage to the dorsolateral frontal region affects appreciation of contextual cues and injury to the orbitofrontal region impairs one's ability to conform actions to perceived cues. Problems in either area thus increase the likelihood of impulsive aggression. In fact, Heinrichs (1989) did find that the existence of a focal frontal lesion was the best single predictor of violent incidents among the psychiatric patients studied. Brain injured individuals are also likely to be prone to increased disinhibition by alcohol or drug abuse. The combined effects of brain injury and/or substance use may serve to increase cortical inhibition more than either factor alone.

Zillman (1983) expanded on the two factor, arousal-aggression theory by including cognition as a third factor. Cognitions enter the model at several points. They may be a source of arousal. Positive thoughts, such as "boy, is my wife going to be pleased when she sees what I've bought her," as well as negative ones, such as "my wife doesn't appreciate how hard I work," are equally capable of producing arousal. Once the individual is aroused, cognitions play a role in defining the arousal as anger. Thus, when the aroused husband (in either of the above scenarios) comes home and the house is in disarray, the kids are fighting, and his wife is annoyed, the arousal may be readily redefined as anger. We can see an interaction between other factors, such as defective self-esteem and cognitive perceptions. Defective self-esteem increases the probability of inflammatory cognitions and perceptions. Goldstein and Rosenbaum (1985) found that abusive men, in addition to having lower self-esteem than their non-aggressive counterparts, were significantly more likely than non-batterers to interpret their wife's behaviors as blows to their self-esteem. Batterers might be more likely to interpret neutral events in a negative way and more likely to label the consequent arousal in a negative way. In the model of impulsive aggression presented by Fogel and Stone (1992) the patient's perception of an event evokes an emotional response that impacts on both the level of arousal and the development of a motive for the impulsive act.

Cognitions next play a mediating role, wherein the angry husband can either calm himself down ("I guess my wife had a pretty tough day, also"), or provoke himself further ("Can't she do anything around here? Do I have to work all day and come home to do her work as well?"). Problems with spouse-specific assertion may enter the model at this point. If the husband is unable or doesn't know how to "check things out" with his wife (e.g., "Do you think I don't work hard?" "Are you angry at me for some reason?" "Did you have a bad day?"), he deprives himself of important input from her that might otherwise counteract the negative cognitions. Deprived of more factual input, he is left to his own cognitive machinations, which again are more probably negative, especially in an individual with low self-esteem. He may also incorporate irrational self-talk and cognitive distortions in his perceptions that tend to exacerbate his anger, reduce his tolerance, and even counter more factual, rational data.

According to Zillman (1983), an important role of cognitions in this process involves validating the emotional reaction ("Do I have a right to be angry?"). The outcome of this validation process may be largely influenced by social learning and cultural factors. A more traditional, patriarchal individual who grew up in a home where Dad was the boss, and where aggression was employed as a conflict resolution strategy, will be more likely to view his anger as justified, and utilize power and control tactics in abusive ways. On the other hand, a more egalitarian, non-sexist individual, brought up in a non-violent environment and accustomed to non-violent conflict resolution strategies may be less likely to view his anger as justified and be better able to short-circuit its build-up. The utilization of cognitive-behavioral anger and stress management techniques can also moderate arousal and threshold levels.

Sociocultural factors also enter the model at several points. We have discussed impulse control, thus far, from the perspective of internal controls which are characteristic of the individual and moderated by neurological function. Impulse control, however, is also influenced by external factors, which include legal constraints on behavior and cultural conventions.

Because domestic aggression has traditionally been socially tolerated, and the sanctions imposed by society's agents (the police and judiciary) have been weaker than those for aggression against non-intimates, external controls exert less influence in domestic situations. This often places greater responsibility for the control of marital aggression on the internal controls. Sociocultural factors also influence marital role expectations, attitudes towards women, and attitudes towards aggression which affect the batterer's cognitions and increase the likelihood that he will feel justified in his anger, think inflammatory thoughts about his wife's behavior, and feel less constrained about the use of aggression towards his partner.

FUTURE RESEARCH DIRECTIONS

Disciplinary parochialism complicates the development of models which integrate biological, psychological, and socio-cultural explanations of behavior, yet despite this problem it is generally acknowledged that all three exert important influences in determining behavior. With respect to relationship aggression, potential biological underpinnings have received the least attention. Empirical evidence is accumulating which suggests the importance of physiological factors for understanding relationship aggression. Several studies have now been completed (Brumm, Rosenbaum & Cohen, 1995; Cohen et al., 1995; Rosenbaum et al., 1994; Rosenbaum & Hoge, 1989; Warnken, Rosenbaum, Fletcher, Hoge, & Adelman, 1994) which demonstrate that history of head injury is a significant risk factor for relationship aggression and that abusive men can be reliably discriminated from non-abusive men on several measures of neuropsychological performance which correspond to frontal-temporal lobe damage. Research (by the first author) is in progress which is assessing differences in serotonergic functioning between batterers and non-batterers. Gottman et al. (1995) have demonstrated that some abusers show differences in cardiac reactivity as compared to non-abusers. Further research on these fronts, as well as on other physiological factors yet to be determined, is very much needed. If, for example, head injury is related to relationship aggression, it might be possible to use neuroimaging techniques, such as Single Photon Emission Computed Tomography (SPECT), Photon Emission Tomography (PET), or Magnetic Resonance Imaging (MRI) scans to identify affected areas. Functional neuroimaging, such as Functional Magnetic Resonance Imaging (FMRI) or activated SPECT could further illuminate the relationship between brain and this type of behavior.

The suggestion that physiological factors may play a role in the etiology of marital aggression may be threatening to those who would view it as providing absolution to batterers. Most batterer's treatment programs emphasize the importance of getting batterers to take responsibility for their aggressive behavior and there is a legitimate concern that physiological factors, like head injury or alcohol use, might be invoked as an excuse for abusive behavior. However, if physiological factors are important, as they are seen to be in other forms of aggressive behavior and as the studies presented above suggest, it would be a mistake not to pursue the etiological and treatment implications of this line of research. Further, biological approaches to treatment have not been sufficiently explored or considered in the relationship aggression/batterer field. A number of medications have been shown to be effective in certain individuals with impulsive aggression. These include lithium, beta blockers, carbamazepine, serotonin reuptake inhibitors, buspirone, depakote (valproic acid), tryptophan, fenfluramine, and various neuroleptics (Stein et al., 1993). If effective, medication might be a useful adjunct to current psychotherapeutic interventions, and thereby prevent additional pain and suffering, and reduce recidivism.

Another implication of the information presented in this article is that marital aggression might be viewed similarly to other forms of aggression. Without diminishing the importance of sociocultural influences, existing theories of aggression might have heuristic value for understanding relationship aggression. At the very least, developing theories which account for the consistencies as well as for the inconsistencies in the research literature may augment and complement subtyping strategies.

Methodologically, future studies should include avoidance of unsophisticated experimental designs which, years ago, might have been excused by the primitive state of marital violence research or the inaccessibility of appropriate subjects. Although there may be exceptions, such as utilizing wives as informants regarding the outcome of batterer's treatment programs, information about batterers or victims should be obtained directly. Reliance on either batterers or their victims as sole informants on their partner/spouse threatens the reliability and validity of the information. Designs which lack comparison groups should generally be avoided, other than in the case of presenting pilot data for purposes of stimulating research. These suggestions are not new (Geffner et al., 1988), yet uncontrolled research, as well as research relying exclusively on informant data, continues to appear.

Finally, while much of the available research on batterers is descriptive or comparative based on surveys or interviews, it is also possible to involve batterers in experimental designs or observational studies. Margolin and colleagues at the University of Southern California (Margolin, John & Gleberman, 1988) and Vivian and O'Leary at State University of New York, Stony Brook (1987), for example, have examined the communication styles of abusive couples by observing them in problem-solving situations. Gottman et al. (1995) have been studying heart rate changes in batterers during arguments with their mates. Rosenbaum and colleagues at the University of Massachusetts, Worcester have conducted neuropsychological examinations of batterers using a computerized battery of tests, and they are currently assessing serotonergic functioning by measuring levels of serum prolactin in response to a fenfluramine challenge. Geffner and colleagues in Tyler, TX collected quantitative electroencephalographic (EEG) data in conjunction with neuropsychological evaluations of batterers (Geffner et al., 1992). With the creative use of computer graphics or other types of audiovisual media, it may be possible to create stimuli that enable us to test a host of behavioral, cognitive, and physiological hypotheses with batterers.

REFERENCES

Asberg, M., Traskman, L., & Thoren, P. (1976). 5-HIAA in the cerebrospinal fluid: A suicide predictor? *Archives of General Psych, 33,* 1193-1197.

Bear, D. M., Blumer, D., Chetham, D., & Ryder, J. (1982). Interictal behavioral in hospitalized temporal lobe epileptics: Relationship to idiopathic psychiatric syndromes. *Journal of Neurology, Neurosurgery & Psychiatry, 45,* 481-488.

Brown, G. F., Goodwin, F., Ballenger, J. C., Goyer, P. F., & Major, L. F. (1979). Aggression in humans correlates with cerebrospinal fluid amine metabolites. *Psychiatric Research, 1,* 131-139.

Browne, A. (1993). Violence against women by male partners: Prevalence, outcomes, and policy implications. *American Psychologist, 48,* 1077-1087.

Brumm, V. L., Rosenbaum, A., & Cohen, R. A. (1995). The neuropsychology of impulsivity and marital violence. Abstract in *Journal of the International Neuropsychological Society, 1* (2), 134.

Caesar, P. L. (1986, August). Men who batter: A heterogeneous group. In L. K. Hamberger (Chair), *The male batterer: Characteristics of a heterogeneous population.* Symposium at the convention of the American Psychological Association, Washington, D.C.

Caesar, P. L. (1988). Exposure to violence in the families-of-origin among wife abusers and maritally non-violent men. *Violence and Victims, 3,* 49-62.

Cantwell, D. P. (1985). Hyperactive children have grown up. *Archives of General Psychiatry, 42,* 1026-1028.

Claes, J. A., & Rosenthal, D. M. (1990). Men who batter women: A study in power. *Journal of Family Violence, 5* (3), 215-224.

Coccaro, E. F., Siever, I. J., & Klar, H. (1989). Serotonergic studies in patients with affective and personality disorders: Correlates with suicidal and impulsive aggressive behavior. *Archives of General Psychiatry, 46*, 587-599.

Cohen, R. A., Rosenbaum, A., Fletcher, K. E., Kane, R. L., Warnken, W. J., & Benjamin, S. (1995). Neuropsychological Correlates of Domestic Violence. Unpublished paper. Butler Hospital, Brown University School of Medicine and University of Massachusetts School of Medicine.

Elliot, F. A. (1982a). Neurologic findings in adult minimal brain dysfunction and the dyscontrol syndrome. *Journal of Nervous Mental Disorders, 170*, 680-687.

Elliot, F. A. (1982b). Clinical approaches to family violence: Biological contributions to family violence. *Family Therapy Collections, 3*, 35-58.

Elliott, F. A. (1987). Neuroanatomy and neurology of aggression, *Psychiatric Annals, 17*, 385-388.

Elliot, F. A. (1992). The neurologic contribution: An overview. *Archives of Neurology, 49*, 595-603.

Fogel, B. S., & Stone, A. B. (1992). Practical pathophysiology in neuropsychiatry: A clinical approach to depression and impulsive behavior in neurological patients. In S. C. Yudofsky & R. E. Hales (Eds.), *The American Psychiatric Press Textbook of Neuropsychiatry* (pp. 329-344). Washington, D.C.: American Psychiatric Press.

Geen, R. G. (1990). *Human aggression.* Pacific Grove, CA: Brooks/Cole.

Geffner, R. (1995, April). State of the art in family violence research and treatment. Unpublished paper presented at the Institute of Human Development and Family Studies, University of Texas, Austin, TX.

Geffner, R., Roberts, R., Ford, K., Marmion, S., Lundberg-Love, P., & Mercer, L. (1992). *Neuropsychological impairment and marital aggression: Preliminary results of a pilot study* (Technical Research Report to Hogg Foundation). Tyler, TX: Family Violence & Sexual Assault Institute.

Geffner, R., & Rosenbaum, A. (1990). Characteristics and treatment of batterers. *Behavioral Sciences and the Law, 8*, 131-140.

Geffner, R., Rosenbaum, A., & Hughes, H. (1988). Research issues in family violence. In M. Hersen & V. B. Van Hasselt (Eds.), *Handbook of family violence* (pp. 457-481). New York: Plenum.

Gelles, R. J. (1974). *The violent home: A study of physical aggression between husbands and wives.* Beverly Hills, CA: Sage.

Golden, R. N., Gilmore, J. H., Corrigan, M. H. N. et al. (1991). Serotonin, suicide, and aggression: Clinical studies. *Journal of Clinical Psychiatry, 52*, 61-69.

Goldstein, D., & Rosenbaum, A. (1985). An evaluation of the self-esteem of maritally violent men. *Family Relations, 34*, 425-428.

Gondolf, E. W. (1988). Who are those guys? Toward a behavioral typology of batterers. *Violence and Victims, 3*, 187-203.

Gottman, J. M., Jacobson, N. S., Rushe, R. H., Shortt, J. W., Babcock, J., La Taillade, J., & Waltz, J. (1995). The relationship between heart rate reactivity, emotionally aggressive behavior and general violence in batterers, *Journal of Family Psychology, 9*, 227-248.

Hamberger, L. K., & Hastings, J. E. (1986). Personality correlates of men who abuse their partners: A controlled comparison. *Violence and Victims, 3*, 31-48.

Hamberger, L. K., & Hastings, J. E. (1991). Personality correlates of men who batter and non-violent men: Some continuities and discontinuities. *Journal of Family Violence, 6*, 131-147.

Hamberger, L. K., Lohr, J. M., Bonge, D. & Tolin, D. (1995, July). A Typology of Men Who Batter: Relationship to Violence Severity. Paper presented at the 4th International Family Violence Research Conference, Durham, N.H.

Hathaway, S., & McKinley, J. (1972). *Minnesota Multiphasic Personality Inventory.* St. Paul: University of Minnesota Press.

Hechtman,, L., & Weiss, G. (1986). Controlled prospective fifteen year follow up of hyperactives as adults. *Canadian Journal of Psychiatry, 31*, 557-567.

Heinrichs, R. W. (1989). Frontal cerebral lesions and violent incidents in chronic neuropsychiatric patients. *Biological Psychiatry, 25*, 174-178.

Holtzworth-Munroe, A., & Stuart, G. L. (1994). Typologies of male batterers: Three subtypes and the differences among them. *Psychological Bulletin, 116*, 476-497.

Holtzworth-Munroe, A., Waltz, J., Jacobson, N. S., Monaco, V., Fehrenbach, P. A., & Gottman, J. M. (1992). Recruiting non-violent men as control subjects for research on marital violence: How easily can it be done? *Violence and Victims, 7*(1), 79-88.

Hornung, C. A., McCullough, B. C., & Sujimoto, T. (1981). Status relationships in marriage: Risk factors in spouse abuse. *Journal of Marriage and the Family, 43*, 675-692.

Hotaling, G. T., & Sugarman, D. B. (1986). An analysis of risk markers in husband to wife violence: The current state of knowledge. *Violence and Victims, 1*, 101-124.

Kalmuss, D. (1984). The intergenerational transmission of marital aggression. *Journal of Marriage and the Family, 46*, 11-19.

Kantor, G.K., & Straus, M.A. (1986). *The drunken bum theory of wife-beating.* Paper presented at the National Alcoholism Forum and Conference on Alcohol and the Family, San Francisco.

Lewis, D. O., Pincus, J. H., Bard, B., Richardson, E., Prichep, L. S., Feld, M., & Yaeger, C. (1988). Neuropsychiatric, psychoeducational, and family characteristics of 14 juveniles condemned to death in the United States. *American Journal of Psychiatry, 145*, 584-589.

Lewis, D. O., Pincus, J. H., Feldman, M., Jackson, L., & Bard, B. (1986). Psychiatric, neurological, and psychoeducational characteristics of 15 death row inmates in the United States. *American Journal of Psychiatry, 143*, 838-845.

Linnoila, M., & Virkkunen, M. (1992). Aggression, suicidality, and serotonin. *Journal of Clinical Psychiatry, 53* (supplement), 4651.

Linnoila, M., Virkkunen, M., Scheinen, M. et al. (1983). Low cerebrospinal fluid 5-hydroxyindoleacetic acid concentration differentiates impulsive from non-impulsive violent behavior. *Life Science, 33*, 2609-2614.

Lundberg-Love, P. K. (1993). Personal communication. Psychology Department, University of Texas at Tyler, Tyler, TX.

Margolin, G., John R., & Gleberman, L. (1988). Affective responses to conflictual discussions in violent and nonviolent couples. *Journal of Consulting and Clinical Psychology, 56* (1), 24-33.

McAllister, T. W. (1992). Neuropsychiatric sequelae of head injuries. *Psychiatric Clinics of North America, 15*, 395-413.

Millon, T. (1983). *Millon Clinical Multiaxial Inventory Manual.* Minneapolis, MN: Interpretive Scoring Systems.

Novello, A., Rosenberg, M., Saltzman, L., & Shosky, J. (1992). From the Surgeon General, U.S. Public Health Service, *The Journal of the American Medical Association, 267* (*23*), 3132.

O'Brien, J. E. (1971). Violence in divorce-prone families. *Journal of Marriage and the Family, 33*, 692-698.

Price, B. H., Daffner, K., Stowe, R. M., & Mesulam, M. M. (1990). The comportmental learning disabilities of early frontal lobe damage. *Brain, 113*, 1383-1393.

Rosenbaum, A. (1988). Methodological issues in marital violence research. *Journal of Family Violence, 3*, 91-104.

Rosenbaum, A., & Hoge, S. K. (1989). Head injury and marital aggression. *American Journal of Psychiatry, 146:8*, 1048-1051.

Rosenbaum, A., Hoge, S. K., Adelman, S. A., Warnken, W. J., Fletcher, K. E., & Kane, R. (1994). Head injury in partner-abusive men. *Journal of Consulting and Clinical Psychology, 62* (*6*), 1187-1193.

Rosenbaum, A., & O'Leary, K. D. (1981). Marital violence: Characteristics of abusive couples. *Journal of Consulting and Clinical Psychology, 49*, 6371.

Ross, E., & Rush, A. (1981). Diagnosis and neuroanatomical correlates of depression in brain-damaged patients: Implications for a neurology of depression. *Archives of General Psychology, 38*, 1344-1354.

Roy, M. (1977). *Battered women.* New York: Van Nostrand Reinhold.

Saunders, D. G. (1992). A typology of men who batter: Three types derived from cluster analysis. *American Journal of Orthopsychiatry, 62* (*2*), 264-275.

Scott, J. P. (1958). *Aggression.* Chicago: University of Chicago Press.

Snyder, D. K., & Fruchtman, L.A. (1981). Differential patterns of wife abuse: A data-based typology. Journal of Consulting and Clinical Psychology, 49, *Journal of Consulting and Clinical Psychology, 49*, 878-885.

Sonkin, D. J., Martin, D., & Walker, L. (1985). *The male batterer: A treatment approach.* New York: Springer.

Star, B. (1983). *Helping the abuser.* New York: Family Service Association of America.

Stein D,, Hollander, E., & Leibowitz, M. (1993). Neurobiology of impulsivity and the impulse control disorders. *Journal of Neuropsychiatry and Clinical Neurosciences, 5*, 9-17.

Straus, M. A., Gelles, R. S., & Steinmetz, J. K. (1980). *Behind closed doors: Violence in the American family.* Garden City, N.J.: Anchor/Doubleday.

Straus, M. A., & Gelles, R. J. (1986). Societal change and change in family violence from 1975 to 1985 as revealed by the national surveys. *Journal of Marriage and the Family*, *48*, 465-479.

Sugarman, D. B., & Hotaling, G. T. (1989). Violent men in intimate relationships: An analysis of risk markers. *Journal of Applied Social Psychology*, *19*, 1034-1048.

U.S. Senate Judiciary Committee (1992, October). *Violence against women: A week in the life of America* (prepared by the majority staff of the Senate Judiciary Committee). (Available from Hart Office Building, Room B04, Washington, D.C. 20510).

Virkkunen, M., Rawlings, R., Tokola, R. et al. (1994). CSF biochemistries, glucose metabolism, and diurnal activity rhythms in alcoholic, violent offenders, fire setters, and healthy volunteers. *Archives of General Psychiatry*, *51*, 20-27.

Vivian, D., & O'Leary, K. D. (1987). *Communication patterns in physically aggressive engaged couples*. Paper presented at the Third National Family Violence Research Conference, University of New Hampshire, Durham.

Warnken, W., Rosenbaum, A., Fletcher, K. E., Hoge, S. K., & Adelman, S. A. (1994). Head injured males: A population at risk for relationship aggression? *Violence and Victims*, *9*, 153-166.

Zillman, D. (1983). Arousal and aggression. In R. G. Geen and E. I. Donnerstein (Eds.), *Aggression: Theoretical and empirical reviews. Vol. 1* (pp. 75-101). New York: Academic Press.

Research Concerning Wife Abuse: Implications for Physician Training

L. Kevin Hamberger

SUMMARY. Violence toward women has been declared a public health epidemic. To date, research on battered women in medical settings has focused primarily on incidence and prevalence and on identification of risk markers. Such research also has elucidated low rates of battered women identified in medical settings, as well as barriers to such identification. Methods of training physicians to identify and help battered women are described in the present article. The unique role of psychologists and other mental health professionals in designing and evaluating such programs is discussed. *[Article copies available for a fee from The Haworth Document Delivery Service: 1-800-342-9678. E-mail address: getinfo@haworth.com]*

KEYWORDS. Family violence, spouse abuse, health care, battered women, characteristics

Violence toward women by their intimate partners has been recognized for several years as a public health problem of epidemic proportions (Koop, 1987; Straus & Gelles, 1986). So prevalent is male-to-female partner assault that some authorities estimate as many as 60% of all mar-

Address correspondence to: Dr. L. Kevin Hamberger, St. Catherine's Family Practice Center, P.O. Box 598, Kenosha, WI 53141.

[Haworth co-indexing entry note]: "Research Concerning Wife Abuse: Implications for Physician Training." Hamberger, L. Kevin. Co-published simultaneously in *Journal of Aggression, Maltreatment & Trauma* (Haworth Maltreatment & Trauma Press, an imprint of The Haworth Press, Inc.) Vol. 1, No. 1 (#1), 1997, pp. 81-96; and: *Violence and Sexual Abuse at Home: Current Issues in Spousal Battering and Child Maltreatment* (ed: Robert Geffner, Susan B. Sorenson, and Paula K. Lundberg-Love) Haworth Maltreatment & Trauma Press, an imprint of The Haworth Press, Inc., 1997, pp. 81-96. Single or multiple copies of this article are available for a fee from The Haworth Document Delivery Service [1-800-342-9678, 9:00 a.m. - 5:00 p.m. (EST). E-mail address: getinfo@haworth.com].

ried women will be assaulted at some time during the course of their lifetime (e.g., Walker, 1979). Furthermore, many of the assaults against battered women result in injury (Foneska, 1974). In addition to physical injuries, battering has been related to psychological reactions including anxiety, depression and post traumatic stress disorder (Appleton, 1980; Douglas, 1987; Walker, 1979). Therefore, many battered women are likely to seek medical and psychological services for their injuries (Goldberg & Carey, 1982; Goldberg & Tomlanovich, 1984; Harway & Hansen, 1990).

Emergency room utilization by battered women has received considerable research attention. For example, Rounsaville and Weissman (1977-78) found that 37 battered women who presented to a university medical center surgical emergency room during a one-month period accounted for 3.8% of all admissions. Moreover, although 20 of these women had presented to the emergency room with injuries in the past, only three had been identified as battered. Stark, Flitcraft and Frazier (1979) estimated that nearly 25% of women seen in an emergency service were battered, although physicians identified only 2.8% of these women. A more recent study of 453 women at an emergency department in Australia revealed that 2% reported assault within the past 24 hours, and 9% reported an assault within the past year (Roberts, O'Toole, Lawrence, & Raphael, 1993). Prevalence statistics for this latter study are generally lower than those reported for American institutions. This difference may reflect culture differences, as well as different methods of defining and measuring partner violence. These and other studies (e.g., Goldberg & Tomlanovich, 1984) suggest that battered women utilize emergency medical services in high numbers, but often are not properly identified by health care providers. Rounsaville and Weissman (1977-78) suggested that battered women often are not identified as such because they have not been asked about being battered. Stark et al. (1979) suggest that battered women are not often identified because their injuries are treated primarily as medical problems.

The psychosocial aspects of victimization, including repeat visits for injuries and secondary problems related to abuse, lead to referral strategies that communicate the message that the woman is responsible for her problems or that the problem may not be that important. This mode of intervention may be viewed as an institutionalized extension of societal sexism and patriarchal authority that revictimizes battered women and further entraps them in violent, abusive relationships. A study by McLeer, Anwar, Herman, and Maquiling (1989) lends support to the viewpoints described above. Prior to instituting a standard protocol for identifying battered women in an emergency department, official prevalence estimates for battered women were around 5.6%. After instituting the protocol, official prevalence rates rose to 30%.

This would suggest that, following the admonition of Rounsaville and Weissman (1977-78) almost two decades ago, clinicians should ask women whether they have been battered. However, after an eight year follow-up of the battered woman identification program, McLeer et al. (1989) reported that official rates returned to nearly the original baseline level (7.7%). The authors suggested that a more general systems failure was responsible: without institutional policies and procedures for identifying battered women, the tendency is to overlook their situation and focus only on treating the medical symptoms. McLeer et al. (1989) called for changes in the entire medical system, including hospital accreditation criteria, to establish the routine assessment and investigation of battered women as a standard of care in emergency departments. Such advocacy has been responded to by the Joint Commission on Accreditation of Healthcare Organizations (JCAHO). In their 1992 Accreditation Manual for Hospitals (JCAHO, 1992), specific standards require both ambulatory care and emergency services to develop written policies and procedures for identifying and intervening with victims of family violence, including partner abuse.

Whereas the medical system has a history of inadequately addressing the problem of battered women, Goldberg and Tomlanovich (1984) also demonstrated that battered women themselves may contribute to the complicated picture of underidentification. These authors specifically encouraged women to disclose their victimization status directly to their physician via a confidential questionnaire. Despite such encouragement, over three-fourths of the known battered women did not do so. The study was unable to elucidate factors related to the battered women's reticence. Surveying both physicians and battered women, Drossman et al. (1990) found that only 17% of the women had actually informed their doctors about the abuse they experienced. Results from these two studies indicate that battered women do not readily disclose their victimization.

ABUSE VICTIMS IN OUTPATIENT CLINICS

As noted above, victims of intimate violence often seek medical treatment for acute injuries in hospital emergency departments. Mehta and Dandrea (1988) and Flitcraft (1990) pointed out that large numbers of battered women also will seek outpatient medical services at primary care and ob-gyn or other specialty clinics. Treatment sought in such clinics may be related directly to physical injuries sustained during an assault. Conversely, many battered women utilize outpatient primary care medical services for alleviation of the "indirect" results of violence victimization. For example, Koss, Woodruff, and Koss (1990) found that female victims of violent crime (not specifically domestic violence) rated their health status lower than nonvictimized women. Furthermore, violence victims made more frequent trips to physicians up to two years after the victimization than did nonvictims (Koss, Koss, & Woodruff, 1991).

Overall, victims of violent crime constituted 57% of the 5,086 surveyed women enrolled in a clinic-based managed care medical program (Koss et al., 1990, 1991); 29-39% were physically or sexually assaulted by intimate partners. Drossman et al. (1990) surveyed women referred to a gastroenterology clinic; among 206 patients surveyed, 44% reported a history of physical or sexual abuse either as a child or as an adult. Although not specifically related to battered women, the studies by Koss et al. (1990, 1991) and Drossman et al. (1990) provide useful estimates of the number and frequency of family violence victim visits in outpatient medical settings.

BATTERED WOMEN IN OUTPATIENT CLINICS

Studies of battered women have been undertaken in various outpatient settings such as obstetrical clinics, general medical clinics and family medicine clinics. These studies are summarized in Table 1. In one obstetrical clinic study (Hillard, 1985), 81 of 742 (10.9%) women interviewed reported having been battered at some time in the history of their relationship. Nearly 4% of the women reported having been battered during the pregnancy. In another study (Helton, McFarlane, & Anderson, 1987), 290 pregnant women randomly selected from a number of private and public obstetrical clinics were interviewed. Of the total, 15.1% reported a history of battering prior to the pregnancy. Another 8.3% reported violence during the current pregnancy. Hence, in obstetrical clinic surveys, both pre-pregnancy and pregnancy battering rates range from 4% to 15% of patients.

Prevalence rates of battering also have been studied in general medicine and family medicine clinics. In a very early study, Dewsbury (1987) found an overall rate of 1.15 battered women per 1,000 women visiting a general medicine clinic. This study's method of inquiry was not entirely clear. Battering was defined as "repeated" physical assault with at least one experience of moderate injury. Hence, many women who sustained little or no injury or one instance of assault were not included in the survey.

A more recent study assessed the prevalence of battered women at two family practice clinics (Rath, Jarratt, & Leonardson, 1989). A total of 218 women were surveyed via an anonymous questionnaire regarding both verbal and physical abuse. A total of 48% of the women reported verbal abuse. Forty-four percent of the women reported some form of "minor" physical abuse and 28% reported severe physical abuse. Unlike the afore-mentioned obstetrical clinic studies (Helton et al., 1987; Hillard, 1985), Rath et al. (1989) did not distinguish between current or recent victimization and lifetime victimization, although such a distinction may be useful to guide assessment, diagnosis and treatment/referral planning. To illustrate, recently or currently battered women may be in immediate crisis and may require crisis stabilization and safety planning, including referral to shelter services. In contrast, women reporting a lifetime, but not recent, history of intimate assault may not require crisis management, but may need to be evaluated for post-traumatic stress disorder or other psychosocial sequelae of victimization.

Rath et al. (1989) conducted a chart review of 100 female patients to determine whether abuse was recorded, either in the problem list or in the progress notes. Whereas about one-third of the charts showed evidence of physician inquiry about stressors in the patient's life, only 4% clearly identified the patient as abused. Gin and colleagues (1991) assessed current and lifetime abuse among women attending three general internal medicine ambulatory clinics. The investigators found a lifetime victimization rate of 28%, and the proportion of women in current violent relationships was 14%.

Hamberger, Saunders, and Hovey (1992) conducted a survey of 374 women who came to an outpatient family medicine clinic. In addition to gathering demographic data, the group administered the Conflict Tactics Scale (CTS; Straus, 1979). Participants were instructed to respond to the CTS in terms of whether the tactics were used against them in the *past year*, as well as at *any time* during their life while in an intimate relationship. The respondents also indicated whether: (a) they were injured (ever or in the past year) by a domestic assault; (b) their physician had inquired during the most recent visit about relationship distress, verbal abuse or physical abuse. With respect to physician inquiry, the data were analyzed *both* without regard for the nature of the most recent visit and only for those respondents whose documented recent visit was extended, and thus afforded a reasonable opportunity for inquiry. Examples of extended visits include appointments for complete histories and physical examinations, first obstetrical visits, or psychosocial counseling sessions.

Of the women who were at risk by virtue of having been in a relationship, 25% reported being assaulted in the past year. Nearly 60% of the recently assaulted women reported an injury of at least the magnitude of

TABLE 1. Summary of Research on Battered Women in Ambulatory Care Clinics

Study	Type of Assault	Injury Rate %	Lifetime or Recent Violence	n/N (%)	Clinic Type
Hillard, 1985	Hit or tried to hit	49% sought treatment for injuries	Prior to pregnancy	81/742 (10.9)	OB
		40% reported multiple injury sites	During pregnancy	29/742 (4)	
Helton et al., 1987	Threats, hit slapped, kicked	2.8% sought treatment for injuries	Prior to pregnancy	44/290 (15.1)	OB
		6.8% reported multiple injury sites	During pregnancy	24/290 (8.3)	

Study	Type	Prevalence	Time frame	Rate (%)	Setting
Dewsbury, 1975	Repeated, injurious assault	Same as violence prevalence	Not determined	1.15/1,000 (0.1)	General Medicine
Gin et al., 1991	Not reported	Not reported	Lifetime	109/319 (34)	General Medicine
			Current	24/139 (17)	
Rath et al., 1989	Verbal abuse	Not reported	Not determined	102/213 (48)	Family Practice
	Minor violence			94/213 (44)	
	Severe violence			60/213 (28)	
Hamberger et al., 1992	Minor violence	24.7%	Lifetime	130/335 (40)	Family Practice
	Severe violence	14.8%	Past year	85/338 (25)	

bruising. Almost 40% of the total sample reported an assault against them during the course of their lives. Sixty-seven percent of the women reporting lifetime assaults also reported having sustained an injury.

Results suggested higher physician inquiry rates when the patient was seen for an extended visit. For all types of visits (including brief encounters), only 6.5% of respondents were asked about relationship distress, 2% were asked about verbal abuse and 1.7% were asked about physical assault.

WHY PHYSICIANS NEED TRAINING ABOUT BATTERING

The literature on incidence and prevalence of battered women seeking medical services in emergency and outpatient clinics holds information which, if better disseminated, might change the way many physicians practice medicine. Large numbers of battered women seek medical services for treatment of acute injuries from assault, for psychosocial sequelae related to the assault or for routine health maintenance and health care. In general, studies based on official documented records of emergency departments suggest that rates of victimization among female patients are roughly comparable to estimates generated from national surveys on domestic violence (i.e., about 4%, Straus & Gelles, 1986). In those studies in which women were surveyed directly about victimization, rates often were comparable to estimates of true rates of violence victimization, or 20%-30% (Straus & Gelles, 1986; Straus, Gelles, & Steinmetz, 1980). Similarly, battered women attend outpatient clinics in numbers roughly proportional to estimates of violence incidence and prevalence in the community, which range from 25% to 44%.

Battering victimization is vastly underdiagnosed in the medical system in both outpatient and emergency settings. In the emergency setting, this problem is highlighted by the several studies reviewed above. Stark et al. (1979) observed an official documented rate of victimization of 2.8%. A review of medical chart notes and records, however, suggested that the true rate of victimization was about ten times higher. Another study revealed similar findings (McLeer et al., 1989). The retrospective review of medical records showed a prevalence rate of 5.6%. However, following introduction of a protocol for specifically asking about domestic violence, the rate rose to 30%, as stated above.

Underdiagnosis of domestic violence also is evident in outpatient settings. For example, Rath et al. (1989) located only four "official" records of victimization among 100 charts. In addition, Hamberger et al. (1992) found inquiry rates of only 1.7%. It appears, therefore, that physicians do not ask their female patients about violence in their lives. Furthermore, battered women themselves often are reluctant to directly report their victimization to a treating physician. The obvious implication is that physicians must ask female patients about violence (e.g., Drossman et al., 1990; Goldberg & Tomlanovich, 1984; Hamberger et al., 1992; Hillard, 1985; McLeer et al., 1989; Rath et al., 1989; Rounsaville & Weissman, 1977-78).

One aspect of physician training, then, will involve teaching specific interviewing skills. At least as important as technical skills training are interventions with physician attitudes and values. Sugg and Inui (1992) found a number of factors related to the reluctance of primary care physicians to ask patients about abuse victimization. These factors included lack of comfort in exploring the issue, fear of offending patients by asking about relationship violence, time constraints, and either not knowing how to intervene, or not having control over the intervention process.

Behavioral Science Professionals as Physician Trainers

Behavioral science professionals, including psychologists, social workers and others in medical settings, are well positioned to train medical staff to identify, assess and intervene with battered women. Although not all mental health professionals are skilled in the area of domestic abuse (Harway & Hansen, 1990), those with expertise in the subject can be effective physician trainers. Mental health physician trainers must keep in mind that the purpose of training is to give physicians the skills to manage the battered women's care as part of a team effort, and not merely the skills to intercept the problem and refer the patient into the mental health services network.

Rounsaville and Weissman (1977-78) found that, although battered women expressed interest in discussing the problem with their treating physician, the vast majority refused to speak with a psychiatrist. Thus, efforts to transfer battered women's problems to the mental health arena are probably doomed to failure. Such efforts may be inappropriate, insofar as such a shift relabels battered women's experiences as clinical pathologies. The physician should remain the battered patient's primary contact for health care and other services; the mental health professional's responsibility is to enable the physician to do so while serving the patient's best interests.

What Should Training Involve?

The main features of training curricula for violence education are highlighted here. The Society of Teachers of Family Medicine has published a comprehensive model violence education curriculum for use in primary care residency training programs (Hendricks-Matthews, 1992). Hamberger (1990) also has compiled an annotated list of training programs and protocols for identifying and intervening with battered women. In addition, Hamberger, Burge, Graham, and Costa (in press) have completed a compendium on violence education issues for health care professionals. The primary areas of training are summarized in Table 2. Major aspects of each of these areas are described briefly.

Understanding the dynamics of domestic violence. Based on this author's experience in training family practice residents, perhaps the most frustrating aspect of intervening with battered women is their tendency to return to their violent partners, only to be battered and return to the emergency room or doctor's office again. This phenomenon seems to lead to a number of physician reactions. One reaction is to begin to view the patient as blameworthy for her victimization. Assignment of blameworthiness can lead to negative labeling such as "masochist," "hysterical," or otherwise mentally ill. Another reaction may be to increasingly withdraw caring assistance from the patient, and to focus only on superficial treatment of wounds.

Understanding some of the dynamics of domestic violence can enhance physician understanding of why battered women often return to their batterers despite knowledge of the risk of further victimization. Strube (1988) and Barnett and LaViolette (1993) reviewed studies of reasons why women stay in abusive relationships. Although there are numerous psychological explanations for why battered women stay in such relationships, physicians must be made aware of the many practical reasons they do so. For example, battered women frequently report having no place to

TABLE 2. Primary Areas of Physician Training for Identification and Intervention with Battered Women

- Dynamics of domestic violence
- Observational skills
- Interviewing skills
- Risk assessment
- Safety planning
- Follow-up
- Documentation

go, no supportive friends or relatives, and no independent financial resources. Furthermore, many battered women are terrified to leave their partners because of previous and ongoing life-threatening violence or verbal threats. Understanding such factors can enable the treating physician to view the battered woman's plight as a legitimate response to an extreme situation, rather than as an internal defect.

Clues from clinical observation. Although the body of empirical literature profiling battered women in medical settings is not extensive, several reports based on clinical observation reveal clues which should heighten a clinician's index of suspicion. Chief among these are presenting complaints of pain (Goldberg & Tomlanovich, 1984), a pattern of injuries not consistent with the patient's explanation, injuries about the head and neck (Foneska, 1974), and symptoms associated with mental health disorders (Saunders, Hamberger, & Hovey, 1993). Additionally, physicians should be alert to other risk factors for battering, such as being divorced or separated.

Rounsaville and Weissman (1977-78) identified battered women as more likely to sustain primary injuries about the head and neck. Similarly, Foneska (1974) found more facial injuries among battered women than among women assaulted by people other than their partners. Drossman et al. (1990) observed that battered women in a gastroenterology clinic had a higher percentage of functional gastrointestinal disorders, whereas nonbattered women had a higher percentage of organic gastrointestinal disorders.

In emergency settings, battered women are more likely to have a history of psychiatric problems, to have been in marital counseling, and/or to be divorced (Appleton, 1980). Goldberg and Carey (1982) identified battered women as manifesting suicidal gestures and attempts. They also found that battered women presented explanations that were incompatible with the injury profiles. Mehta and Dandrea (1988) found that battered women in an obstetrics clinic showed more emotional problems, were less educated and more likely to be divorced or separated than nonbattered women. Similarly, Hamberger et al. (1992) found that, compared to nonbattered women, battered women were younger, more likely to be separated or divorced, and to have been in a relationship for less time.

Although more rigorous and systematic evaluation is needed, this information suggests that battered women present multiple clues which, if investigated, would lead the physician to discover that she was battered. Psychologists and other mental health professionals can assist physicians in identifying known cues, following the leads for further information, and initiating appropriate interventions.

Interviewing skills. Authorities such as Goldberg and Tomlanovich

(1984) and Rath et al. (1989) correctly suggest that *how* a battered woman is approached on an interpersonal level may have important implications and influence her response. However, the literature on underidentification suggests that any questioning about violence would constitute a significant improvement. Social science professionals on medical school faculties often oversee medical student and resident training in interviewing and doctor-patient relationship skills. A number of battered woman identification protocols have been published which provide detailed examples of interview strategies (Braham, Furniss, Holtz, & Stevens, 1986; Goldberg & Carey, 1982; Saunders, 1991). In general, such strategies include empathizing with the victim and providing emotional support for her situation. Also important is avoiding judgmental responses that either suggest she is to blame or are too prescriptive, which deny her the opportunity to take control and choose a course of action.

The primary goal of interviewing a battered woman is to provide support and validation for her experience, and information for her safety. Physicians need to understand that merely because they cannot elicit an admission of battering from a battered woman does not mean she has not benefitted from their efforts. More than a few battered women have suggested to this author that although they did not respond to initial physician inquiries, the effort facilitated future doctor visits, subsequent safety planning and escape efforts. In contrast, other battered women have indicated reluctance to seek subsequent medical help because the physician either did not question or respond to cues, or responded by suggesting the woman caused her victimization in some way. Physician educators can assist in teaching necessary interviewing skills by directly observing physician interactions and providing feedback and practice opportunities.

Safety planning. In this author's experience with training physicians, a common concern is what to do after identifying a battered woman. In addition to providing appropriate support and validation, discussed previously, physicians can be instructed in initiating safety planning strategies. Such strategies include, but are not limited to, providing education about battered women's resources, social services and police arrest policies. Furthermore, an assessment of lethality should be conducted (Browne, 1987; Campbell, 1995). Such an assessment focuses on factors that differentiate battered women who used lethal violence or were at risk for serious injury or death from those who were not. Such factors include frequency and severity of injuries, a man's threats to kill, a man's drug use and frequency of intoxication, forced or threatened sexual acts, and the woman's suicidal threats. Saunders (1991) provided a list of highly serious, potentially lethal risk markers in cases of partner violence. Some of these are similar to those identified by Browne (1987). Others include: abuser violently jealous, violent outside the home, violent toward the children, and violence during pregnancy. Lethality determination should be followed up by an expression of concern for the woman's safety, as well as the development of concrete safety-enhancing strategies. Such strategies include inquiring directly about the woman's sense of safety and, if present, the children's safety. Identifying safe havens outside the house and supportive social networks also is important. Finally, arrangements should be made for follow-up contacts with the physician.

Follow-up. Battered women identified in a clinic should not be sent home without making follow-up appointments or arrangements. Follow-up affords the battered woman a place she can return to for further support and assistance. Although referral to a women's shelter is important, follow-up with the treating physician may facilitate safety for a battered woman who chooses to remain with the batterer. Going to a physician, particularly in an outpatient clinic, is usually construed as a legitimate yet confidential activity, and thus is conducive to further problem solving and safety planning.

Documentation. Physicians need to document carefully their battered patients' injuries, and the etiology of these injuries. Additional training by medical members of a sexual assault team or forensic scientists can add to the physician's ability to interpret physical evidence of assault. Mental health professionals can help prepare the physician to receive such knowledge and to unravel and record salient facts of the patient's social history. As with the basic identification of battered women, physicians appear to have underdocumented domestic violence even when detected (Warshaw, 1989). For example, although an assault may be documented as such, the fact that the assailant was a domestic partner often is ignored. Warshaw (1989) found that in nearly three-quarters of assault cases, the woman's relationship to the assailant was not recorded. Careful documentation of the effects and the known causes is essential for legal purposes, especially if charges are filed. Such documentation also should facilitate any necessary future medical interventions.

CONCLUSION

Battered women appear to be frequent users of medical services, both in emergency departments and ambulatory care centers. Physicians are well positioned to intercept acts of domestic violence and offer support as well as medical treatment. Nonetheless, domestic violence is grossly underdiagnosed in medical settings. Physician training is greatly needed if inroads are to be made into this problem.

Mental health professionals can improve the detection and treatment of battered women in medical settings by educating physicians, conducting research, and disseminating findings. Despite a plethora of articles on the topic, there is very little empirical information about characteristics of battered women in medical settings. Areas of future research could include utilization patterns and frequencies, problem complaints, and physician diagnoses. The few studies that have been done are based on fairly small samples, often in specialty clinics such as ob-gyn or gastroenterology. Research conducted by Koss et al. (1990, 1991) on female victims of violent crime could serve as a model for similar research on battered women. Accessing large patient databases such as those maintained by managed care programs can facilitate large-scale studies needed to document utilization patterns, diagnostic profiles, and other factors.

Finally, psychologists may be particularly well suited to assess the effectiveness of physician training programs. Although physician training is important, as noted above, the costs of medical education will require that clear benefits be shown. Hence, program evaluation research will be an important contribution of the mental health professional in medical education.

REFERENCES

Appleton, W. (1980). The battered woman syndrome. *Annals of Emergency Medicine, 9,* 84-91.

Barnett, O. W., & LaViolette, A. D. (1993). *It could happen to anyone: Why battered women stay.* Newbury Park, CA: Sage Publications.

Braham, R., Furniss, K., Holtz, H., & Stevens, M. E. (1986). *Hospital protocol on domestic violence.* Morristown, NJ: Jersey Battered Women's Service.

Browne, A. (1987). When battered women kill. New York: Free Press.

Campbell, J. C. (Ed.). (1995). *Assessing dangerousness: Violence by sexual offenders, batterers, and child abusers.* Thousand Oaks, CA: Sage Publications.

Dewsbury, A. R. (1987). Family violence as seen in the general practice. *Royal Society of Health Journal, 95,* 290-294.

Douglas, M. A. (1987). The battered woman syndrome. In D.J. Sonkin (Ed.), *Domestic violence on trial* (pp. 276-300). New York: Springer.

Drossman, D. A., Leserman, J., Nachman, G., Zhiming, L., Gluck, H., Toomey, T.C., & Mitchell, C. M. (1990). Sexual and physical abuse in women with functional or gastrointestinal disorders. *Annals of Internal Medicine, 113,* 828-833.

Flitcraft, A. (1990, October 15). Battered women in your practice? *Patient Care*, 107-118.

Foneska, S. (1974). A study of wife-beating in the Camberwell area. *British Journal of Clinical Practice, 28,* 400-404.

Gin, N. E., Rucker, L., Frayne, S., Cygan, R., & Hubbel, A. (1991). Prevalence of domestic violence among patients in three ambulatory care internal medicine clinics. *Journal of General Internal Medicine, 6,* 317-322.

Goldberg, W., & Carey, A. L. (1982, January). Domestic violence victims in the emergency setting. *Topics in Emergency Medicine, 3,* 65-75.

Goldberg, W. G., & Tomlanovich, M. C. (1984). Domestic violence victims in the emergency departments: New findings. *Journal of the American Medical Association, 251,* 3259-3264.

Hamberger, L. K. (1990, May). *Training curricula in the detection of violence in family medicine: Models, methods and materials.* Roundtable discussion presented at the meeting of the Society of Teachers of Family Medicine, Philadelphia, PA.

Hamberger, L. K., Burge, S., Graham, A., & Costa, A. (Eds.). (In Press). *Violence issues for health care educators and providers.* Binghamton, NY: The Haworth Press, Inc.

Hamberger, L. K., Saunders, D. G., & Hovey, M. (1992). The prevalence of domestic violence in community practice and rate of physician inquiry. *Family Medicine, 24,* 283-287.

Harway, M., & Hansen, M. (1990). Therapists' recognition of wife battering: Some empirical evidence. *Family Violence Bulletin, 6,* 16-18.

Helton, A. S., McFarlane, J., & Anderson, E. T. (1987). Battered and pregnant: A prevalence study. *American Journal of Public Health, 77,* 1337-1339.

Hendricks-Matthews, M. (Ed.). (1992). *Violence education: Toward a solution.* Kansas City, MO: Society of Teachers of Family Medicine.

Hillard, P. J. (1985). Physical abuse in pregnancy. *Obstetrics and Gynecology, 66,* 185-190.

Joint Commission on Accreditation of Healthcare Organizations (1992). *Accreditation manual for hospitals* (pp. 22-23, 33-34). Washington, DC: JCAHO.

Koop, C. E. (1987). *Healing interpersonal violence. Making health a full partner.* Keynote address at the Surgeon General's Northwest Conference on Interpersonal Violence, Seattle, WA. Washington, DC: U.S. Public Health Service.

Koss, M. P., Koss, P. G., & Woodruff, W. J. (1991). Deleterious effects of criminal victimization on women's health and medical utilization. *Archives of Internal Medicine, 151,* 342-347.

Koss, M. P., Woodruff, W. J., & Koss, P. G. (1990). Relation of criminal victimization to health perceptions among women medical patients. *Journal of Consulting and Clinical Psychology, 58,* 147-152.

McLeer, S. V., Anwar, R. A. H., Herman, S., & Maquiling, K. (1989). Education is not enough: A systems failure in protecting battered women. *Annals of Emergency Medicine, 18,* 651-653.

Mehta, P., & Dandrea, L. A. (1988). The battered woman. *American Family Physician, 37,* 193-199.

Rath, G. D., Jarratt, L. G., & Leonardson, F. (1989). Rates of domestic violence against adult women by men partners. *Journal of the American Board of Family Practice, 2,* 228-233.

Roberts, G. L., O'Toole, B. I., Lawrence, J. M., & Raphael, B. (1993). Domestic violence victims in a hospital emergency department. *The Medical Journal of Australia, 159,* 307-310.

Rounsaville, B., & Weissman, M. M. (1977-78). Battered women: A medical problem requiring detection. *International Journal of Psychiatry in Medicine, 8,* 191-202.

Saunders, D. G. (1991). Family violence. *Emergency Care Quarterly, 7,* 51-61.

Saunders, D. G., Hamberger, L. K., & Hovey, M. (1993). Indicators of woman abuse based on a chart review at a family practice center. *Archives of Family Medicine, 2,* 537-543.

Stark, E., Flitcraft, A., & Frazier, W. (1979). Medicine and patriarchal violence: The social construction of a "private" event. *International Journal of Health Services, 9,* 461-493.

Straus, M. A. (1979). Measuring intrafamily conflict and violence: The Conflict Tactics Scales (CTS). *Journal of Marriage and the Family, 4,* 75-88.

Straus, M. A., & Gelles, R. J. (1986). Societal change and change in family violence from 1975 to 1985 as revealed by two national surveys. *Journal of Marriage and the Family, 48,* 465-479.

Straus, M. A., Gelles, R. J., & Steinmetz, S. K. (1980). *Behind closed doors: Violence in the American family.* New York: Anchor.

Strube, M. J. (1988). The decision to leave an abusive relationship: Empirical evidence and theoretical issues. *Psychological Bulletin, 104,* 236-250.

Sugg, N. K., & Inui, T. (1992). Primary care physicians' response to domestic violence: Opening Pandora's box. *Journal of the American Medical Association, 267,* 3157-3160.

Walker, L. E. A. (1979). *The battered woman.* New York: Harper and Row.

Warshaw, C. (1989). Limitations of the medical model in the care of battered women. *Gender and Society, 3,* 506-517.

Battered Women:
A Historical Research Review
and Some Common Myths

Mildred Daley Pagelow

SUMMARY. This review of research findings on woman battering reveals how research has played a major role in changing social policy and challenging common myths and stereotypes. The earliest literature contained the ideas of a few psychotherapists who viewed woman battering as a rare phenomenon that involved masochistic women and sadistic men, which led to the myth of psychopathology as the mediating factor. Research following the birth of the battered women's movement destroyed this and some subsequent myths. It led to changes in medical practitioners' attitudes toward battered women patients and law enforcement's reaction to battering victims and their abusers. It also revealed important facts about the courts' handling of abusers and their victims and about violent relationships that result in homicide. The myth that children living in violent households are unharmed has been soundly discredited, yet despite these findings, many battered women continue to face serious difficulties when they attempt to divorce their abusers and obtain custody of their children. Other myths have been exposed by researchers on the basis of their findings. However, once ideas gain popular public acceptance, they tend to continue to exert influence. Nevertheless, positive changes have occurred in the entire spectrum of medical, legal, and social services with which battered women must interface. The research

---

Address correspondence to: Mildred Daley Pagelow, PhD, Department of Sociology, California State University, Fullerton, CA 92634.

[Haworth co-indexing entry note]: "Battered Women: A Historical Research Review and Some Common Myths." Pagelow, Mildred Daley. Co-published simultaneously in *Journal of Aggression, Maltreatment & Trauma* (Haworth Maltreatment & Trauma Press, an imprint of The Haworth Press, Inc.) Vol. 1, No. 1 (#1), 1997, pp. 97-116; and: *Violence and Sexual Abuse at Home: Current Issues in Spousal Battering and Child Maltreatment* (ed: Robert Geffner, Susan B. Sorenson, and Paula K. Lundberg-Love) Haworth Maltreatment & Trauma Press, an imprint of The Haworth Press, Inc., 1997, pp. 97-116. Single or multiple copies of this article are available for a fee from The Haworth Document Delivery Service [1-800-342-9678, 9:00 a.m. - 5:00 p.m. (EST). E-mail address: getinfo@haworth.com].

findings reviewed here help highlight current needs and suggest future directions. *[Article copies available for a fee from The Haworth Document Delivery Service: 1-800-342-9678. E-mail address: getinfo@haworth. com]*

KEYWORDS. Wife abuse, characteristics, domestic violence, homicide, custody shelters

The "battered women's movement" started in England in 1971 with the establishment of the first shelter for abused wives. Slowly it spread and a second shelter opened in 1974 in the Netherlands. Finally, stimulated by a grassroots movement in the United States in the mid-1970s, shelters gradually increased from three to hundreds (Pagelow, 1981a, 1984; Tierney, 1982). It quickly became apparent that activists needed research findings to bolster their claims about the magnitude of the problem and service providers needed them to guide provision of their services. Since then, some early popular ideas about woman-battering have been discounted by research although some linger on, and other myths and issues calling for research have developed over time.

BATTERED WOMEN, MEDICINE, AND THE MYTH OF PSYCHOPATHOLOGY

In March 1976, exhaustive computer searches of the literature on battered women produced only four to six citations, most of which were written by psychoanalysts who described wife abuse as a rare phenomenon in which either or both parties were neurotic or psychotic. Researchers and other professionals in the social and behavioral sciences became keenly interested in this newly discovered social problem. Before long, the first myth of woman battering (that it occurred rarely and only between psychologically disturbed individuals) was shattered.

Frequently the only, or the first, practitioners who come in contact with victims are medical professionals (Stark et al., 1981). Early research reports found that medical professionals tended to engage in victim blaming (Pagelow, 1981a). Worse yet, medical intervention methods tended to accelerate battered women's problems especially when family maintenance was the therapeutic goal (Stark, Flitcraft, & Frazier, 1979). Medical professionals frequently expressed the myth that female patients who left medical care and returned home with the men who inflicted their injuries were masochists rather than women who perceived no viable alternatives. Many physicians believed that their duty was to attend to their patients' physical trauma and dismiss them as having "mental problems" which were not their responsibility. Since then, the "myth of female masochism" regarding battered women has not been supported by research evidence (Kuhl, 1981).

In October, 1985, Flitcraft and Stark were co-chairs of the Spouse Abuse Prevention work group at the Surgeon General's workshop on violence and public health in Leesburg, Virginia. About 150 researchers and practitioners participated and each work group offered their recommendations, which were subsequently published by the U. S. Department of Health and Human Services (1986). The following month, at the opening session of the First National Nursing Conference, nurses presented recommendations from the Leesburg workshop on Violence Against Women. The Nursing Network on Violence Against Women was established at the conference. Since then, nurses and some physicians have contributed greatly to the accumulation of knowledge about battered women in the health care field. In general, nurses appear to be more helpful to battered women and less victim-blaming than some physicians, but gender appears to play a greater role than professional category in attitudes toward battered women (Rose & Saunders, 1986).

Most research finds that abused women are not identified as such in clinics and emergency rooms. Medical practitioners focus on the women's psychosocial problems such as depression, drug abuse, and suicide attempts, and ignore symptoms of injuries inflicted by others (Bullock, McFarlane, Bateman, & Miller, 1989; Campbell, 1986; Kurz, 1989; Randall, 1990a, 1990b; Rose & Saunders, 1986; Warshaw, 1989).

In an effort to alert physicians to the need for education and sensitization to the identification and treatment of battering victims, Randall (1990a, 1990b) notes the tendency of physicians to ignore strong indicators of abuse. Mark Rosenberg, former director of injury control at the Centers for Disease Control states that: "The only physicians who ask about violence are psychiatrists, and they're only interested if it occurs in a dream. They rarely ask about the violent events that occur in real life" (cited in Randall, 1990a, p. 939).

Stark et al. (1981) was the first to report that battering accounts for more than 25% of visits by women who use emergency services, yet even in hospitals that developed a protocol for identifying battering, fewer than 1 in 25 were accurately diagnosed. Since then, there have been many studies to establish the prevalence of battering among women seeking medical services, to discover how many battering victims are identified, and to ascertain what kind of treatment, if any, follows (Bullock et al., 1989; Kurz, 1987; Kurz & Stark, 1988).

Warshaw (1989) examined medical records of cases from a hospital emergency department which has a formal protocol for recognizing and caring for women at risk of abuse. Both medical doctors and nurses failed to deal with the evidence of ongoing domestic violence. Warshaw (1989, p. 510) stated, "Physicians, in other clinical situations, would not discharge a patient from the emergency room with a potentially life-threatening condition."

Campbell's (1992) review of nursing research on battering found that at least 10-22% (and perhaps as high as 25%) of women using emergency services were battered, yet only 2-8% were identified correctly. The research showed that identification increased after staff training and abuse protocols were implemented. Campbell suggests that future research should empower the women and children involved, not blame or pathologize them.

Improvements are occurring. Nurses in some hospital emergency rooms voluntarily report all suspected cases of wife abuse to police departments, which can help build a "paper trail" to document a history of violence (Pagelow, 1990a). They also urge victims to allow pictures to be taken of their injuries at the hospital which are kept in a locked file, in case victims need them later. Some also distribute printed victim-assistance information to suspected victims which gives names and telephone numbers of shelters and victim services, as well as brief explanations of victims' legal and civil rights (Pagelow, 1987). For a description of a successful hospital-based program, see Randall (1991).

BATTERED WOMEN, LAW ENFORCEMENT, AND THE MYTH OF DANGEROUSNESS

Police officers also may become involved when wife abuse occurs (Lavoie, Jacob, Hardy, & Martin, 1989; Stith, 1990). Historically, one of the most frequent complaints of victims has been that police did little or nothing helpful when (and if) they responded to domestic violence calls (Pagelow, 1981a). Conversely, police complained that these were nuisance calls because they repeatedly had to go to the same homes, these were "lovers' quarrels" that required them to play social worker, and even when victims asked them to make arrests, battered women seldom pressed charges. Officers' instructions were based on an official non-arrest policy (Parnas, 1967). As the President of the Police Association explains, "Physical violence within the home was thought to be exempt from the same laws which kept acquaintances or strangers from assaulting each other on the streets" (Murphy, 1984, p. 3). Arrests were correspondingly rare, occurring in only 3-27% of all domestic disturbance calls (Elk & Johnson, 1989; Sherman & Berk, 1984a).

Another feature of law enforcement attitudes was a commonly accepted belief that these calls resulted in the highest injury and death rate for officers. Police were reluctant to place themselves in great personal danger responding to calls that were unofficially viewed as nuisance calls. Some researchers contributed to the myth's acceptance by repeatedly stating that domestic disturbances were the single most frequent cause of police injuries and deaths. However, Pagelow (1981a) warned that these statistics came from an FBI catch-all category of "domestic disturbance" which included other combinations of victims and abusers, so such claims could be greatly exaggerated. This idea was supported by research. A study by Gardner and Clemmer (1986) found "the danger to police in these cases has been overstated. . . . other police assignments are far more dangerous" (Stewart, 1986, p. 1). Although it was shown that robberies are the most dangerous calls leading to officer assaults, injuries, and deaths, many police officers still believe "domestic disputes" are most dangerous for them.

Major changes in police policy occurred after a unique research experiment conducted in Minneapolis in 1981 and 1982 (Sherman & Berk, 1984a, 1984b). The experiment showed that arrests clearly are an improvement over sending the suspect away. The latter intervention produced two and a half times as many repeat incidents as talking to suspects or arrests. Sherman and Berk said, "on the basis of this study alone, police should probably employ arrest in most cases of minor domestic violence" (1984b, p. 7). Very quickly, law enforcement departments across the country began revising their non-arrest policies to policies favoring arrest for probable cause (Elk & Johnson, 1989; Goolkasian, 1986a). Although there were other factors arguing for a change in police response to spouse assault (Eigenberg & Moriarity, 1990), the Minneapolis experiment's results undoubtedly exerted the greatest influence for change.

Berk and Newton (1985) attempted to replicate the experiment and found that arrests substantially reduced the number of new incidents of wife battery. On the other hand, the first of six replications funded by the National Institute of Justice failed to find differences in the prevalence and frequency of repeat offenses between treatment groups six months after the presenting offense (Dunford, Huizinga, & Elliott, 1990). Although arrest did not deter future violence, it did not place victims in greater danger of increased violence, either. Additional replications have suggested that arrest alone may be effective for certain types of batterers in certain situations. It appears that other interventions (e.g., treatment) must also occur in conjunction with arrest for better reduction of recidivism. We still need other research and an accumulated knowledge base to guide policies on the most effective police response to battering incidents.

Other research focuses on police response and whether and how police are following new laws and departmental guidelines. Elk and Johnson (1989) found no increase in arrests or filing charges even when weapons were involved. Others found no increases (Lerman, 1981) or a decrease (Buzawa, 1982) in arrests in areas where police powers to arrest have been expanded.

Research on police response to domestic violence calls has proliferated (Berk, Berk, & Newton, 1984; Eigenberg & Moriarity, 1990; Lavoie et al., 1989; Stith, 1990). Dolon, Hendricks, and Meagher (1986) reported that arrest occurs most often when: (1) the officer's safety is threatened, (2) a felony is committed, (3) a weapon is used, (4) the victim is seriously injured, (5) future violence appears likely, (6) many calls come from the same residence, (7) the suspect is under the influence of alcohol or other drugs, (8) the officer's authority is disregarded, (9) there have been previous injuries to victim, (10) prior legal action was taken, such as obtaining a restraining order, and (11) the victim insists on arrest.

Friday, Metzgar, and Walters (1989) found that the impact of arrest on future behavior was weaker than in the Minneapolis experiment. They conclude that the greatest impact from arrest occurs when there have been no prior arrests, noting that these are the cases in which police are least likely to arrest. This conclusion is in direct contradiction to that drawn by Berk and Newton (1985) who found that arrests are especially effective for batterers whom police would ordinarily be inclined to arrest: repeat offenders. Future research may resolve this issue. As research findings continue to accumulate, it is likely we will find other contradictions and some puzzles about attitudes and behaviors.

Research has helped propel the "non-crime" of assault and battery of wives into becoming officially defined as criminal behavior. However, the need for scientifically sound studies, replications, and longitudinal studies is still great.

BATTERED WOMEN, THE LEGAL SYSTEM, AND THE MYTH OF EQUAL JUSTICE FOR ALL

In 1982, the President's Task Force on Victims of Crime recommended that a task force be established to study violence in the family (Herrington,

1982, 1986). The Attorney General's Task Force on Family Violence (U.S. Department of Justice, 1984) offered recommendations for prosecutors and judges. By 1989, 27 states had established committees or task forces to study gender bias in the courts, and more states followed (Response, 1989). One task force found, "The most compelling and moving testimony that the committee received during hearings that it conducted throughout the state concerned domestic violence" (Maryland Special Joint Committee on Gender Bias in the Courts, 1989, p. 8).

The California committee said virtually the same thing:

> Again and again, this committee heard testimony that police officers, district and city attorneys, court personnel, mediators, and judges— the justice system—treated the victims of domestic violence as though their complaints were trivial, exaggerated, or somehow their own fault. (Judicial Council Advisory Committee on Gender Bias in the Courts, 1990, Sec. 6, p. 5)

Many researchers and advocates of battered women concur. Some find particular fault with judges, such as Archer (1989), who stated:

> If a woman manages to pass through the obstacle course set up by the District Attorney's office, and actually gets her charges into a courtroom, she still will have problems getting a conviction. Many judges have traditional views as to male/female roles, and like the police, many do not view spouse abuse as a true crime. (p. 154)

In 1987, the National Council of Juvenile and Family Court Judges began working to find ways to develop a more effective system. Three years later the Council officially adopted recommendations for improving court practices in family violence cases (Family Violence Project, 1990). Their recommendations and accompanying explanations show a substantial depth of understanding. Although the report recommended that judges should not issue mutual restraining orders (Family Violence Project, 1990), judges sometimes still impose mutual restraining orders, even when existing state law seems to preclude such decisions (Hart, Bricklin, & Zorza, 1991).

All judges must have at least a rudimentary grasp of the issue and of battering victims, and the best way to educate juries may be through expert testimony (Archer, 1989; Maryland Special Joint Committee on Gender Bias in the Courts, 1989). Qualified authorities can speak generally about the nature of battering and can explain why victims are reluctant (or refuse) to testify against their abusers (Goolkasian, 1986b).

Sentences for convicted batterers have traditionally been much lighter than violent crimes involving strangers (Archer, 1989; Goolkasian, 1986b). Thus, it would help if the justice system dealt with abusers as violent criminals rather than as misbehaving husbands. The law is clear regarding battery involving serious injuries, threat of continued harm, a long pattern of abuse, or earlier legal contact because of spouse abuse. But there is a wide range of other sentencing options. Alternatives include restitution and/or fines, weekend incarceration, specifically tailored probation, and diversion programs. Many states passed laws to divert certain offenders from the criminal justice system into psychological counseling programs. But findings about whether diversion and treatment programs are truly effective are ambiguous (Pirog-Good and Stets, 1986; Saunders & Azar, 1989; Tolman & Bennett, 1990).

One problem is that in some jurisdictions, the opportunity for diversion is given to suspects before they enter a plea; thus, they can be diverted into counseling and out of the justice system without a record, as permitted under the law in California. The judges' report takes a firm stand on the subject, saying, "Diversion should only occur in extraordinary cases, and then only after an admission before a judicial officer has been entered" (Family Violence Project, 1990, p. 38). This would effectively control those who take diversion lightly and drop out because they could be sentenced swiftly without re-setting the trial. It should be noted that some jurisdictions rigorously prosecute battering cases, and some states do not allow pre-trial diversions.

The literature focusing on battered women and the legal system continues to grow. Recommendations come from government-sponsored task forces and individual researchers who have studied the complexities of the system with which battered women must deal in order to obtain protection and justice. But battered women continue to face unmet needs. In time, statistics will begin to reflect the effects of new state laws and improvements over old statutes. For example, laws on temporary restraining orders have been greatly improved, but more changes are still needed (Judicial Council Advisory Committee on Gender Bias in the Courts, 1990; Pagelow, 1992).

BATTERED WOMEN AND HOMICIDE:
TILL DEATH DO US PART

Woman battering, formerly viewed as a "non-crime," sometimes continues until the suicide, homicide or attempted homicide of victims, abusers, and/or their children. Writers have paid much more attention to the instances when battered women strike back at their abusers with deadly force, despite the fact that battering is more likely to culminate in the death of the woman. In spouse homicides, wives are 1.3 times more likely to be killed than are husbands (Mercy & Saltzman, 1989).

Woman battering tends to escalate in severity and frequency over time (Pagelow, 1981b), and may end in homicide, suicide, or both. In 1985, for example, over 1,300 women, 30% of the total homicides of females, were killed by a husband or boyfriend (Uniform Crime Reports, 1986). Six percent of all male victims of homicide were killed by their wives or girlfriends. In 1992, 41% of female homicides were committed by a husband or boyfriend where the offender was identified (Bachman & Saltzman, 1996). Men tend to kill and be killed in far greater numbers than women. The statistics for spouse homicides tend to remain consistent over time (Bachman & Saltzman, 1996). Browne (1987) reported that in 1984, of the over 2,000 persons killed by spouses, two-thirds (1,300) were wives killed by husbands and one-third (806) were husbands killed by wives. However, as Campbell (1986) noted, "when women kill, they are far more likely than men to be responding to, rather than initiating, violence" (p. 37).

Murder/suicide is most likely to occur between a husband and wife, and almost always is perpetrated by the male who first kills his wife, girlfriend, or estranged partner and then himself (Stuart & Campbell, 1989). In other instances, the wife and some or all of the children and/or other family members are targets (Browne, 1987; Pagelow, 1990b).

Campbell (1986; 1995) developed and tested an instrument for assessing battered women's risk of homicide, the Danger Assessment instrument. Another instrument has been published by Sonkin, Martin, and Walker (1985). Campbell's tool was designed to be administered to battered women by nurses, and although the nurse makes no actual predictions, its value is in helping the victim determine for herself how dangerous her current situation is. It does not attempt to predict the direction of the danger, whether it is likely that the battered woman will kill or be killed, because the sequence of events may be determined almost entirely by circumstances.

Researchers began early to study the lethal effects of woman battering. Most were scholars concerned about legal defenses for battered women who strike back (Eisenberg, 1979; Eisenberg & Seymour, 1979). Later, others tried to understand why some battered women resort to homicide (Ewing, 1987). Browne (1987) compared battered women who kill to others who do not.

One study compared battered women who killed with those who did not and identified seven factors that were present in the experiences of women who killed: (1) the men became intoxicated every day, (2) the men used recreational drugs, (3) they had made threats to kill the wife, (4) their physical attacks were more frequent, (5) victims sustained more and more severe injuries, (6) the women were more likely to have been raped by the abusers, and (7) the women were forced into other sexual acts against their will (Browne, 1987).

Other studies on battered women who kill assume a variety of viewpoints. Some address theoretical questions (Mahan & Swebilius, 1989), resources that might prevent female-perpetrated homicides (Browne & Williams, 1989), predicting jury verdicts in such cases (Follingstad et al., 1989), the use of expert witnesses in these trials (Lafferty, 1990), and the "battered woman syndrome" as a trial defense (Stuesser, 1990). Gillespie (1989) looks at homicide by battered women from the perspective of American criminal law, and describes an unbalanced and unjust legal system.

When violent relationships culminate in homicide, the children always pay a heavy price, as expressed by Stuart and Campbell (1989):

> Children who lose a parent at the hand of the other parent face not only the loss of the significant person, but also the stigma of the event and the complex legal processes that accompany homicide. The outcome of legal proceedings may result in the incarceration of the remaining parent. . . . When a murder-suicide occurs, the child is abandoned by the two people who were to protect and nurture the child. (p. 246)

Much more research is needed on marital partners who strike with lethal force, whether they are male batterers or battering victims. Many women do not leave their abusers until they become convinced that their own or their children's lives are at stake.

BATTERED WOMEN, CUSTODY, AND THE MYTH THAT CHILDREN ARE UNHARMED

Abused women remain tied to their abusers for a diverse combination of economic, social, legal, and psychological reasons (Barnett & LaViolette, 1993). There also are physical reasons for staying with abusive spouses, such as chronic illness of the children or themselves, or physical handicaps (National Battered Women's Law Project, 1991; Pagelow, 1988). When they do try to get away, battered women often enter the most dangerous period of the entire relationship, after which they may find that their abusers are obsessed with continuing their control and domination (Pagelow, 1993). Many years later, some women are still trying to hide from their ex-spouses, or they constantly endure harassment, intimidation, stalking, and damaged property.

Children provide batterers a means of maintaining control and domination over wives who seek to escape. Changes in the courts may assist them (Geffner & Pagelow, 1990). Some abusers use the courts to continue their control over their ex-wives and children by taking advantage of the current trend of courts favoring joint custody or granting sole custody to fathers. Women usually are the primary caretakers of children before and after divorce, and they have profound fears of losing custody, whereas the batterer has little to lose by using custody as a bargaining and power tactic (Liss & Stahly, 1993; Marks, 1988; Pagelow, 1992).

Influenced in some measure by the fathers' rights movement and some research that suggested children's best interest is served by frequent and continuing contact with both parents (Wallerstein & Kelly, 1980), over two-thirds of the states have passed laws authorizing or recommending joint custody (Geffner & Pagelow, 1990; Pagelow, 1992). Some state laws permit joint custody awards even when one parent objects, a decision which Wallerstein (1988) opposes in abusive relationships. Problems incurred by joint custody in conflictual relationships are substantial (Steinman, 1986; Steinman, Zemmelman, & Knoblauch, 1985). Research shows that some children in these families fare better when sole custody is awarded and there is little or no paternal contact (Furstenberg, Morgan, & Allison, 1987; Johnston, Kline, Tschann, & Campbell, 1988). According to the Family Violence Project report (1990), "Judges should not presume that joint custody is in the best interest of the children. . . . Court orders which force victims to share custody with their abusers place both victims and children in danger" (p. 26). The power and control will be perpetuated and abused spouses and their children will tend to be revictimized (American Psychological Association, 1996; Geffner & Pagelow, 1990).

Many custody disputes are not adjudicated but are sent to mediation first. Mediation for disputes in custody and visitation issues began in 1981. Most states make exceptions and/or special provisions for cases involving domestic violence (Sun & Thomas, 1987), but in some states, mediation is still mandatory with no exceptions, even when battering has occurred. Mediation has been defined as:

[A] cooperative dispute resolution process in which a neutral [trained] third party tries to help contesting parties reach a settlement of their differences. . . . Its objective is to cause disputing parties to compromise and thereby reach a voluntary and mutually acceptable agreement. (Pearson, Thoennes, & Kool, 1982, p. 337)

All definitions include reference to the voluntary nature of mediation. Marks (1988) notes that "mandatory mediation" is a contradiction in terms and may carry stigma for the person who does not cooperate.

Battle lines have been drawn between battered women's advocates and court-affiliated mediators regarding forcing battered women to mediate with their abusers (Dies, 1985; Geffner & Pagelow, 1990; Germane, Johnson, & Lemon, 1985; Hart, 1990; Keenan, 1985; Pagelow, 1990b; Sun & Thomas, 1987). Various task forces oppose mandated mediation for couples with a history of violence (American Psychological Association, 1996; Family Violence Project, 1990; Judicial Council on Gender Bias in the Courts, 1990). A few articles support mediation for couples with a history of violence (e.g., Erickson & McKnight, 1990) although almost no research findings have supported that position.

Much research attention has focused on whether interparental violence is harmful to children (i.e., the children who are exposed to the violence). Two assumptions shared by many in the court system have been: (1) abuse directed only at a spouse is not necessarily damaging to a child, and (2) being a violent spouse is unrelated to that person's ability to be a good parent. In response to those suppositions, the flood of research reports is impressive. First, it has been fairly well established that children in these families are aware of the violence (Walker, 1984; Wallerstein & Kelly, 1980), even if they do not personally observe the violence (Geffner & Pagelow, 1990; Pagelow, 1990b). Children who live in households where their fathers beat their mothers are victims of domestic violence, whether their abuse is direct or indirect (Hughes, 1991; 1997, in this volume; Rossman & Rosenberg, 1997, in this volume). Children who both observe the violence and are directly abused by one or both parents are doubly victimized (Pagelow, 1982, 1990b). Research evidence of double victimization is extensive: the children suffer even more pervasive and long-lasting harm (Bowker, Arbitell, & McFerron, 1988; Forsstrom-Cohen & Rosenbaum, 1985; Hughes, 1997, in this volume; Rosenbaum & O'Leary, 1981). Children whose mothers are battered are twice as likely as children from nonviolent homes to be abuse victims, and their fathers are three times more likely to be their abusers than their mothers (Stark & Flitcraft, 1985; Walker, 1984).

A history of wife abuse must be seriously considered in custody awards, partly because a violent man also is likely to abuse his children (Archer, 1989; Family Violence Project, 1990). The literature reveals a plethora of evidence that children in abusive families are harmed by interparental violence (Davis & Carlson, 1987; Hershorn & Rosenbaum, 1985; Hughes, 1997, in this volume; Jaffe, Wolfe, Wilson, & Zak, 1986a, 1986b; Rosenberg & Rossman, 1990; Sun & Thomas, 1987; Wolfe, Jaffe, Wilson, & Zak, 1985).

The issues of child custody court battles when battered women attempt to end their violent marriages, joint custody, and mediation have all engendered a sudden growth in the literature. Many unanswered questions can be addressed by longitudinal research only. Rigorously designed studies are needed to examine the implementation and long-term effects of mandated mediation agreements and court-decreed parenting plans. We need to address questions such as: How do abusers abide by the agreements they make in mediation as compared to court-mandated decisions?, How does the system respond when the father refuses to abide by the terms of custody and visitation in either case?, What about safety factors in the lives of women who mediated with their abusers compared to those under court discretion?, Is there any difference in post-divorce harassment, threats, and physical abuse between the two methods? and, Which method is better for the children?

There is sufficiently strong evidence that battering is harmful to children living in violent households, a finding that should influence court decisions favoring "the best interests of the children." Unfortunately, parental vs. children's rights is an issue still being argued in the courts.

GENDER DIFFERENCES AND THE MYTH OF THE BATTERED HUSBAND SYNDROME

There is substantial evidence showing that the vast majority of victims of spouse abuse are female, and the vast majority of abusers are male. Marital violence studies reveal an average of only 5-10% of abused spouses are husbands (Dunford et al., 1990; Elk & Johnson, 1989; Goolkasian, 1986b; Judicial Council on Gender Bias in the Courts, 1990; Sherman & Berk, 1984b; U.S. Department of Justice, 1984).

The first national study of family violence (Straus, Gelles, & Steinmetz, 1980) found a large percentage of the violence involved both husband and wife, and from this arose the claims of "mutual combat." Mutual combat claims have been denounced by many researchers on the basis of the scale used in that study, and that most women who strike out against their spouses do so in self-defense (Pagelow, 1992; Saunders, 1988).

Berk, Berk, Loseke, and Rauma (1983) examined criminal justice records and found that women suffer physical consequences of spousal violence far more than men in terms of incidence and in terms of severity of injuries. They conclude, "we can find no substantial evidence for the battered husband syndrome; our data show that it is women who are battered" (Berk et al., 1983, p. 210).

There are some battered husbands, but there are not enough to match the exaggerated image that has been promulgated by some researchers and the mass media. The myth of mutual combat has firmly taken root in the public consciousness and among many professionals in a variety of fields. Despite evidence to the contrary, these myths continue to influence attitudes about and actions affecting battered women (Hart et al., 1990).

CONCLUSION

This review of research findings relating to certain issues and myths has highlighted some accomplishments, new directions taken by researchers, and future research needs. The past two decades have shown great progress in our understanding of the formerly concealed subject of woman battering. Because many advocates and researchers persisted, most people today reject many of the myths about spouse abuse, the abusers, and their victims. Changes in the social, legal, and health care systems undoubtedly have saved many lives and helped others escape lives of pain. Most who have labored in this field can take pleasure in acknowledging that there has been some measure of success.

There is much more to be done. Without massive social and structural changes to eliminate the root causes of woman battering, the future holds no promise of its elimination. More scientifically sound research can help guide social policy and legislation. Given a better informed medical, legal, judicial, and social system, society may be able to stop the violence permanently and provide peaceful lives for women and their children.

REFERENCES

American Psychological Association (1996). *Violence and the family: Report of the American Psychological Association Presidential Task Force on Violence and the Family.* Washington, DC: Author.

Archer, N. H. (1989). Battered women and the legal system: Past, present, and future. *Law and Psychology Review, 13,* 145-163.

Bachman, R., & Saltzman, L. E. (1996). *Violence against women: Estimates from the redesigned survey* (Bureau of Justice Statistics special report). Rockville, MD: U.S. Department of Justice (NCJ No. 154348).

Barnett, O. W., & LaViolette, A. D. (1993). *It could happen to anyone: Why battered women stay.* Newbury Park, CA: Sage.

Berk, R. A., Berk, S. F., Loseke, D. R., & Rauma, D. (1983). Mutual combat and other family violence myths. In D. Finkelhor, R. J. Gelles, G. T. Hotaling & M. A. Straus (Eds.), *The dark side of families: Current family violence research* (pp. 197-212). Beverly Hills, CA: Sage Publications.

Berk, R. A., Berk, S. F., & Newton, P. J. (1984). *An empirical analysis of police responses to incidents of wife battery.* Unpublished paper, University of California, Santa Barbara.

Berk, R. A., & Newton, P. J. (1985). Does arrest really deter wife battery? An effort to replicate the findings of the Minneapolis spouse abuse experiment. *American Sociological Review, 50,* 253-292.

Bowker, L. H., Arbitell, M., & McFerron, J. R. (1988). On the relationship between wife beating and child abuse. In K. Yllo & M. Bograd (Eds.), *Feminist perspectives on wife abuse* (pp. 158-174). Newbury Park, CA: Sage.

Browne, A. (1987). *When battered women kill.* New York: Free Press.

Browne, A., & Williams, K. R. (1989). Exploring the effect of resource availability and the likelihood of female-perpetrated homicides. *Law and Society Review, 23,* 75-94.

Bullock, L., McFarlane, J., Bateman, L. H., & Miller, V. (1989). The prevalence and characteristics of battered women in a primary care setting. *Nurse Practitioner, 14,* 47-55.

Buzawa, E. (1982). Police officer response to domestic violence legislation in Michigan. *Journal of Police Science and Administration, 10,* 415-423.

Campbell, J. C. (1986). Nursing assessment for risk of homicide with battered women. *Advances in Nursing Science, 8,* 36-51.

Campbell, J. C. (1992). Review of nursing research on battering. In C. M. Sampselle (Ed.), *Violence against women: Nursing research, education, and practice issues* (pp. 69-81). New York: Hemisphere.

Campbell, J. C. (Ed.). (1995). *Assessing dangerousness: Violence by sexual offenders, batterers, and child abusers.* Thousand Oaks, CA: Sage Publications.

Davis, L. V., & Carlson, B. E. (1987). Observation of spouse abuse: What happens to the children? *Journal of Interpersonal Violence, 2,* 278-291.

Dies, M. (1985). California's answer: Mandatory mediation of child custody and visitation disputes. *Ohio State Journal on Dispute Resolution, 1,* 168-169.

Dolon, R., Hendricks, J., & Meagher, M. (1986). Police practices and attitudes toward domestic violence. *Journal of Police Science and Administration, 14,* 187-192.

Dunford, F. W., Huizinga, D., & Elliott, D. S. (1990). The role of arrest in domestic assault: The Omaha police experiment. *Criminology, 28,* 183-206.

Eigenberg, H., & Moriarty, L. (1990). Domestic violence and local law enforcement in Texas: Examining police officers' awareness of state legislation. *Journal of Interpersonal Violence, 5,* 1283-1289.

Eisenberg, A. D. (1979). An overview of legal remedies for battered women [Part I]. *Trial, 15,* 28-31.

Eisenberg, A. D., & Seymour, E. J. (1979). An overview of legal remedies for battered women [Part II]. *Trial, 15*, 42-45, 60-69.

Elk, R., & Johnson, C. W. (1989). Police arrest in domestic violence. *Response, 12*, 7-13.

Erickson, S. K., & McKnight, M. S. (1990). Mediating spousal abuse divorces. *Mediation Quarterly, 7*, 377-388.

Ewing, C. P. (1987). *Battered women who kill: Psychological self-defense as legal justification*. Lexington, MA: Lexington Books.

Family Violence Project. (1990). *Family violence: Improving court practices* [Recommendations from the National Council of Juvenile and Family Court Judges' Family Violence Project]. Washington, DC: U.S. Department of Justice.

Follingstad, D. R., Polek, D. S., Hause, E. S., Deaton, L. H., Bulger, M. W., & Conway, Z. D. (1989). Factors predicting verdicts in cases where battered women kill their husbands. *Law and Human Behavior, 13*, 253-269.

Forsstrom-Cohen, B., & Rosenbaum, A. (1985). The effects of parental marital violence on young adults: An exploratory investigation. *Journal of Marriage and the Family, 47*, 467-472.

Friday, P. C., Metzgar, S., & Walters, D. (1989, October). *Policing domestic violence: Perceptions, experience, and reality*. Paper presented at the Midwest Criminal Justice Association, Chicago, IL.

Furstenberg, F. F., Morgan, S. P., & Allison, P. D. (1987). Paternal participation and children's well-being after marital dissolution. *American Sociological Review, 52*, 695-701.

Gardner, J., & Clemmer, E. (1986). Danger to police in domestic disturbances–A new look. *National Institute of Justice: Research in Brief*. Washington, DC: U.S. Department of Justice.

Geffner, R., & Pagelow, M. D. (1990). Mediation and child custody issues in abusive relationships. *Behavioral Sciences and the Law, 8*, 151-159.

Germane, C., Johnson, M., & Lemon, N. (1985). Mandatory custody mediation and joint custody orders in California: the danger for victims of domestic violence. *Berkeley Women's Law Journal, 1*, 188-189.

Gillespie, C. K. (1989). *Justifiable homicide: Battered women, self-defense and the law*. Columbus, OH: Ohio State University Press.

Goolkasian, G. A. (1986a, November). Confronting domestic violence: A guide for criminal justice agencies. In *National Institute of Justice, Research in Brief*. Washington, DC: U.S. Department of Justice.

Goolkasian, G. A. (1986b, November). Confronting domestic violence: The role of criminal judges. In *National Institute of Justice, Research in Brief*. Washington, DC: U.S. Department of Justice.

Hart, B. J. (1990). Gentle jeopardy: The further endangerment of battered women and children in custody mediation. *Mediation Quarterly, 7*, 317-330.

Hart, B. J., Bricklin, S., & Zorza, J. (1991, 10 August; 26 September). Appeal from the orders of the Court of Common Pleas of Allegheny County [*Amici*

Curiae Brief in Support of Appeal of Heard vs. Heard]. Pittsburgh, Pennsylvania.

Herrington, L.H. (1982). *President's task force on victims of crime*. Washington, DC: U.S. Government Printing Office.

Herrington, L.H. (1986, May). *President's task force on victims of crime: Four years later*. Washington, DC: U.S. Department of Justice.

Hershorn, M., & Rosenbaum, A. (1985). Children of marital violence: A closer look at the unintended victims. *American Journal of Orthopsychiatry, 55*, 260-266.

Hughes, H. M. (1991, August). *Research concerning children of battered women: Clinical and policy implications*. Paper presented at the annual meeting of the American Psychological Association, San Francisco, CA.

Hughes, H. M. (1997). Research concerning children of battered women: Clinical implications. In R. Geffner, S. B. Sorenson, & P. K. Lundberg-Love (Eds.), *Violence and sexual abuse at home: Current issues in spousal battering and child maltreatment*. Binghamton, NY: The Haworth Press, Inc.

Jaffe, P., Wolfe, D. A., Wilson, S. K., & Zak, L. (1986a). Similarities in behavioral and social maladjustment among child victims and witnesses to family violence. *American Journal of Orthopsychiatry, 56*, 142-146.

Jaffe, P., Wolfe, D. A., Wilson, S. K., & Zak, L. (1986b). Family violence and child adjustment: a comparative analysis of girls' and boys' behavioral symptoms. *American Journal of Psychiatry, 14*, 74-77.

Johnston, J. R., Kline, M., Tschann, J. M., & Campbell, L. E. G. (1988, March). *Ongoing postdivorce conflict in families contesting custody: Does joint custody and frequent access help?* Paper presented at the 65th annual meeting of the American Orthopsychiatric Association, San Francisco, CA.

Judicial Council Advisory Committee on Gender Bias in the Courts. (1990). *Achieving equal justice for women and men in the courts* [The draft report of the Judicial Council Advisory Committee on Gender Bias in the Courts]. San Francisco, CA: Administrative Office of the Courts.

Keenan, L. (1985). Domestic violence and custody litigation: The need for statutory reform. *Hofstra Law Review, 13*, 437-438.

Kuhl, A. F. (1981). *A preliminary profile of abusing men*. Paper presented at the Academy for Criminal Justice Sciences, Boston, MA.

Kurz, D. (1987). Emergency department responses to battered women: Resistance to medicalization. *Social Problems, 34*, 69-81.

Kurz, D. (1989). Social science perspectives on wife abuse: Current debates and future directions. *Gender and Society, 3*, 489-505.

Kurz, D., & Stark, E. (1988). Not-so-benign neglect: The medical response to battering. In K. Yllo & M. Bograd (Eds.), *Feminist Perspectives on Wife Abuse* (pp. 249-266). Beverly Hills, CA: Sage.

Lafferty, G. P. (1990). Battered woman syndrome. *Dickinson Law Review, 94*, 553-560.

Lavoie, F., Jacob, M., Hardy, J., & Martin, G. (1989). Police attitudes in assigning responsibility for wife abuse. *Journal of Family Violence, 4*, 369-388.

Lerman, L. (1981). *Prosecution of spouse abuse: Innovations in criminal justice response*. Washington, DC: Police Executive Research Forum.

Liss, M. B., & Stahly, G. B. (1993). Domestic violence and child custody. In M. Hansen & M. Harway (Eds.), *Battering and family therapy: A feminist perspective* (pp. 175-187). Newbury Park, CA: Sage.

Mahan, S., & Swebilius, J. (1989, November). *Battered women who murder their mates*. Paper presented at the American Society of Criminology meeting, Reno, NV.

Marks, L. A. (1988). Mandatory mediation of family law and domestic violence cases. *NCADV Voice, Special edition*, 18-22.

Maryland Special Joint Committee on Gender Bias in the Courts. (1989). Domestic violence and the courts: Maryland Special Joint Committee on gender bias in the courts. *Response to the Victimization of Women and Children, 12*, 3-6.

Mercy, J. A., & Saltzman, L. E. (1989). Fatal violence among spouses in the United States, 1976-85. *American Journal of Public Health, 79*, 595-599.

Murphy, P. V. (1984, April). [Sidebar, untitled]. *Police Foundation Reports* (p. 3).

National Battered Women's Law Project. (1991). Vulnerability of disabled women to domestic abuse. *The Women's Advocate, 12*, 3. New York: National Center on Women and Family Law.

Pagelow, M. D. (1981a). *Woman-battering: Victims and their experiences*. Beverly Hills, CA: Sage.

Pagelow, M. D. (1981b). Factors affecting women's decisions to leave violent relationships. *Journal of Family Issues, 2*, 391-414.

Pagelow, M. D. (1982). Children in violent families: Direct and indirect victims. In S. Hill & B. J. Barnes (Eds.), *Young children and their families* (pp. 47-72). Lexington, MA: Lexington.

Pagelow, M. D. (1984). *Family violence*. New York: Praeger.

Pagelow, M. D. (1987, July). *Application of spouse abuse research to policy*. Paper prepared for presentation at the Third National Family Violence Research Conference. Durham, NH.

Pagelow, M. D. (1988). Marital rape. In V. B. Van Hasselt, R. L. Morrison, A. S. Bellack & M. Hersen (Eds.), *Handbook of family violence* (pp. 207-232). New York: Plenum.

Pagelow, M. D. (1990a, 18 March). Stricter measures are needed to protect the lives of victims of abuse. *The Los Angeles Times*, p. B-10.

Pagelow, M. D. (1990b). Effects of domestic violence on children and their consequences for custody and visitation agreements. *Mediation Quarterly, 7*, 347-363.

Pagelow, M.D. (1992). Adult victims of domestic violence: Battered women. *Journal of Interpersonal Violence, 7*, 87-120.

Pagelow, M. D. (1993). Justice for victims of spouse abuse in divorce and child custody cases. *Violence and Victims, 8*, 69-83.

Parnas, R. I. (1967). The police response to the domestic disturbance. *Wisconsin Law Review*, 914-960.

Pearson, J., Thoennes, N., & Kool, L. V. (1982). Mediation of contested child custody disputes. *The Colorado Lawyer, 11*, 337-355.

Pirog-Good, M. A., & Stets, J. (1986). Programs for abusers: Who drops out and what can be done. *Response to the Victimization of Women and Children, 9*, 17-19.

Randall, T. (1990a). Domestic violence intervention calls for more than treating injuries. *Journal of the American Medical Association, 264*, 939-940.

Randall, T. (1990b). Domestic violence begets other problems of which physicians must be aware to be effective. *Journal of the American Medical Association, 264*, 940-944.

Randall, T. (1991). Hospital-wide program identifies battered women; offers assistance. *Journal of the American Medical Association, 266*, 1177-1179.

Response. (1989). Conference proceedings. *Response to the Victimization of Women and Children, 12*, 29.

Rose, K., & Saunders, D. G. (1986). Nurses' and physicians' attitudes about women abuse: The effects of gender and professional role. *Health Care for Women International, 7*, 427-438.

Rosenbaum, A., & O'Leary, K. D. (1981). Children: The unintended victims of marital violence. *American Journal of Orthopsychiatry, 51*, 692-699.

Rosenberg, M. S., & Rossman, B. B. R. (1990). The child witness to marital violence. R. T. Ammerman & M. Hersen (Eds.), *Treatment of family violence* (pp. 183-210). New York: John Wiley.

Rossman, B. B. R., & Rosenberg, M. S. (1997). Psychological maltreatment: A needs analysis and application for children in violent families. In R. Geffner, S. B. Sorenson, & P. K. Lundberg-Love (Eds.), *Violence and sexual abuse at home: Current issues in spousal battering and child maltreatment.* Binghamton, NY: The Haworth Press, Inc.

Saunders, D. G. (1988). Wife abuse, husband abuse, or mutual combat? A feminist perspective on the empirical findings. K. Yllo & M. Bograd (Eds.), *Feminist perspectives on wife abuse* (pp. 90-113). Newbury Park, CA: Sage.

Saunders, D. G., & Azar, S. T. (1989). Treatment programs for family violence. L. Ohlin & M. Tonry (Eds.), *Family violence* (pp. 481-546). Chicago: University of Chicago Press.

Sherman, L. W., & Berk, R. A. (1984a). The specific deterrent effects of arrest for domestic assault. *American Sociological Review, 49*, 261-272.

Sherman, L.W., & Berk, R. A. (1984b). The Minneapolis domestic violence experiment. *Police Foundation Reports*, 1-8.

Sonkin, D. J., Martin, D., & Walker, L. E. (1985). *The male batterer: A treatment approach.* New York: Springer.

Stark, E., & Flitcraft, A. (1985). Woman-battering, child abuse, and social heredity. In N. Johnson (Ed.), *Marital Violence* (pp. 147-171). London: Routledge and Kegan Paul.

Stark, E., Flitcraft, A., & Frazier, W. (1979). Medicine and patriarchal violence: The social construction of a "private" event. *International Journal of Health Services, 9*, 461-493.

Stark, E., Flitcraft, A., Zuckerman, D., Grey, A., Robison, J., & Frazier, W. (1981, April). *Wife abuse in the medical setting: An introduction for health personnel.* Domestic Violence Monograph Series. Washington, DC: National Clearinghouse on Domestic Violence, U.S. Government Printing Office.

Steinman, S. B. (1986, April). *Children in joint custody: a report of a study of children in voluntary and court-determined joint custody.* Paper presented at the annual meeting of the Association for Orthopsychiatry, Chicago, IL.

Steinman, S. B., Zemmelman, S. E., & Knoblauch, T. M. (1985). A study of parents who sought joint custody following divorce: Who reaches agreement and sustains joint custody and who returns to court. *Journal of the American Academy of Child Psychiatry, 24,* 554-562.

Stewart, J. K. (1986, Nov.). National Institute of Justice Research in Brief. Washington, DC: U.S. Dept. of Justice, Office of Justice Programs.

Stith, S. M. (1990). Police response to domestic violence: The influence of individual and familial factors. *Violence and Victims, 5,* 37-49.

Straus, M. A., Gelles, R. J., & Steinmetz, S. (1980). *Behind closed doors: Violence in the American family.* New York: Doubleday.

Stuart, E. P., & Campbell, J. C. (1989). Assessment of patterns of dangerousness with battered women. *Issues in Mental Health Nursing, 10,* 245-260.

Stuesser, L. (1990). The "defense" of "battered woman syndrome" in Canada. *Manitoba Law Journal, 19,* 195-210.

Sun, M., & Thomas, E. (1987). *Custody litigation on behalf of battered women.* New York: National Center on Women and Family Law.

Tierney, K. J. (1982). The battered women movement and the creation of the wife beating problem. *Social Problems, 29,* 207-220.

Tolman, R. M., & Bennett, L. W. (1990). A review of quantitative research on men who batter. *Journal of Interpersonal Violence, 5,* 87-118.

U.S. Department of Health and Human Services. (1986, May). *Surgeon General's workshop on violence and public health report* [DHHS Publication No. HRS-D-MC 86-1]. Washington, DC: Health Resources and Services Administration.

U.S. Department of Justice. (1984, September). *Attorney general's task force* [Final Report]. Washington, DC: U.S. Department of Justice.

Uniform Crime Reports. Federal Bureau of Investigation. (1986). *Crime in the United States, 1985.* Washington, DC: U.S. Department of Justice.

Walker, L.E. (1984). *The battered woman syndrome.* New York: Springer.

Wallerstein, J.S. (1988, May). *Keynote address.* Paper presented at the annual conference of the Association of Family and Conciliation Courts, Long Beach, CA.

Wallerstein, J.S., & Kelly, J.B. (1980). *Surviving the breakup: How children and parents cope with divorce.* New York: Basic Books.

Warshaw, C. (1989). Limitations of the medical model in the care of battered women. *Gender and Society, 3,* 506-517.

Wolfe, D.A., Jaffe, P., Wilson, S.K., & Zak, L. (1985). Children of battered women: The relation of child behavior to family violence and maternal stress. *Journal of Counseling and Clinical Psychology, 33,* 657-664.

Female Offenders in Domestic Violence:
A Look at Actions in Their Context

L. Kevin Hamberger

SUMMARY. It is well accepted that large numbers of men batter women. Although some data also reveal that women report assaulting men in large numbers, interpretation of the latter data has been fraught with controversy. The present article reports on a sample of women arrested for domestic violence. When questions were asked about frequency of violence initiation, which partner began the overall pattern of violence in the relationship, and the women's reasons for using violence, it was found that about two-thirds of the women were battered and using violence to protect themselves or to retaliate for previous violence against them. Implications of these findings for conceptualizing women's violence as well as for training law enforcement personnel are discussed. *[Article copies available for a fee from The Haworth Document Delivery Service: 1-800-342-9678. E-mail address: getinfo@haworth.com]*

KEYWORDS. Family violence, spouse abuse, domestic violence, arrests, law enforcement, characteristics

Theories about the causes of domestic violence reflect deeply held social and political views which color both the design and interpretation of

Address correspondence to: L. Kevin Hamberger, PhD, St. Catherine's Family Practice Center, P.O. Box 598, Kenosha, WI 53141.

[Haworth co-indexing entry note]: "Female Offenders in Domestic Violence: A Look at Actions in Their Context." Hamberger, L. Kevin. Co-published simultaneously in *Journal of Aggression, Maltreatment & Trauma* (Haworth Maltreatment & Trauma Press, an imprint of The Haworth Press, Inc.) Vol. 1, No. 1 (#1), 1997, pp. 117-129; and: *Violence and Sexual Abuse at Home: Current Issues in Spousal Battering and Child Maltreatment* (ed: Robert Geffner, Susan B. Sorenson, and Paula K. Lundberg-Love) Haworth Maltreatment & Trauma Press, an imprint of The Haworth Press, Inc., 1997, pp. 117-129. Single or multiple copies of this article are available for a fee from The Haworth Document Delivery Service [1-800-342-9678, 9:00 a.m. - 5:00 p.m. (EST). E-mail address: getinfo@haworth.com].

117

research in ways that are not always acknowledged. The controversy, passion and heated debate which arise when paradigms clash may interfere with obtaining a dispassionate understanding of domestic violence to guide our legal, therapeutic, and political actions. A re-examination of the literature and preliminary new evidence suggests that context plays a very important role in domestic violence. Although the incidence of recognized woman-initiated violence appears to be higher than originally believed, the women who initiate acts against their partners usually have been abused by those partners repeatedly, and have become violent themselves as a response of desperation or self-defense or both. The history of violence, how the pattern began and developed, and personal definitions are parts of the contextual pattern which must be understood.

TWO VIEWPOINTS: A BRIEF BACKGROUND

One view on the controversy surrounding female-to-male violence holds that intimate violence is primarily directed against women. Woman assault is woven into the patriarchal, sexist fabric of our society, the pattern which includes institutional values and practices that reinforce male privilege and condone violence as an "allowable" strategy to dominate women. Based on this tenet, the battered women's movement aims to achieve political and social change to end men's violence toward women (Dobash & Dobash, 1979; Pagelow, 1984; Schechter, 1982).

Another view is that the sexes have equal power to inflict injury, fear and terror in their partners. This position holds that women are as likely as men to initiate violence, and to use it effectively, in relationships. Although some characterize the "equal combatant" notion as an attempt to halt progress in controlling domestic violence, adherents have made some headway. In the early 1980s, funding sources for battered women's shelters and programs were threatened as policy makers called for funds to develop "battered men's" shelters and programs (Pagelow, 1984). (Readers interested in a detailed history of the controversy are referred to Steinmetz, 1977-1978; also see Pagelow, 1984; McNeely & Robinson-Simpson, 1987; and Saunders, 1988.) Indeed, this author has heard some battered women's advocates discussing "the husband beating problem" or "female batterers" at state and national level domestic violence conferences.

Viewing women's violence as the equivalent to men's violence has profound implications for both individuals and social movements. Consider an example of a woman who slaps her husband and is apprehended under domestic violence mandatory arrest laws. On first impression, she appears as likely as her husband to initiate violence. However, a thorough review of her history shows that her husband has been arrested twice for violence against her. He initiated the overall pattern of violence early in the 16 years of their violent marriage, and only in the last two years has she used force against him, usually in self-defense or out of hopeless desperation. She did indeed slap her husband, but only as he was coming toward her, making gestures that he always has used before assaulting her. Closer scrutiny reveals a battered woman who is responding to threatening cues that reliably have predicted violence against her in the past. For her attempt at self-defense, she gains a police record and the humiliation of being handcuffed in front of her children, taken from her home, and held in jail for 24 hours. If we look only at her act of violence, outside the context of her long history of victimization, it might be concluded that she is a primary aggressor in her relationship. If, however, we contextualize her violence, we can make a number of observations. First, she has been battered by her husband for 16 years. Second, despite police intervention, the battering against her has persisted. Third, although she has been battered on a regular basis, she has begun using force against her husband only recently. Furthermore, her motivation for using violence was self-defense. She reacted to behaviors by her partner previously associated with attacks upon her. Hence, in discussions of female-to-male partner violence, the concept of self-defense must be disentangled from that of perpetration for purposes of domination or control. In this article, the importance of understanding the context of women's violence will be explored.

GENERAL POPULATION STUDIES OF WOMAN-INITIATED VIOLENCE

One study attempting to shed light on the issue of violence initiated by women is the nonclinical sample of Straus and associates (Straus, 1989). Using a nationally representative sample, Straus found that women reported initiating both minor and severe violence about as frequently as men. This finding rests upon the question: "Let's talk about the last time you and your partner got into a physical fight and the (MOST SEVERE ACT) happened. In that particular instance, who started the physical conflict, you or your partner?" This question has been criticized for a number of reasons (Saunders, 1989). First it is possible that respondents mistook the question to refer to initiation of the *argument* that led to physical assault, rather than the physical assault itself. In the study, interviewers were instructed to be alert for this misunderstanding and rephrase the question if necessary. Second, even if the wife did strike first, such an act could still be considered self-defense if she defined the situation as threatening. Finally, the overall context of the male-initiated assault could be that of a relationship in which the husband started the *pattern* of abuse which created an environment of terror for the woman. Her initiation of violence could then be related to her realistic fear of attack by the partner on whom she is economically dependent, and from whom she is unable to escape.

CLINICAL STUDIES OF WOMAN-INITIATED VIOLENCE

It has been argued that clinical samples or samples derived from shelter or law enforcement settings may not be relevant to the general population because they can represent extremes (McNeely & Robinson-Simpson, 1987). Nevertheless, such identified populations are of interest in their own right. After all, it is individuals who have been identified as needing services who are most likely affected by policies such as shelter funding or mandatory arrest and court-ordered counseling.

Studies of clinical populations include Browne's (1987) report of reasons battered women kill their partners and Saunders' (1986) survey of battered women's use of nonlethal violence toward their partners. That women in such groups use violence against their partners is not in dispute. Indeed, Saunders reported that 75% of the battered women reported using minor violence as measured by the Conflict Tactics Scale (CTS) (Straus, 1979). At issue is the context in which women are violent, such as when terrified, feeling helpless to escape brutality, and fearing death at the hands of their partners. Saunders reported that self-defense was the most common justification battered women offered for their use of violence.

Another clinical population that has recently emerged is women arrested for domestic violence and ordered to domestic violence counseling. In a brief descriptive article, Hamberger and Arnold (1990) reported that seven months after mandatory arrest for domestic violence was instituted, domestic violence arrests of women increased 12-fold. After two years, the rate of female arrests was still about 10 times higher than before mandatory arrest. During the same pre-post interval, rates of arrest for men increased about two-fold. Hence, although mandatory arrest did result in more male offenders being arrested, women actually exhibited a larger proportional increase in arrest rates. When these data are combined with the national survey reported by Straus (1989), a casual reader might conclude that women are the primary initiators of violence. Because many of these women have attended court-required counseling, however, a clinical approach to investigating the context of their violence has been possible.

A description follows of the context of violence committed by a group of 52 women arrested for domestic violence, both before and after institution of mandatory arrest. Only those data pertaining to the context of the violence will be presented here. The reader is cautioned that these data are preliminary, and based on a very small sample, the generalizability of which is wholly untested and unknown. Nevertheless, with the burgeoning of domestic violence arrest laws, it is likely that other communities may experience increases in arrests of women, as well as increased demand for counseling services for such women. In that regard, the present report can provide leads for further research and policy making.

Characteristics of Domestically Violent Women

In this study, most participants were Caucasian (84%) or African American (14%); about 2% were Hispanic. With respect to marital status, 37.2% were in intact marriages, 15.7% were separated, and 19.6% were divorced; the remainder (27.4%) were never married. A total of 67.3% of the sample reported at least a high school education. Over half (56.8%) were employed outside the home and the remainder were either homemakers or unemployed. Sixty-eight percent of the women denied having an alcohol problem. Age range of the participants was 19-51 years, with a mean age of 29.5 years.

Many of the women reported experiencing abuse within their families of origin (see Table 1). Forty-eight percent of the women reported having experienced emotional abuse, physical abuse, or both. For illustrative purposes, these findings compare with 22% for male offenders from the same community (Hamberger & Hastings, 1986). Furthermore, almost 54% of the women reported having been exposed to father-to-mother violence. Male offenders from the same community reported a father-to-mother violence exposure rate of 28%. Over one-third of the women reported some type of sexual victimization, either within their families or by nonfamily members. Finally, almost half (49%) of the women reported having been battered in a previous relationship.

Mandatory arrest procedure. When the police are called to a domestic disturbance, the mandatory arrest law requires the police to arrest the primary perpetrator if they find probable cause that a domestic assault has occurred. The vast majority of arrested women are adjudicated through municipal court, where a large fine is levied (i.e., $625). If the woman completes a counseling program the fine is reduced to $85. A few of the women are referred through criminal court under a deferred prosecution agreement. Under such an agreement, the case is held open in court and, upon successful completion of the counseling the charge is either reduced

TABLE 1. Violence Victimization in Women Arrested for Domestic Violence Compared to a Sample of Domestically-Violent Men

Family of origin	Males* %	Females %
Abuse history		
Emotional	6.6	6.0
Physical	7.0	8.0
None	74.2	52.0
Both	8.3	34.0
Witnessed father-to-mother violence		
Yes	28.0	53.8
Sexual abuse	—	35.0
Previous relationship violence victimization	—	49.0

* Data for males from Hamberger and Hastings (1986)

or dropped. The counseling program consists of three one-hour pretreatment evaluation sessions and 12 two-hour group sessions.

Assessment. A complete description of the assessment and intervention program is beyond the scope of the present article and is described elsewhere (Hamberger & Potente, 1994). However, a detailed description of the part of assessment which elucidates the history and defines the context of the women's violence is provided below.

To assess the context of violence committed by women, participants first are asked about direct abuse experiences in the family of origin, including emotional, physical and sexual abuse. The women also are asked whether they had witnessed parental violence. Second is an attempt to ascertain whether the women had been assaulted in previous intimate relationships. Third, rather than ask whether the woman had ever initiated a "physical fight" with her partner, the following inquiry is made: "In the course of an argument or conflict with your partner, have you ever been the first to use physical force or aggression, such as grab, push, hit or any other type of physical force?" The same question also is asked with respect to her partner's initiation of physical force. Following the latter inquiry, the woman is asked: "Over the entire history of violence in your relationship, what percent of the times when physical violence occurred were you the person to actually initiate the use of physical force?" The same question is asked with respect to the partner's initiation of force.

To assess which partner started the overall pattern of violence in the relationship, the woman is asked: "Which person was the first ever to initiate physical force in the history of your relationship, you or your partner?" Finally, to assess the woman's typical motivation for using physical force against her partner, the following question is asked: "When you think about the times that you have used some type of physical violence against your partner, what was the primary reason for your use of violence?" If this question is not readily comprehended, it is clarified by further discussion of the purpose or "payoff" from the violence. The woman's response is recorded verbatim.

Results. In this sample of 52 arrested women, 73% reported ever having initiated the use of violence at some time in their relationship, as compared to about 77% of their partners, also based on the women's report. If the question is rephrased to ask about the percent of occasions the woman or her partner are the first to use physical force or aggression in a conflict, the picture changes from that described above. Twenty-five percent of the women reported initiating violence 100% of the time. A total of 37% of the women reported that their partners initiated violence 100% of the time. Fifty-five percent of the women reported that their male partner initiated violence more than half of the time violence occurred. In contrast, about one-third of the women reported initiating violence over half the time. Equal initiation rates (50-50) were reported in only 12.5% of the cases. Therefore, asking who initiates violence in a simple "yes/no" format can lead to the impression that women initiate violence as often as men in a relationship.

In response to the question, "Who started the overall pattern of violence in the relationship?" (i.e., who was the first ever to hit?), women reported that 51% of the men began the pattern, compared to 27.4% of the women. It was unclear who started the pattern in the other 21.5% of the cases. At least three women who reported initiating violence more often than their partners qualified their responses by noting that their partners had initiated the violence exclusively for several years prior to the point at which they initiated the violence. Two women who reported equal percentages of violence initiation between partners also noted that their partners started the pattern of violence.

Although the differences between domestically violent men and women in this sample are not large, in no category of violence initiation described above did women, as a group, exceed the men. Hence, although many of these arrested women acknowledge having initiated violence against their partners, they typically did so in the context of a relationship in which the male partner initiated violence more often, and in which he was more likely to have initiated the overall pattern of violence in the relationship. In the present study, over two-thirds of the women met at least one of the following conditions for being a battered woman: (a) battered in a previous relationship; (b) male partner initiated assaults more than 50% of the time; (c) partner began the overall pattern of violence in the relationship.

Women's verbatim responses to direct inquiry as to the reasons for using violence against their partners was studied (see Table 2). Some women gave more than one reason which accounts for the greater number of reasons than women in the sample. The most frequent reason for using aggression was self-defense/protection from an attack (n = 24). Five women reported retaliation for a previous assault, and one reported retaliation for emotional abuse as the reasons for using aggression. Ten used violence to reduce tension or express negative feelings. Getting a partner to talk, listen or stop nagging/shut up were reasons for violence given by 11 women, with two using force to assert authority or to be "one up" on their partner. Hence, some women did report using violence as a way to attempt to control their partners. Nevertheless, data need to be interpreted with caution. For example, one woman who reported using force to get her husband out of the house had been severely battered by him and was trying to get him to leave to ensure her safety. Another woman reported using force to "get one up" on her partner and explained that the strategy was used to keep him from assaulting her further. Hence, motivations for violence that suggest control can actually be construed as counter-control measures to ensure protection from additional attacks.

TABLE 2. Reasons for Using Violence by Women Arrested for Domestic Violence

Reason	Number of responses
Self-defense/protection	24
Retaliate for previous assault	5
Retaliate for emotional abuse	1
Express feeling/tension	10
Get partner to talk, attend, listen/do something	5
Stop nagging/get other to shut up	6
Assert authority/be "one up"	2
Don't know why	1
No data	11

Implications for Training

Research on women arrested for domestic violence is too preliminary to suggest concrete training protocols. A few equally preliminary ideas are worthy of mention, however. First, research such as that presented above can be used to sensitize law enforcement and criminal justice personnel: most women (e.g., 67% in the present study) who are arrested for using violence against their partners do not appear to be "husband beaters" or "mutual combatants." Rather, in many instances, they are battered women who are fighting to defend themselves from an assault by their partners. Even many women who appear to have initiated more assaults upon their partners than vice versa may, upon further exploration, be found to be caught in a pattern of violence begun and stabilized (often years ago) by their partner.

Some workers in the field would point to the one-third of the present sample who reported initiating violence more frequently than their male partners as evidence that women do batter or abuse their male partners. Pagelow (1984) has acknowledged that "Undoubtedly, many women are violent and able to create an atmosphere of fear for their husbands" (p. 274). However, as Pagelow noted, there was no scientific evidence for a large-scale "battered husband syndrome." Pagelow (1991) subsequently estimated the prevalence of such primary-abusive women at between 5-10%.

The present study revealed that about one-third of the arrested women studied could not be classified as battered using the criteria of: (1) having been battered in a previous relationship, (2) her partner initiated more than half the assaults, or (3) her partner started the overall pattern of violence in the relationship. In interpreting these results, one must remain cognizant that all of the women were violent with their partners. Furthermore, about three-fourths reported having initiated violence against their partner at some time in the relationship. Therefore, it may be expected that many of the women were of the abusive type described by Pagelow (1984, 1991). That two-thirds of the women among this violent sample were battered women was particularly noteworthy.

One moral position is that all forms of violence are wrong, and that whoever uses force is morally responsible for that utilization and its cessation, whether battered or not. Such a view may be, at least in part, reflected in mandatory arrest laws that often seem interpreted by law enforcement personnel as meaning "if somebody hits, we have to take them in." Hence, training could focus on enhancing officers' knowledge that women's violence frequently occurs in a different sociopsychological context than men's violence, as well as enhancing officers' skills in determining such a context. By asking questions and determining that a particular woman's violence was motivated by a need for self-protection from imminent danger, the officer may be less likely to arrest her as a "mutual combatant."

Similarly, for women who are arrested, advocacy work can be done to assist prosecutors and judges in making charging or sentencing decisions, or perhaps to assist in the defense of battered women arrested for domestic violence. Without such educational advocacy efforts, battered women who act to protect themselves may be victimized further by not getting protection from the system, and actually being blamed for their plight, prosecuted and inappropriately labeled as "mutual combatants" or "husband beaters."

The experience of this author in working with women arrested for domestic violence over the past several years has led to the decision to eschew such terms as "mutual combatant," "husband beater," and "female batterer." These terms connote a sense of equality in the use of violence. They also imply the creation of an environment of fear, terror and control which does not often exist in relationships in which women assault men. Instead of such inappropriate terms, more descriptive and neutral terms such as "domestically violent women" or "women arrested for domestic violence" are used to characterize most women who have been arrested for domestic violence.

Future Directions

Because this area of research is new, much work remains to determine whether findings from this sample generalize to other samples of women arrested for domestic violence elsewhere. Another area for further research will be the continued refinement of interview/assessment strategies for evaluating contextual aspects of women's violence. For example, this author has found that asking about the percentage of violent acts initiated by either partner provides more information than simply asking about initiation of violence in a "yes/no" format.

Another way to get at similar information would be to ask about the frequency of use of violence by either partner. It also is important to ask about who initiated the *pattern* of violence in the relationship. The present program demonstrates the importance of exploring, in much more detail, the meaning and temporal sequencing of women's violence. For example, a woman who endured beatings for five years without responding but who now initiates more violence than her abusive partner is emerging from a different context than a woman who initiated the pattern of violence and always initiates violence in conflicts with her partner. Such individual differences in context may also lead to individually tailored interventions for domestically violent women.

Of course, the overall validity of women's stated reasons for using violence has yet to be determined. It may be, for example, that reasons given by women for using violence are self-generated excuses. This research does not assess the "truth value" of such statements. Future research should determine the relationship between stated reasons for use of violence and other indices of victimization, including injury, fearfulness of violence, post-traumatic stress disorder, to name a few. Of course, the pattern and context of violence of females should be compared with that of males to determine gender differences in reasons for and patterns of partner violence. Determination of such differences will help establish the validity of the current findings. For example, recent research by Hamberger, Lohr and Bonge (1994) did find gender differences in reasons given for partner violence. Although reasons given by male and female perpetrators were different and varied, female offenders identified self-defense and retaliation as important motivators for partner violence. Male offenders tended to report using violence against female partners for purposes of control and punishment. While promising, this is but one study. More research needs to be done to further refine and identify our knowledge of gender differences in use of partner violence.

CONCLUSION

Within the criminal justice system, battered women who use violence often are not identified, nor is their context. Instead, they are often mislabeled as "mutual combatants" or "husband beaters." As such, their plight goes unnoticed as they are shuttled through the system. They are prosecuted, held responsible for their situation and thus are victimized by domestic violence laws and policies that were originally designed to protect them.

Psychologists and other mental health professionals who work in collaboration with criminal justice personnel or who serve on domestic violence task forces are well suited to bring their specialized knowledge and skills to bear upon educational and policymaking programs that affect battered women. Such skills include training law enforcement and criminal justice personnel about the dynamics of victimization. Research skills can be utilized to generate relevant information, measure training programs, and expand and use knowledge to further inform policies about battered women in these settings.

Research on battered women in criminal justice settings is presently in its infancy. Much needs to be done to further elucidate issues that hinder as well as facilitate the appropriate identification of and intervention with battered women, particularly in those settings that are both ideally suited and expected to provide protection and advocacy for battered women.

SPECIFIC RECOMMENDATIONS

As noted previously, this appears to be a new area of inquiry, with potentially profound implications. Research that enhances the identification of battered women in such settings can be used to advocate and lobby for changes in investigation procedures, both at the scene as well as with prosecutors who must make charging decisions. Specific areas of future research include the development of interview and other assessment techniques that aim to determine the context of women's violence. It is insufficient and misleading, at least in clinical settings, simply to ask an arrested woman whether she used violence or ever initiated it. Such a method of inquiry ignores factors such as history of violence, how the pattern was initiated, how the pattern evolved, and the meaning of the violence to the woman including factors related to her first use of force in any given specific instance.

Of course, similar assessment techniques should be used with male perpetrators as well. Comparable assessment methods used with male offenders will facilitate investigation of gender differences in context, motivation and impact of partner violence.

Furthermore, methods need to be developed and tested for associating specific instances of women's violence to the broader pattern of violence against the woman and its associated brutality and terror. Such research can be used to inform police and policymakers in avoiding viewing such women, a priori, as "husband beaters" or "mutual combatants."

Finally, an additional area of research centers upon refining our understanding of the underlying concepts and the connotative value of terminology. Concepts such as "mutual combatant" often are used in a facile manner, with little or no consensus, nor any operational definition to support their use. It is time to begin debate, dialogue and research on the parameters which constitute "mutuality" of violence. For example, Saunders (1989) has suggested that minimal preconditions for assuming the existence of mutual violence would include equal size of the combatants, equal training and socialization in the use of violence, equal propensities to use violence, equal ability to inflict pain from the violence and equal ability to instill fear and terror as a result of the use of violence. However, these factors have not been studied systematically, and there appears to be no clarity in the domestic violence literature regarding the meaning of "mutual violence." There is also no consensus opinion on the meaning of that term and related concepts.

REFERENCES

Browne, A. (1987). *When battered women kill.* New York: Free Press.

Dobash, R. E., & Dobash, R. P. (1979). *Violence against wives: A case against the patriarchy.* New York: Free Press.

Hamberger, L. K., & Arnold, J. (1990). The impact of mandatory arrest on domestic violence perpetrator counseling services. *Family Violence Bulletin, 6,* 10-12.

Hamberger, L. K., & Hastings, J. E. (1986). Personality correlates of men who abuse their partners: A cross validation study. *Journal of Family Violence, 1,* 323-346.

Hamberger, L. K., Lohr, J. M., & Bonge, D. (1994). The intended function of domestic violence is different for arrested male and female perpetrators. *Family Violence and Sexual Assault Bulletin, 10,* 40-44.

Hamberger, L. K., & Potente, T. (1994). Counseling women arrested for domestic violence: Implications for theory and practice. *Violence and Victims, 9,* 125-137.

McNeely, R. L., & Robinson-Simpson, G. (1987). The truth about domestic violence: A falsely framed issue. *Social Work, 32,* 485-490.

Pagelow, M. D. (1984). *Family violence.* New York: Praeger.

Pagelow, M. D. (1991, August). Battered women: Current and future research directions. In R. Geffner (Chair), *Family violence: Current research and future directions.* Symposium presented at the meeting of the American Psychological Association, San Francisco, CA.

Saunders, D. G. (1986). When battered women use violence: Husband abuse or self-defense? *Violence and Victims, 1,* 47-60.

Saunders, D. G. (1988). Other "truths" about domestic violence: A reply to McNeely and Robinson-Simpson. *Social Work, 33,* 179-183.

Saunders, D. G. (1989, November). *Who hits first and who hurts most? Evidence for the greater victimization of women in intimate relationships.* Paper presented at the 41st Annual Meeting of the American Society of Criminology, Reno, NV.

Schechter, S. (1982). *Women and male violence: The visions and struggles of the battered women's movement.* Boston: South End Press.

Steinmetz, S. K. (1977-78). The battered husband syndrome. *Victimology: An International Journal, 2,* 499-509.

Straus, M. A. (1979). Measuring intrafamily conflict and violence: The Conflict Tactics (CT) Scales. *Journal of Marriage and the Family, 4,* 75-88.

Straus, M. A. (1989, November). *Assaults by wives on husbands: Implications for primary prevention on marital violence.* Paper presented at the meeting of the American Society of Criminology, Reno, NV.

Multifaceted Approaches
in Spouse Abuse Treatment

Eve Lipchik
Elizabeth A. Sirles
Anthony D. Kubicki

SUMMARY. The understanding of spouse abuse has changed considerably in the last 30 years, shifting from a perspective based on individual psychopathology to that of a pervasive social problem. Current treatment solutions for stopping violence are limited to those that address resocializing the batterer. Several states often restrict the use of state funds for batterers' groups and forbid couples treatment as a primary treatment option in spite of the fact that most couples choose to remain in their relationships in the presence of repeated violence. This article argues for broadening options to include a specific type of couples treatment as a part of a coordinated community response to remediate domestic violence. Solution-focused therapy is described as an example of treatment of relationships that makes safety a priority and is not victim-blaming. It is suitable treatment both for couples who wish to stay together and those seeking a safe way to separate. *[Article copies available for a fee from The Haworth Document Delivery Service: 1-800-342-9678. E-mail address: getinfo@haworth.com]*

Address correspondence to: Eve Lipchik, ICF Consultants, Inc., 1524 N. Farwell Avenue, Milwaukee, WI 53202.

[Haworth co-indexing entry note]: "Multifaceted Approaches in Spouse Abuse Treatment." Lipchik, Eve, Elizabeth A. Sirles, and Anthony D. Kubicki. Co-published simultaneously in *Journal of Aggression, Maltreatment & Trauma* (Haworth Maltreatment & Trauma Press, an imprint of The Haworth Press, Inc.) Vol. 1, No. 1 (#1), 1997, pp. 131-148; and: *Violence and Sexual Abuse at Home: Current Issues in Spousal Battering and Child Maltreatment* (ed: Robert Geffner, Susan B. Sorenson, and Paula K. Lundberg-Love) Haworth Maltreatment & Trauma Press, an imprint of The Haworth Press, Inc., 1997, pp. 131-148. Single or multiple copies of this article are available for a fee from The Haworth Document Delivery Service [1-800-342-9678, 9:00 a.m. - 5:00 p.m. (EST). E-mail address: getinfo@haworth.com].

KEYWORDS. Family violence, couples, solution focused treatment, battering

On the surface, the prognosis for the field of domestic violence looks good. Over the last three decades, theories of spousal abuse have evolved from male prerogative, to female pathology, to a pervasive societal problem. The police response is changing from "buddy, take a walk until she cools down" to mandatory arrest of the primary aggressor. Prosecution rates of batterers are rising steadily in many American cities. National legislation to remedy this crime has been approved in the form of the Violent Crime Control and Law Enforcement Act of 1994. Yet physical and sexual violence against women by current or past partners continues to put 8-12 million women in the United States at risk annually (American Medical Association, 1992). Advocates for battered women have expended tremendous effort, and continue to do so, to educate and to influence policy makers and the public about the consequences of abuse of women and their families. However, upon closer investigation, there is one area in the domestic violence movement that has been at a relative standstill for the last 10 years: treatment.

Treatment options seem to present a dilemma between the sociopolitical philosophy that describes all domestic violence as men using power to control women, and the reality of the prevalence of multifaceted acts of domestic violence. Domestic violence advocates, who represent the former philosophy, lobby for batterers programs as the primary treatment option and against couples and family counseling as another option. Those who view the problem from psychological and relational perspectives as well look for additional options that will be safe and effective.

Grassroots movements are very important for social change. They are driven by a single-minded focus on ideology. When their mission captures the public conscience, professionals at all levels enter the picture and contribute their particular skills to the cause. Scientific thinking and methodology begin to find shades of gray where once there was no question about what was black or white. This has happened in the field of domestic violence. Advocates for battered women can be credited for an historic change in society's awareness of men's power and control over women. They have worked hard to justify and maintain their focus on the resocialization of men. However, studies from various fields which joined their efforts to promote the safety of women and to end domestic violence, such as sociology, psychology, social work, and criminal justice, indicate disappointing outcomes for what were believed to be the most significant interventions developed to date (i.e., education/treatment groups and mandatory arrest) (Hoffman, 1992; Sherman et al., 1991). The logical solution appears to be to expand options to encourage research and development of safe and effective interventions based on alternative philosophies and strategies. However, this does not seem to be happening. Some options, such as couples and family treatment are being discouraged categorically (Brandl, 1990) without really having been explored or tested. The purpose of this article is to introduce a sociopolitically informed, solution-focused treatment alternative for stopping violence.

THE STATE OF CURRENT TREATMENT OPTIONS

The feminist movement of the 1960s laid the foundation for redefining battering of females by male partners as a pervasive social problem. It laid to rest any explanations that blamed women for asking for or provoking violence. It challenged ingrained attitudes of patriarchal punishment of women. Society's consciousness was raised to the reality that violence is perpetrated by men of all socioeconomic classes and all psychological types. Sociopolitical philosophy taught us that male and female behavior is more the result of socialization and institutionalized sex roles than of genetic heritage or psychological makeup, and that women's inferior position in society is so ingrained that many men are often not even conscious of their attitudes toward women. In short, we have learned that male criminal behavior is an insidious part of normal everyday life in America (Hamberger & Hastings, 1986; Tolman & Bennett, 1990). It is under this light that clinicians, researchers, policy makers and the public have sought to understand and remediate the problem of domestic violence the past three decades. Unfortunately, this once helpful light has established a rigid parameter of acceptable treatment and intervention options that is not based upon nor supported by research or clinical data.

One clear direction so far is a strong trend by individual states to set standards for batterers treatment funded with state monies. This was spearheaded by the state of Colorado which established a pro-arrest policy in 1984 (Brandl, 1990), and followed it with such standards in 1988. These standards prescribed group programs for batterers as the primary treatment method and forbade couples treatment except under special circumstances. Numerous states now also provide state funding for abuser education/ treatment groups, and 11 states have already established mandated standards to control which programs will be eligible to receive client referrals from the courts. Many other states are currently working on mandating such standards. This trend may lead toward similar legislation and policies on the national level.

One would presume that the process of setting standards is based on conclusive evidence. This may not always be the case. For example, in 1991, the State of Wisconsin set standards for the treatment of batterers which prohibited funding any programs that do not offer batterers groups as the primary treatment method and that do offer couples counseling or family therapy as a primary treatment method. These standards were based on a discussion paper on programs for batterers authorized by the State of Wisconsin (Brandl, 1990). The author of the study concluded that "Based on the current research, it is difficult to determine whether abuser education/treatment is effective. Group education/treatment may end physical violence for some batterers but in most cases psychological battering and terrorist tactics continue. Other areas of concern include attrition rates, special populations and length of treatment" (Brandl, p. 68). The report also concluded that there is so little information available about treatment of couples that further research is needed before it can be considered a viable intervention tool. A recent article discussed the dangers of setting standards prohibiting or authorizing specific treatment modalities since evidence is lacking to justify this (Geffner, 1995).

Further evidence against setting standards without proof of successful outcome is a description of the Duluth program started by Ellen Pence in 1981 (Paymar & Pence, 1993). The Duluth program is considered the prototype for batterers' programs all over the world. In an article, founder Pence seems very hopeless as she talks about recidivism rates of up to 60% for batterers who complete the program (Hoffman, 1992). She advises women in battering relationships to leave their partners because even the best programs cannot insure that a violent man will change.

So in three decades we have come a long way in terms of social consciousness about spouse abuse, but we do not seem to know much more about how to treat it. What we do know is that:

1. Batterers and their victims are not a homogeneous population; they come from all social, economic and racial groups (Hamberger & Hastings, 1986; Hotaling & Sugarman, 1986; Tolman & Bennett, 1990);
2. 50-75% of couples continue their relationship despite the best efforts of police, prosecutors, shelters and advocates (Feazell, Mayers, & Deschner, 1984; Purdy & Nickle, 1981);
3. The results of education/resocialization batterers groups, the only sanctioned treatment option, are disappointing (Brandl, 1990; Hamberger & Hastings, 1993).

One of the dilemmas that may be impeding progress is that from a political standpoint, group treatment for batterers is the only treatment consistent with the feminist philosophy that aims to correct the faulty socialization of men raised in a patriarchal society. Individual or couples treatment methods have been declared politically incorrect. They are accused of keeping batterers from assuming full responsibility for their violent behaviors because they utilize empathic techniques. Furthermore, treating the couple implies to some that the woman, or victim, needs to change. Some see this as classic victim blaming which service providers and activists are trying to fight. But most of all, couples treatment has been labeled as dangerous, unethical and ineffective. It is believed to be dangerous because if the woman tells her side of the story in front of the man, she may pay the price later. It is believed to be unethical because it expects her to change and thereby supposedly does not hold him accountable for his violence. It is believed to be ineffective because the batterer will deny and lie, and nothing will get accomplished. Furthermore, there appears to be the assumption that couples treatment values saving the relationship above stopping physical and mental abuse (Bograd, 1984; Willbach, 1989).

It is striking that the domestic violence literature usually refers to couples treatment as if it were a generic approach without indicating a particular theoretical orientation (e.g., psychodynamic, behavioral, cognitive, systemic). This may change with increased research in this area. One study which has compared various treatment modalities found little difference in outcome among them (Jacobson & Addis, 1993). Similar results were obtained by O'Leary and his colleagues (e.g., O'Leary, 1996; O'Leary & Neidig, 1993). There has not been much other research investigating effectiveness of various types of treatment approaches. Therefore, speculations that one approach may be the best for all clients, or that a particular approach, such as couples treatment, may be dangerous for any client, is premature and not supported by any research.

This article describes an approach for treating couples in relationships that have experienced abusive, controlling and/or violent behaviors. The authors have found this program to be very helpful for couples who express the desire to stay together, and it is sensitive to the major concerns that have been expressed about couples treatment.

AN OPTION: SOLUTION-FOCUSED TREATMENT

At the very least, one essential primary intervention should be a treatment which is as safe and effective as other recommended interventions for couples who choose to stay together. Solution-focused therapy (de Shazer, 1985, 1988; de Shazer et al., 1986; Lipchik, 1991) will be described here as an example of a type of treatment for the relationship that could fill this void of working with couples but focusing on the violence and safety of the battered woman.

Over the past decade, various approaches to couples therapy based on a systemic, interactional theory have been described in the literature (Erchak, 1984; Fraser, 1988; Gelles & Maynard, 1987; Gelles & Wasserstrom, 1984; Margolin, 1979; Neidig & Friedman, 1984; Taylor, 1984). Each approach is designed to help couples deal with their relationship if they want to stay together, while attempting to be sensitive to the issues of safety and individual responsibility. Lipchik and colleagues have been adapting the solution-focused brief therapy model for use with batterers and their partners since 1985 (Lipchik, 1991). This model is based on systemic principles but includes the therapist as part of the system. It differs from traditional medical models in that it does not conceptualize human problems in terms of individual psychopathology, but as arising from and being maintained by the interactions between people. Interactions between people are thought of as taking place through verbal and non-verbal communication and language. Language creates meaning for individuals and between individuals, therefore change can take place through conversations that create opportunities for more ways of understanding particular situations. Relationships are thought of as the product of the interactions (exchange of language) between two or more unique individuals. Individuals influence each other through the meaning that is created between them about their interactions and they each are responsible for the behavioral choices they make in response to the meaning they ascribe to their interactions. This therapeutic model also emphasizes individual characteristics and strengths of each member of a relational system as building blocks toward a better future.

One of the salient features of this model is how it deals with clients' resistance and denial, an approach founded on the work of Milton Erickson (Zeig, 1985). Erickson's work demonstrated that clients are more cooperative when therapists listen to and accept their point of view rather than tell them what is wrong and what has to change. Domestic violence professionals are well aware of the fact that most perpetrators and victims resist being told what to do. A very important aspect of solution-focused therapy is how the therapist's accepting and respectful attitude toward the batterer, as well as the battered woman, provides for her greater safety from the start. This therapeutic stance reduces distrust and denial, particularly on the part of the batterer, and enables both partners to face their situation and the necessary changes more honestly. When the therapist does not take sides, gender issues can be discussed constructively as well. The therapist's role is that of a partner in the co-construction of a future reality (von Foerster, 1981) that includes a solution to the stated problem, not that of an expert who sees him or herself as responsible for the solution of the particular relationship problem (except for elimination of violence and emotional control). Studies indicate that when clients define their own goals for treatment, they achieve them faster and maintain them longer (Gurman & Kniskern, 1981). Therapeutic models founded on such ideas are therefore particularly useful for involuntary clients, such as batterers.

Solution-focused therapy is best thought of as a team approach with a therapist in the room conducting the session and one or more therapists behind a one-way mirror. However, it also can be effective when practiced without a team. Each session is one hour and is divided into an interview, a consultation break, and a summation message which may include the suggestion of a task. The criteria for whether a particular couple is appropriate for this treatment of their relationship are evaluated clinically as well as with psychological instruments. The clinical part consists of three sessions, first a conjoint session with the couple then an individual one with each partner. In the first session the couple is seen together so the therapist can observe their interaction. The individual sessions allow each person to say things they might not say in front of the other. It gives the therapist a chance to talk with the woman confidentially about a present or future safety plan, if necessary, and with the man about a strategy for self-control. We have found the accepting climate and focus on positives in the first joint session makes both partners feel safe enough to be very honest with us in their individual sessions. Upon rare occasion, solution-focused therapists may reinforce safety by asking for a non-violence contract before committing to treat the couple. These contracts are always framed as protective for the batterer as well as the victim.

The written instruments are filled out the hour before the couple meets the therapist for the first time. They consist of:

1. A detailed intake form that covers personal history, including present physical and mental status; use of medications and drugs and alcohol; extensive details about family history, such as sexual and physical abuse;
2. the Dyadic Adjustment Scale (Spanier, 1976);
3. the Conflict Tactics Scale (Straus, 1979).

After completion of the conjoint and individual sessions the therapist or team review their findings from the clinical sessions and compare them with the information on the forms to make the final decision whether it is safe to work with a couple. The couple is asked to fill these forms out again after treatment is completed for comparison.

Sessions are scheduled one week apart until positive change occurs, then bi-monthly, and eventually monthly for at least six months. Three months and 12 months after termination, a separate follow-up call is made to both partners. The questions are formulated to reinforce the positive changes that occurred in treatment. These questions will be discussed in some detail in a subsequent section of the article.

The criteria used for assessing appropriateness for treatment are:

1. *Intensity and chronicity of abuse.* As a rule, the less chronic the abuse the better the prognosis.
2. *Quality of relationship.* Both partners must be able to give some concrete examples of what they appreciate about each other and about their relationship. There should be some evidence of the capacity for empathy and mutuality.
3. *Mental status.* Clients who manifest signs of possible neurological or psychological impairment should be evaluated by a psychiatrist.
4. *Alcohol and other drug abuse* (AODA). Does drug or alcohol consumption usually precede abusive or violent behavior? If the relationship is judged mutually satisfying and free of abuse except after substances are used, assessment for AODA treatment is indicated.
5. *Previous interventions.* Find out what has worked and not worked for the couple in their past efforts (their own attempts or professional interventions) to improve the relationship.
6. *Clients' goals.* Both partners must agree that they want no further violence, they want to preserve the relationship, and there is one small change they want to work on.
7. *Motivation.* Both partners must appear willing to do something different, not only expect changes from the other.

The therapist makes the decision whether to keep seeing the clients together or separately during the course of treatment. Safety always is the first consideration for separate treatment. Other times separate treatment is conducted because the couple no longer seems to have the same goals or because they request it. In the event that tempers flare during a session to the degree that the therapist sees conjoint work as counterproductive, the clients are separated and the therapist advocates for both of them. The woman is seen first and helped to leave safely if that is what she wants. In talking with the man, the therapist tries to help him find a way not to do anything he will regret later. In the 15 years that this model has been used for treating couples in whose relationship battering has occurred, there has been almost no reoccurrence of violence during treatment. In the rare times when it happens, treatment is not discontinued because the therapist should not be seen as punitive and because it could endanger the woman. Instead, the therapist allows the legal system to provide consequences, and continues to work with the couple separately and together to meet their goals. It often is at that point that the woman or man may decide to end the relationship. An established, supportive therapeutic relationship with both partners can help accomplish this in a healthy manner and lay some groundwork to prevent violence in future relationships.

Throughout therapy the therapist focuses the clients' thoughts on exceptions to their complaints, their existing and potential strengths and how to reinforce those strengths. In domestic violence cases this means examining what is going on when the couple gets along well (i.e., when coercion and violence do not occur). Although the therapist does not avoid the issues of power, control and violence that brought the couple to treatment, she/he aims to create and to maintain an emotionally comfortable climate for both of them which will promote hope and motivation to change. In this environment it is also easier for couples to face the reality that it may be better for both of them if they do not stay together.

A therapeutic climate in which the therapist accepts and advocates for both partners empowers each of them as participants in the relationship. Because the relationship is seen as the product of two individuals in interaction, both of whom have freedom of choice about how to behave toward one another, each partner is held responsible for his or her behaviors. For example, he cannot accuse her of "making him hit her." She may have done something to make him angry, but he has a choice about how to respond. In this context the violence becomes the responsibility only of the person who perpetrates it. The thrust of treatment is away from a win-lose situation in which both partners are focusing on their feelings to a win-win situation in which both partners will want to make choices that are good for the relationship because that will benefit them most individually.

CASE STUDY

In the following case study, names have been changed to protect confidentiality. Italicized print highlights material important for assessment.

The Browns are a white couple who have been married for 16 years. Joe, a Vietnam veteran, is 40 and Marge is 38. They have two children, a daughter, age 14, and a son, age 10. Joe suffered a disabling stroke four years ago and has lost the function of his right arm and leg. He and Marge, who is unemployed as well, exist on Joe's disability insurance. Joe writes spiritual poetry as a hobby. Marge always has been a homemaker and continues to keep busy with housekeeping and the children. The couple was mandated to treatment by the District Attorney after Marge reported Joe to the police for battery. Several incidents occurred in the past 18 months but Marge dropped the charges. *At the District Attorney's office both partners insisted they wanted to stay together under all circumstances.*

Joe and Marge presented as poorly dressed and groomed, and very depressed. *They both agreed that the battery occurs only when Joe drinks too much brandy. When he confines himself to drinking beer, which he drinks daily, there is no violence. (The fact that there is no violence when Joe drinks beer would rule out immediate referral for alcohol treatment and we would assess the relationship further.) Joe said he felt terrible whenever he hurt Marge and wanted to stop this. Marge also wanted it to stop* and said she recognizes that Joe did not mean to harm her. *(It is important for assessment that the man expresses the unconditional desire to stop and takes responsibility for it. Expressing some feeling of guilt also is diagnostic in terms of possible capacity for empathy. The battered woman must express the desire to have the violence stop as well. Some women minimize physical violence and say it is more important for the emotional abuse to stop. Such a case is not considered appropriate for couples treatment.)* The first session moved very slowly because both partners seemed to be low in energy and to be feeling very hopeless. The reality of the situation was that Joe would never have healthy mobility again. The message to both of them at the end of the first session emphasized positives such as their mutual goals, their loyalty to each other, and their desire to be each others' best friend. It acknowledged the difficulty of their situation and complimented them for having overcome so many difficulties together in the past.

Individual assessment indicated that the partners were deeply committed to each other and felt physically and emotionally satisfied a good deal of the time. Marge felt she and Joe were good partners as parents and agreed with each other most of the time. Her description of the relationship implied a foundation of friendship and respect. *Exploration of how she perceived the balance of power in the relationship indicated that she saw him as more intelligent and creative than herself, but that she experienced him as admiring her ability to be calm and think things through before acting. Marge stated her present goal as wanting more closeness and for Joe to be less "grumpy" than he had been in the recent past. (Here are two important pieces of the assessment: Marge does not experience herself as without power and control in the relationship, and so far she is expressing the same goal as Joe.) On the other hand, Marge appeared very depressed and lethargic and was not able to describe any plan for keeping herself safe from future violence.* Helping her formulate a plan was the major focus of the individual session.

In his individual session *Joe said he had decided to stop drinking brandy in order to prevent any future violence and he had some excellent ideas about how he was going to follow through with that. He described his goal for therapy as wanting to feel closer to Marge again. He felt she distanced from him by sleeping a lot. Joe also expressed respect and admiration for Marge and considered her his best friend. (Again, two important points for assessment: Joe's goal appears to be the same as Marge's and he presents evidence that the relationship has some positive foundation.) But he also expressed frustration with her present passivity and wanted her to take more initiative to help him exercise his body and stimulate his mind.* It was his perception that he always had to provide the energy for the relationship and he felt burned out.

The assessment from the individual sessions was that both partners appeared to have the same goal, to be closer again, and that the quality of the relationship in the past reflected mutuality, love and respect. Because they both mentioned that they usually felt closer when they got more positive attention from each other it was suggested to them separately that they think of three ways to surprise the other person before the next meeting and to notice the reaction. They were told not to discuss the assignment or its results with each other until their next session together.

The couple returned as depressed as before and said they had "forgotten" the assignment. Obviously the therapist had succumbed to her own agenda of lightening the relationship and had not been willing to accept Joe and Marge's lack of energy at that point. She had tried to move them out of their depressed state too fast. The couple did report, however, that they had bickered less and that they had not stayed angry with each other as long as usual. In this session, the talk centered on how they had overcome difficulties in the past, such as a period of unemployment Joe had experienced before going into the service, his stroke, and his subsequent heroin addiction. (*Their ability to resolve problems in the past had been determined in the first three sessions and was part of the assessment.*) They described this process as a team effort in which Joe initiated some action and Marge picked up on it, and provided support and additional ideas for implementation. They mentioned that they did not really know what it is that keeps them "on an even plateau" or moves them ahead. When pressed, Joe came up with the idea that they "just have to be in synch" to move forward; that "we might be on such a plateau now." However, he admitted he was frustrated and was looking for some changes. He wanted Marge to put some more energy into their lives now. She agreed to try in what appeared to be a halfhearted way.

What became evident in that session was a pattern of Joe pushing Marge to be more energetic and the more he pushed the more she distanced and lost energy. In response he would increase his intake of alcohol and the potency of what he drank. The message at the end of the session commented on positives, namely, the couple's way of working as a team, their recognition of their interactional patterns, and their honesty about what they wanted from each other. To ease the pressure for change that they appeared to be feeling, which may in fact have immobilized them, the therapist agreed with their perception that they may be on one of their "plateaus" and should not be looking for any changes from each other until they felt "in synch" with each other.

As soon as they had been given permission to stay the way they were, both partners started to change slightly. Joe developed additional plans for drinking less beer as well as abstaining totally from anything stronger, and Marge added some ideas about how to do this and what to do instead. The couple's sense of humor began to return, and they became more active together in parenting, outings and playing board games. Their own solutions were reinforced at the end of each session. Joe and Marge discussed with the therapist how to recognize conflict, deal with it, and avoid all possibility of violence in the future. By the end of treatment, which lasted seven sessions over a period of six months, they even solved a problem they had with Marge's parents that had been a source of conflict since they were married. Both partners looked healthier, more energetic and were more well groomed.

Follow-up calls were made three months and one year later. After two years the therapist had contact with the couple again because she requested permission to show a piece of videotape of their treatment. When doing follow-up it is important to talk to both partners, and to try to arrange it so they do not talk in front of each other. The list of questions we ask are:

1. How have things been going?
2. What is different, if anything?
3. What are you doing to keep things going well?
4. Have you had any fights like you used to have? (If yes, did they get physical? If yes, ask them to schedule an appointment. If no, ask what they are doing to keep fights from getting physical.)
5. What do you think was the most helpful thing you gained for your relationship from therapy? (If the answer does not fit with what happened in therapy ask them to elaborate further to get an idea of what they are doing that works.)

6. I recall at the end of treatment that you said what helped you most to improve your relationship was. . . . . and your partner said it was. . . . . Is that still true? (The purpose of this question is to remind them of their solution at the end of treatment and to reinforce it.)
7. For the woman only if she says the violence has ceased: Do you feel your partner is respectful of your feelings and needs? (If not, ask if some additional sessions might be useful.)

Both partners reported things had been going well given their circumstances and there was no repetition of violence or excessive drinking. Joe had continued to confine his drinking to beer. Marge was still unemployed because they had decided that her contact with "whole, healthy men" as Joe put it, was more of a threat to their relationship than the shortage of money they frequently experienced. Realistically it would have been a very large change for her to go to work under any circumstances because she had never worked outside the home before, and Joe had always provided money for them. Some of Joe's poetry had been published in the interim.

This case demonstrates three of the most basic assumptions of solution-focused brief therapy: a small change can lead to bigger changes, when something works don't fix it, and clients have resources to help themselves. This couple came to treatment with the goals of stopping violence and feeling closer to each other again. They were assessed to be appropriate for treatment of their relationship because they were judged to have similar goals, Joe wanted to change and take responsibility for his behaviors, they had a history of solving problems together, there did not seem to be an undue desire for power and control on Joe's part, he was not violent when he drank beer, only when he drank hard liquor, and the couple had many positives in their relationship and seemed empathic toward each other.

The therapist in this case quickly recognized that she was trying to move the couple too quickly when she gave a task to try to lighten their relationship at the end of the first session and they did not respond to it. In a way, the therapist was demanding something of the couple which they were demanding of each other and were not able to do. Therapists have to start where a couple is, not where they want them to be. She recognized this and moved more slowly, listening to the clients about their past way of solving problems and then actually suggesting they do nothing until they found themselves "in synch" again given that this is what had worked in the past. What was happening in the meantime in therapy was that they were recalling positives in their past problem solving and in their relationship. It can be assumed that this intervention countered their hopelessness just enough to mobilize both of them again. They appear to have gotten stuck focusing on what they were not getting from each other. The conversations with the therapist reminded them that they both needed change but that they also had love and commitment in their relationship. This small shift seems to have motivated them to make some different choices.

Some readers might feel that there are many other issues that were not addressed here, including the beer drinking. Considering this man's physical disability and life style, and the fact that drinking beer did not affect his behavior, it seemed unrealistic to suggest he stop unless his physicians demanded it. Marge also did not see it as a problem. Finally, their decision that Marge stay home instead of supplementing the income with work was agreeable to both of them. While it may appear to some people that it would be healthier if this couple would spend less time together and Joe would learn to trust Marge's love enough to feel comfortable with her working outside the home, from a solution-focused point of view this would be seen as imposing the therapist's agenda upon the couple. The therapeutic collaboration should not go beyond what clients want for their particular relationship as long as it is safe and ethical.

CONCLUSION

Some voices in the field of domestic violence are beginning to speak out for evaluation of couples treatment as a possible option:

> In my experience, however, there are couples for whom the violence is not so pervasive or severe; the woman still has some agency and power within the relationship and outside of it, and the man shows some readiness and capacity to take genuine responsibility for being violent. Under these circumstances, I now believe that there is a reasonable potential for ending violence using a conjoint approach; (Goldner, 1992, p. 58)

> In setting policies to effectively contain and prevent physical aggression, multifaceted intervention is warranted. Strategies that address interpersonal psychological variables are likely to be effective in deterring physical violence between intimates. (Pan, Neidig, & O'Leary, 1994, p. 980)

It is also encouraging that in the past few years, findings from research in the field of psychology is providing us with typologies of batterers and their partners (e.g., Holtzworth-Munroe & Stuart, 1994; Jacobson et al., 1994; O'Leary, Malone & Tyree, 1994; Pan, Neidig & O'Leary, 1994) which will provide a much more scientific basis for decisions about the safety and appropriateness of couples treatment, and about which couples may benefit from this approach. Of course, assessment will be a critical component in a future of varied treatment. Barnhill and colleagues (1980) suggested a multifaceted approach that uses physiological, psychological, interpersonal and family resources as well as focuses on life stresses and resources. Dutton (1988) has developed a nested ecological theory based on the work of developmental psychologists and ethnologists which allows for hierarchical levels of assessment on the ontogenetic (verbal skills, emotional response, empathy), microsystemic (the relationship), exosystem (environmental stress such as unemployment, racial discrimination) and the macrosystemic (socialization) levels.

One could hope that in the future, family therapists would join police, courts, shelters, hospitals, probation and parole agents as part of a holistic coordinated community response. A treatment intervention such as solution-focused treatment of relationships would be one choice for offenders and their partners. A systemic assessment would be made based on safety first and then the goals expressed by both partners. Treatment recommendations would be based on how safely and quickly the couple's goals could be met considering their strengths and resources and how they fit with the goals and recommendations of other community organizations involved in the case. In other words, it would become an important part of the response to ascertain that everyone involved in the case agrees on and coordinates efforts toward the same goals. As much as possible, these should be the ones defined by the batterer and the battered woman because people are clearly more motivated to work toward what they want rather than what others want for them.

When couples who want to stay together are assessed as not appropriate for treatment of their relationship, they would be directed to other interventions and subsequently be reassessed for couples work if they so desire. The present trend for a batterers group as the primary intervention would be very appropriate for a male partner who says he wants to stay in the relationship but thinks he has the right to hit his partner when she "makes him angry."

If the present trend toward a monolithic view of violence in intimate relationships and the resulting constraint of treatment options is allowed to continue, we are in danger of impeding the progress toward solutions for violence. The goal of stopping violence and emotional abuse must become more of a priority than maintaining the philosophical beliefs about how such goals are achieved. Openness to the further study of existing options and the development and study of new ones must prevail. The search for one solution for all cases must be abandoned in favor of the acceptance of multiple options that depend on particular situations. The challenge to all who are dedicated to helping couples to stop violence is to create a reliable assessment tool and a variety of safe, effective treatment interventions. Solution-focused therapy for relationships experiencing physical and emotional abuse is one response to that challenge.

REFERENCES

American Medical Association (1992). American Medical Association diagnostic and treatment guidelines on domestic violence. *Archives of Family Medicine, 1*, 39-47.

Barnhill, L., Bloomgarden, R., Berghorn, G., Squires, M., & Siracusa, A. (1980). Clinical and community interventions in violent families. In L. R. Wolberg & M. L. Aronson (Eds.), *Group and family therapy* (pp. 234-249). New York: Brunner/Mazel.

Bograd, M. (1984). Family systems approaches to wife battery: A feminist critique. *American Journal of Orthopsychiatry, 54*, 558-565.

Brandl, B. (1990). *Programs for batterers: A discussion paper.* Madison, WI: Dept. of Health and Social Services, Division of Community Services, Bureau for Children, Youth and Families.

de Shazer, S. (1985). *Keys to solutions in brief therapy.* New York: W. W. Norton.

de Shazer, S. (1988). *Clues: Investigating solutions in brief therapy.* New York: W.W. Norton.

de Shazer, S., Berg, I. K., Lipchik, E., Nunnally, E., Molar, A., Gingerich, W., & Weiner-Davis, M. (1986). Brief therapy: Focused solution development. *Family Process, 25*, 207-227.

Dutton, D. G. (1988). *The domestic assault of women: Psychological and criminal justice perspectives.* Newton, MA: Allyn & Bacon.

Erchak, G. M. (1984). The escalation and maintenance of spouse abuse: A cybernetic model. *Victimology, 2*, 247-53.

Feazell, C. S., Mayers, R. S., & Deschner, J. (1984). Services for men who batter: Implications for programs and policies. *Family Relations, 33*, 217-233.

Fraser, J. S. (1988). Strategic rapid intervention in wife beating. In E. Nunnally, C. Chilman & F. Cox, (Eds.), *Families in Trouble, 3*, (pp. 163-191). Newbury Park, CA: Sage.

Geffner, R. (1995). Standards for batterer intervention: Editor's response. *Family Violence & Sexual Assault Bulletin, 11* (3-4), 29-32.

Gelles, J. A., & Wasserstrom, J. (1984). Conjoint therapy for the treatment of domestic violence. In A. R. Roberts (Ed.), *Battering women and their families* (pp. 33-49). New York: Springer.

Gelles, R. J., & Maynard, P. E. (1987). A structural family systems approach to intervention in cases of family violence. *Family Relations, 36*, 270-275.

Goldner, V. (1992). Making room for both/and. *Family Therapy Networker, 16*, 54-62.

Gurman A., & Kniskern, D. P. (1981). Family therapy outcome research: Knowns and unknowns. In A. S. Gurman & D. P. Kniskern (Eds.), *Handbook of family therapy* (pp. 742-775). New York: Brunner/Mazel.

Hamberger, L. K. & Hastings, J. E. (1993). Court-mandated treatment of men who assault their partners. In N. Z. Hilton (Ed.), *Legal responses to wife assault: Current trends and evaluation* (pp. 188-229). Newbury Park, CA: Sage.

Hamberger, L. K., & Hastings, J. (1986). Personality correlates of men who abuse their partners: A cross-validation study. *Journal of Family Violence, 1*, 323-341.

Hoffman, J. (1992, February 16). When men hit women. *New York Times Magazine*, pp. 26-28, 66, 72.

Holtzworth-Munroe, A., & Stuart, G. L. (1994). Typologies of male batterers: Three subtypes and the differences among them. *Psychological Bulletin, 116(3)*, 476-497.

Hotaling, G., & Sugarman, D. (1986). An analysis of risk markers in husband to wife violence: The current state of knowledge. *Victims and Violence, 1*, 101-124.

Jacobson, N. S., Gottman, J. M., Waltz, J., Rushe, R., Babcock, J., & Holtzworth-Munroe, A. (1994). Affect, verbal content, and psychophysiology in the arguments of couples with a violent husband. *Journal of Consulting and Clinical Psychology, 62(5)*, 982-988.

Jacobson, N. S., & Addis, M. E. (1993). Research on couples and couple therapy: What do we know? Where are we going? *Journal of Consulting and Clinical Psychology, 61*, 85-93.

Lipchik, E. (1991). Spouse abuse: Challenging the party line. *The Family Therapy Networker, 15*, 59-63.

Margolin, G. (1979). Conjoint marital therapy to enhance anger management and reduce spouse abuse. *American Journal of Family Therapy, 7*, 13-24.

McKain, J. L. (1987). Family violence: A treatment program for couples. *Journal of Independent Social Work, 1*, 71-83.

Neidig, P. H., & Friedman, D. H. (1984). *Spouse abuse: A treatment approach for couples*. Champaign, IL: Research Press.

O'Leary, K. D. (1996). Physical aggression in intimate relationships can be treated within a marital context under certain circumstances. *Journal of Interpersonal Violence, 11(3)*, 450-452.

O'Leary, K. D., Malone, J., & Tyree, A. (1994). Physical aggression in early marriage: Prerelationship and relationship effects. *Journal of Consulting and Clinical Psychology, 62*, 594-602.

O'Leary, K. D., & Neidig, P. H. (1993). *Couple and gender specific treatment for decreasing physical and psychological aggression in marriage*. Paper presented at the Association for Advancement of Behavior Therapy, Atlanta, GA.

Pan, H. S., Neidig, P. H., & O'Leary, K. D. (1994). Predicting mild and severe husband-to-wife physical aggression. *Journal of Consulting and Clinical Psychology, 62,* 975-980.

Paymar, M., & Pence, E. (1993). *Education groups for men who batter: The Duluth Model.* New York, NY: Springer Publishing.

Purdy, F., & Nickle, N. (1981). Practice principles for working with groups of men who batter. *Social Work Groups, 4,* 111-123.

Sherman, L. W., Schmidt, J. D., Rogan, D. P., Gartin, P. R., Cohn, E. G., Collins, D. J., & Bacich, A. R. (1991). From initial deterrence to long-term escalation: Short-term custody arrest for poverty ghetto domestic violence. *Criminology, 29,* 821-850.

Spanier, G. B. (1976). Measuring dyadic adjustment: New scale for assessing the quality of marriage and similar dyads. *Journal of Marriage and the Family, 38,* 15-28.

Straus, M. A. (1979). Measuring intrafamily conflict and violence: The Conflict Tactics (CT) Scales. *Journal of Marriage and the Family, 41,* 75-88.

Taylor, J. W. (1984). Structured conjoint therapy for spouse abuse cases. *Social Casework, 63,* 11-18.

Tolman, R., & Bennett, L. (1990). A review of quantitative research on men who batter. *Journal of Interpersonal Violence, 5,* 87-118.

Von Foerster, H. (1981). *Observing systems.* Seaside, CA: Intersystemic Publications.

Willbach, E. (1989). Ethics and family therapy: The case management of family violence. *Journal of Marital and Family Therapy, 15,* 43-53.

Zeig, J. (Ed.) (1985). *Ericksonian psychotherapy: Clinical applications.* Vol. 2. New York: Brunner/Mazel.

CHILD PHYSICAL MALTREATMENT AND EXPOSURE TO VIOLENCE IN FAMILIES: ISSUES, INTERVENTIONS, AND RESEARCH

Risk Factors for the Occurrence of Child Abuse and Neglect

Andrea J. Sedlak

Address correspondence to: Andrea J. Sedlak, PhD, Westat, Inc., 1650 Research Boulevard, Rockville, MD 20850.

The author gratefully acknowledges the contributions of Keith Rust, PhD, and Huseyin Goksel to the research.

The analyses reported here were sponsored by the National Center on Child Abuse and Neglect (NCCAN), Administration on Children, Youth and Families (ACYF), Administration for Children and Families (ACF), in the U.S. Department of Health and Human Services, under Contract 105-89-1739 to Westat, Inc. The database was collected previously for the second national incidence study on child abuse and neglect (NIS-2). NCCAN also sponsored the NIS-2, which was conducted by Westat under Contract 105-85-1702.

The views and conclusions are those of the author and do not necessarily represent the opinions or official positions of the sponsors.

SUMMARY. A large, nationally representative database of child abuse and neglect cases was analyzed to identify demographic risk factors for the occurrence of different types of abuse and neglect. The analyses used the data collected in the second National Incidence Study of Child Abuse and Neglect (the NIS-2) concerning children who were harmed by abuse or neglect. Multiple-factor logistic models were developed to identify risk factors for the occurrence of abuse or neglect in six categories of maltreatment: physical abuse, sexual abuse, emotional maltreatment, physical neglect, educational neglect, and multiple maltreatment. A key finding was that children in families with incomes under $15,000 per year were at far greater risk in every category of maltreatment. Also, older children were generally at greater risk in every category, and risk was related to family structure, family size, child's sex and race/ethnicity, and metropolitan status of the county. However, these relationships applied to only certain types of abuse or neglect or took different forms in different maltreatment categories. Interactions among risk factors were the rule rather than the exception. Findings emphasize the need for better coordination between human services and income support services to families. The results imply that risk assessment would be appreciably advanced by going beyond simple matrix approaches that independently consider different factors by developing assessment models that include interactions between different risk factors. *[Article copies available for a fee from The Haworth Document Delivery Service: 1-800-342-9678. E-mail address: getinfo@haworth.com]*

KEYWORDS. Child maltreatment, incidence rates, sexual abuse, neglect, demographic factors

This article summarizes the results of recent efforts to use a large, nationally representative database of child abuse and neglect cases in order to examine demographic risk factors for the occurrence of different types of abuse and neglect. The data used were obtained through the sentinel survey conducted in the second National Incidence Study of Child Abuse and Neglect, also called the NIS-2.

THE NIS METHODOLOGY AND PREVIOUS FINDINGS

The NIS-2, like the NIS-1 before it, was designed to go beyond cases of child maltreatment that come to the attention of child protective services (CPS) by obtaining data on cases of child abuse and neglect that are recognized by a broad spectrum of community professionals serving children and families in various arenas. The sentinel survey method used in the NIS is based on the assumption that children who are officially reported to CPS agencies represent only the "tip of the iceberg," and that there are considerable numbers of children who are recognized as abused or neglected by community professionals who are not investigated by CPS. The NIS-1 was conducted in 1979 and 1980 and its findings were published in 1981 (National Center on Child Abuse and Neglect, 1981). The NIS-2 data were collected in 1986 and prevalence estimates were published initially in 1988 (U.S. Department of Health and Human Services, 1988) and revised in 1991 (Sedlak, 1991a). The NIS-3 provided updated national estimates of the numbers of abused or neglected children in the United States. The NIS-3 data were collected in 1993 and the findings were published in September 1996.[1]

In order to provide estimates of the prevalence and distribution of all categories of abuse and neglect in the U.S., the NIS is conducted in a nationally representative sample of counties, a sample of 29 counties in the NIS-2. In every sampled county, the county CPS agency was a key participant. The data collected in the 29 participating CPS agencies represented all the children who were reported and accepted for investigation during the study data period. The data period for the NIS-2 was from September 7 through December 6, 1986. Non-CPS participants in each county included professional staff who were likely to come into contact with maltreated children in public schools, day care centers, short-stay general and children's hospitals, voluntary social services agencies, mental health agencies, the county juvenile probation and public health departments, municipal police departments, and the county sheriff or state police division with jurisdiction over any unincorporated areas not served by municipal law enforcement. Non-CPS participants in the NIS-2 included 3,137 sentinels in 706 non-CPS agencies. Data collection was prospective in that the community professionals at non-CPS agencies served as sentinels by remaining on the lookout for child maltreatment cases. They were trained in the study definitions of maltreatment at the outset and submitted a data form on each maltreated child they encountered during the data period. The NIS-2 collected a total of 7,185 data forms over the 3-month study period, 3,909 from CPS agencies and 3,276 from non-CPS sentinels.

In order to provide a common standard across the broad range of sentinel sources, each child reported to the study was evaluated as to his or her "countability" as abused or neglected in relation to the study definitions, and only children who fit the standards were used in the national estimates.[2] The NIS-2 applied two definitional standards and generated estimates of prevalence based on each. The Harm Standard was developed in the NIS-1 and it was designed to provide as objective a basis as possible. This standard generally required that a child already have experienced demonstrable harm as a result of maltreatment in order to be countable.[3] In contrast, the more lenient Endangerment Standard permitted a child to be countable as long as the sentinel considered that he or she had been seriously endangered by abuse or neglect. This standard also automatically included all the children whose cases were substantiated by CPS. The analyses of the NIS-2 data that are reported here used the data on Harm Standard cases because it reflects the more objective definition and should, therefore, be less vulnerable to subjective differences as to what different sentinel groups consider "endangerment" to be.

Duplicate data forms about the same child were identified and "unduplicated" so that each child was counted by the study only once. Following unduplication, the NIS-2 database consisted of records on 5,317 children, 2,235 of whom were countable under the Harm Standard and 3,276 of whom were counted under the Endangerment Standard. Finally, the data were weighted to represent the number of children who were maltreated in 1986 in the U.S. Further information about these aspects of NIS-2 data processing and weighing can be found in Sedlak, McFarland, and Rust (1987). The unique methodological challenges and limitations characteristic of this type of survey were discussed by Sedlak (1993a).

The NIS-1 revealed that an estimated 625,100 children had experienced Harm Standard abuse or neglect in the U.S. in 1980. The NIS-2 indicated that a significantly higher number of children had been harmed by maltreatment in 1986, an estimated 931,000. In addition, the NIS-2 showed that an estimated 1,424,000 children met the Endangerment Standard, having been endangered (or harmed) by abuse or neglect.

Since the NIS-2 was completed, additional analyses of these data were undertaken, in part, to capitalize on the information relevant to risk factors for the occurrence of different types of abuse and neglect. This article presents the method and key findings from these subsequent analyses. Further details can be found in Sedlak (1993b).

OTHER RELEVANT LITERATURE

Apart from the NIS-2 data, two other databases provided information about the national prevalence of child maltreatment in the mid-1980s and the demographic correlates of child abuse and neglect cases: (1) the American Association for Protecting Children (AAPC) of the American Humane Association collected data from state CPS agencies on cases reported to CPS during 1986 (1988), and (2) Straus and Gelles (1986, 1988a, 1988b, 1990) conducted a national telephone survey of parents concerning their physically assaultive behaviors toward their children.

The AAPC (1988) found there were 2.1 million reports of abused or neglected children in 1986. The average maltreatment profile involved a child 7.2 years old, although this varied with type of maltreatment, ranging from a mean of 5.5 years for physical abuse to a mean of 9.2 years for sexual abuse. Overall, 52% of the reports involved females, but this characteristic also differed across maltreatment types, with a slight majority of male victims (54.2%) of physical abuse and a substantial majority of female victims (77%) of sexual abuse. Some variation was evident in race/ethnicity distributions of maltreatment, and the types of abuse depended strongly on family structure, with female-headed households overrepresented.

The NIS-2 and the AAPC data differ in the definition of child abuse and neglect, in their information basis, and in their duplicate counting of children. The NIS-2 estimates went beyond children who had been reported to CPS to include children who were recognized as abused or neglected by community professionals, whereas the AAPC totals were restricted to those children who had been reported to CPS (and whose report was accepted for investigation by that agency). The NIS-2 totals included only those abused or neglected children who fit the NIS-2 definitions (whether or not they had been reported to CPS). In contrast, although the AAPC estimates were only of children who had been reported to CPS, they included all such children (whether or not they were countable under NIS-2 definitional standards). It is possible, however, to extract an estimate from the NIS-2 data that is more comparable to the figures obtained by the AAPC by considering corresponding children (i.e., all those NIS-2 children who had been investigated by CPS regardless of their countability in the study). Using this approach, the NIS-2 data showed that CPS agencies investigated an estimated 1,657,000 children in the U.S. in 1986. This figure is below the corresponding AAPC total for the same year, most likely because of the third important difference between the two studies: the inclusion or exclusion of duplicate reports on the same children. States typically were unable to identify duplicate reports, so the AAPC estimate includes an unknown proportion of children who are counted multiple times. In contrast, as noted above, the NIS methodology attempts to avoid the double-counting problem insofar as possible. Given these three differences between the NIS-2 and the AAPC methods, the data from the two studies may well reveal different demographic correlates of abuse and neglect.

The National Family Violence Survey[4] (NFVS) conducted by Straus and Gelles (1990) affords another perspective on the national prevalence and correlates of child abuse in the mid-1980s. Telephone interviews were conducted in 1985 with 3,229 parents of children under age 18 living at home. Based on parents' answers concerning their physically assaultive actions toward their children, it was estimated that 110 out of every 1,000 children in the general population experienced severe violence by their parents in 1985,[5] and that 23 in 1,000 had experienced *very* severe violence.[6] Severe violence evidenced a curvilinear relationship with child's age, peaking in the three to ten year old range, but very severe violence was unrelated to child's age. Child's gender was not related to physical abuse, but family socioeconomic status (SES) was. The rate of physical abuse among blue collar parents was almost twice the rate among White collar parents, and families earning less than $20,000 per year had the highest rates of child abuse while those earning $40,000 or more had the lowest rates. Race/ethnicity differences also emerged, with both Black children and Hispanic children abused at significantly higher rates than White children. Family size also appeared to be related to the rate of physical child abuse in that families with one or two children had higher rates than those with three or more children.

The NFVS and the NIS-2 differ in three crucial respects: the type of maltreatment studied, the definition of countable cases, and the informant basis. The NIS-2 studied all categories of abuse and neglect, whereas the NFVS data pertain only to physical abuse. The comparison most similar to the NFVS estimate of child abuse is the NIS-2 estimate of physically abused children. Even the lowest rate from the NFVS (i.e., the rate of very severe violence, or 23 per 1,000 children) was more than five times the rate of Harm Standard physical abuse found in the NIS-2 (i.e., 4.3 per 1,000 children) and more than four times the rate of Endangerment Standard physical abuse in the NIS-2 (i.e., 4.9 per 1,000 children; cf. Sedlak, 1991a). This discrepancy probably stems from the fact that the two studies used very different definitions of physical abuse and obtained their data from very different informants. The NIS-2 definitions are more congruent with federal and state laws and child welfare practice which give primary emphasis to the outcomes or effects of parent/caretaker actions (i.e., actual harm or injury to the child or what sentinels perceived to be serious endangerment), whereas the NFVS estimates included all children whose parents acknowledged specific actions toward the child. Also, the informant basis of the two studies was entirely different. Recall the conceptual "iceberg" model that inspired the NIS methodology, in which CPS agencies encounter only the top-most portion of abuse and neglect cases while non-CPS sentinels in the NIS provide information about some deeper levels of cases which do not come to CPS attention. By surveying the general population, the NFVS delved even deeper into the "iceberg" than did the NIS. The NFVS data probably include some cases that also would be tapped by the NIS methodology, but the opposite also is true; the NIS methodology probably includes cases that are not acknowledged by respondents in the NFVS.[7] The differences between the NIS-2 and the NFVS in their definitions and informant basis imply that the NIS-2 data may reveal different demographic risk factors.

The NIS-2 data were used by Jones and McCurdy (1992) to provide both descriptive analyses of the percentage distributions of countable children on different characteristics and a series of logistic analyses examining the predictors of abuse and neglect. Their logistic analyses addressed conditional questions of the form: "Given that a child is maltreated, what are the characteristics that distinguish children who suffer maltreatment type A from those who suffer maltreatment type B?" They found the child's age to be important in distinguishing all categories of maltreatment from each other. The logistic models they provided show that, with increasing age, maltreated children were more likely to be physically or emotionally abused than neglected, and younger children who were maltreated were more likely to be sexually abused than to be physically or emotionally abused. Among maltreated children, females were more likely to be sexually abused than to be physically abused, emotionally abused, or neglected. Given that they were maltreated at all, children in families with incomes over $15,000 were more likely to be physically, sexually, or emotionally abused than they were to be neglected, and those in single-parent families were more likely to be neglected than to be physically, sexually, or emotionally abused.

Unfortunately, there are several problems with the analysis methods Jones and McCurdy used which cast doubt on the validity of the findings they reported: they used unweighted data, excluded a nonrandom subset of the NIS-2 cases, and failed to take into account the sample design effect. First, the fact that they used the unweighted NIS-2 data means that the results of the descriptive analyses are likely to be misleading. That is, the percentage distributions are distorted by differences in sampling rates between different types of cases (e.g., fatalities were always taken with certainty but other cases often were sampled) and between cases seen by different categories of sentinels. Although statisticians disagree about whether it is always necessary to use weighting information in regression analyses (cf. Lepkowski, Landis, Parsons, & Stehouwer, 1988; Smith, 1984), there is considerable consensus on the need to take sample design factors into account in the model. Thus, as a consequence of their use of unweighted data, one cannot generalize the Jones and McCurdy findings beyond the specific sample that was selected in the NIS-2.

Second, although Jones and McCurdy reported that their analyses were based on an expanded Endangerment Standard criterion (one which allowed cases to count even when the maltreatment had occurred outside of the 3-month study time frame), the totals they provided indicate that they omitted a substantial number of Endangerment Standard cases. In order to derive mutually-exclusive maltreatment categories, they adopted the strategy of using only the first-mentioned maltreatment in each child's data record (E. D. Jones, personal communication, June 2, 1990). This approach had the unfortunate consequence of reducing the data in a non-random way, especially in the category of emotional maltreatment where at least 46% of the countable Endangerment Standard cases were excluded.[8] Moreover, because the elimination of cases was nonrandom, the subset of data Jones and McCurdy used for analyses was not nationally representative, despite having been derived from a larger nationally representative database. As a result, their findings cannot be generalized beyond the specific subset of cases they extracted.

Third, Jones and McCurdy used a standard logistic regression approach. Standard statistical packages assume that the data derive from simple random samples with zero covariance between the elements of the sample. However, the NIS-2 used a multi-level sampling design which involved the clustering of sentinels within agencies and of agencies within counties, so there is a considerable degree of positive covariance in the NIS-2 data. For significance tests to yield meaningful results in this context, unbiased variance estimates must be obtained (Lee, Forthofer, & Lorimor, 1989). Otherwise, findings will be distorted by the misspecification effect (Skinner, 1989). This effect is particularly severe for the NIS-2 data. In fact, some early analyses suggested that the misspecification effect can be as high as a factor of 10. Because the Jones and McCurdy analyses did not take this into account, one cannot draw meaningful conclusions from their results.[9]

The analyses reported in this article differ from those conducted by Jones and McCurdy in a number of respects. First, they are based on Harm Standard cases in order to minimize the influence of distortions due to sentinels' beliefs and subjective judgments. Second, they differed in their principal focus. As described earlier, the Jones and McCurdy analyses addressed *conditional* questions that were predicated on some type of maltreatment having occurred and inquired about the characteristics that distinguish children who experience different kinds of maltreatment. The analyses reported here are concerned with identifying the risk factors for the occurrence of different forms of abuse and neglect. As such, they address unconditional questions of the form: "What characteristics distinguish children who suffer maltreatment type A from children in the general U.S. population?" Finally, these analyses use the weighted NIS-2 data and apply methods that appropriately take account of the NIS-2 design effect in computations of variances and tests for significant patterns.

METHOD

To the extent that the NIS-2 provides a nationally representative sample of maltreated children, the risk factors identified in this database should be broadly generalizable. By comparing the characteristics of these children to the characteristics of non-maltreated children in the general population, it was possible to identify the important features that distinguished maltreated from non-maltreated children. Specifically, the nationally representative sample of 2,235 children in the NIS-2 who met the Harm Standard were combined with a comparison database of 3,798 nationally representative nonmaltreated children obtained in the U.S. Bureau of Census Current Population (USBCCP) Surveys conducted in March 1986 and March 1987. The decision was made to use the data from both of the USBCCP surveys in combination because neither data period exactly matched the data period of the NIS-2, but together the data period of both surveys straddled that of the NIS-2. Also, the combined data from both surveys were expected to provide more reliable estimates of general population characteristics than either survey alone could provide.

Early exploratory analyses revealed strong risk factor differences across maltreatment types. For this reason, the NIS-2 Harm Standard cases were divided for separate analyses into the six mutually-exclusive categories listed in Table 1. Earlier reports of the NIS-2 findings (e.g., U.S. Department of Health & Human Services, 1988; Sedlak, 1991a) classified children into all categories that applied to them,[10] whereas the present scheme places children who had experienced multiple forms of maltreatment into a separate category. Thus, earlier reports gave the rate of 4.3 per 1,000 children physically abused according to the Harm Standard (Sedlak, 1991a) while this report indicates a rate of 3.7 per 1,000 children.

To maximize the likelihood that respondents will submit information to the study, the NIS data forms are fairly short which limits the information that is available about the children and families. The forms ask only about a few key demographic features and focus primarily on the data items needed for deciding on the child's countability under the study definitions.

TABLE 1. Distribution of NIS-2 Harm Standard Cases Across Six Mutually-Exclusive Maltreatment Categories

Type of Maltreatment	Unweighted n	Weighted N	Rate per 1,000
Physical abuse[a]	664	231,000	3.7
Sexual abuse[a]	446	107,000	1.7
Emotional maltreatment[a]	274	146,000	2.3
Physical neglect[a]	430	151,000	2.4
Multiple maltreatment[a,b]	164	56,000	0.9
Educational neglect	257	240,000	3.8
All maltreatment	2,235	931,000	14.8

[a]With or without Educational neglect

[b]Combinations of the first 4 categories.

Because of these limitations, it was possible to examine the predictive strength of only seven demographic factors (see Table 2).

Except for county metropolitan status, there were few cases of missing data in the NIS-2 database. Missing values were imputed within each maltreatment category by randomly assigning values using the unweighted distribution of values from cases not missing data.

Although a nationally representative sample of non-maltreated children was not available for comparison, the USBCCP surveys done in March 1986 and March 1987 provided information about the distribution of demographic characteristics in the general population. Given the NIS-2 information concerning the numbers and characteristics of maltreated children in the nation, the distribution of characteristics among non-maltreated children could be derived from the general population information by subtraction. In this way, the USBCCP survey data were adjusted to reflect only the non-maltreated sector of children in the U.S. child population.

Specifically, the procedures used in combining the three databases (the NIS-2 data and the two USBCCP surveys) followed a three-step process, each step of which operated on the full cross-classification table of the seven demographic factors identified earlier. The full cross-classification of the seven factors yielded a table with 5,184 cells (i.e., 6 × 4 × 2 × 3 × 4 × 3 × 3). First, the data from the two USBCCP surveys were combined. An estimate of the general population in each cell was developed from each USBCCP survey, and the average of the estimates from the two surveys was taken as the estimate of children in the general population with that combination of characteristics. Second, within-cell estimates of

TABLE 2. Variables and Categories Used in Analysis of Factors Associated with Maltreatment

Variable	Categories
Age	0 - 2 years 3 - 5 6 - 8 9 - 11 12 - 14 15 - 17
Race	White, not Hispanic Black, not Hispanic Hispanic Other
Sex	Male Female
Family Income	Under $15,000 $15,000 - $29,999 $30,000 or more
Family Structure	Both parents Mother only Father only Neither parent
Family Size	One Child 2 or 3 children 4 or more children
County Metropolitan status	Metropolitan Statistical Area (MSA) of 1,000,000 or more in population Other MSA Non-MSA

the prevalence of each type of Harm Standard maltreatment in the NIS-2 were calculated.[11] Third, for each cell, the NIS-2 estimate for all maltreatment was subtracted from the combined USBCCP survey estimate in order to derive an estimate of the size of the unmaltreated population in the cell. Fourth, replicate weights were developed for each record in order to permit appropriate standard errors of model parameters and significance tests using replicated logistic regression procedure. This was an important feature because, as discussed earlier, the nature of the NIS-2 sample design was such that if the NIS-2 data had been treated as coming from a simple random sample, the resulting tests of significance would have severely overstated the statistical significance of the results. Details of these preparatory steps can be found in Sedlak (1993b, especially Appendix B).

The replicated logistic regression procedure used was WESLOG (Flyer & Mohadjer, 1989). Six series of logistic models were independently developed to identify the factors that predicted occurrence of each category of Harm Standard maltreatment. The analyses began with single-factor WESLOG models within each maltreatment category, assessing the degree to which each of the seven demographic factors predicted the classification of cases as maltreated or not maltreated. After computing the single-factor models for each variable, three interaction terms were assessed, Race × Age, Sex × Age, and Family Structure × Age, when any of their component variables appeared to be important according to the single-factor models. In deciding whether a variable was important, consideration was given both to the overall model significance and to the t-values associated with individual parameters in the model. Next, a multi-factor model to account for occurrence of maltreatment in the category was developed by simultaneously including all the terms associated with risk of the maltreatment in the single factor and simple interaction tests. Finally, terms were eliminated from the multi-factor model when their parameter t-values fell below ± 1.00 in the context of the other predictors. Using this approach, a final, multi-factor model was identified for each maltreatment type by simultaneously considering the marginal statistical significance of the model terms, the estimated size of the effect of the model parameters as indicated by the parameter coefficients, the adjusted proportion of total likelihood attributed to model fit (analogous to the adjusted R^2 statistic, or variance accounted for, in multiple regression, see Harrell, 1986), and the overall statistical significance of the model fit.

Throughout this report, expected rates were computed from the applicable multi-factor logistic model by using the model formula and parameters to compute the value of the logit for children with specified combinations of characteristics. Then, the exponential transform was used to compute a probability from the logit, and this was multiplied by 1,000 to obtain the expected rate per 1,000 children in the population with the specified combination of characteristics. Details on the method of using the parameters of a logistic model to derive probabilities for specific subgroups can be found in Sedlak (1993b, especially Appendix C).

RESULTS

Table 3 summarizes the substantive findings on risk factors for Harm Standard abuse or neglect. (The Appendix presents the model parameters and significance statistics for the final multiple factor model accounting for occurrence of each type of maltreatment.) The effects described in each column of Table 3 are those that emerged when all of the other effects in the column were taken into account. Harrell's R^2 statistic indicated that the multi-factor models accounted for 8-20% of the variance in the occurrence of abuse and neglect. Specifically, the variance accounted for by the final multi-factor model was 8.2% in the case of physical abuse, 12.0% for sexual abuse, 12.0% for emotional maltreatment, 20.2% for physical neglect, 9.5% for multiple maltreatment, and 17.4% for educational neglect. All seven characteristics examined were found to relate to risk of abuse or neglect in some way. The specific factors that predicted risk and the nature of their relation to risk depended on the type of maltreatment and often on the circumstances of other important predictive factors.

Child's Age

Regardless of the type of maltreatment, children's risk of being maltreated varied with their age. For all maltreatment categories, older children were at greater risk, but the relationship with age generally was modified by interactions with other factors. Only emotional maltreatment evidenced a simple, unqualified age effect: older children were at greater risk. In all other maltreatment categories, significant effects emerged in connection with one or more of the three age interactions that were examined (Race/ethnicity × Age, Sex × Age, and Family Structure × Age). Interestingly, age effects were not evident in the single-factor analyses predicting physical neglect and multiple maltreatment, perhaps because the overall age distributions in those categories showed curvilinear patterns, with notably low representation among 6 to 8 year olds. However, the multi-factor models did reveal age-related changes in risk in these categories.

For four types of maltreatment, the impact of age depended on family structure. Nevertheless, the exact nature of the interactions differed across these categories. For sexual abuse and physical neglect, older children were at greater risk only in father-only families. Figure 1 illustrates this interaction, showing the model-based predictions of the likelihood of physical neglect among children whose other characteristics place them at relatively high risk. The graph shown here presents the probability of

TABLE 3. Risk Factors for the Occurrence of Harm Standard Maltreatment

	PHYSICAL ABUSE	SEXUAL ABUSE	EMOTIONAL MALTREAT-MENT	PHYSICAL NEGLECT	EDUCATIONAL NEGLECT-ONLY	MULTIPLE MALTREAT-MENT
Child's Sex	No relationship	Females at greater risk	No relationship	Depends on age: females at greater risk at 15-17 years	No relationship	Females at greater risk
Child's Age	Depends on race and family structure; older at greater risk especially blacks and Hispanics and with both parents present	Depends on race and family structure; older at greater risk for whites, blacks, and Hispanics, (but not other minorities) and for children in father-only households	Older children at greater risk	Depends on sex and family structure; older at greater risk for females and in father-only families	Depends on family structure; older children at greater risk with both parents present	Depends on race; older at greater risk for whites, blacks, and Hispanics, not other minorities
Child's Race/ Ethnicity	Depends on age; blacks and Hispanics at greater risk as age progresses	Depends on age; whites, blacks & Hispanics at greater risk than Other Races at older ages	Other minorities at greater risk than whites, blacks, or Hispanics	Related to risk of maltreatment when other factors ignored; not relevant when other important factors in this column are taken into account	Whites and blacks at greater risk than Hispanics and other minorities	Depends on age; whites at greater risk than other race/ethnicities at older ages

162

Family Income	Higher risk in lower income families	Higher risk in lower income families	Higher risk in lower income families	Higher risk in lower income families	Higher risk in lower income families	Higher risk in lower income families
County Metropolitan Status	No relationship	No relationship	No relationship	Higher risk in very large urban counties (pop 1 million +)	Higher risk in urban than in rural counties	Higher risk in urban than in rural counties
Number of Children in Household	Higher risk with only one child in household	No relationship	Related to risk of maltreatment when other factors ignored; not relevant when other important factors in this column are taken into account	Related to risk of maltreatment when other factors ignored; not relevant when other important factors in this column are taken into account	Higher risk with only one child in household	No relationship
Family Structure	Depends on age; two parent families at greater risk above 5 years of age	Depends on age; father-only families at greater risk at older ages	No relationship	Depends on age; 15-17 yr olds at greater risk in father-only families	Depends on age; both parent families at greater risk at older ages	Both parent and mother-only families at greater risk than father-only families

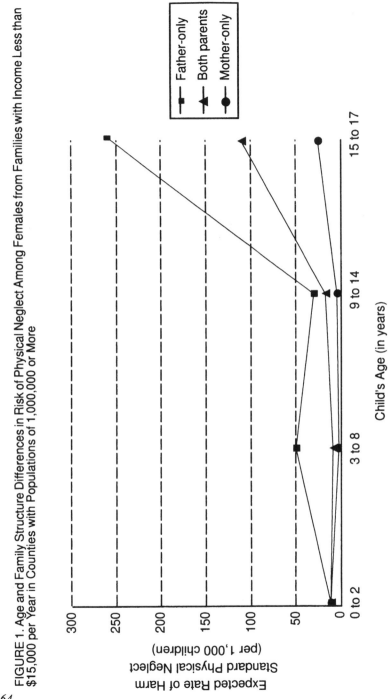

FIGURE 1. Age and Family Structure Differences in Risk of Physical Neglect Among Females from Families with Income Less than $15,000 per Year in Counties with Populations of 1,000,000 or More

physical neglect for females in households where the family income was below $15,000 per year and lived in large metropolitan counties.

Figure 1 indicates that different family structures have widely different implications for adolescents' risk of physical neglect, with father-only household composition associated with a much higher risk level for the older age group. The figure was constrained to present the relationship for a very specific subset of children because interaction effects in a multi-factor logistic model can be only specified by making explicit assumptions about the status of all the other important predictors included in the model. However, the focus here and in the other graphs presented is on the general pattern that is depicted, because the NIS-2 data generally are not sufficient to provide reliable individual cell-level estimates at these detailed levels of classification. (The data are sufficient to provide unbiased and reliable estimates at the level of one-way and two-way marginal totals, which are required to assess the final multi-factor models.) The same pattern shown in Figure 1 generally was true for children with other combinations of characteristics and in the model predicting the likelihood of sexual abuse. These similar patterns differed only in the shift in scale values on the Y-axis, reflecting different average levels of risk for the maltreatment in question.

A different type of interaction between age and family structure emerged for physical abuse and educational neglect. The interaction of age and family structure in the logistic model predicting risk of physical abuse is graphed for children who generally were at high risk for physical abuse on the basis of their other characteristics (see Figure 2). Although different family structures had fairly similar risk implications for children under age 12, older children were at greater risk of physical abuse when they lived in two-parent households. Again, this general pattern applied to children with other characteristics and the Age × Family Structure interaction was very similar in connection with risk of educational neglect.

Race/ethnicity modified the influence of age on risk for three types of maltreatment. Higher levels of risk among older children held for Whites, Blacks, and Hispanics (but not for other minorities) for sexual abuse and multiple maltreatment. Figure 3 shows the pattern of multiple maltreatment for children who are at high risk. Moreover, in the case of multiple maltreatment, the age-related increases in risk were slightly stronger for Whites than for Blacks or Hispanics. The findings for children at other overall risk levels conformed to the general relationships shown here, and the Race/ethnicity × Age pattern was similar in risk of sexual abuse except that Whites, Blacks, and Hispanics did not differ in their risk of sexual abuse.

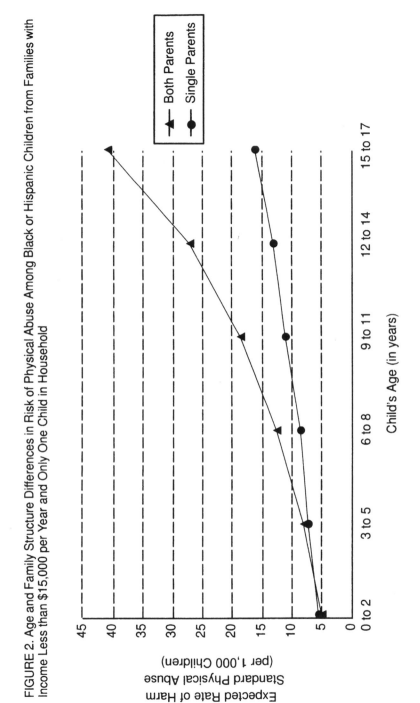

FIGURE 2. Age and Family Structure Differences in Risk of Physical Abuse Among Black or Hispanic Children from Families with Income Less than $15,000 per Year and Only One Child in Household

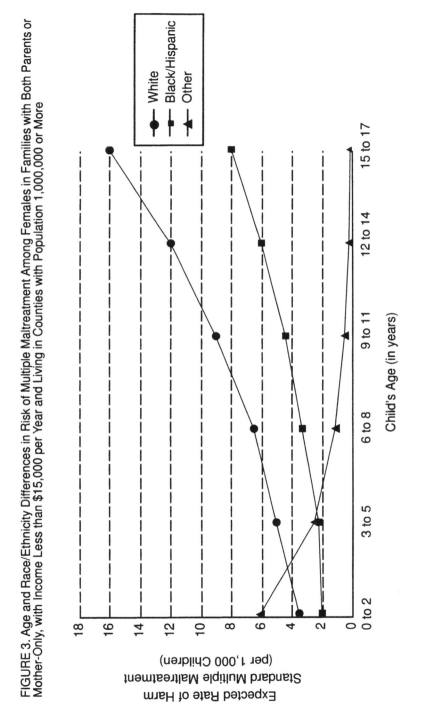

FIGURE 3. Age and Race/Ethnicity Differences in Risk of Multiple Maltreatment Among Females in Families with Both Parents or Mother-Only, with Income Less than $15,000 per Year and Living in Counties with Population 1,000,000 or More

167

In contrast, the general nature of the interaction of age and race/ethnicity was quite different for physical abuse (see Figure 4). The age effect was stronger for Black and Hispanic children compared with White children and those of other races/ethnicities. The figure shows the pattern for children who were otherwise at high risk of physical abuse. The pattern for other subgroups of children was similar except that when overall levels of risk were lower the age effect essentially disappeared altogether among White children and those of other races/ethnicities.

The child's sex affected the relation between age and risk of physical neglect. Figure 5 shows the pattern in which the older children's greater risk is expected to be much higher among females. Although this graph depicts only children whose other characteristics placed them at generally high risk, the pattern also held true for children with other combinations of characteristics.

Child's Sex

In the single-factor analyses, the child's sex was significantly related only to risk of sexual abuse. However, after taking other important predictors into account, the child's sex also was related to risk in two other maltreatment categories (i.e., physical neglect and multiple maltreatment). In all cases, females were at greater risk than males. Moreover, the influence of a child's sex on risk of physical neglect was modified by age. As seen in Figure 5, females were at greater risk than males in the 15 to 17 year old group but not at younger ages.

Child's Race/Ethnicity

The child's race/ethnicity was an important predictor of risk of maltreatment for all except physical neglect, where the impact it displayed in the single-factor model disappeared in the multi-factor analyses. On the other hand, race/ethnicity had not shown even a marginal effect in the single-factor model predicting risk of sexual abuse and risk of multiple maltreatment, but was important in the multi-factor analyses. In the final multi-factor models, race/ethnicity had a simple effect on risk of emotional maltreatment and of educational neglect but its effect was nearly opposite in the two cases. Other minorities were at greater risk of emotional maltreatment than were Whites, Blacks, or Hispanics, whereas Whites and Blacks were at greater risk of educational neglect than were Hispanics and other minorities. As described above, race/ethnicity effects on risk of physical abuse, sexual abuse, and multiple maltreatment were modified by

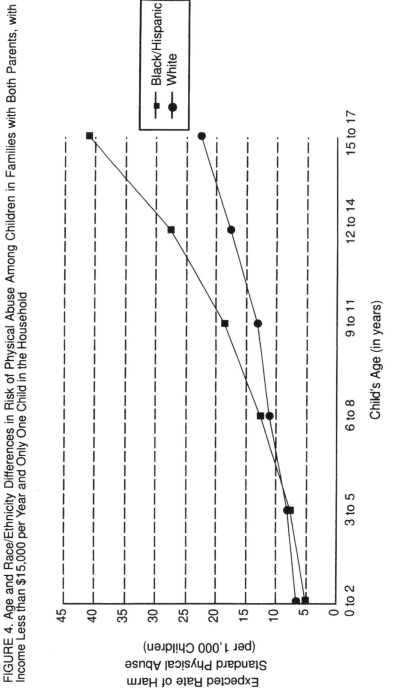

FIGURE 4. Age and Race/Ethnicity Differences in Risk of Physical Abuse Among Children in Families with Both Parents, with Income Less than $15,000 per Year and Only One Child in the Household

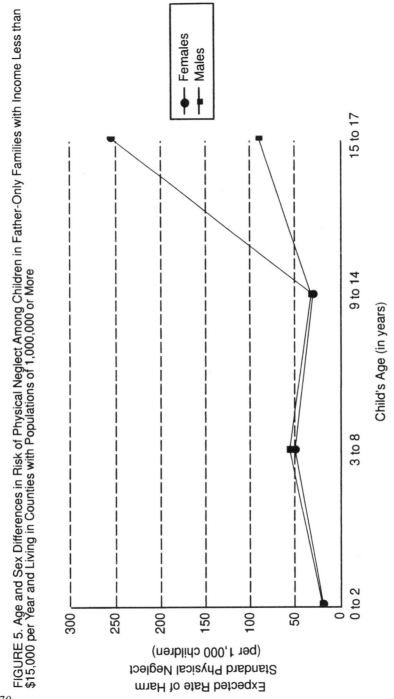

FIGURE 5. Age and Sex Differences in Risk of Physical Neglect Among Children in Father-Only Families with Income Less than $15,000 per Year and Living in Counties with Populations of 1,000,000 or More

170

the child's age and different race/ethnicity distinctions were important across these categories.

Family Income

Family income had highly significant effects on risk for every category of maltreatment both in the single-factor analyses and in all the final multi-factor models. To date, the potency of this effect has emerged consistently in the NIS-2 data regardless of the analytic approach taken (U.S. Department of Health and Human Services, 1988; Sedlak, 1991a, 1991b). Compared to children whose families had incomes of $30,000 per year or more, children from families with incomes below $15,000 per year were found to have:

1. 21 times greater risk of physical abuse,
2. more than 24 times greater risk of sexual abuse,
3. between 20 and 162 times greater risk of physical neglect (depending on the children's other characteristics),
4. more than 13 times greater risk of emotional maltreatment,
5. 16 times greater risk of multiple maltreatment, and
6. between 78 and 97 times greater risk of educational neglect (depending on the children's other characteristics).

County Metropolitan Status

County metropolitan status did not evidence a noteworthy relationship with risk in any category in the single-factor analyses, but it did play a role in the multi-factor models in connection with the risk of physical neglect, educational neglect, and multiple maltreatment. In all cases, children in more populous, urbanized counties were at greater risk of maltreatment. For physical neglect and multiple maltreatment, children who lived in counties with populations of 1,000,000 or more were at greater risk than children in less populous counties. Children were at greater risk of experiencing educational neglect if they lived in urban (whether large or not) rather than in rural counties.

Number of Other Children in the Household

The single-factor analyses indicated that the number of children in the household significantly predicted risk of physical abuse, physical neglect, and educational neglect; in the multi-factor analyses, this factor remained an important predictor of risk for physical abuse and educational neglect. In both cases, children in families where they were the only child were at greater risk than those living in households where there were other children. The effect for physical abuse was non-linear; risk did not decrease consistently with increasing numbers of children. In fact, children from families with four or more children had a slightly higher probability of abuse than children from families with two to three children.

Family Structure

When family structure was examined in single-factor logistic models, it demonstrated a significant association with physical abuse and physical neglect and a marginal relationship with educational neglect. In all cases, the single-factor analyses showed that children in single-parent families were at greater risk. However, family structure exhibited dramatically different relationships with risk when the effects of other important predictors (most notably family income) were taken into account. In the final multi-factor models, family structure had an unqualified effect only on the risk of multiple maltreatment, where it emerged that children in both-parent and mother-only families were at greater risk. In the four other categories of maltreatment, the impact of family structure depended on the child's age. Fifteen to seventeen-year-olds were at substantially greater risk of physical abuse and of educational neglect if they lived in two-parent families. These same older children were at greater risk of sexual abuse and physical neglect in father-only families than they were in mother-only families or families with both parents.

DISCUSSION

Family Income

Family income was the only factor that strongly and consistently related to risk in all categories of abuse and neglect. Despite the fact that the NIS data forms gather only rudimentary information about family income, and despite the fact that 20% of the cases had missing data on this item (because participants did not always have enough information to confidently answer it), family income emerged as important in every analysis.

It is possible that these findings derive from biases in the information provided by the NIS-2 sentinels, either because of their differential contacts with lower income families, because of a greater tendency to report the poorer families, or because of their stereotypical beliefs about the connection between income and child maltreatment. However, there are several reasons why it is unlikely that the remarkably strong effects of family income observed here are simply and solely due to distortions of this sort.

First, the majority of children were encountered by sentinels who were likely to see children and families at all income levels. School sentinels identified more than half the abused and neglected children who met the Harm Standard in the NIS-2. Given that approximately 90% of the U.S. population of school-age children attend public schools (National Center for Education Statistics, 1988),[12] the population of children who are in public school represents a broad spectrum of income levels. Similarly, the NIS-2 hospitals encounter a broad spectrum of the population. They were not limited to public hospitals, but included private as well as public hospitals that provided general medical and surgical services, were primarily short-stay facilities, and met the required minimum of 4,000 admissions annually. Also, social service and mental health agencies were nongovernmental (i.e., voluntary) agencies and included private agencies. Thus, it appears unlikely that the strong relationship between income and child maltreatment derives entirely from differential observation of lower income families by NIS sentinels.

Second, some have attributed the overrepresentation of lower socioeconomic families in the maltreatment statistics to the reluctance of service providers to interfere in the lives of more affluent and influential individuals (U.S. Department of Health, Education, and Welfare, 1977), so a related explanation for the findings here is that sentinels simply are more likely to report on cases of maltreatment they observe when family income is low. There is no reason to expect sentinels' reports to the study and their reports to CPS to follow different dynamics. If the overrepresentation of low-income families among the maltreated sectors was due to a stronger tendency to report maltreatment in these cases to the study, then this same pattern should be found among their reports to CPS. Yet, other analyses of the NIS-2 data have shown that once a NIS-2 sentinel has recognized a case of Harm Standard maltreatment, family income was generally not related to the likelihood of CPS receiving and investigating a report on the case. In fact, family income emerged as a predictor of the likelihood of CPS investigation only for cases of physical neglect, and that relationship was in the opposite direction: physically neglected children in lower income families were less likely to have their maltreatment investigated by CPS (Sedlak, 1993b).[13]

Third, although it is possible that subjective perceptions by the NIS-2 sentinels contributed to the income findings to some degree, the circumstances here probably minimized the extent to which such stereotypes biased the findings. Some influence from stereotypes is possible because NIS-2 participants typically were not in a position to know actual family income, so the data on this question probably include a number of educated guesses. Thus, it is theoretically possible that the observed relationships were partially a function of respondents' beliefs (or stereotypes) about the relation between income and the occurrence of maltreatment. However, research shows that distortions due to subjective impressions typically diminish with increased personal familiarity (Deaux, 1976). Considering that school sentinels recognized a majority of the maltreated children in the NIS-2 and that these people should, in general, be rather familiar with the children and their family circumstances, one could expect minimal bias by stereotypes concerning the relationship between maltreatment and poverty.

Fourth, if these results are an artifact of differential observation of lower income families, then it means that the number of maltreated children in the nation who met the Harm Standard in 1986 was more than twice the number indicated by the NIS-2 data. That is, if children from middle and upper income families experience abuse and neglect at the same rates as those from the lower income families as documented in the NIS-2, there would have to be approximately 1,105,400 additional maltreated children in middle and upper income families who remained hidden from NIS-2 observers.

Moreover, if the income findings reported here were derived solely from differential observation of low income families and/or stereotypical beliefs of sentinels, then they should disappear in the context of a methodology such as that used by Straus and Gelles (1990) in the NFVS, where households were nationally representative and respondents self reported their physically abusive behaviors. Instead, that approach revealed significantly higher rates of child abuse among blue collar families and among families earning less than $20,000 per year. The very pervasive and robust nature of income differences in risk of abuse and neglect implies that the pattern observed here most likely reflects real risk differences among children in the different income sectors of the population.

Many other researchers also have noted the effects of income on risk of child maltreatment (Kinard & Klerman, 1980; Pelton, 1981; Russell & Trainor, 1984). In addition, a number of problems associated with low income are plausible causal contributors to child maltreatment, including factors such as social mobility, lack of education, and the daily stressors of poverty. In this connection, Garbarino (1980, 1981) noted that socioeconomic factors are associated with the availability of social support systems that can assist parents in their child care responsibilities. He concluded that although economic factors remain the most important variable, their influence is mediated by the social structure of the community. The idea that child maltreatment has an essentially classless distribution has persisted despite the multiple studies using widely varying methods that have documented its strong relationship with socioeconomic class. As suggested by Biller and Solomon (1986), the longevity of the myth of classlessness may stem from the popularity of models of the etiology of child maltreatment that focus on intrapsychic factors and view the problem as a disease. The findings here indicate that, although abuse and neglect does occur in every social class, it is substantially overrepresented in low-income families.

Other Demographic Factors

The child's age ranked a distant second as a predictor of risk of abuse and/or neglect. Age did play some role in the risk of all categories of maltreatment, and wherever age did influence risk of maltreatment, it was the older children who were at greater risk. Age-related differences in risk were nearly always qualified in some way, such that they appeared only in specific subgroups or were stronger for some subsets of children than for others. The characteristics that defined the subgroups that showed differential age patterns varied across the maltreatment categories but included all the variables for which age interactions were examined: family structure, child's race/ethnicity, and child's sex.

Family structure and child's race/ethnicity predicted risk in nearly all categories of maltreatment, but the specific family structures and races/ethnicities whose risk was greater varied from one type of maltreatment to another. In addition, the effects that did emerge often were qualified by the child's age, meaning that they appeared only at certain ages or were stronger in some age brackets than others. The simple effects of family structure disappeared or reversed when family income was taken into account (but not vice versa). This implies that the attention paid to the "breakdown in the family" as an underlying cause of abuse and neglect may be to some degree misplaced. Child abuse and neglect may be more prevalent in single-parent families simply because they are likely to have lower family income than families with both parents in the home. These findings indicate that, when income is controlled for, single-parent families do not necessarily engender greater maltreatment risk. In fact, when the same resources are available to the family, children in mother-only households are less likely to be mal-treated—less likely to be sexually abused and less likely to be physically neglected. Given the same resources, children in single-parent households (whether mother-only or father-only households) were less likely to be physically abused or educationally neglected.

The remaining three factors, county metropolitan status, family size, and child's sex, had more limited relationships to risk and predicted three or fewer of the six maltreatment categories studied. Nevertheless, all three showed consistent patterns in the nature of their relationship to risk, with children in urban areas, only-children, and females at greater risk than their respective counterparts.

Study Strengths and Limitations

One of the most important advantages of the findings concerning predictors of risk for child abuse and neglect presented here is their nationally representative character and, hence, their generalizability. Much of the previous research on risk factors of child abuse and neglect was based largely on observations of nonrepresentative samples, which were identified only among the clientele who use different services (including CPS) and which typically had very limited geographical scope. In contrast, these analyses provide nationally representative estimates of the relationships between various characteristics and experiences of abuse and neglect.

Multi-factor logistic models predicting risk of maltreatment accounted for only 8 to 20 percent of the variance in the occurrence of abuse and neglect in this research. This probably stemmed from two methodological issues. First, it may derive from the limitations of the statistic, Harrell's R^2, used to gauge the degree of variance accounted for. Whereas there have been a number of proposals for methods of calculating a goodness-of-fit statistic for logistic models that is analogous to the R^2 statistic used in evaluating standard regression models, there are disadvantages with all the measures that have been proposed to date, and none is universally accepted or employed (Aldrich & Nelson, 1984; Hosmer & Lemeshow, 1989). One problem with Harrell's statistic is that it appears to depend on the overall likelihood of the event under study, in that when one attempts to account for a relatively rare event, the values of the statistic are substantially lower than the values obtained when the phenomenon under study is relatively common. Second, the relatively low estimates of the variance accounted for may, in part, be a valid reflection of the fact that many other characteristics of children and their family circumstances are important determinants of the risk of abuse and neglect beyond the few demographic characteristics examined in this study. Simple demographic characteristics may be significantly related to the likelihood of occurrence of maltreatment, but they do not appear to serve very well as risk markers for the underlying determinants of abuse and neglect.

CONCLUSIONS

The strength of family income as a risk factor for all categories of abuse and neglect suggests that the separation of income support and human services may be a bureaucratic fiction that is not in the best interests of the children who are at risk of abuse or neglect. Income support services include Aid for Dependent Children (AFDC), food stamps, the Special Supplemental Food Program for Women, Infants, and Children (WIC), job training, and other economic survival support services. Exploring methods by which income support and human services can be coordinated and better integrated with each other would be useful. When a family is reported for abuse or neglect and found to have an income dramatically below that needed for adequate functioning, intervention needs to explicitly include strategies geared toward enhancing their economic resources. Special demonstration projects could be funded to assess the relative feasibility and effectiveness of different approaches. These conclusions are consistent with the recent report of the U.S. Advisory Board on Child Abuse and Neglect (1991), which recommended that the federal government take measures to insure "the development of linkages with other service providers and community resources to ensure that children and families are receiving coordinated, integrated services" (p. 71).

There are a substantial number of interactions among important predictors across the maltreatment categories. In fact, interaction effects emerged in every category where analyses explicitly tested for their presence. Thus, simplistic, single-factor approaches to predicting abuse or neglect will be incorrect because they will not address the complexity of these events and their multiple determinants and modifiers. To be effective, policies and programs will need to acknowledge this complexity explicitly by taking multiple factors into account simultaneously rather than focusing on single issues or individual factors. Administrators and policy makers will need to build mechanisms for obtaining the multi-factor information base they will require to adequately design and monitor these complex policies and programs.

NOTES

1. The NIS-3 was conducted by Westat under Contract 105-91-1800 from NCCAN.

2. In addition to the definitional criteria concerning the harm or endangerment of the child, which are discussed here, there was also a countability requirement concerning the degree of credible evidence available to support the assumption

that the maltreatment had occurred as alleged. The survey design itself also imposed other criteria concerning what cases were "in-scope": the children had to meet age, residence, and custody status standards, the maltreatment had to meet specific requirements concerning date of occurrence and perpetrator's relation to the child. These and other details of the NIS-2 definitional standards are described in Sedlak, McFarland, and Rust (1987).

3. Exceptions were made in a few categories where the nature of the maltreatment itself was so egregious that harm could be inferred when direct evidence of it was not available. Those categories included abandonment, the more extreme types of sexual abuse, and the emotional abuse category of tying and binding or close confinement.

4. Straus and Gelles (1990) refer to it as the "1985 National Survey" and as the "National Family Violence Resurvey" to distinguish it from their earlier 1975 survey.

5. This included kicking, biting, punching, hitting (or trying to hit) with something, beating up, threatening with a knife or gun, or using a knife or gun.

6. Including all the acts subsumed under "severe violence" except hitting (or trying to hit) with something.

7. The actual extent of overlap of the cases identified in these two methodologies is unknown.

8. Exclusions for the other maltreatment categories ranged from 6-10%.

9. Because of the combined effects of stratification and clustering in complex sample designs, one cannot draw a general conclusion about the direction in which variances will be distorted. Moreover, the degree of distortion generally varies across different classification cells. Thus, the problem cannot be addressed by a simple strategy such as making an overall adjustment in the alpha level required for significance.

10. Thus, all physically abused children were counted in the category of physical abuse, even those who had also suffered countable abuse in other categories (e.g., those who had also been neglected, sexually abused, etc.).

11. Obviously, with so many cells, the reliability of cell-level estimates from these sources, particularly from the NIS-2, was very low. However, the data were examined in analyses that employed a multivariate modeling approach rather than analyze individual cells. As a result, reliable estimates at the cell level were not necessary; all that was necessary were unbiased and reliable estimates at the cell-aggregate levels regarding the one-way and two-way marginal totals. The available data were more than sufficient to support this need.

12. Moreover, not all children who attend private school should be assumed to live in higher income families. Between two-thirds and three-fourths of them attend Catholic schools that often provide sliding-scale tuition fees to accommodate children from lower-income families.

13. This pattern may reflect the fact that poverty-related deprivation does not constitute physical neglect by most CPS agencies' definitions (Berkowitz & Sedlak, 1993).

REFERENCES

Aldrich, J. H., & Nelson, F. D. (1984). *Linear probability, logit, and probit models*. Beverly Hills, CA: Sage.

American Association for Protecting Children. (1988). *Highlights of official child neglect and abuse reporting, 1986*. Denver, CO: American Humane Association.

Berkowitz, S., & Sedlak, A. J. (1993). *Study of high risk child abuse and neglect groups: State survey report*. Rockville, MD: Westat, Inc. Technical Report (Contract no. 105-89-1739). Washington, DC: National Center on Child Abuse and Neglect, Administration for Children and Families, U.S. Dept. of Health and Human Services.

Biller, H., & Solomon, R. (1986). *Child maltreatment and paternal deprivation: A manifesto for research, prevention, and treatment*. Lexington, MA: Lexington Books.

Deaux, K. (1976). Sex: A perspective on the attribution process. In J. H. Harvey, W. J. Ickes & R. F. Kidd (Eds.), *New directions in attribution research, Vol. 1* (pp. 336-352). Hillsdale, NJ: Lawrence Erlbaum Associates.

Flyer, P., & Mohadjer, L. (1989). *The WESLOG procedure*. Unpublished manuscript. Rockville, MD: Westat, Inc.

Garbarino, J. (1980). What kind of society permits child abuse? *Infant Mental Health Journal, 1*, 270-281.

Garbarino, J. (1981). An ecological approach to child maltreatment. In L. H. Pelton (Ed.), *The social context of child abuse and neglect*. New York: Human Sciences Press.

Harrell, F. E. (1986). The LOGIST Procedure. Chapter 23 in *SUGI supplemental library user's guide*. Version 5 Edition. SAS Institute: Cary, NC.

Hosmer, D. W., Jr., & Lemeshow, S. (1989). *Applied logistic regression*. New York: John Wiley & Sons.

Jones, E. D., & McCurdy, K. (1992). The links between types of maltreatment and demographic characteristics of children. *Child Abuse & Neglect, 16*, 201-215.

Kinard, E. M., & Klerman, L. V. (1980). Teenage parenting and child abuse. Are they related? *American Journal of Orthopsychiatry, 50*, 481-488.

Lee, E. S., Forthofer, R. N., & Lorimor, R. J. (1989). *Analyzing complex survey data*. Newbury Park, CA: Sage.

Lepkowski, J. M., Landis, J. R., Parsons, P. E., & Stehouwer, S. A. (1988). Statistical methodologies for analyzing a complex sample survey. Series A, Methodological Report No. 4. In National Center for Health Statistics, *National medical care utilization and expenditure survey*. DHHS Pub. No. 88-20004. Public Health Service. Washington, DC: U.S. Government Printing Office.

National Center for Education Statistics (1988, December). *Key statistics for private elementary and secondary education: School year 1988-89*. Washington, DC: Government Publication No. CS-89-067.

National Center on Child Abuse and Neglect (1981). *Study findings: National study of incidence and severity of child abuse and neglect*. Washington, DC: Department of Health, Education, and Welfare.

Pelton, L. (Ed.) (1981). *The social context of child abuse and neglect.* New York: Human Sciences Press.

Russell, A. B., & Trainor, C. M. (1984). *Trends in child abuse and neglect: A national perspective.* Denver, CO: American Association for Protecting Children, American Humane Association.

Sedlak, A. J. (1991a). *National incidence and prevalence of child abuse and neglect: 1988–Revised report.* Rockville, MD: Westat, Inc.

Sedlak, A. J. (1991b). *Supplementary analyses of data on the national incidence of child abuse and neglect–Revised report.* Rockville, MD: Westat, Inc. Technical Report to the American Enterprise Institute, Washington, DC.

Sedlak, A. J. (1993a, January). *Estimating the national prevalence of child abuse from sentinel data.* Paper presented at the winter conference of the American Statistical Association, Fort Lauderdale, FL.

Sedlak, A. J. (1993b). *Study of high risk child abuse and neglect groups: NIS-2 reanalysis report.* Rockville, MD: Westat, Inc. Technical Report (Contract no. 105-89-1739). Washington, DC: National Center on Child Abuse and Neglect, Administration for Children and Families, U.S. Dept. of Health and Human Services.

Sedlak, A. J., McFarland, J., & Rust, K. (1987). *Study of the national incidence and prevalence of child abuse and neglect: Report on data processing and analysis.* Technical Report (Contract no. 105-85-1702). Washington, DC: National Center on Child Abuse and Neglect, Office of Human Development Services, U.S. Department of Health and Human Services.

Skinner, C. J. (1989). Domain means, regression and multivariate analysis. In C. J. Skinner, D. Holt & T. M. F. Smith (Eds.), *Analysis of complex surveys* (chap. 3). New York: Wiley.

Smith, T. M. F. (1984). Present position and potential developments: Some personal views/sample surveys. *Journal of the Royal Statistical Society, 147* (part 2), 208-221.

Straus, M. A., & Gelles, R. J. (1986). Societal change and change in family violence from 1975 to 1985 as revealed by two national surveys. *Journal of Marriage and the Family, 48,* 465-479.

Straus, M. A., & Gelles, R. J. (1988a). How violent are American families? Estimates from the National Family Violence Resurvey and other studies. In G. T. Hotaling et al. (Eds.), *New directions in family violence research.* Newbury Park, CA: Sage.

Straus, M. A., & Gelles, R. J. (1988b). Violence in American families: How much is there and why does it occur? In C. C. Chilman, F. Cox & E. Nunnally (Eds.), *Families in trouble* (pp. 141-162). Newbury Park, CA: Sage.

Straus, M. A., & Gelles, R. J. (1990). *Physical violence in American families: Risk factors and adaptations to violence in 8,145 families.* New Brunswick, NJ: Transaction Publishers.

U.S. Advisory Board on Child Abuse and Neglect. (1991, September 15). *Creating caring communities: Blueprint for an effective federal policy on child abuse and neglect. Second report.* Washington, DC: Administration for Children and Families, U.S. Department of Health and Human Services.

U.S. Department of Health and Human Services. (1988). *Study findings: Study of the national incidence and prevalence of child abuse and neglect: 1988.* Washington, DC: U.S. Department of Health and Human Services Publication, Office of Human Development Services.

U.S. Department of Health, Education, and Welfare. (1977). *Child abuse and neglect programs: Practice and theory.* Washington, DC: U.S. Government Printing Office.

APPENDIX

TABLE A-1. Multi-factor Logistic Model to Predict the Occurrence of Physical Abuse

Parameter	Parameter Estimate	t
Intercept	−5.23856	−21.43
Age categories	0.24421	4.09
Black or Hispanic	−0.37504	−1.11
Income $15,000-29,999	−0.75037	−4.22
Income $30,000+	−2.89336	−8.17
2 to 3 children	−0.37216	−2.79
4 or more children	−0.25048	−1.06
Single parents	0.31873	0.67
Black/Hispanic x Age	0.16690	1.96
Single parent x Age	−0.20806	−1.76
Model R^2 Value	0.0819	
Model F-value	22.579 ** ($p < .005$)	
Model df	9,13	

TABLE A-2. Multi-factor Logistic Model to Predict the Occurrence of Sexual Abuse

Parameter	Parameter Estimate	t
Intercept	−6.76845	−12.17
Female	1.21550	2.72
Age categories	0.28048	2.99
"Other" races	1.11882	1.49
Income $15,000-29,999	−1.42888	−5.26
Income $30,000+	−3.28111	−6.83
Mother-only	−1.30187	−1.44
Father-only	−1.39673	−0.95
"Other" races x Age	−0.57852	−2.58
Mother-only x Age	0.13012	0.54
Father-only x Age	0.42413	1.13
Model R^2 Value	0.1195	
Model F-value	48.439 ** ($p < .005$)	
Model df	10,12	

TABLE A-3. Multi-factor Logistic Model to Predict the Occurrence of Physical Neglect

Parameter	Parameter Estimate	t
Intercept	−4.14428	−13.18
3-8 year olds	−0.39700	−1.31
9-14 year olds	0.19562	0.50
15-17 year olds	0.83387	0.58
Income $15,000-29,999	−1.89876	−3.55
Income $30,000+	−5.24725	−6.83
Other MSA & NonMSA	−1.31109	−2.18
Mother-only	−0.01197	−0.04
Father-only	0.15599	0.30
Mother-only x 3-8 yr olds	−0.78401	−2.43
Mother-only x 9-14 yr olds	−1.12620	−2.94
Mother-only x 15-17 yr olds	−1.45642	−2.35
Father-only x 3-8 yr olds	1.54030	2.70
Father-only x 9-14 yr olds	0.42254	0.71
Father-only x 15-17 yr olds	0.85520	1.35
Females	−0.06718	−0.25
Females x 15-17 yr olds	1.32303	1.01
Model R^2 Value	0.202	
Model F-value	7.483 * ($p < .025$)	
Model df	16,6	

TABLE A-4. Multi-factor Logistic Model to Predict the Occurrence of Emotional Maltreatment

Parameter	Parameter Estimate	t
Intercept	−7.40889	−26.12
Age categories	0.53820	8.06
"Other" races	1.49757	3.39
Income $15,000-29,999	-1.02085	−4.23
Income $30,000+	−2.55762	−6.39
Model R^2 Value	0.1201	
Model F-value	24.778 * * ($p < .005$)	
Model df	4,18	

TABLE A-5. Multi-factor Logistic Model to Predict the Occurrence of Multiple Maltreatment

Parameter	Parameter Estimate	t
Intercept	−6.50494	−8.10
Females	0.61677	1.71
Age categories	0.29579	2.04
Blacks & Hispanics	−0.70775	−1.25
"Other" races	1.64811	2.19
Income $15,000-29,999	−1.41213	−3.34
Income $30,000+	−2.79076	−5.04
Other MSA & Non-MSA	−1.11120	−1.45
Father-only	−1.52179	−1.44
"Other" races x Age	−1.10573	−3.67
Model R^2 Value	0.0954	
Model F-value	9.623 ** ($p < .005$)	
Model df	9,13	

TABLE A-6. Multi-factor Logistic Model to Predict the Occurrence of Educational Neglect[a]

Parameter	Parameter Estimate	Standard Error	t
Intercept	−3.40916	0.79979	−4.26
9-11 year olds	−0.71875	0.65961	−1.09
12-14 year olds	0.57907	0.64590	0.90
15-17 year olds	1.18165	0.77790	1.52
Hispanic	−1.27429	0.28229	−4.51
"Other" races	−2.15894	1.63740	−1.32
Income $15,000-29,999	−1.53964	0.29540	−5.21
Income $30,000+	−4.34692	1.00078	−4.34
Non-MSA	−1.26482	0.72016	−1.76
2-3 children	−0.35559	0.20226	−1.76
4 or more children	−0.18371	0.15131	−1.21
Single parents	−0.23430	0.63455	−0.37
Single parents x 9-11 yr olds	0.80254	0.92189	0.87
Single par's x 12-14 yr olds	−0.20929	0.80326	−0.26
Single par's x 15-17 yr olds	−1.51455	0.69083	−2.19

Model R^2 Value	0.1738
Model F-value	27.222 ** ($p < .005$)
Model df	14,8

[a]This model was based on 2,544 nonmaltreated cases (rather than the 3,798 nonmaltreated cases in the combined USBCCP survey data), because preschoolers were omitted from this analysis.

Child Homicide
in the City of Los Angeles:
An Epidemiologic Examination
of a Decade of Deaths

Susan B. Sorenson
Julie G. Peterson
Barbra A. Richardson

SUMMARY. Homicide is the only leading cause of child death which has increased in rank in the past 30 years. This investigation describes the deaths of 0-14 year olds which were classified as homicides by the Los Angeles Police Department from 1980 to 1989. Special focus is given to suspect-to-victim relationship and victim race/ethnicity because of their relevance to prevention and program planning. Family members were suspects in 49.8% of the cases (mother, 14.5%; father, 13.6%; mother's paramour, 8.5%; male and

Address correspondence to: Dr. Susan B. Sorenson, UCLA School of Public Health, 10833 Le Conte Avenue, Los Angeles, CA 90095-1772.

The authors would like to thank former Los Angeles Police Chief Darryl Gates and Captain William Gartland for making the homicide case summaries available. Special thanks to Officer David Strandgren of the Special Robbery Homicide Division for his assistance.

This work was supported by the Southern California Injury Prevention Research Center through a grant from the Centers for Disease Control (R49/CCR903622).

[Haworth co-indexing entry note]: "Child Homicide in the City of Los Angeles: An Epidemiologic Examination of a Decade of Deaths." Sorenson, Susan B., Julie G. Peterson, and Barbra Richardson. Co-published simultaneously in *Journal of Aggression, Maltreatment & Trauma* (Haworth Maltreatment & Trauma Press, an imprint of The Haworth Press, Inc.) Vol. 1, No. 1 (#1), 1997, pp. 189-205; and: *Violence and Sexual Abuse at Home: Current Issues in Spousal Battering and Child Maltreatment* (ed: Robert Geffner, Susan B. Sorenson, and Paula K. Lundberg-Love) Haworth Maltreatment & Trauma Press, an imprint of The Haworth Press, Inc., 1997, pp. 189-205. Single or multiple copies of this article are available for a fee from The Haworth Document Delivery Service [1-800-342-9678, 9:00 a.m. - 5:00 p.m. (EST). E-mail address: getinfo@haworth.com].

189

female caretaker, 11.1%; other family members, 2.1%). Few differences emerged among the Black, Hispanic, and non-Hispanic White child victims. Non-Hispanic White victims had the highest proportion (67.7%) and Hispanic victims had the lowest proportion (42.7%) of within-family suspects. Prevention implications include the need to focus on the actions of male caregivers and the observation that the substance and content of prevention programs (e.g., an emphasis on reducing blunt force trauma to young children) can be consistent across race/ethnic groups. *[Article copies available for a fee from The Haworth Document Delivery Service: 1-800-342-9678. E-mail address: getinfo@haworth.com]*

KEYWORDS. Child abuse, fatalities, risk factors, demographic factors, family violence

CHILD HOMICIDE IN THE CITY OF LOS ANGELES: AN EPIDEMIOLOGIC EXAMINATION OF A DECADE OF DEATHS

The deliberate killing of children typically is met with shock and horror. Nonetheless, homicide was the fourth leading cause of death for United States children 1 to 14 years old in 1994 (Singh, Kochanek, & MacDorman, 1996), and remains the leading cause of injury death from birth to one year of age (Waller, Baker, & Szocka, 1989). The purpose of the present investigation is three-fold: to update previous research by examining recent patterns of child homicide in a socioeconomically and ethnically diverse population; to describe homicides in which a family member was a suspect; and to compare patterns across racial/ethnic groups (Hispanic, Black, and non-Hispanic White children).

The identification of likely perpetrators can help lead to the development of appropriately-targeted prevention and intervention programs. By examining the relationship of the suspect to the victim, groups of children at risk and likely perpetrators can be identified. Knowledge about within-family homicides of children is especially important because families may be more accessible for prevention measures than other categories of victim-perpetrator relationships (e.g., stranger) and because children typically have extensive contact with family members (i.e., they have high levels of exposure and time at risk).

Some epidemiologic studies based upon law enforcement data (e.g., Goetting, 1990; Jason, 1983; Jason, Gilliland, & Tyler, 1983; Paulson & Rushforth, 1986) have included victim-suspect relationship as one of the variables of interest. Investigations using medical examiner files or death certificates typically do not contain data on the victim-suspect relationship (e.g., Muscat, 1988) although there are some exceptions (e.g., Abel, 1986; Copeland, 1985). Still other research has focused solely on homicides of children by their parents (e.g., Korbin, 1987; Silverman & Kennedy, 1988). The present research updates these investigations and examines patterns of child homicide with emphasis on the relationship of the suspect to the victim.

The present study also contributes to the literature by examining the phenomenon of child homicide among Hispanics. Hispanics are a rapidly growing ethnic group. The Hispanic population of the U.S. is expected to increase 173% from 1980 to 2000 as compared to a 131% increase for Blacks and a 113% increase for all Whites during the same time (calculated from data provided by the U.S. Bureau of the Census, *Current Population Reports*). The Hispanic population increase is related both to a relatively high fertility rate (U.S. Bureau of the Census, 1983) and immigration patterns. To our knowledge, this is the first population-based investigation of child homicide which includes significant numbers of Hispanic as well as Black and non-Hispanic White children.

METHOD

As part of a study of child homicide risk (Sorenson & Peterson, 1994; Sorenson, Richardson, & Peterson, 1993), data were abstracted from the case summaries of all child deaths from 1980 through 1989 which were investigated and filed as homicides by the Los Angeles Police Department (LAPD). Police department records were surveyed because they contain information about the victim, the suspect, and the homicide incident, a range of information typically not available in other data sources (e.g., coroner records). Data collected include: the sex, race/ethnicity, and age of the victim; the sex, race/ethnicity, and age of the suspect(s); the relationship of the suspect(s) to the victim; the context of the homicide; and the motive. The LAPD is responsible for the investigation of all homicides in the city of Los Angeles, a population base of nearly three million people. The present study included all cases in which the victim was 14 years old or younger.

Previous research on child homicide has focused on the imputed motive of the perpetrator, an approach that would not necessarily capture all of the family-related child homicides. For example, family member perpetrators often are studied in cases of a relatively narrowly defined type of homicide, fatal child abuse and neglect (e.g., Jason & Andereck, 1983). One problem with this approach is that the motive and context of the event are inferred by the law enforcement investigator through a hypothetical reconstruction of the event. Despite relative consistency in training, individual differences among officers may lead to unique interpretations of the suspect's motive. The death of a child at the hands of a parent may be attributed to motives as diverse as child abuse, child endangering, sex (i.e., sex was the primary motive), and murder/suicide.[1]

Copeland's (1985) study of child homicide deaths in Metro-Dade County (Florida) from 1956 to 1982 illustrates the potential problem of limiting an investigation to child abuse and neglect fatalities. In 152 homicides of persons under the age of 13, family members (biological fathers, mothers, step-fathers) perpetrated 66.1% of the child abuse and neglect fatalities and were responsible for 31.7% of the homicides attributed to other motives. Thus, if we focus primarily on child abuse and neglect fatalities, we would underestimate the magnitude of family-perpetrated homicide.

A broad social definition of "family" was adopted in order to include persons who were likely to assume a caretaking role upon occasion.[2] Suspects who were labelled "family members" included: biological parents, siblings, and grandparents; step-parents, step-siblings, and step-grandparents; common-law spouse or boy/girlfriend of the parent; and aunts, uncles, and half-siblings. The "known non-family" category included neighbors, friends, and gang members. "Strangers" included persons who were specified as not known to the victim. The "unknown" group included cases in which the relationship of the victim to the perpetrator was not specified and cases in which the relationship could not be ascertained from the report. The "no suspect" group included cases which specifically were designated as such. If any of the suspects was a family member, the relationship was categorized as "family." Crosstabulations, frequencies, and chi-square analyses were used to describe distributions of the data and to test for significant differences between the suspect-victim relationship groups.

RESULTS

A total of 246 deaths of children aged 0-14 years were investigated and filed as homicides by the LAPD from 1980 through 1989. Eleven of these deaths were in a single residential arson fire which killed 25 people. Due to the uniqueness of this event, these 11 cases were omitted from the analyses. The 235 child homicide cases are described in detail below.

Relationship of Suspect to Victim

Family members were the most common suspects (49.8%) in the homicides of children (see Table 1). In nearly one-tenth (9.4%) of the cases, there was no suspect. In another 11.1% of cases, neither the specific nor general relation of the suspect(s) to the victim was known. Although the

TABLE 1. Relationship of Suspect to Child Victim by Victim Age, City of Los Angeles, 1980-1989

Relation[a]	Victim age		
	0-4 years	5-14 years	0-14 years
Family[b]	93 (76.9%)	24 (21.0%)	117 (49.8%)
Mother only	27 (22.3%)	7 (6.1%)	34 (14.5%)
Father only	24 (19.9%)	8 (7.0%)	32 (13.6%)
Mother & Father	23 (19.0%)	3 (2.6%)	24 (11.1%)
Mother's paramour	16 (13.2%)	4 (93.5%)	20 (8.5%)
Other family	3 (2.5%)	2 (1.8%)	5 (2.1%)
Non-family[c]	9 (7.4%)	46 (40.4%)	55 (23.3%)
Rival gang	0 (0.0%)	37 (32.5%)	37 (15.7%)
Other	9 (7.4%)	9 (7.9%)	18 (7.7%)
Stranger	3 (2.5%)	12 (10.5%)	15 (6.4%)
Unknown[d]	12 (9.9%)	14 (12.3%)	26 (11.1%)
No suspect[e]	4 (3.3%)	18 (15.8%)	22 (9.4%)
Total	121 (100.0%)	114 (100.0%)	235 (100.0%)

[a]If any one of the three listed suspects included a family member, the relationship was classified as "Family."
[b]Includes: mother, father, step-parent, parent's common-law spouse, parent's boy/girlfriend, siblings, step-siblings, half-siblings, grandparents, aunt, uncle.
[c]Non-family cases in which the suspect was known to victim.
[d]Cases in which the suspect to victim relationship could not be determined.
[e]Cases in which the police did not identify a suspect.

specific relationship could not be determined in these cases, about one-third (38.5%) of the victims were either living with or in the suspect's care at the time of death. Fathers and mothers were about equally likely (13.6% and 14.5%, respectively) to be the sole suspect; the paramour of the victim's mother was the sole suspect in 8.5% of the cases. In another 11.1% of the cases both the female and male caregiver (e.g., mother and father, mother and her boyfriend) were suspects.

Victim Characteristics

Age. Consistent with previous research, over half (51.5%) of the child homicide victims were four years old or younger. When a child under the age of five was killed, a family member typically was the suspect (76.9%), whereas non-family members and strangers were suspects in 7.4% and 2.5% of the cases, respectively (see Table 1). A different pattern of relation to the suspect (family vs. other suspects) emerges for child victims based upon their age ($\chi^2(1, N = 213) = 63.2, p < .001$). Children four or fewer years old were 3.7 times as likely as those age five or older to be killed by family members.

Race/Ethnicity. Most of the child homicide victims were Black (51.5%) or Hispanic (31.9%); 13.2% were non-Hispanic White and 3.4% were of other ethnic/racial origins. As shown in Table 2, a family member was the most common suspect for all racial/ethnic groups. Although Black victims were most numerous, non-Hispanic Whites had the highest proportion of cases of family member suspects (67.7%). Blacks had a higher proportion of cases with unknown or no suspects than Hispanics and non-Hispanic Whites (24.8%, 16.0%, and 12.9%, respectively).

Sex. Most of the child homicide victims (64.7%) were boys. Within-family homicide victims were slightly more likely to be male than female (1.2:1.0). In contrast, the non-family and stranger groups had a 3.7:1.0 ratio of boy to girl victims (see Table 3). Therefore, a different pattern of victimization occurs for within-family homicides than for other child homicides ($\chi^2(1, N = 213) = 9.4, p = .002$). If a girl child is killed, she is 1.5 times as likely as a boy child to have been killed by a family member.

Suspects

Sex. For the 235 victims, there were a total of 322 suspects. Data were collected on the first three suspects listed in each case, resulting in information on 303 suspects. As shown in Table 4, there were nearly three times as many male as female suspects (2.9:1.0). The pattern of data on

TABLE 2. Relationship of Suspect to Child Victim by Victim Race, City of Los Angeles, 1980-1989

Relation[a]	Victim race/ethnicity			
	Black	Hispanic	White	Total
Family	59 (48.8%)	32 (42.7%)	21 (67.7%)	112 (47.7%)
Non-family	25 (20.7%)	25 (33.3%)	4 (12.9%)	54 (23.0%)
Stranger	7 (5.8%)	6 (8.0%)	2 (6.5%)	15 (6.4%)
Unknown	15 (12.4%)	7 (9.3%)	3 (9.7%)	25 (10.6%)
No suspect	15 (12.4%)	5 (6.7%)	1 (3.2%)	21 (8.9%)
Total[b]	121 (100.1%)	75 (100.0%)	31 (100.0%)	227 (96.6%)[c]

[a]Same relationship category definitions as in Table 1.
[b]Columns may not sum to 100.0% due to rounding.
[c]The remaining 8 victims (3.4%) include Asian, Filipino, East Indian, and Native American children.

TABLE 3. Relationship of Suspect to Child Victim by Victim Sex, City of Los Angeles, 1980-1989

Relation[a]	Victim sex		
	Male	Female	Total
Family	64 (42.1%)	53 (63.9%)	117 (49.8%)
Non-family	43 (28.3%)	12 (14.5%)	55 (23.3%)
Stranger	12 (7.9%)	3 (3.6%)	15 (6.4%)
Unknown	17 (11.2%)	9 (10.8%)	26 (11.1%)
No suspect	16 (10.5%)	6 (7.2%)	22 (9.4%)
Total	152 (100.0%)	83 (100.0%)	235 (100.0%)

[a]Same relationship category definitions as in Table 1.

relation of suspect to victim varies by suspect sex ($\chi^2(1, N = 303) = 48.1$, $p < .001$). Although more men than women were suspects overall, when a woman is a suspect in the homicide of a child, the child is 2.2 times more likely to be a family member.

Motive. Child abuse or neglect was the primary motive in over one-

TABLE 4. Relationship of Suspect(s) to Child Victim by Suspect Sex, City of Los Angeles, 1980-1989

Relation[a]	Suspect sex		Total
	Men	Women	
Family	85 (37.8%)	65 (83.3%)	150 (49.5%)
Non-family	88 (39.1%)	2 (2.6%)	90 (29.7%)
Stranger	23 (10.2%)	1 (1.3%)	24 (7.9%)
Unknown	29 (12.9%)	10 (12.6%)	39 (12.9%)
Total	225 (100.0%)	78 (100.0%)	303 (100.0%)[b]

[a]Same relationship category definitions as in Table 1.
[b]Exceeds case total of 235 as 146 cases had one suspect, 43 cases had two suspects, 16 cases had three suspects, and 8 cases had more than three suspects. No suspects were identified in 22 of the cases.

third (34.9%) of the cases. Family members were suspects in most (85.4%) of these child abuse or neglect cases. Additionally, family members were suspects in a number of the cases (30.7%) which were attributed to causes other than abuse or neglect (e.g., murder-suicide, sex).

Event Characteristics

Location. As shown in Table 5, the victim's home was the most common (55.7%) site of the homicide. A great majority (87.2%) of the homicides in which family members were suspects occurred in the victim's home. An additional 7.7% of all killings occurred in the home or yard of another. A total of 22.1% of the child victims were killed in a street or alley. Most (59.6%) street homicides were by non-family members, very few (1.7%) family members were killed in the street.

Mode of Death. Bludgeoning and gunshot wounds were the most common causes of death for child homicide victims (34.5% and 36.6%, respectively). Family members were much less likely than others to use a firearm (9.4% vs. 78.2%, respectively, $\chi^2(1, N = 213) = 75.8, p < .001$). Family members were three times as likely to beat or bludgeon a child to death as all other cases in which a suspect was identified (53.0% vs.

TABLE 5. Relationship of Suspect to Child Victim by Location of the Homicide, City of Los Angeles, 1980-1989

Relation[a]	Location					
	victim's home/yard	another home/yard	street/alley	other	n.s.[b]	total[c]
Family	102 (87.2%)	4 (3.4%)	2 (1.7%)	2 (1.7%)	7 (6.0%)	117 (100.0%)
Non-family	7 (12.7%)	6 (10.9%)	31 (56.4%)	5 (9.1%)	6 (10.9%)	55 (100.0%)
Stranger	4 (26.7%)	1 (6.7%)	7 (46.7%)	2 (13.3%)	1 (6.7%)	15 (100.1%)
Unknown	13 (50.0%)	6 (23.1%)	2 (7.7%)	1 (3.9%)	4 (15.4%)	26 (100.1%)
No suspect	5 (22.7%)	1 (4.6%)	10 (45.5%)	3 (13.6%)	3 (13.6%)	22 (100.0%)
Total	131 (55.7%)	18 (7.7%)	52 (22.1%)	13 (5.5%)	21 (8.9%)	235 (99.9%)

[a]Same relationship category definitions as in Table 1.
[b]Not specified
[c]Columns may not sum to 100.0% due to rounding.

197

17.7%, respectively, $\chi^2(1, N = 213) = 28.1, p < .001$). Table 6 shows the relationship of the victim to the suspect by the mode of death.

Within-Family Homicides by Race/Ethnicity

Patterns in the data indicate that Black and Hispanic children may be more likely than non-Hispanic Whites to have been killed by a non-family member. This finding is of borderline statistical significance ($p < .06$). As demonstrated in Table 2, a family member was the most common suspect for all racial/ethnic groups.

There were no statistically significant findings when examining race/ethnicity by victim age, victim sex, suspect sex, motive, location of death, and mode of death. Several findings may be of interest, although not statistically significant. One-fourth (23.8%) of the non-Hispanic White victims were killed by females compared to 42.4% of the Black and 43.8% of the Hispanic victims. Although Hispanics accounted for only 28.6% of the within-family child homicide victims, they accounted for 54.6% of the homicide victims in murder/suicides (27.3% and 18.2% of the murder/suicide victims were non-Hispanic White and Black, respectively). Most children (42.0%) were killed by being hit with hands or feet; a majority of the Hispanic children (56.3%) were killed this way compared to 39.0% of the Black and 28.6% of the non-Hispanic White children.

DISCUSSION

Using a social definition of family, family members were suspects in over one-half of the deaths of children which were classified as homicides by the Los Angeles Police Department from 1980 to 1989. Mothers and fathers were about equally likely to be the sole suspect in the death of a child (14.5% and 13.6%, respectively). The paramour of the child's mother was the sole suspect in 8.5% of the cases. The female and male caregiver (e.g., mother and father, mother and common-law husband) both were suspects in another 11.1% of the cases. Previous epidemiologic studies (Blaser, 1983-85; Copeland, 1985; Jason et al., 1983) have found remarkably similar patterns of suspect-to-victim relationship; that is, relatively equal percentages of the child homicides are committed by mothers, fathers, and intimates of the mothers. The one exception to an otherwise uniform pattern of similar numbers of homicides committed by fathers and by mothers (Abel, 1986) may be due to the fact that only about one-half of the medical examiner's files reviewed by Abel contained information on

TABLE 6. Relationship of Suspect to Child Victim by Victim Mode of Death, City of Los Angeles, 1980-1989

Relation[a]	Victim mode of death					
	BFT[b]	Firearm	Pierce[c]	Asphyx[d]	Other[e]	Total[f]
Family	62 (53.0%)	11 (9.4%)	13 (11.1%)	9 (7.7%)	22 (18.8%)	117 (100.0%)
Non-family	7 (12.7%)	43 (78.2%)	3 (5.5%)	0 (0.0%)	2 (3.6%)	55 (100.0%)
Stranger	1 (6.7%)	12 (80.0%)	1 (6.7%)	0 (0.0%)	1 (6.7%)	15 (100.1%)
Unknown	9 (34.6%)	9 (34.6%)	2 (7.7%)	1 (3.9%)	5 (19.2%)	26 (100.0%)
No suspect	2 (9.1%)	11 (50.0%)	2 (9.1%)	3 (13.6%)	4 (18.2%)	22 (100.0%)
Total	81 (34.5%)	86 (36.6%)	21 (8.9%)	13 (5.5%)	34 (14.5%)	235 (100.0%)

[a]Same relationship category definitions as in Table 1.
[b]Blunt force trauma
[c]Piercing or cutting instrument
[d]Asphyxiation
[e]Fire, burn, malnourishment, exposure, other
[f]Rows may not sum to 100.0% due to rounding.

offenders. Thus, research to date indicates that the mother's male intimate (husband or boyfriend) is nearly twice as likely as the mother to be a suspect in a case of child homicide.

Child homicide cases in which a family member was a suspect are distinct from those in which the suspect was not related to the victim. Homicides with family member suspects have young victims (0-4 years old) who are equally likely to be male or female, are most often killed in the home by blunt force trauma, and in two thirds of the deaths the male caretaker is suspected of committing the homicide. Child homicide cases in which the suspect is not related to the victim have older victims (5-14 years) who are three times more likely to be male than female, and are most often killed by an acquaintance or a stranger in a street or alley with a firearm. Characteristics which do not statistically differentiate family from non-family member suspect-victim relationship include the number of suspects, number of victims, and motive.

Children 0-4 years old were more likely than 5-14 year olds to be killed by family members than non-family members. Neonates, infants, and toddlers are biologically vulnerable to certain caretaker behaviors which are not likely to cause damage to an older child (e.g., being shaken). Thus, this age-related finding may account for blunt force trauma being the mechanism of death for over one-half of the children in which a family member was a suspect.

Family members were the most common suspects in all cases of child homicide, regardless of race or ethnicity (67.7% for non-Hispanic Whites vs. 48.8% for Blacks and 42.7% for Hispanics). The large percentage of homicides of non-Hispanic White children with family member suspects may reflect less victimization by other persons. For example, non-Hispanic White children are less likely to be victims of gang-related homicide, which accounts for a significant minority of the non-family homicides of Black and Hispanic children.

Race/ethnicity differences in mode of death were not statistically significant although trends indicate that Hispanic children are more likely to be killed by hands and fists, and to be victims of a murder/suicide. Statistically non-significant findings also indicate that Hispanic and Black children were more likely to be killed by a woman than non-Hispanic White children. Of interest is the trend for the suspect to be a non-family member in the homicide of Black and Hispanic children. Potential differences by race/ethnicity in the relation of the suspect to the child victim deserve further investigation as this information is crucial in developing and directing appropriate prevention efforts.

Data Source Strengths and Limitations

Los Angeles Police Department records, the data source for this research, provided information about child deaths for a large and diverse population base. The records contained a range of information about the victim, the suspect, and the incident itself which is not available through other data sources such as coroner reports. Furthermore, the records included cases of child death for which intention was most established; if a child was believed to have been killed intentionally by another person, the case was filed as a police homicide case. Thus, police department records were the best way to obtain data about the victim, suspect, and incident when a child was killed intentionally.

Although the population base is large and ethnically diverse, these findings may have limited generalizability to other parts of the United States and to other groups. Most of the Hispanics in Los Angeles are of Mexican heritage and, although Mexican Americans comprise the largest subgroup of Hispanics in the U.S. (U.S. Bureau of the Census, 1981), investigations of child homicide among those of Cuban, Puerto Rican, Central American, and additional Latin origins are needed to assess the applicability of these findings to other Hispanic subgroups. This investigation precluded the possibility that observed differences could be attributed to regional variations by investigating ethnic/racial group differences within the same geographic area (O'Carroll & Mercy, 1989).

As is increasingly admitted (e.g., Newlands & Emery, 1991), a portion of child deaths attributed to natural or accidental causes are likely to be homicides. In 1978, Los Angeles County established ICAN (the Interagency Council on Child Abuse and Neglect) and began to hold meetings of the agencies involved in child deaths which may have been intentional. Representatives of the Department of Children's Services, Medical Examiner's Office, Police Department and Sheriff's Office, Probation, District Attorney, Department of Mental Health, Fire Department (paramedic services), Office of Education, and local hospitals continue to meet monthly to review and discuss cases of suspicious child death. Collaborative interagency efforts such as this may serve to identify more fully the scope of homicide of children. (For a review of the work of child death review teams across the U.S., see Durfee, Gellert, & Tilton-Durfee, 1992). In recognizing the grim possibility that police and coroner data may not identify all cases of child homicide, we acknowledge that the patterns of child homicide found in this and other investigations may not accurately depict the homicide of children.

CONCLUSIONS AND IMPLICATIONS

Family members are the most likely suspects in a child homicide when the victim is very young, whereas extrafamilial perpetration is more common at older ages. Because over one-half of the homicides of 0-14 year olds occur to children under the age of five, successful prevention and intervention with family members is likely to reduce homicides of young children substantially. Young children are more physically vulnerable than their older counterparts. (For an analysis of children's homicide risk by developmental level see Crittenden and Craig, 1990). If these children are victims of single violent episodes, traditional social service intervention is likely to have less preventive impact simply because such cases are not brought to their attention until it is too late (see Sorenson and Peterson, 1994, for a case control study of child protective service history among child homicide victims).

Single suspects and single victims may be characteristics of the general act of homicide, regardless of age of the victim, in that adult homicides also reflect this pattern. When a victim is quite young, a sole family member may be the suspect because: (1) severe aggression toward a child may be inhibited in the presence of another adult; (2) another adult may serve as an escape valve for the caretaker by providing back-up care or other sources of support; (3) another adult may become the primary target of aggression, as in the case of wife battering; and (4) another adult may intervene on the child's behalf.

The relationship of the victim to the suspect is an important component for both understanding and preventing child homicide. When homicide perpetration comes from within the victim's own family, a history of relational patterns and external events that may affect relational patterns can be identified. Fathers and the paramour of the mother (most often the mother's boyfriend or step-father of her child) are suspects in child homicide cases more often than mothers. Nevertheless, both research reports and intervention programs focus disproportionately on the maternal offender (e.g., Korbin, 1987; Lesnik-Oberstein, 1986; Lomis, 1986). The present study and other investigations of both fatal and nonfatal cases of severe child abuse (e.g., Bergman, Larsen, & Mueller, 1986) indicate that the data do not directly support a program emphasis on mothers as perpetrators.

Abuse prevention activities (e.g., Amundson, 1989; Taylor & Beauchamp, 1988) also tend to focus on the mother rather than the adult male intimates of the mother. Concentration on the mother may be due to several reasons including: the fact that the mother often is the primary caretaker and strengthening her ability to protect and care for her child is crucial to the child's well-being; mothers, not fathers, typically are the ones who seek health care services; and, homicide by a mother, rather than a father or male intimate of the mother, may be perceived as a more severe transgression of social and biological norms and, thus, may be more closely scrutinized. Prevention programs, therefore, may effectively reduce what otherwise would be higher rates of child homicide by mothers and other women. Alternatively, prevention efforts may be misplaced by directing the attention toward women. Hence, both researchers and practitioners need to take into account more fully the research findings about who commits and is suspected of committing child homicide. Mass media campaigns aimed at men who physically abuse children is one example of redirected prevention efforts.

As with other health, social, and criminal justice activities, prevention and intervention programs designed to reduce fatal and nonfatal violence toward children need to be culturally-specific and culturally-sensitive. It is important to note that risk patterns of within-family homicide appear to be similar across race/ethnicity although rates differ by age and race/ethnicity (Sorenson et al., 1993). Thus, whereas prevention activities need to be tailored to specific audiences, research findings lend support to the idea that the substance and content of the programs (e.g., an emphasis on reducing blunt force trauma) can be consistent across groups. Potential differences by race/ethnicity in the relation of the suspect to the child victim deserve further investigation as this information is crucial in targeting prevention efforts.

NOTES

1. The terms child abuse, child endangering, and murder/suicide are socially-defined labels for specific behaviors and their consequences. These terms are not impulses, drives, or intentions and, thus, do not meet the typical definition of motive. These examples of motives were drawn from police records and reflect the actual practice of a law enforcement agency.

2. Some research indicates that a social definition of family more accurately describes patterns of relatedness than biological definitions especially in some minority communities (for a review of this and related issues, see Bass, Wyatt, & Powell, 1982).

REFERENCES

Abel, E. L. (1986). Childhood homicide in Erie County, New York. *Pediatrics*, *77*, 709-713.

Amundson, M. J. (1989). Family crisis care: A home based intervention program for child abuse. *Issues in Mental Health Nursing*, *10*, 285.

Bass, B., Wyatt G. E., & Powell, G. J. (1982). *The Afro-American family.* New York: Grune & Stratton.

Bergman, A. B., Larsen, R. M., & Mueller, B. A. (1986). Changing spectrum of serious child abuse. *Pediatrics, 77,* 113-116.

Blaser, M. J. (1983-85). Epidemiologic characteristics of child homicides in Atlanta, 1970-1980. *Pediatrician, 12,* 63-67.

Copeland, A. R. (1985). Homicide in childhood. The Metro-Dade County experience from 1956 to 1982. *American Journal of Forensic Medicine and Pathology, 6,* 21-24.

Crittenden, P. M., & Craig, S. E. (1990). Developmental trends in the nature of child homicide. *Journal of Interpersonal Violence, 5,* 202-216.

Durfee, M. J., Gellert, G. A., & Tilton-Durfee, D. (1992). Origins and clinical relevance of child death review teams. *Journal of the American Medical Association, 267,* 3172-3175.

Goetting, A. (1990). Child victims of homicide: A portrait of their killers and the circumstances of their deaths. *Violence and Victims, 5,* 287-293.

Jason, J. (1983). Child homicide spectrum. *American Journal of Diseases of the Child, 137,* 578-581.

Jason, J., & Andereck, N. D. (1983). Fatal child abuse in Georgia: The epidemiology of severe physical child abuse. *Child Abuse and Neglect, 7,* 1-9.

Jason, J., Gilliland, J. C., & Tyler, C. W. (1983). Homicide as a cause of pediatric mortality in the United States. *Pediatrics, 72,* 191-197.

Korbin, J. E. (1987). Incarcerated mothers' perceptions of their fatally maltreated children. *Child Abuse and Neglect, 11,* 397-407.

Lesnik-Oberstein, M. (1986). Multitherapeutic approach to clinical treatment for a child at risk for maternal filicide. *Child Abuse and Neglect, 10,* 407-410.

Lomis, M. J. (1986). Maternal filicide: A preliminary examination of culture and victim sex. *International Journal of Law and Psychiatry, 9,* 503-506.

Muscat, J. E. (1988). Characteristics of childhood homicide in Ohio, 1974-1985. *American Journal of Public Health, 78,* 822-824.

Newlands, M., & Emery, J. S. (1991). Child abuse and cot deaths. *Child Abuse and Neglect, 15,* 275-278.

O'Carroll, P. W., & Mercy, J. A. (1989). Regional variation in homicide rates: Why is the *west* so violent? *Violence and Victims, 4,* 17-25.

Paulson, J. A., & Rushforth, N. B. (1986). Violent death in children in a metropolitan county: Changing patterns of homicide, 1958 to 1982. *Pediatrics, 78,* 1013-1020.

Silverman, R. A., & Kennedy, L. W. (1988). Women who kill their children. *Violence and Victims, 3,* 113-127.

Singh, G. K., Kochanek, K. D., & MacDorman, M. F. (1996). Advance report of final mortality statistics, 1994. Monthly Vital Statistics Report; Vol 45, No 3, suppl. Hyattsville, MD: National Center for Health Statistics, 1996. (Calculated from Table 7).

Sorenson, S. B., & Peterson, J. G. (1994). Traumatic child death and maltreatment history. *American Journal of Public Health, 84,* 623-627.

Sorenson, S. B., Richardson, B. A., & Peterson, J. G. (1993). Race/ethnicity patterns in homicides of 0-14 year olds in Los Angeles, 1980-89. *American Journal of Public Health, 83,* 725-727.

Taylor, D. K., & Beauchamp, C. (1988). Hospital-based primary prevention strategy in child abuse: A multi-level needs assessment. *Child Abuse and Neglect, 12,* 343-354.

U.S. Bureau of the Census. (1981). *1980 census of population: Vol.1. Characteristics of the population. Chapter B. General population characteristics. Part 1. United States Summary.* Washington, D.C.: U.S. Government Printing Office.

U.S. Bureau of the Census. (1983). *Census of the Population: 1980. General social and economic characteristics.* PC80-1C-1 (Table 166). Washington, D.C.: U.S. Government Printing Office.

U.S. Bureau of the Census. *Current Population Reports,* Series P-25, Nos. 995, 1018, 1045, and 1057.

Waller, A. E., Baker, S. P., & Szocka, A. (1989). Childhood injury deaths: National analysis and geographic variations. *American Journal of Public Health, 79,* 310-315.

Physical Abuse and Childhood Disability: Risk and Treatment Factors

Robert T. Ammerman

SUMMARY. Several authors have hypothesized that children with disabilities are at increased risk for physical abuse. Such a finding would be consistent with current ecological models, which posit that certain child characteristics (e.g., behavior problems) in combination with other risk factors can lead to abuse. The paucity of research in this area makes it difficult to draw firm conclusions at this time. However, the few studies conducted suggest that child characteristics play a minor role in the etiology of abuse. Despite the lack of evidence indicating that children with disabilities are at significantly greater risk for abuse than their nondisabled peers, the presence of a disability raises some unique issues in the identification, assessment, and treatment of special needs children. This article reviews the literature linking abuse and disability as a risk factor. In addition, impediments encountered in the assessment and treatment of abused children with disabilities and their families are discussed and guidelines

Address correspondence to: Robert T. Ammerman, PhD, Allegheny General Hospital, 320 East North Avenue, Pittsburgh, PA 15212 (e-mail: rammerma@ asri.edu).

Preparation of this manuscript was facilitated in part by grant Nos. H133G10008 and H133A40007 from the National Institute on Disabilities and Rehabilitation Research, U.S. Department of Education, and a grant from the Vira I. Heinz Endowment. However, the opinions reflected herein do not necessarily reflect the position of policy of the U.S. Department of Education or the Vira I. Heinz Endowment, and no official endorsement should be inferred.

[Haworth co-indexing entry note]: "Physical Abuse and Childhood Disability: Risk and Treatment Factors." Ammerman, Robert T. Co-published simultaneously in *Journal of Aggression, Maltreatment & Trauma* (Haworth Maltreatment & Trauma Press, an imprint of The Haworth Press, Inc.) Vol. 1, No. 1 (#1), 1997, pp. 207-224; and: *Violence and Sexual Abuse at Home: Current Issues in Spousal Battering and Child Maltreatment* (ed: Robert Geffner, Susan B. Sorenson, and Paula K. Lundberg-Love) Haworth Maltreatment & Trauma Press, an imprint of The Haworth Press, Inc., 1997, pp. 207-224. Single or multiple copies of this article are available for a fee from The Haworth Document Delivery Service [1-800-342-9678, 9:00 a.m. - 5:00 p.m. (EST). E-mail address: getinfo@haworth.com].

for practice are presented. *[Article copies available for a fee from The Haworth Document Delivery Service: 1-800-342-9678. E-mail address: getinfo@haworth.com]*

KEYWORDS. Child abuse, maltreatment, child characteristics, child assessment, treatment issues

Child abuse has become one of the major societal problems facing children and families in the United States. Reports of child maltreatment (comprising physical abuse, neglect, sexual abuse, and emotional abuse) in general, and physical abuse in particular, are on the rise. For example, in 1993 there were almost 2 million reports of child maltreatment (National Center on Child Abuse and Neglect, 1995). Moreover, it is widely believed that many cases of child abuse go undetected, and that official reports represent only "the tip of the iceberg."

Recently, there has been a heightened interest in the maltreatment of children with disabilities. This interest stems in part from the belief, for reasons presented in subsequent sections, that some disabled children are at increased risk for abuse. Unfortunately, very little empirical research has been conducted on abuse and disability. The incidence of disability in abused children is inconclusive, with studies reporting rates of 3%-70% (see Ammerman, Van Hasselt, & Hersen, 1988). Likewise, the documented occurrence of abuse in disabled populations ranges from 3% to 40% (Ammerman et al., 1988). No investigation has examined directly whether children with disabilities are at higher risk for abuse than their nondisabled peers. However, there is little doubt that the unique features of disability influence efforts in treatment and prevention.

This review examines several aspects of disability and abuse. First, theoretical models of child abuse are presented, and the role of disability in these formulations is discussed. Second, hypothesized mechanisms of increased abuse risk in disabled children are critically examined. And third, assessment and treatment of families implicated in the abuse of their disabled child are addressed, and specific treatment approaches are presented.

THEORETICAL MODELS:
IMPLICATIONS FOR THE ROLE OF THE CHILD IN ABUSE

As research has increasingly documented the complexity of child abuse, models describing the etiology (or causes) of abuse have also become more detailed and sophisticated. It is now universally acknowledged that child abuse is a multidetermined phenomenon in which individual, situational, and societal forces mix and interact to bring about violence. Within this context, it has been hypothesized that the child, or at least certain characteristics in some children, can contribute to bringing about abuse in selected circumstances.

Early formulations of child abuse emphasized single cause explanations (see Table 1 for an overview of predominant child abuse models). The psychopathology model focused on parental personality disorders, psychosis, sadistic traits, or other forms of mental illness as primary determinants of abuse. This orientation partly grew out of case reports describing the newly recognized "battered child syndrome" (Kempe, Silverman, Steele, Droegemueller, & Silver, 1962), the majority of which represented the most severe cases of abuse. More recent empirical research, however, has shown that only about 10% of abusive parents exhibit documented psychopathology or psychiatric disorders (Wolfe, 1985). Indeed, there is no specific syndrome or constellation of symptoms or characteristics that uniquely typifies the abusive parent.

Sociological models underscore the importance of social factors in causing abuse. Included here are poverty, crowding, chronic unemployment, educational underachievement, neighborhood violence, racism, and cultural acceptance of violence, to name a few. Evidence supporting the role of social factors is compelling. Crowding is strongly associated with abuse (Garbarino & Crouter, 1978), and abuse is more prevalently reported among lower socioeconomic groups (Masten & Garmezy, 1985). Once again, however, social influences are neither necessary nor sufficient to cause abuse; the majority of families in poverty do not abuse their children, and abuse occurs in all aspects of society.

The social-situational model, introduced in the mid-1970s (Parke & Collmer, 1975), stresses the interaction of individual and situational contributors to abuse. According to this formulation, parent and child factors combine during certain high-risk situations (e.g., difficult bedtime) to trigger an abusive incident. Empirical support for this view is impressive. Abuse is most likely to occur during times of discipline (Kadushin & Martin, 1981). Also, Reid and colleagues (e.g., Reid, Patterson, & Loeber, 1982) have shown that mutual aversive interchanges between abusive parents and their children serve to escalate conflict, sometimes to the point of physical violence.

The social-situational model fueled interest in multidimensional formulations, in which different forces interact, eventually resulting in abuse. These "integrative" models are exemplified by the ecological model (e.g., Belsky,

TABLE 1. Models of Child Maltreatment and Their Distinctive Features

Model		Distinctive Features
Traditional Models		
PSYCHOPATHOLOGY	(e.g., Steele & Pollock, 1968)	Focuses on parental psychiatric disorders as the cause of maltreatment.
SOCIAL-CULTURAL	(e.g., Gelles, 1973)	Emphasizes the role of stress engendered by poverty, unemployment, and educational disadvantage.
SOCIAL-SITUATIONAL	(Parke & Collmer, 1975)	Views child abuse as stemming from the combined contributions of parental, child, and situational characteristics.
Integrative Models		
ECOLOGICAL	(Belsky, 1980)	Delineates four levels of causative influence in the etiology of abuse and neglect: Ontogenetic, Microsystem, Exosystem, and Macrosystem.
TRANSACTIONAL	(Cicchetti & Rizley, 1981)	Proposes the interaction between potentiating and compensating factors that increase or decrease the likelihood of maltreatment, respectively. Distinguishes between enduring and transient factors that differentially affect risk for maltreatment on a temporal dimension.
TRANSITIONAL	(Wolfe, 1987)	Hypothesizes three stages of parent-child interactions that progressively heighten the probability of abuse. Destabilizing factors facilitate escalation of conflict, while compensatory factors prevent passage into other stages.

From Ammerman, R. T. (1990). Etiological models of maltreatment: A behavioral perspective. *Behavior Modification, 14,* 230-254. Reprinted with permission.

1980). In this viewpoint, four levels of sequentially embedded and mutually interactive spheres of influence and causation are proposed: ontogenetic, microsystem, exosystem, and macrosystem. Ontogenetic factors consist of characteristics of the individual that may contribute to abuse, such as low parental intellectual functioning or difficult infant temperament. The microsystem comprises dyadic and family aspects, such as marital distress or lack of social support. The exosystem refers to the community, in which absence of important service providers or presence of neighborhood crime can have a negative impact. Finally, the macrosystem is composed of societal forces, such as cultural sanctioning of violence.

Two additional integrative models, both derived in part from the ecological formulation, bear mentioning. The transactional model (Cicchetti & Rizley, 1981) delineates potentiating and compensatory factors, which heighten or lower the probability of abuse, respectively. Thus, extensive social support and steady employment can serve as buffers that prevent the parent from resorting to physical violence in the face of other stressors. This model further stipulates that some factors are stable (e.g., parental experience of abuse in childhood), while others are transient, or in a state of flux (e.g., stressful life events). The transactional model (Wolfe, 1987) of abuse adopts an ecological perspective, and acknowledges the interaction of potentiating and compensatory factors in precipitating abuse. It goes on to hypothesize that families progressively move through phases that increase the likelihood of violent conflict. According to this view, families may be at risk for abuse for some time before crossing into the abusive stage. With intervention, families may continue to be viewed as being at risk even though they are not engaging actively in abuse.

Comment

The models described above provide a framework for understanding the complex ways in which abuse develops. The strength of the integrative models is that they acknowledge that maltreatment is multidetermined, growing out of the interaction of several forces. A limitation of these models, however, is that they fail to explain how such causative influences combine to bring about abuse. Understanding the processes that directly lead to abuse is, of course, critical in designing prevention and treatment programs.

The relevance of these theoretical models to the abuse of children with disabilities is clear. Social situational and integrative models suggest that certain childhood factors, such as severe behavior problems, difficult temperament, or other characteristics that add to household stress, can play a role in bringing about abuse. However, it is essential to note that childhood contributions play only a relatively minor role in abuse; research has documented that parental and societal factors exert a more powerful influence than child characteristics (see Ammerman, 1991). Thus, it is now thought that some disabled children are at risk for abuse only in those families that are already vulnerable to perpetrating abuse. However, even a small causative role for disability helps us understand the complex relationship between abuse and disability, and has important implications for assessment and treatment.

ASSOCIATION BETWEEN ABUSE AND DISABILITY

The association between abuse and disability has been a source of debate for several decades. For some (e.g., Helfer, 1973), it was clear that disability (or, more precisely, characteristics of some disabled children) heightened risk for abuse. Others (e.g., Martin & Beezley, 1974) disagreed, arguing that disabled children with more overt handicapping conditions were actually at lower risk for abuse, in that parents would attribute disruptive behavior to the disabling condition and not to purposeful intent on the part of the child. Still others (e.g., Ammerman et al., 1988) have pointed out that, in the absence of empirical data specifically investigating abuse in disabled children, conclusive statements about the relationship between abuse and disability cannot be made at this time.

Several converging hypotheses point toward increased risk for abuse in disabled children. Risk may be manifested via three pathways: disruptions in caregiver-infant attachment, stress, and increased vulnerability. A caveat is in order, however, before moving on to these topics, which are described below. Research in this area is not strong and many of the studies are plagued by serious methodological problems. Critical examinations of research in this area are made by Ammerman et al. (1988) and Starr, Dietrich, Fischoff, Ceresnie, and Zweier (1984).

Child Risk Factors Associated with Maltreatment

Several investigations have found a connection between early mother-infant separation and physical abuse. Low birthweight, prematurity, and medical complications at birth are three factors that can contribute to early mother-infant separation. For example, Klein and Stern (1971) found that 23% of one abused sample were low-birthweight infants. Additional studies (all retrospective in design) have documented a high degree of frequent and prolonged mother-infant separations due to medical complications at birth (e.g., Lynch & Roberts, 1977). These findings are particularly relevant for children with disabilities, given that they may suffer from medical problems that result in frequent hospitalizations and prolonged separations from their mothers.

A large body of research demonstrates a relationship between insecure mother-infant attachment and child maltreatment. Numerous investigations have found insecure attachment in abused and neglected infants (e.g., Schneider-Rosen & Cicchetti, 1984), and it has been suggested that factors disrupting formation of the affective bond can lead to subsequent child maltreatment (Ainsworth, 1980). A number of these factors are exhibited by some families with a disabled child, and include: (1) the initial shock and disappointment often experienced by parents at the birth of a disabled child; (2) maternal depression which may occur following birth; (3) possible rejection and accompanying hostile feelings toward the disabled child; (4) deficits in behaviors exhibited by the disabled infant that promote formation of the attachment bond; and (5) disappointment due to unrealistic expectations regarding the disabled child's development and/or abilities.

Unfortunately, there is little empirical evidence that these disruptions in attachment occur with any significant frequency in families of disabled children, and there is no support that such problems lead to abuse in this population. Equally important is the finding that, when a strong methodological design is used, prematurity and mother-infant separations are poor predictors of subsequent abuse in nondisabled children (Egeland & Vaughn, 1981).

The relationship between stress and maltreatment has been well documented (e.g., Browne, 1986). Factors that exacerbate stress and are associated with abuse include poverty (Meier, 1985), unemployment (Oates & Hufton, 1977), social isolation (Elmer, 1967), and single-parent status (Sack, Mason, & Higgins, 1985). Families that engage in maltreatment not only experience increased stress, but typically do not exhibit adequate coping skills (Egeland, Breitenbucher, & Rosenberg, 1980). This issue is particularly important for families with a disabled child. Indeed, introduction of a disabled child into the family typically raises parental stress levels (e.g., Konstantareas & Homatidis, 1989). Disabled children can require additional time and effort compared to their nondisabled peers. Frequent visits to the hospital and the financial burden resulting from additional care needs may worsen an already stressful family environment. Such stress may be compounded when the child is multiply disabled.

The behavioral problems evidenced by some disabled children often exacerbate parental stress. Multiply disabled children, in particular, exhibit behavioral disturbances that can be especially aversive and difficult to control. Some examples of these include rocking, eye poking, hand flapping, disruptiveness, aggression, screaming, and tantrums. Moreover, the inability to control a child's behavior is a frequent precipitant of abuse (Kadushin & Martin, 1981). The aforementioned problems typically require consistent behavior management techniques to bring them under control. Many parents of disabled children require specific training to use behavior management techniques in an effective manner. Thus, the chronicity and pervasiveness of more severely disabled children's behavioral dysfunctions may place them at high risk for abuse. As an example, it has been demonstrated that the persistent cry of a premature infant is sufficient to elicit physiological arousal in adults (Frodi et al., 1978). Furthermore, such arousal has been associated with episodes of maltreatment (Kadushin & Martin, 1981).

Finally, evidence suggests that more vulnerable children are at higher risk for maltreatment (Gelles, 1978). For example, infants are the most frequent targets of abuse in nondisabled populations, perhaps because during infancy a child is least responsive and most vulnerable. It is possible, however, that the higher risk in infancy might be an artifact of reporting, given that the infant's fragility (as contrasted with that of older children) makes it more likely that the effects of maltreatment will be evident (Gelles, 1973). Many disabled children, however, can be viewed as vulnerable. They, too, are relatively defenseless (depending on the type and extent of the handicap). Severely disabled children with profound intellectual deficits or language deficits are "easy targets" since they obviously cannot report instances of maltreatment.

Comment

Although the lines of argument suggesting that children with disabilities are at greater risk for abuse as compared to their nondisabled peers are compelling, supporting data are lacking. No research has been conducted examining whether specific characteristics of *disabled* children lead to abuse. Studies of nondisabled abused children, consistently have downplayed the role of the child in the etiology of abuse (see Ammerman, 1991). Also, in one study of mothers of psychiatrically hospitalized children and adolescents with disabilities, parental psychopathology and reports of stress were more predictive of potential for child abuse than child behavior problems (Ammerman, Hersen, Lubetsky, & Van Hasselt, 1990). However, Ammerman, Hersen, Van Hasselt, Lubetsky, and Sieck (1994) found that mothers who were severely isolated, reported a high degree of anger reactivity, and had children with mild disabilities, were more likely to use harsh physical punishment with their children. These results underscore the importance of interactive models of maltreatment, in which the role of disability and child characteristics are examined within the context of other risk factors.

Although the relationship between disability and abuse remains relatively understudied, the limited data suggest that disabled children, as a whole, are probably not at a significantly increased risk for physical abuse. Rather, it is more likely that a subset of disabled children are at heightened risk if they have parents and families who also display characteristics (such as unemployment, substance abuse, etc.) that disinhibit the expression of abuse. Identifying this subset of children is a major goal of future research, both in terms of screening for at-risk children and for developing effective interventions.

ISSUES IN ASSESSMENT AND TREATMENT

Although the precise nature of potential risk of abuse in disabled populations is inconclusive, the fact remains that many disabled children are abused each year. The literature contains several examples of interventions with disabled populations (e.g., Wolfe et al., 1982). These interventions are primarily behavioral in orientation, emphasizing general parental coping, and problem-solving skills to reduce risk and lower the probability of abuse.

Assessment

The heterogeneity of abused children with disabilities and their families necessitates a broad and comprehensive approach to assessment. Each child and family is unique. No set of problems, symptoms, or skills deficits will be found in all families. As a result, clinical assessment consists of an evaluation of multiple areas of child and parent functioning in order to identify targets for treatment. Table 2 presents a list of problems, skill deficits, and symptoms often found in abusive mothers and abused children, respectively. The list is not exhaustive, but underscores the numerous influences on the child, parent, and family that are potentially important for treatment planning. Also, note that although fathers are implicated in almost half of child abuse cases, the research literature almost exclusively focuses on abusive mothers due to their greater willingness to participate in research of this type (see Fantuzzo & Twentyman, 1986). Detailed reviews of the characteristics of abusive parents and abused children are found in Ammerman, Cassisi, Hersen, and Van Hasselt (1986) and Wolfe (1987).

TABLE 2. Frequently Exhibited Characteristics of Abusive Mothers and Abused Children

Characteristics of Abusive Mothers	Characteristics of Abused Children
Low frustration tolerance	Hypervigilant
Inadequate parenting skills	Aggressive
Anger responsivity	Depressed and/or anxious
Inconsistent discipline methods	Academic underachievement
Unrealistic expectations of child	Poor infant attachment with caregiver
Socially isolated	Social insensitivity
Increased report of stress	Inadequate social skills
Unhappiness and dissatisfaction	Socially withdrawn

Accordingly, the assessment battery needs to reflect the diversity of potential problem areas in abusive families. Although no standard battery of tests and measures has been developed for child abuse, most agree that a thorough assessment is needed. Table 3 presents examples of measures used in assessing child abuse in children with disabilities. Note that a variety of areas are examined. Once again, this battery suggests guidelines for assessment. Additional measures can be added based upon the unique needs of the family.

Treatment

There is no standard behavioral approach to the treatment of child abuse. Most interventions are parent-child focused, with the intention of enhancing parenting skills to improve the relationship and prevent future abuse. Parent training forms the crux of behavioral interventions, while other treatment components or services are often offered at the same time to address the multiple problem areas exhibited by parents, children, and families.

Comprehensive Behavioral Treatment (CBT), described below, is a multi-component, in-home behavioral intervention for maltreating parents of disabled children. CBT was developed at the Western Pennsylvania School for Blind Children. It is a comprehensive intervention consisting of 16 weekly sessions lasting 1 1/2 to 2 hours, followed by 8-16 monthly or bimonthly "booster" sessions over an additional 8 months. Families first receive an assessment battery (many of the instruments used are listed in Table 3), after

TABLE 3. Instruments Frequently Used in the Psychometric Assessment of Child Abuse and Neglect

Instrument	Authors	Completed By	Area Measured
Minnesota Multiphasic Personality Inventory - 2	Hathaway & McKinley, 1989	Parent	Psychopathology
Beck Depression Inventory	Beck, 1993	Parent	Depression
Wechsler Adult Intelligence Scale-Revised	Wechsler, 1987	Parent	Intellectual functioning
Parenting Stress Index	Abidin, 1995	Parent	Parent stress
Parent-Child Relationship Inventory	Gerard, 1994	Parent	Parent - child relationship issues
Social Provisions Scale	Russell & Cutrona, 1984	Parent	Social network
Novaco Provocation Inventory	Novaco, 1975	Parent	Anger responsivity
Child Abuse Potential Inventory	Milner, 1986	Parent	Abuse potential
Child Behavior Checklist	Achenbach, 1991	Parent and/or Teacher	Child behavior problems
Aberrant Behavior Checklist	Aman & Singh, 1983	Parent and/or Teacher	Child behavior problems
Vineland Adaptive Behavior Scales Revised	Sparrow, Balla, & Cicchetti, 1984	Parent and/or Teacher	Developmental functioning
Child Abuse and Neglect Interview Scale (CANIS)	Ammerman, Hersen, & Van Hasselt, 1988	Parent*	Factors related to child abuse and neglect

*Administered by clinician in special education settings.

which 3-4 components are selected based upon the specific and unique needs of the family. The CBT components are drawn primarily from the child abuse (see Ammerman, 1989) and disability intervention literatures. Thus, CBT combines these previously developed programs to provide a specialized intervention for parents who abuse their disabled children.

Child Management Skills Training

Many parents who engage in maltreatment exhibit deficits in child management skills. Child management skills training is designed to teach such parents more effective methods in controlling their child's maladaptive behaviors. Parents are trained to use techniques of positive reinforcement, differential reinforcement, extinction, and time-out to handle a variety of child problems, including non-compliance, aggression, disruptiveness, self-injury, and self-stimulating behaviors. In addition, knowledge and expectations of behavior in disabled children are discussed. Concrete examples of specific child behavior problems are presented, and appropriate management techniques specifically designed to remediate these difficulties are taught. Parents rehearse newly acquired skills within the session and practice them at home through weekly homework assignments. Promoting effective child management skills has two primary benefits in that it: (1) provides parents with strategies to reduce child behavior problems, thus decreasing the likelihood of subsequent physical abuse; and (2) encourages and increases positive interactions between parent and child, which serves to strengthen their bond.

Parenting Skills Training

Parenting skills training seeks to teach parents how to be more effective and nurturant with their child (e.g., Lutzker, Megson, Webb, & Dachman, 1985; Wolfe et al., 1982). Parenting skills training is designed for parents who have been either physically abusive or neglectful. Using a didactic approach, parents are taught how to: (a) be sensitive to their child's emotional needs; (b) provide for the child's care and nutritional requirements; (c) increase their use of praise and positive social attention; and (d) use positive physical attention (i.e., physical affection). Newly learned skills are practiced at home to promote generalization. Parenting skills training is designed to improve the parent-child relationship in general, in order to prevent further occurrence of physical abuse or neglect.

Impulse and Anger Control Training

This component is administered primarily to parents who abuse their children. Here, the parent is trained to eliminate violent expressions of anger. Also, more effective handling of situations that precipitate anger outbursts are taught (Denicola & Sandler, 1980). Anger control training involves identifying and anticipating events that elicit anger, learning self-control through the behavioral techniques of thought-stopping and cognitive restructuring (substituting anger-promoting cognitions with those that encourage self-control), and using alternative conflict resolution strategies. Parents practice impulse control skills through role playing in treatment sessions and apply them in the natural environment via weekly homework assignments. Impulse control training is designed to break the cycle of anger and frustration that often leads to abusive behavior. Furthermore, it provides the parent with a new behavioral repertoire to deal with difficult parent-child situations.

Leisure Skills Training

Few data are available on training parents effectively to utilize leisure time as a way of reducing stress in the household. Use of leisure time is, however, a problem of paramount importance in parents with disabled children. Because the care requirements of disabled children can require almost continual attention and supervision, it is crucial for parents to schedule time away from their child in order to decrease stress. Thus, leisure skills training consists of teaching parents to organize their day so that scheduled breaks occur. Leisure skills training also involves arranging for alternative care providers for the disabled child during leisure periods, which is often difficult for many parents.

Household Organization Training

Household organization training is designed to prevent stress and ensure that a disorganized household does not interfere with other aspects of parenting and family life. Implementation of this protocol involves teaching specific skills needed to organize the household effectively. Indeed, such skills are of paramount importance for children with disabilities given their need for consistency, structure, and increased care. Areas to be targeted include meal planning, planned family activities, keeping doctor's appointments, coordinating shopping trips, and promoting safety strategies to prevent accidents. Research has demonstrated that household organization skills often are prerequisites for parenting and child management skills among maltreating parents (Barone, Greene, & Lutzker, 1986). Moreover, the use of such procedures contributes to a less stressful and more positive home environment.

Stress Reduction Training and Problem-Solving Skills

This component is divided into two parts: (1) learning how to relax to reduce feelings of anxiety and discomfort that accompany stress, and (2) acquiring new strategies and approaches to solving day-to-day problems and difficult-to-handle situations with disabled children. First, the parent is taught deep-muscle relaxation, as adapted by Kelly (1983) for use with parents of abused children. Audiotapes of a 30-minute relaxation session are given to facilitate practice at home each day. Once relaxation has been mastered, parents are instructed to use such newly-acquired skills during stressful situations. Examples of stressful situations include problematic parent-child interactions, family disagreements and arguments, and job-related difficulties. Second, parents are taught how to cope with a variety of life stressors and daily problem situations. This component involves increasing social supports and expanding social networks, dealing with financial pressures, and effectively utilizing leisure time to provide breaks from the often fatiguing task of child care. Problem-solving skills training is individually tailored to meet the specific needs of each parent. For example, one parent may experience increased stress due to unemployment and financial concerns, while another may complain of social isolation and overwork because of his/her child's care needs.

Developmental Psychoeducational Training

Children with disabilities vary considerably as a function of type and severity of impairment. The developmental course of these children often is difficult to predict. Parents frequently have unrealistic or inaccurate expectations regarding the development of their children and the specific skills and abilities they will display. This is especially true of parents involved in maltreatment. The purpose of developmental psychoeducational training is to provide the parent with information about what to expect from the child's growth and development.

Specific Behavioral Strategies to Be Carried Out

The format of Comprehensive Behavior Treatment follows the model typically used in parent training approaches in general (e.g., Forehand & McMahon, 1981), and behavioral interventions with parents who maltreat in particular (Kelly, 1983). The procedure for training involves: (1) direct instructions, (2) modeling, (3) behavioral rehearsal, and (4) feedback. Direct instructions provide parents with specific guidelines for handling a problematic situation. For example, a mother might be taught precisely what to do in a situation in which her child cries continuously. Modeling is used to provide the parent with a clear example of how to perform the behavior. Thus, the therapist enacts the role of the parent and performs the appropriate response. By observing and then practicing the correct behavior, the parent may be more likely to utilize it successfully in the home environment. At this point, the parent is asked to perform the behavior within the context of a simulated role play of the problematic situation. Such behavioral rehearsal permits the parent to practice in the session. With therapist-provided feedback, the parent can enhance newly acquired skills before applying them in the home situation. Finally, weekly homework assignments are given to promote practice in the home environment and to increase the generalizability of training.

CONCLUSION

The recent interest in child abuse in general has seen a parallel increase in attention directed toward the maltreatment of children with disabilities. Unfortunately, little research has been conducted in this area. Despite strong suggestions that disabled children might be at heightened risk for abuse, current data do not support this broad contention. Rather, it appears that a subset of children, all of whom are already members of at-risk families, may be at high risk for abuse. Interventions have been developed to treat abusive parents of disabled children. These involve behavioral programs that are individually tailored, based upon comprehensive assessment, to meet the needs of the family.

REFERENCES

Abidin, R. R. (1995). *Parenting Stress Index* (3rd ed.). Odessa, FL: Psychological Assessment Resources.

Achenbach, T. M. (1991). *Manual for the Child Behavior Checklist 4-18 and 1991 Profile*. Burlington, VT: University of Vermont Department of Psychiatry.

Ainsworth, M. D. (1980). Attachment and child abuse. In G. Gerber, C. Ross, & E. Zigler (Eds.), *Child abuse: An agenda for action* (pp. 35-47). New York: Oxford University Press.

Aman, M. G., & Singh, N. N. (1983). *Aberrant Behavior Checklist*. Canterbury, New Zealand: University of Canterbury.

Ammerman, R. T. (1989). Child abuse and neglect. In M. Hersen (Ed.), *Innovations in child behavior therapy* (pp. 353-394). New York: Springer.

Ammerman, R. T. (1990) Etiological models of maltreatment: A behavioral perspective. *Behavior Modification, 14,* 230-254.

Ammerman, R. T. (1991). The role of the child in physical abuse: A reappraisal. *Violence and Victims, 6,* 87-101.

Ammerman, R. T., Cassisi, J. E., Hersen, M., & Van Hasselt, V. B. (1986). Consequences of physical abuse and neglect in children. *Clinical Psychology Review, 6,* 291-310.

Ammerman, R. T., Hersen, M., & Lubetsky, M. J. (1990). Assessment of child maltreatment in special education settings. *International Journal of Special Education, 5,* 51-65.

Ammerman, R. T., Hersen, M., Lubetsky, M. J., & Van Hasselt, V. B. (1990, November). Child maltreatment and handicap: Preliminary findings and implications for behavioral interventions. In R. T. Ammerman & J. W. Fantuzzo (Co-chairpersons), *New directions in child abuse and neglect.* Symposium presented at the 24th Annual Convention of the Association for Advancement of Behavior Therapy, San Francisco.

Ammerman, R. T., Hersen, M., & Van Hasselt, V. B. (1988). *The Child Abuse and Neglect Interview Schedule (CANIS).* Unpublished instrument, Western Pennsylvania School for Blind Children, Pittsburgh, PA.

Ammerman, R. T., Hersen, M., Van Hasselt, V. B., Lubetsky, M. J., & Sieck, W. R. (1994). Maltreatment in psychiatrically hospitalized children and adolescents with developmental disabilities: Prevalence and correlates. *Journal of the American Academy of Child and Adolescent Psychiatry, 33,* 567-576.

Ammerman, R. T., Van Hasselt, V. B., & Hersen, M. (1988). Maltreatment of handicapped children: A critical review. *Journal of Family Violence, 3,* 53-72.

Barone, V. J., Green, B. F., & Lutzker, J. R. (1986). Home safety with families being treated for child abuse and neglect. *Behavior Modification, 10,* 93-114.

Beck, A. T. (1993). *Beck Depression Inventory (BDI).* San Antonio, TX: Psychological Corporation.

Belsky, J. (1980). Child maltreatment: An ecological integration. *American Psychologist, 35,* 320-335.

Browne, D. H. (1986). The role of stress in the commission of subsequent acts of child abuse and neglect. *Journal of Family Violence, 1,* 289-297.

Cicchetti, D., & Rizley, R. (1981). Developmental perspectives on the etiology, intergenerational transmission, and sequelae of child maltreatment. *New Directions for Child Development, 11,* 31-55.

Denicola, J., & Sandler, J. (1980). Training abusive parents cognitive behavioral techniques. *Behavior Therapy, 11,* 263-270.

Egeland, B., Breitenbucher, M., & Rosenberg, D. (1980). Prospective study of significance of etiology of child abuse. *Journal of Consulting and Clinical Psychology, 48,* 195-205.

Egeland, B., & Vaughn, B. (1981). Failure of "bond formation" as a cause of abuse, neglect, and maltreatment. *American Journal of Orthopsychiatry, 51,* 78-84.

Elmer, E. (1967). *Children in jeopardy*. Pittsburgh, PA: University of Pittsburgh Press.

Fantuzzo, J. W., & Twentyman, C. T. (1986). Child abuse and psychotherapy research. Merging social concerns and empirical investigation. *Professional Psychology: Research and Practice, 17*, 375-380.

Forehand, R. L., & McMahon, R. J. (1981). *Helping the noncompliant child: A clinician's guide to parent training*. New York: Guilford.

Frodi, A. M., Lamb, M., Leavitt, L., Donovan, W., Neff, C., & Sherry, D. (1978). Fathers' and mothers' responses to the appearance and cries of premature and normal infants. *Developmental Psychology, 14*, 490-498.

Garbarino, J., & Crouter, A. (1978). Defining the community context of parent-child relations: The correlates of child maltreatment. *Child Development, 49*, 604-616.

Gelles, R. J. (1973). Child abuse as psychopathology: A sociological critique and reformulation. *American Journal of Orthopsychiatry, 43*, 611-621.

Gelles, R. J. (1978). Violence toward children in the United States. *American Journal of Orthopsychiatry, 48*, 580-592.

Gerard, A. B. (1994). *Parent-Child Relationship Inventory (PCRI)*. Los Angeles, CA: Western Psychological Services.

Hathaway, S. R., & McKinley, J. C. (1989). *Minnesota Multiphasic Personality Inventory-2 (MMPI-2)*. Minneapolis, MN: University of Minnesota Press.

Helfer, R. (1973). The etiology of child abuse. *Pediatrics, 51*, 777-779.

Kadushin, A., & Martin, J. A. (1981). *Child abuse: An interactional event*. New York: Columbia University Press.

Kelly, J. A. (1983). *Treating child abusive families: Intervention based an skills-training or principles*. New York: Plenum Press.

Kempe, C. H., Silverman, F. N., Steele, B. F., Droegemueller, W., & Silver, H. K. (1962). The battered child syndrome. *Journal of American Medical Association, 181*, 105-112.

Klein, M., & Stem, L. (1971). Low birth weight and the battered child syndrome. *American Journal of Diseases in Childhood, 122*, 15-18.

Konstantareas, M. M., & Homatidis, S. (1989). Assessing child symptom severity and stress in parents of autistic children. *Journal of Child Psychology and Psychiatry, 30*, 459-470.

Lutzker, J. R., Megson, D. A., Webb, M. E., & Dachman, R. S. (1985). Validating and training adult-child interaction skills to professionals and to parents indicated for child abuse and neglect. *Journal of Child and Adolescent Psychotherapy, 2*, 91-104.

Lynch, M. A., & Roberts, J. (1977). Predicting child abuse: Signs of bonding failure in the maternity hospital. *British Medical Journal, 1*, 624-626.

Martin, H. P., & Beezley, P. (1974). Prevention and the consequences of child abuse. *Journal of Operational Psychiatry, 6*, 68-77.

Masten, A. S., & Garmezy, N. (1985). Risk, vulnerability, and protective factors in developmental psychopathology. In B. B. Lahey & A. E. Kazdin (Eds.), *Advances in clinical child psychology* (Vol. 8, pp. 1-52). New York: Plenum.

Meier, J. H. (Ed.). (1985). *Assault against children: Why it happens and how to stop it.* San Diego, CA: College-Hill Press.

Milner, J. S. (1986). *The Child Abuse Potential Inventory (2nd ed).* DeKalb, IL: Psytec.

National Center on Child Abuse and Neglect. (1995). Child maltreatment 1993: Reports from states to the National Center on Child Abuse and Neglect. Washington, D.C.: U.S. Department of Health and Human Services, U.S. Government Printing Office.

Novaco, R. W. (1975). *Anger control: The development and evaluation of an experimental treatment.* Lexington, MA: Heath.

Oates, R. K., & Hufton, I. W. (1977). The spectrum of failure to thrive and child abuse: A follow-up study. *Child Abuse and Neglect, 1,* 119-124.

Parke, R. D., & Collmer, C. W. (1975). Child abuse: An interdisciplinary analysis. In E. M. Hetherington (Ed.), *Review of child development research* (Vol. 5, pp. 509-590). Chicago: University of Chicago Press.

Reid, J. B., Patterson, G. R., & Loeber, R. (1982). The abused child: Victim, instigator, or innocent bystander? *Nebraska Symposium on Motivation, 29,* 47-68.

Russell, D., & Cutrona, C. E. (1984). *The Social Provisions Scale.* Unpublished manuscript, University of Iowa, College of Medicine, Iowa City.

Sack, W. H., Mason, R., & Higgins, J. E. (1985). The single-parent family and abusive child punishment. *American Journal of Orthopsychiatry, 5,* 252-259.

Schneider-Rosen, K., & Cicchetti, D. (1984). The relationship between affect and cognition in maltreated infants: Quality of attachment and the development of visual self-recognition. *Child Development, 55,* 648-658.

Sparrow, S. S., Balla, D. A., & Cicchetti, D. V. (1984). *The Vineland Adaptive Behavior Scales.* (Revised). Circle Pines, MN: American Guidance Services.

Starr, R. H., Dietrich, K. N., Fischoff, J., Ceresnie, S., & Zweier, D. (1984). The contribution of handicapping conditions to child abuse. *Topics in Early Childhood Special Education, 4,* 55-69.

Steele, B. J., & Pollock, C. (1968). A psychiatric study of parents who abuse infants and small children. In R. Helfer & C. H. Kempe (Eds.), *The battered child* (pp. 89-133). Chicago: University of Chicago Press.

Wechsler, D. (1987). *Manual for the Wechsler Adult Intelligence Scale–Revised.* San Antonio, TX: Psychological Corporation.

Wolfe, D. A. (1985). Child abusive parents: An empirical review and analysis. *Psychological Bulletin, 97,* 462-482.

Wolfe, D. A. (1987). *Child abuse: Implications for child development and psychopathology.* Newbury Park, CA: Sage.

Wolfe, D. A., St. Lawrence, J., Graves, K., Brehony, K., Bradlyn, A., & Kelly, J. A. (1982). Intensive behavioral parent training for a child abusive mother. *Behavior Therapy, 13,* 438-451.

Research Concerning Children
of Battered Women:
Clinical Implications

Honore M. Hughes

SUMMARY. Although the negative impact on children exposed to
spouse abuse is well documented, little empirical research is available to guide clinical interventions. A brief review of the research
literature describing these detrimental influences on children's adjustment is presented. Factors are discussed which mediate the consequences for children exposed to spouse abuse. These variables
include those that are child-related as well as factors which are situa-
tional/contextual. Next, several theoretical/conceptual models are
presented to assist with an understanding of how this impact on
youngsters' psychological and emotional functioning takes place.
These models suggest both direct and indirect mechanisms of influence. Finally, recommendations regarding clinical interventions are
delineated based on these models as well as the available literature
on the treatment of children of battered women. Suggestions related
to appropriate types of treatment, including symptom-and mecha-
nism-specific interventions, are made. *[Article copies available for a fee
from The Haworth Document Delivery Service: 1-800-342-9678. E-mail
address: getinfo@haworth.com]*

Address correspondence to: Honore M. Hughes, Saint Louis University,
Department of Psychology, 221 North Grand Boulevard, St. Louis, MO
63103-2006 (e-mail hugheshm@sluvca.slu.edu).

[Haworth co-indexing entry note]: "Research Concerning Children of Battered Women: Clinical
Implications." Hughes, Honore M. Co-published simultaneously in *Journal of Aggression, Maltreat-
ment & Trauma* (Haworth Maltreatment & Trauma Press, an imprint of The Haworth Press, Inc.) Vol. 1,
No. 1 (#1), 1997, pp. 225-244; and: *Violence and Sexual Abuse at Home: Current Issues in Spousal
Battering and Child Maltreatment* (ed: Robert Geffner, Susan B. Sorenson, and Paula K. Lundberg-Love)
Haworth Maltreatment & Trauma Press, an imprint of The Haworth Press, Inc., 1997, pp. 225-244. Single
or multiple copies of this article are available for a fee from The Haworth Document Delivery Service
[1-800-342-9678, 9:00 a.m. - 5:00 p.m. (EST). E-mail address: getinfo@haworth.com].

225

KEYWORDS. Family violence, emotional abuse, child maltreatment, treatment, child adjustment

Researchers studying children of battered women have concentrated to date on documenting the negative impact of spouse abuse. Thus, there is a paucity of empirical research available to guide clinical interventions. Clinicians furnishing services to children in families in which there is spouse abuse often find themselves relying on types of information other than research to assist them in providing treatment. Much of the writing that is available comes from clinical experience with this population of children. In addition, clinicians often rely on empirical studies of other maltreated populations that might be extrapolated as appropriate (e.g., Hughes & Fantuzzo, 1994).

In order to address the clinical implications of spouse abuse for intervention with children, a brief review of the research literature describing the negative influence on children's adjustment will be presented. Then, several new theoretical/conceptual models for understanding how this impact occurs will be offered. Finally, recommendations regarding clinical interventions will be made based on these models as well as on the literature on treatment of children of battered women.

CURRENT STATE OF KNOWLEDGE

Consequences for Children

Concern regarding the psychological adjustment of children of battered women has intensified within recent years as more evidence became available supporting the negative impact of being exposed to marital violence (Cummings & Davies, 1994; Fincham, 1994; Hughes & Fantuzzo, 1994; Rossman, Hughes, & Hanson, in press; Rossman & Rosenberg, 1997, this volume). Although the connection between marital or couple violence and children's behavioral and emotional difficulties has been well documented, reasons for this association are not well understood. Many of the researchers presently pursuing investigations in this area are exploring variables and combinations of factors which may provide explanations. Two facts seem clear at this point: (a) there are multiple causes for the difficulties children experience (e.g., Cummings & Davies, 1994; Fincham, 1994), and (b) there continues to be a need to search for more precise explanations for these youngsters' problems. When the specific reasons for the detrimental influence on children are better understood, then more effective intervention and prevention strategies can be designed. The following is a brief overview of current knowledge.

Prevalence. Estimates regarding the prevalence of spouse abuse range from 10% to 30% of U.S. families (Geffner & Pagelow, 1990; Pagelow, 1984; Straus & Gelles, 1986); thus, it is apparent that a substantial number of children live in violent homes. While most researchers have not inquired about this specifically, when investigators ask women who have been beaten where their children are while they are being assaulted, in 90% of the cases the children are either in the same, or the next room (e.g., Hughes, 1988; Rosenberg & Rossman, 1990).

Types of difficulties. Research findings indicate that exposure to parental violence is a traumatic experience for children. A number of researchers have found that both behavioral and emotional problems are significantly higher in the children of battered women (e.g., Christopoulos et al., 1987; Graham-Bermann, 1996; Hershorn & Rosenbaum, 1985; Hughes, 1988; Hughes, Parkinson, & Vargo, 1989; Hughes, Vargo, Ito, & Skinner, 1991; Rossman et al., in press; Sternberg et al., 1993; Wolfe, Zak, Wilson, & Jaffe, 1986). Overall, there are consistent emotional and behavioral differences between children of battered women and other children in both internalizing (e.g., depressed, anxious) and externalizing (e.g., aggressive, disobedient) behaviors.

Other difficulties which have been reported include: an increase in somatic symptoms (Rosenberg & Rossman, 1990), lower cognitive skills and school achievement (Moore, Pepler, Weinberg, Hammond, Waddell, & Weiser, 1990), and difficulties with social problem-solving (Moore et al., 1990; Rossman, Heaton, Moss, Malik, Lintz, & Romero, 1991; Wilson, 1991), as well as tendencies to be more external in locus of control (Moore et al., 1990). In addition, Jouriles, Barling and O'Leary (1987) found that children of battered women were four times more likely to show psychopathology as were children living in non-violent homes.

Extent of impact. It is also important for purposes of intervention to investigate the impact of spouse abuse on the children by examining the proportion of children who are reported to exhibit more severe difficulties, problems that are beyond those of the normative group for behavior problem measures, and at a level indicating problems severe enough that the children are in need of clinical treatment (upper 2-10% of the standardization sample). Several researchers have investigated the percentages of children in shelter samples who have behavior problem checklist scores above the cut-offs indicating need for clinical services. Depending on the gender of the child, the type of violence experienced, and the T-score used as the cut-off, the percentages reported range from 25% to 65%, with, on the average, approximately 35% to 50% of the children falling above that cut-off (e.g., Christopoulos et al., 1987; Hughes et al., 1991; Sternberg et al., 1993; Wolfe et al., 1986). By comparison, approximately 25% of children in comparably low income families have scores within the clinical range (Burns, Patterson, Nussbaum, & Parker, 1991). Thus, a substantial proportion of children of battered women are reported by them to be in need of clinical treatment.

Variables That Mediate the Impact on Children

Many of the investigators in this area have emphasized the need to better understand the consequences through the identification of variables which mediate the impact of marital violence on children. The following list of potential mediators (see Table 1) has been adapted from a number of sources, including Cummings and Davies (1994), Grych and Fincham (1990), Hughes and Fantuzzo (1994), Hughes et al. (1991) and Moore et al. (1990). This model includes both child factors and situational/contextual factors.

Child factors to be considered consist of characteristics of individual children which are relatively stable and more like "traits." Qualities such as temperament, self-esteem, cognitive abilities, coping skills, attributional style, cognitive-developmental capabilities, age and gender are important to understand more fully, especially as they are related to their role in a child's psychological functioning. Situational/contextual factors include those situational factors related more directly to the children, such

TABLE 1. Mediating Variables

Child factors

- temperament, self-esteem, cognitive abilities, coping abilities, attributional style, gender, age: cognitive-developmental capabilities

Situational/contextual factors

- more or less stable factors related to the child (e.g., past experience with violence, perceived emotional climate of the family)
- marital conflict factors: frequency, intensity, duration, content, resolution, overt, covert, age at onset

---

as their past experience with violence, perceived emotional climate in their family, etc., and those that are less directly related, including aspects of the marital conflict, such as its frequency, intensity, duration, content, resolution, and a child's age at the onset.

Few of the variables which potentially moderate the impact of spouse abuse on children's psychological adjustment have been investigated extensively for children of battered women. Those that have received the most in-depth examination are gender, and past experience with violence, focusing on child factors and child-related situational variables, respectively.

Gender. Impact on the psychological adjustment of children based on gender seems to be inconsistent, depending on whether one examines mean scores, or looks at percentages above a clinical cut-off. When researchers examine average scores, few differences between boys and girls in shelters are seen (e.g., Hughes et al., 1991; Pepler & Moore, 1993). Both boys and girls receive high scores, significantly above the comparison children, on both internalizing and externalizing behaviors.

However, when adjustment is examined in terms of the percentage of children who receive ratings which are at or above a certain score indicating the need for clinical intervention, differences by gender are noted. In these instances, most researchers find that girls, rather than boys, have greater percentages of total problem scores above the clinical level. For example, Christopoulos et al. (1987) reported that more girls receive scores above the clinical cut-off, with 36% of the girls and 28% of the boys above that level on externalizing behaviors. Other researchers who also have found more girls to be above the cut-off points, include Moore and Pepler (1996), who reported three times as many girls as boys within the clinical range on internalizing and externalizing problems. One exception to this was Wolfe, Jaffe, Wilson & Zak (1985) who reported that 34% of boys and 20% of girls were above the cut-off on total problem behaviors.

Hughes et al. (1989, 1991) also found that more girls were above the clinical level. In addition, they examined the impact of physical abuse on the child, and found that there was a cumulative impact as children were exposed to more types of violence and that the influence interacted with gender. In a study investigating the proportion of youngsters exposed to marital violence and abused/exposed children who were considered to be within the clinically problematic range of behavioral difficulties, on total problems, a greater proportion of girls were found to have difficulties within the clinical range (45% and 65% of the girls vs. 30% and 43% of the boys for the exposed and abused/exposed children, respectively).

Thus, gender is likely to be an important mediator, in that more girls than boys have been reported to experience problems above the clinical level.

Type of violence experienced. The co-occurrence of different types of violence is rather high, with estimates in the 40-60% range (Forsstrom-Cohen & Rosenbaum, 1985; Rosenbaum & O'Leary, 1981; Ross, 1996; Straus, Gelles, & Steinmetz, 1980). Thus, spouse abuse and child abuse are both likely to occur in the same family. Several investigators have studied children who have been exposed to more than one type of family violence. Hughes and colleagues have been investigating what they call the "double whammy": the hypothesis that though the effect of being exposed to spouse abuse is negative, the impact is even worse when children are also physically abused. This idea has been tentatively borne out in several studies (Hughes, 1988; Hughes et al., 1989; Hughes et al., 1991).

Other researchers examining children exposed to multiple types of family violence include Sternberg and colleagues (1993). These research-ers studied depression and behavior problems in 8-12 year-old children who composed four groups: physically-abused; non-abused but exposed to parental violence; physically-abused and exposed to parental violence; and non-abused, non-exposed children. Also, in two studies, Rossman and colleagues (Rossman et al., 1991; Rossman et al., 1993) examined 4-9 year old children divided into comparison, exposed, or mixed abuse-ex-posed to marital violence groups. In these investigations as well, past experience with different types of violence had an impact on the children's psychological adjustment: the more types of violence children were exposed to, the less well adjusted they were (Rossman et al., in press).

Marital conflict factors. A large body of research addressing marital conflict is instructive for understanding children's difficulties (see Cum-mings & Davies, 1994); however, the majority of it pertains to non-violent conflict. There is evidence to indicate that physically violent confronta-tions have an impact on children which is different than that seen with non-violent friction. Researchers have suggested that physically aggres-sive marital discord has a greater impact than marital conflict which is not violent. For example, Jouriles and colleagues (1987) found that physical aggression directed toward the children's mothers was an independent predictor of risk for psychopathology in children, beyond that of non-vio-lent conflict. Moreover, Fantuzzo and colleagues (1991) reported that verbal conflict was related to low to moderate rates of psychopathology in children. Laumakis, Margolin, and John (1994) also found that physical conflict between the adults was more distressing to children than verbal conflict.

Mechanisms by Which Spouse Abuse Exerts an Impact

Perhaps some of these results can be better understood when several of the hypothesized mechanisms by which spouse abuse exerts an impact on children are examined. Understanding the potential moderators of behavioral and emotional outcomes as well as likely mechanisms of impact has implications for clinical intervention. Once mechanisms are delineated, better treatment and prevention programs can be implemented. A number of researchers recently proposed models based on theory and research to help explain the psychological and behavioral consequences for the children. Several investigators have suggested that the mechanisms of impact likely work in both direct and indirect ways (Cummings & Davies, 1994; Fincham, Grych, & Osborne, 1994; Grych & Fincham, 1990; see Table 2). Direct mechanisms first mentioned by Grych and Fincham (1990) and elaborated by several others (Cummings & Davies, 1994; Fincham et al., 1994) include modeling of aggressiveness and stress in the family.

Direct mechanisms. Related to the fact that both boys and girls exhibit externalizing symptoms, the aggressiveness on the part of both likely has been acquired through modeling, with children copying what they see the abusive parent (usually their father) doing. Grych and Fincham (1990) point out that children tend to imitate their parents and learn about interpersonal relationships from them. In addition, Cummings and Davies (1994) suggest that children learn "scripts" from parents (i.e., general strategies for using aggressive behavior because they see their father being reinforced for using aggression to obtain what he wants).

Moreover, not only do children learn to be aggressive by watching

TABLE 2. Proposed Mechanisms by Which Spouse/Partner Abuse Exerts an Impact on Children

---

Direct Mechanisms

- Modeling of aggressiveness
- Stress in family

Indirect Mechanisms

- Characteristics of the parent-child interaction (quality of attachment; emotional availability of mothers)
- Disciplinary practices (disrupted; harsh; negative)

---

others act in that fashion, there is a "disinhibitory" impact as well. Watching someone else be aggressive gives one permission to also be aggressive (Cummings & Davies, 1994; Grych & Fincham, 1990). Since children are more likely to imitate a model they view as powerful and successful in achieving goals (Bandura, 1973; Pagelow, 1984), modeling in the case of spouse abuse can be especially influential.

The second direct mechanism operates through the fact that the violent family environment is very stressful for the children (e.g., Cummings & Davies, 1994; Laumakis et al., 1994). Cummings and Davies (1994) describe typical responses to stress on the part of children as those of physiological arousal and emotional dysregulation. Thus, being subject to chronic stress depletes the resources of the children over time and reduces the quality of the child's functioning. Therefore, the anxiety and depressive-type symptoms experienced by children are apt to be a result of the family stress created by the spouse abuse. As Jaffe, Wolfe, and Wilson (1990) point out, many of the signs of distress in children of battered women are very similar to Post-Traumatic Stress Disorder (PTSD) symptoms.

Indirect mechanisms. Indirect mechanisms discussed by these same researchers (Cummings & Davies, 1994; Fincham et al., 1994; Grych & Fincham, 1990) include characteristics of the parent-child relationship (for example, quality of attachment or emotional availability, emotional negativity, parent-child aggression), and disciplinary practices (e.g., those that are exceedingly negative, harsh, inconsistent, ineffective; see Table 2).

Abuse of the mother can be indirectly related to children's behavior problems because it can lead to a deterioration in the mental health of the mother and the quality of the parent-child relationship. For example, Wolfe et al. (1985) investigated the extent to which shelter mothers' physical and mental health influenced children's adjustment. They found that maternal stress variables predicted child adjustment better than physical violence between parents, and suggested that the impact on the child of observing spouse abuse may be partially a function of the mother's impairment following specific events, such as being beaten, as well as the accompanying disruption and uncertainly in the family.

Moreover, a likely outcome of being beaten is to become depressed (e.g., Cascardi & O'Leary, 1992; Hughes & Rau, 1984; Orava, McLeod, & Sharpe, 1996). Depending on the length of time the women have experienced depressive symptoms and the severity of their dysfunction, the parent-child relationship could be negatively affected. Research indicates that children of depressed women are at-risk for adjustment difficulties (Downey & Coyne, 1990; Lee & Gotlib, 1989). Moreover, evidence from areas such as child psychopathology indicates that depression can disrupt parenting (Downey & Coyne, 1990).

In addition, hostility and aggression expressed during the marital conflict can spill over to the parent-child relationship (Fincham et al., 1994). Similarly, the negative emotions experienced by the parent(s) as a result of the conflict could result in parents' responses to those feelings being either overt hostility toward the child or withdrawal and neglect of the child. McDonald and Jouriles (1991) also provide support for physically aggressive marital discord exerting a negative impact on parenting skills.

Stress related to parenting also has been found to be a potential influence on the parent-child relationship. Holden and Ritchie (1991; Holden, 1996) found that battered women who report greater parenting stress are more likely to have children who are experiencing adjustment problems. In addition, mothers' parenting stress levels was one of two significant predictors of child behavior problems (Holden & Ritchie, 1991).

As additional support for the importance of the parent-child relationship, Rossman and Rosenberg (1997, this volume) present a model in which they delineate how marital conflict can interfere with parenting, resulting in caregiving which is insufficient for meeting a child's developmental needs. Through parenting which does not meet the youngsters' emotional needs, disruption of children's personality and psychological functioning occurs, resulting in difficulties for the children in the areas of competence, autonomy, and relatedness.

In addition, Cummings and Davies (1994) propose a model based on attachment theory in which they present evidence for their hypothesis that marital conflict causes children to have concerns about their emotional security. The authors suggest that marital conflict undermines the children's feelings of emotional security, leading to adjustment problems in children. According to this hypothesis, emotional security is a central mediating mechanism, a link between parents' destructive styles of conflict and children's behavioral/emotional outcomes.

Concerning disciplinary practices as an indirect mechanism, a number of variables are important to consider. Inadequate parenting in the form of inconsistent and/or negative discipline puts children at especially high risk for aggressiveness through modeling. With that type of ineffective parenting, much aggressiveness occurs among family members within the home (e.g., Fauber, Forehand, Thomas, & Wierson, 1990; Patterson, De Baryshe, & Ramsey, 1989). Similarly, Cummings and Davies (1994) also point out that interparental conflict can lead to ineffective child management, inconsistent discipline, and lax monitoring of the children. Not only can there be inconsistent parenting, but disagreements over child rearing can be the source of some disputes (Grych & Fincham, 1990).

These direct mechanisms of modeling and stress, plus indirect mechanisms of the quality of the parent-child relationship and the nature of the discipline, provide some guidance for clinical interventions. These implications are delineated in the following section.

CLINICAL IMPLICATIONS OF RESEARCH AND THEORY

Goals of Interventions

The general goals of treatment are to reduce children's symptoms of distress and increase their functioning and competence, with interventions directed toward personality functioning and psychological adjustment as well as behavior. Thus, based on research discussed above, it is clear that children's distress can be alleviated by reducing their externalizing and internalizing behaviors. In addition, based on theory, children's needs to feel emotionally secure must be met, and improvements in their competence, autonomy and ability to relate to people must be seen.

Moreover, symptoms the children experience would be attended to only after the youngsters have had their more immediate requirements met, most specifically their needs for safety and shelter. Thus, the interventions directed toward the children would be primarily related to the direct mechanisms of modeling and stress as discussed above. Addressing the indirect mechanisms would require an approach centered on the primary caregiver.

Symptoms Related to Direct Mechanisms

Regarding interventions for children exposed to potential abuse, focusing on the impact issues would include addressing both externalizing and internalizing behavior, as well as social competence and social problem-solving. (For readers who are interested in more detail than it is possible to include here, consult Hughes and Marshall (1995), Jaffe et al. (1990) and Rosenberg and Rossman (1990) for more information about assessment and intervention issues for children of battered women.) Behaviors likely to result from the mechanism of modeling are usually externalizing-type problems, especially aggressiveness, for both boys and girls. PTSD-type symptoms, those that are more internalizing, are the kinds of difficulties likely to result from the mechanism of stress, again for both boys and girls. Several sources indicate that cognitive-behavioral techniques can be quite effective with both internalizing and externalizing behaviors (e.g., Finch, Nelson, & Ott, 1993; Kendall & Panichelli, 1995). (See Table 3.)

For intervention with aggressiveness, empirical support has been obtained for the efficacy of training older children and adolescents on an individual basis in problem-solving skills (e.g., Kazdin, Esveldt-Dawson, French, & Unis, 1987) and anger control (Feindler & Ecton, 1986). Two additional excellent resources for dealing with more severe levels of violence on the part of children and adolescents are by Kazdin (1987; 1991).

To very briefly summarize these latter resources, Kazdin (1991) points out that treatment methods depend on the age and severity of the aggressive behavior, with the most evidence for success achieved with treatment of younger children and with oppositional and non-compliant behaviors. Options for intervention, especially for younger children, include parent management training. For older children, anger management and the development of prosocial skills, such as social perspective-taking or empathy training, have been found to be effective. Finch, Nelson, and Moss (1993) provide additional strategies for intervention with aggressiveness. In addition, Polyson and Kimball (1993) discuss social skills training for aggressive children.

Although these techniques have been shown to reduce aggressiveness among youngsters in a number of different populations, they have not been tested specifically with children who have been exposed to spouse abuse or who have been physically abused. Clearly, additional treatment

TABLE 3. Clinical Interventions

Direct Mechanisms (Modeling of aggressiveness; Stress in the family)

- Individual or Group treatment of children
- Cognitive-behavioral for aggression, anxiety, depression
- Relationship-oriented for feelings of emotional security and competence
- Combination of approaches

Indirect Mechanisms (Characteristics of the parent-child interaction; Disciplinary practices)

- Treat women's depression
- Teach more effective child management skills

---

outcome research is needed. Given the similarities in presenting problems and the range of backgrounds among the children studied, however, extrapolating from the studies in which effectiveness has been demonstrated seems to be quite reasonable.

Related to children's emotional symptoms, a cognitive-behavioral approach to treating both anxious and depressive symptoms has been shown to be helpful. For example, with children of battered women, Wilson (1991) suggests focusing on negative cognitive errors and other characteristic thought patterns which seem to be conducive to depression, as well as attributions and locus of control. Specific to children experiencing anxiety-related distress, Forman (1993) provides a stress and coping framework and discusses relaxation training, social problem-solving, decreasing irrational beliefs, and learning stress-reducing thought patterns. Kendall and colleagues (1991) also supply suggestions for treating anxiety disorders in children and adolescents, while Stark, Rouse, and Livingston (1991) discuss interventions for depression. See also Grace, Spirito, Finch, and Ott (1993) for development of coping skills for anxiety, and Carey (1993) for the treatment of depression.

Because children of battered women also show difficulties in social problem solving, enhancing those skills as well as children's empathy will be beneficial and will assist in reducing aggressiveness (see Kazdin, 1991; Kazdin et al., 1987). Working on the skills deficits that are observed in the areas of social problem-solving also can help with these emotionally-based symptoms (Forman, 1993).

Play therapy (either nondirective or focused) to deal with inter-personal and intra-personal issues is also likely to be beneficial (e.g., Gil, 1991; Silvern, Karyl, & Landis, 1995). Concerns regarding children's problems with emotional security, feelings of competence, and ability to relate to people would be appropriate to treat with such an approach.

Indirect Mechanisms Focus on Parenting

Research from other areas in psychology plus the model and mechanisms presented above suggest that clinicians need to concentrate on parenting issues in a number of ways. One goal is to focus on characteristics of the mother which influence the parent-child relationship. For example, clinicians would want to reduce the spillover of hostility and negative affect toward the children, as well as to improve the mother's mental health.

Therefore, clinicians need to attend to and treat the mother's likely depression (e.g., Webster-Stratton & Herbert, 1994). Doing so with an empowerment focus (e.g., Bilinkoff, 1995) will not only relieve depression, but will also improve her ability to be attached to her children and meet their emotional needs. Webster-Stratton and Hammond (1988) emphasize the need to take any depression on a mother's part as a "signal," and attend to her distress. According to their experience, intervention programs for mothers regarding parenting have not worked unless treatment was provided for depression as well as the children's behavior problems.

Another important aspect of parenting is to help a mother decrease her discipline and child management problems. She can be a much better parent with more successful disciplinary techniques, and will feel empowered by her improved efficacy as a mother. Blechman (1981, 1984) provides an excellent discussion of a comprehensive approach to parenting, one which addresses the individual needs of the women as well as their parenting skills. Webster-Stratton and Herbert (1994) also suggest a number of strategies which could be used by therapists to help battered women learn new skills and improve the effectiveness of their discipline.

Modes of Intervention

Interventions need to be specifically tailored to the individual child and her/his situation. Because little empirical information is available to guide interventions, service providers rely primarily on clinical and theoretical writing.

Rosenberg and Rossman (1990) is an especially valuable resource for clinicians because they discuss crisis intervention procedures. In addition, they consider the pros and cons of individual and family treatment for children of battered women, and recommend either individual or group interventions for the children. Moreover, the authors discuss frameworks utilized for group treatment. They also include helpful guidance for addressing issues related to parent-child relationships and parenting practices. Another good source for crisis intervention is Arroyo and Eth (1995).

Group interventions. Most of the literature available on interventions with children of battered women focus on discussions of group treatments. This treatment modality often is undertaken in conjunction with a family's residence in a shelter or after they have sought other assistance for the battering. Group interventions have been recommended for children with mild to moderate levels of difficulty (e.g., Hughes, 1986; Peled & Edleson, 1992; Rosenberg & Rossman, 1990). The purpose of this type of intervention is to supply the children with information and to teach them some coping strategies. In addition, group leaders often provide the youngsters with a more systems-level understanding of why spouse abuse takes place, in an effort to prevent the children from using violence as a problem-solving method in the future.

Regarding the treatment of children of battered women, no systematic investigations of the effectiveness of various treatment approaches for these children are available, though two studies present some information regarding efficacy. Jaffe et al. (1990) and Grusznski, Brink, and Edleson (1988) conducted informal evaluations of their group interventions with children in shelters. Pre-and post-group interviews were conducted and mothers and children completed several paper-and-pencil measures. The authors' results were encouraging, though no comparison groups were included. According to Jaffe et al. (1990), mothers felt satisfied with the children's participation, while the children noted that they enjoyed the 10-week group as well as learned some safety skills. In addition, more positive perceptions of the parents were reported by the children. Peled and Edleson (1992, 1995) also discuss a group intervention and present results of a qualitative investigation of both process and outcome.

Individual interventions. For more severe problems (e.g., those children with scores above the cut-off for needing clinical intervention), clinicians would likely find individual treatment to be more effective than the group modality alone. Children benefit from the focused, more intensive opportunity to learn new behaviors as well as understand and work through their negative feelings. As described above, children would profit from cognitive-behavioral treatment, play therapy approaches, or an integration of both. Cognitive-behavioral interventions are usually more focused on aggressiveness, anxiety and depression, whereas with a relationship-oriented treatment, the therapist typically concentrates on feelings of competence, autonomy and relatedness as well as emotional security. A chapter on individual intervention with children of battered women by Silvern et al. (1995) provides much useful information.

It is apparent that much more research regarding treatment of children of battered women remains to be conducted. Researchers in the field of child psychotherapy recommend investigations with a precise focus to determine which types of treatment are most effective with children with what kinds of particular difficulties, in which types of circumstances, provided by what types of therapists (e.g., Friedheim & Russ, 1993). A substantial amount of work remains to be conducted in order to ascertain the most effective methods of intervention for children with specific characteristics who have experienced particular types of violence. However, by utilizing theory, current research findings, and clinical experience to guide treatment outcome research, steps can be taken in the direction providing the most heuristic results.

CONCLUSION

Very little outcome research has been conducted with battered women and their children, with informal evaluations of group interventions being the sole exception. Whereas recommendations were made in this article on the basis of both current knowledge regarding psychological adjustment of children of battered women, and of theory growing out of that research, treatment outcome studies are sorely needed to further elucidate the most effective types of interventions for the specific problems faced by children of battered women.

REFERENCES

Arroyo, W., & Eth, S. (1995). Assessment following violence-witnessing trauma. In E. Peled, P. G. Jaffe & J. L. Edleson (Eds.), *Ending the cycle of violence: Community responses to children of battered women* (pp. 27-42). Newbury Park, CA: Sage.

Bandura, A. (1973). *Aggression: A social learning analysis.* Englewood Cliffs, NJ: Prentice-Hall.

Bilinkoff, J. (1995). Empowering battered women as mothers. In E. Peled, P. G. Jaffe & J. L. Edleson (Eds.), *Ending the cycle of violence: Community responses to children of battered women* (pp. 97-105). Newbury Park, CA: Sage.

Blechman, E. A. (1981). Toward comprehensive behavioral family interventions: An algorithm for matching families and interventions. *Behavior Modification, 5,* 221-235.

Blechman, E. A. (1984). Competent parents, competent children: Behavioral objectives of parent training. In R. A. Polster & R. F. Dangel (Eds.), *Parent training: Foundations of research and practice* (pp. 34-66). New York: Guilford.

Burns, G. L., Patterson, D. R., Nussbaum, B. R., & Parker, C. M. (1991). Disruptive behaviors in an outpatient pediatric population: Additional standardization data on the Eyberg Child Behavior Inventory. *Psychological Assessment: A Journal of Consulting and Clinical Psychology, 3,* 202-207.

Carey, M. P. (1993). Child and adolescent depression: Cognitive-behavioral therapy strategies and interventions. In A. J. Finch, Jr., W. M. Nelson III & E. S. Ott (Eds.), *Cognitive-behavioral procedures with children and adolescents* (pp. 289-314). Boston: Allyn and Bacon.

Cascardi, M., & O'Leary, K. D. (1992). Depressive symptomatology, self-esteem, and self-blame in battered women. *Journal of Family Violence, 7,* 249-259.

Christopoulos, C., Cohn, D. A., Shaw, D. S., Joyce, S., Sullivan-Hanson, J., Kraft, S. P., & Emery, R. E. (1987). Children of abused women: I. Adjustment at time of shelter residence. *Journal of Marriage and the Family, 49,* 611-619.

Cummings, E. M., & Davies, P. (1994). *Children and marital conflict: The impact of family dispute and resolution.* New York: Guilford.

Downey, G., & Coyne, J. C. (1990). Children of depressed parents: An integrative review. *Psychological Bulletin, 108,* 50-76.

Fantuzzo, J. W., De Paola, L. M., Lambert, L., Martino, T., Anderson, G., & Sutton, S. (1991). Effects of interpersonal violence on the psychological adjustment and competencies of young children. *Journal of Consulting and Clinical Psychology, 59,* 258-265.

Fauber, R., Forehand, R., Thomas, A. M., & Wierson, M. (1990). A mediational model of marital conflict on adolescent adjustment in intact and divorced families: The role of disrupted parenting. *Child Development, 61,* 1112-1123.

Feindler, E. L., & Ecton, R. B. (1986). *Anger control with adolescents.* Elmsford, NJ: Pergamon.

Finch, Jr., A. J., Nelson, III, W. M., & Moss, J. H. (1993). Childhood aggression: Cognitive-behavioral therapy strategies and interventions. In A. J. Finch, Jr., W. M. Nelson III & E. S. Ott (Eds.), *Cognitive-behavioral procedures with children and adolescents* (pp. 148-205). Boston: Allyn and Bacon.

Finch, Jr., A. J., Nelson III, W. M., & Ott, E. S. (Eds.). (1993). *Cognitive-behavioral procedures with children and adolescents.* Boston: Allyn and Bacon.

Fincham, F. D. (1994). Understanding the association between marital conflict and child adjustment: An overview. *Journal of Family Psychology, 8,* 123-127.

Fincham, F. D., Grych, J. H., & Osborne, L. N. (1994). Does marital conflict cause child maladjustment? Directions and challenges for longitudinal research. *Journal of Family Psychology, 8,* 128-140.

Forman, S. G. (1993). *Coping skills interventions for children and adolescents.* San Francisco: Jossey-Bass.

Forsstrom-Cohen, B., & Rosenbaum, A. (1985). The effects of parental marital violence on young adults: An exploratory investigation. *Journal of Marriage and the Family, 47,* 467-472.

Friedheim, D. K., & Russ, S. W. (1993). Psychotherapy with children. In C. E. Walker & M. R. Roberts (Eds.), *Handbook of clinical child psychology* (pp. 765-782). New York: Wiley.

Geffner, R., & Pagelow, M.D. (1990). Victims of spouse abuse. In R. T. Ammerman & M. Hersen (Eds.), *Treatment of family violence* (pp. 113-135). New York: Wiley.

Gil, E. (1991). *The healing power of play: Working with abused children.* New York: Guilford.

Grace, N., Spirito, A., Finch, Jr., A. J., & Ott, E. S. (1993). Coping skills for anxiety control in children. In A. J. Finch, Jr., W. M. Nelson III & E. S. Ott (Eds.), *Cognitive-behavioral procedures with children and adolescents* (pp. 257-288). Boston: Allyn and Bacon.

Graham-Bermann, S. A. (1996). Family worries: Assessment of interpersonal anxiety in children from violent and nonviolent homes. *Journal of Clinical Child Psychology, 25,* 280-287.

Grusznski, R. J., Brink, J. C., & Edleson, J. L. (1988). Support and education groups for children of battered women. *Child Welfare, 67,* 431-444.

Grych, J. H., & Fincham, F. D. (1990). Marital conflict and children's adjustment: A cognitive-contextual framework. *Psychological Bulletin, 108,* 267-290.

Hershorn, M., & Rosenbaum, A. (1985). Children of marital violence: A closer look at the unintended victims. *American Journal of Orthopsychiatry, 55,* 260-266.

Holden, G. W. (1996, June). *The stability and change of childrearing in battered women.* Paper presented at the National Conference on Children Exposed to Family Violence, Austin, TX.

Holden, G. W., & Ritchie, K. L. (1991). Linking extreme marital discord, child reading, and child behavior problems: Evidence from battered women. *Child Development, 62,* 311-327.

Hughes, H. M. (1986). Research with children in shelters: Implications for clinical services. *Children Today, 15,* 21-25. (DHHS Publication No. 86-30014)

Hughes, H. M. (1988). Psychological and behavioral correlates of family violence in child witnesses and victims. *American Journal of Orthopsychiatry, 58,* 77-90.

Hughes, H. M., & Fantuzzo, J. W. (1994). Family violence: Child. In R. T. Ammerman, M. Hersen & L. Sisson (Eds.), *Handbook of aggressive and destructive behavior in psychiatric patients* (pp. 491-508). New York: Plenum.

Hughes, H. M., & Marshall, M. (1995). Advocacy for children of battered women. In E. Peled, P. G. Jaffe & J. L. Edleson (Eds.), *Ending the cycle of violence: Community responses to children of battered women* (pp. 97-105). Newbury Park, CA: Sage.

Hughes, H. M., Parkinson, D. L., & Vargo, M. C. (1989). Witnessing spouse abuse and experiencing physical abuse: A "double whammy?" *Journal of Family Violence, 4,* 197-209.

Hughes, H. M., & Rau, T. J. (1984, August). *Psychological adjustment of battered women in shelters.* Paper presented at the annual meeting of the American Psychological Association, Toronto.

Hughes, H. M., Vargo, M. C., Ito, E. S., & Skinner, S. K. (1991). Psychological adjustment of children of battered women: Influences of gender. *Family Violence Bulletin, 7,* 15-17.

Jaffe, P. G., Wolfe, D. A., & Wilson, S. K. (1990). *Children of battered women.* Newbury Park, CA: Sage.

Jouriles, E. N., Barling, J., & O'Leary, K. D. (1987). Predicting child behavior problems in maritally violent families. *Journal of Abnormal Child Psychology, 15,* 165-173.

Kazdin, A. E. (1987). *Conduct disorders in children and adolescents.* Newbury Park, CA: Sage.

Kazdin, A. E. (1991). Aggressive behavior and conduct disorder. In T. R.

Kratochwill & R. J. Morrison (Eds.), *The practice of child psychotherapy* (pp. 174-221). Elmsford, NJ: Pergamon.

Kazdin, A. E., Esveldt-Dawson, K., French, N. H., & Unis, A. S. (1987). Problem-solving skills and relationship therapy in the treatment of antisocial child behavior. *Journal of Consulting and Clinical Psychology, 55*, 76-85.

Kendall, P. C., Chansky, T. E., Friedman, M., Kim, R., Kortlander, E., Sessa, F. M., & Siqueland, L. (1991). Treating anxiety disorders in children and adolescents. In P. C. Kendall (Ed.), *Child and adolescent therapy: Cognitive-behavioral procedures* (pp. 131-164). New York: Guilford.

Kendall, P. C., & Panichelli, S. M. (1995). Cognitive-behavioral treatments. *Journal of Abnormal Child Psychology, 23*, 107-124.

Laumakis, M. A., Margolin, G., & John, R. S. (1994, October). *The emotional, physiological and cognitive reactions of boys and girls from high-conflict and low-conflict homes to simulated marital conflict*. Paper presented at the Clinical Child Conference, Lawrence KS.

Lee, C. M., & Gotlib, I. H. (1989). Maternal depression and child adjustment: A longitudinal analysis. *Journal of Abnormal Psychology, 98*, 78-85.

McDonald, R., & Jouriles, E. N. (1991). Marital aggression and child behavior problems: Research findings, mechanisms, and intervention strategies. *The Behavior Therapist, 14*, 189-192.

Moore, T. E., & Pepler, D. J. (1996, June). *Children exposed to family violence: Gender differences*. Paper presented at the National Conference on Children Exposed to Family Violence, Austin, TX.

Moore, T., Pepler, D., Weinberg, B., Hammond, L., Waddell, J. & Weiser, L. (1990). Research on children from violent families. *Canada's Mental Health Journal, 38*, 19-23.

Orava, T. A., McLeod, P. J., & Sharpe, D. (1996). Perceptions of control, depressive symptomatology, and self-esteem of women in transition from abusive relationships. *Journal of Family Violence, 11*, 167-186.

Pagelow, M. D. (1984). *Family violence*. New York: Praeger.

Patterson, G. R., De Baryshe, B. D., & Ramsey, E. (1989). A developmental perspective on antisocial behavior. *American Psychologist, 44*, 329-335.

Peled, E., & Edleson, J. L. (1992). Multiple perspectives on groupwork with children of battered women, *Violence & Victims, 7*, 327-346.

Peled, E., & Edleson, J. L. (1995). Process and outcome in small groups for children of battered women. In E. Peled, P. G. Jaffe & J. L. Edleson (Eds.), *Ending the cycle of violence: Community responses to children of battered women* (pp. 77-96). Newbury Park, CA: Sage.

Pepler, D., & Moore, T. (1993, August). *Daughters of abused women: At risk?* Paper presented at the annual meeting of the American Psychological Association, Toronto, Canada.

Polyson, S., & Kimball, W. (1993). Social skills training with aggressive children. In A. J. Finch, Jr., W. M. Nelson III & E. S. Ott (Eds.), *Cognitive-behavioral procedures with children and adolescents* (pp. 206-232). Boston: Allyn and Bacon.

Rosenbaum, A. & O'Leary, K. D. (1981). Children: The unintended victims of marital violence. *American Journal of Orthopsychiatry, 51*, 692-699.

Rosenberg, M. S., & Rossman, B. B. R. (1990). The child witness to marital violence. In R. T. Ammerman & M. Hersen (Eds.), *Treatment of family violence* (pp. 183-210). New York: Wiley.

Ross, S. M. (1996). Risk of physical abuse to children of spouse abusing parents. *Child Abuse & Neglect, 20*, 589-598.

Rossman, B. B. R., Bingham, R. D., Cimbora, D. M., Dickerson, L. K., Dexter, R. M., Balog, F. A., & Mallah, K. (1993, August). *Children in violent families: Treatment issues and techniques.* Paper presented at the annual meeting of the American Psychological Association, Toronto, Canada.

Rossman, B. B. R., Heaton, M. K., Moss, T. A., Malik, N., Lintz, C. & Romero, J. (1991, August). *Functioning in abused and nonabused witnesses to family violence.* Paper presented at the annual meeting of the American Psychological Association, San Francisco, CA.

Rossman, B. B. R., Hughes, H. M., & Hanson, K. L. (in press). Victimization of school-aged children. In B. B. R. Rossman & M. S. Rosenberg (Eds.), *Multiple victimization of children: Conceptual, developmental, research, and treatment issues.* Newbury Park, CA: Sage.

Rossman, B. B. R., & Rosenberg, M. S. (1997). Psychological maltreatment: A needs analysis and application for children in violent families. In R. Geffner, S. B. Sorenson, and P. K. Lundberg-Love (Eds.), *Violence and sexual abuse at home: Current issues in spousal battering and child maltreatment.* Binghamton, NY: The Haworth Press, Inc.

Silvern, L., Karyl, J., & Landis, T. Y. (1995). Individual psychotherapy for the traumatized children of abused women. In E. Peled, P. G. Jaffe & J. L. Edleson (Eds.), *Ending the cycle of violence: Community responses to children of battered women* (pp. 43-76). Newbury Park, CA: Sage.

Stark, K. W., Rouse, L. W., & Livingston, R. (1991). Treatment of depression during childhood: Cognitive-behavioral procedures for the individual and the family. In P. C. Kendall (Ed.), *Child and adolescent therapy: Cognitive-behavioral procedures* (pp. 165-208). New York: Guilford.

Sternberg, K. J., Lamb, M. E., Greenbaum, C., Cicchetti, D., Dawud, S., Cortes, R. M., Krispin, O., & Lorey, F. (1993). Effects of domestic violence on children's behavior problems and depression. *Developmental Psychology, 29*, 44-52.

Straus, M. A., & Gelles, R. J. (1986). Societal change and change in family violence from 1975 to 1985 as revealed by two surveys. *Journal of Marriage and the Family, 48*, 465-479.

Straus, M., Gelles, R., & Steinmetz, S. (1980). *Behind closed doors: Violence in the American family.* New York: Anchor.

Webster-Stratton, C., & Hammond, M. (1988). Maternal depression and its relationship to life stress, perceptions of child behavior problems, parenting behaviors, and child conduct problems. *Journal of Abnormal Child Psychology, 16*, 299-315.

Webster-Stratton, C., & Herbert, M. (1994). *Troubled families, problem children.* New York: Wiley.

Wilson, S. K. (1991, March). *Improving social problem-solving skills in children from violent homes.* Paper presented at the annual meeting of the American Orthopsychiatric Association, Toronto, Canada.

Wolfe, D. A., Jaffe, P., Wilson, S., & Zak, L. (1985). Children of battered women: The relationship of child behavior to family violence and maternal stress. *Journal of Consulting and Clinical Psychology, 53,* 657-665.

Wolfe, D. A., Zak, L., Wilson, S., & Jaffe, P. (1986). Child witnesses to violence: Critical issues in behavioral and social adjustment. *Journal of Abnormal Child Psychology, 14,* 95-104.

Psychological Maltreatment:
A Needs Analysis and Application
for Children in Violent Families

B. B. Robbie Rossman
Mindy S. Rosenberg

SUMMARY. Current issues regarding the definition of psychological maltreatment and its impact on children are discussed. The argument is made that psychological maltreatment can be understood as parenting and socialization practices that leave a child's basic psychological needs unmet, and that children exposed to interparental violence should be viewed as victims of psychological maltreatment. A needs analysis based on developmental theory and research is presented as a context within which to view psychological maltreatment. Using that conceptualization, research findings concerning the behavioral, cognitive, and social-emotional difficulties of children exposed to marital violence are examined. Based on this developmental analysis, recommendations are made regarding research that is needed in the areas of these children and psychological maltreatment. *[Article copies available for a fee from The Haworth Document Delivery Service: 1-800-342-9678. E-mail address: getinfo@haworth.com]*

KEYWORDS. Family violence, child maltreatment, battering, child adjustment, child development

---

Address correspondence to: B. B. Robbie Rossman, Department of Psychology, University of Denver, Denver, CO 80208.

[Haworth co-indexing entry note]: "Psychological Maltreatment: A Needs Analysis and Application for Children in Violent Families." Rossman, B. B. Robbie, and Mindy S. Rosenberg. Co-published simultaneously in *Journal of Aggression, Maltreatment & Trauma* (Haworth Maltreatment & Trauma Press, an imprint of The Haworth Press, Inc.) Vol. 1, No. 1 (#1), 1997, pp. 245-262; and: *Violence and Sexual Abuse at Home: Current Issues in Spousal Battering and Child Maltreatment* (ed: Robert Geffner, Susan B. Sorenson, and Paula K. Lundberg-Love) Haworth Maltreatment & Trauma Press, an imprint of The Haworth Press, Inc., 1997, pp. 245-262. Single or multiple copies of this article are available for a fee from The Haworth Document Delivery Service [1-800-342-9678, 9:00 a.m. - 5:00 p.m. (EST). E-mail address: getinfo@haworth.com].

Within the past decade, the problem of child abuse has received unprecedented attention from researchers, clinicians, the media, and policy makers. Psychologists have made significant strides in proposing theoretical models to guide research on the etiology and consequences of child maltreatment (e.g., Cicchetti & Carlson, 1989), and in designing empirically-based intervention and prevention programs (e.g., Willis, Holden, & Rosenberg, 1992). However, as we enter the next phase of research in this field, it is necessary to take stock of our knowledge base and to identify critical areas for future inquiry. The purpose of this article is to discuss a timely issue relating to children in abusive families and to address the implications for theory-building and future research directions in the field: psychological maltreatment with specific emphasis on children who are exposed to marital violence. We will define what is meant by psychological maltreatment and present a developmental framework of children's psychological needs that may be helpful for understanding the variety of behavioral and socioemotional outcomes we have seen among children from violent marital relationships. We then review the literature and research issues for these children, and discuss future research directions.

PSYCHOLOGICAL MALTREATMENT

In some ways, the study of psychological maltreatment is not a new area of inquiry for psychology. Clinicians have long been aware of the potential psychological damage from childhood experiences of gross emotional abuse or neglect, yet their interventions have been based more on intuition than on empirical findings. Although early definitions of child abuse (e.g., the Child Abuse Prevention and Treatment Act of 1974) alluded to "mental injury," a formal definition of psychological maltreatment did not appear until 1983, as a result of the International Conference on Psychological Abuse of Children and Youth in Indianapolis. This definition states:

> Psychological maltreatment of children and youth consists of acts of omission and commission which are judged by community standards and professional expertise to be psychologically damaging. Such acts are committed by individuals, single or collectively, who by their characteristics (e.g., age, status, knowledge, organizational form) are in a position of differential power that renders a child vulnerable. Such acts damage immediately or ultimately the behavioral, cognitive, or physical functioning of the child. Examples of psychological maltreatment include acts of rejecting, terrorizing,

isolating, exploiting, and mis-socializing. (Office for the Study of the Psychological Rights of the Child, 1983, p. 2)

Further elaborating the effects of psychological maltreatment on children's development, Garbarino, Guttman, and Seeley (1986) describe it as a "concerted attack by an adult on a child's development of self and social competence" (p. 8). Hart and Brassard (1990) argue that the different forms of psychological maltreatment can be organized into one or more of the following categories: verbal and emotional assault; passive and passive-aggressive inattention to needs; prevention or punishment of the development of self-esteem and interpersonal skills; interference with the development of personal autonomy; and impairment of the child's ability to function within an expected range of performance. Some researchers consider psychological maltreatment to be the core component of physical and sexual abuse, and to be more prevalent and harmful to children than either form of abuse alone (e.g., Claussen & Crittenden, 1991; Hart & Brassard, 1990). Others propose that researchers measure each form of abuse separately, and they would not include acts of physical and sexual assault under the rubric of psychological maltreatment (McGee & Wolfe, 1991).

Turning formal definitions into operational definitions for research purposes continues to remain an unresolved issue in the field (McGee & Wolfe, 1991; Rosenberg, 1987a; Shaver, Goodman, Rosenberg, & Orcutt, 1991). Many operational definitions are possible, and Hart and Brassard (1990) have suggested several. They have focused on providing behavioral examples of general categories, including *spurning* (e.g., a type of verbal aggression that combines rejection and hostile degradation such as ridiculing, shaming, belittling); *isolating* (e.g., locking a child in a closet or room for an extended period of time or forbidding social interaction outside the family); *exploiting/corrupting*, which involves modeling or encouraging antisocial behavior (e.g., prostitution, criminal activities, substance abuse); *denying emotional expressiveness* (e.g., ignoring a child's attempts to interact or reacting to a child in a mechanistic way without affection); and *terrorizing* (e.g., forcing a child to watch verbal or physical aggression directed toward loved ones or objects; threatening to physically hurt, kill, or abandon the child if expectations are not met). It is this latter category of psychological maltreatment that describes the experiences of children who are exposed to their parents' violence; however, it should be noted that these children also frequently are exposed to multiple forms of psychological and physical abuse.

For purposes of this article, psychological maltreatment can be understood as parenting and socialization practices in which a child's fundamental psychological needs are unmet or met in a deviant fashion, and which require the child to develop unhealthy adaptive strategies to meet those needs. Examples of psychological needs include competence, interpersonal, and autonomy-related needs. In the following sections, we consider the literature on children's psychological needs in conjunction with outcome research on children exposed to marital violence.

A DEVELOPMENTAL NEEDS FRAMEWORK

We adopted a developmental needs framework based on Connell's (1988) work to help understand the psychological outcomes of children exposed to marital violence. Connell derived his framework from an integration of over 30 years of research in child development, drawing on concepts from attachment, object relations, social learning, and ego-analytic theories, and research on intrinsic motivation and emotion regulation. He identified three need domains that are essential for children's psychological growth: competence, autonomy, and relatedness. Connell (1988) proposed that children develop self-system processes (i.e., coping strategies that include both self-appraisals and behaviors) to coordinate the fulfillment of these needs with the demands and provision of their environment (e.g., family, school, peers). Within this framework, children's psychological outcomes are considered a reflection of the extent to which certain needs have or have not been fulfilled, and children's self-system processes are defined as strategies that children develop to accommodate to their environment. Researchers could identify specific psychological outcomes that reflect the extent to which certain needs have been filled and the associated self-system processes developed, and investigate the features of the child's home, school, and peer environment that may have left needs unmet or been met in deviant ways. Alternatively, researchers could assess environmental characteristics (e.g., degree and type of violence exposure or experience, quality of parent-child interaction) to predict how self-system processes develop to accommodate to those circumstances.

Connell's (1988) developmental needs framework makes several assumptions. In order for a child to experience a sense of competence within a particular situation, it is critical to develop self-system processes that include knowledge of how to accomplish specific outcomes ("I know what it takes to do well") and beliefs about one's personal capacity to perform the strategy ("I have the skills to do well"). Aspects of the caretaking environment that support the development of a sense of capacity and knowledge of strategies to obtain goals are structure and consistency. Caretakers who communicate clear and realistic expectations for children's behavior, apply consequences consistently, and provide useful feedback about their children's performance are thought to facilitate the development of competence-related strategies and skills. Alternatively, the lack of structure, inconsistency, unrealistically high expectations and non-contingent responding by caretakers and others in the child's environment are thought to interfere with the healthy development of competence strategies and diminish the fulfillment of competence needs.

The self-system processes associated with autonomy are considered "self-regulation processes" and include cognitions and behaviors that involve children's personal choice and sense of personal control that enable them to initiate, inhibit, maintain, and redirect their behavior and emotions. Features of the caretaking environment that support the development of autonomy self-system processes include providing children with opportunities to make personal choices, acknowledging their feelings, and teaching them how to initiate and regulate their behavior and emotional expression. Caretakers who are overly controlling and model dysregulation of behavior and affect should not be surprised that their children may have difficulty in this domain.

Finally, the development of relatedness self-system processes involves cognitions and behaviors associated with the child feeling secure in his/her relationship with significant others, valued by others, and experiencing him/herself as worthy and capable of affection. Aspects of the caretaking environment that support the development of relatedness strategies include sensitive, involved caretaking that communicates interest, enjoyment, and acceptance to the child. Isolating, ignoring, or shaming children communicates lack of worthiness and children may have difficulty accepting and valuing themselves when feedback about their self-worth has been so negative and damaging. Thus, the environment plays a role in shaping which types of self-system processes (i.e., healthy or unhealthy) a child develops while attempting to fulfill basic psychological needs and in the degree to which those needs are met.

The developmental needs analysis presented here facilitates an understanding of children exposed to marital violence and other victims of psychological maltreatment in at least two ways. First, the three need domains identified by Connell (1988) are those that are highlighted in every major definition of psychological maltreatment as being frustrated, misdirected, or unfulfilled. Second, the framework emphasizes the interaction between need fulfillment, characteristics of the caretaking environment, and the child's development of self-system processes. Therefore, we propose that the psychological outcomes described in research on children exposed to marital violence are the result of the interplay between the child's attempts to fulfill significant needs and the manner in which the environment facilitates or hinders the child's attempts to do so.

In the following section, we review the outcome research on children exposed to marital violence in the context of Connell's (1988) needs analysis. We review what is known about these children in terms of competence, autonomy, and relatedness domains, what is known about family environmental characteristics that either facilitate or obstruct children's need development, and offer some speculations about the connection between them. Because marital violence constitutes a chronic rather than an acute stressor for many children, the psychological outcomes for these children would be expected to reflect more chronic adaptations in self-system processes rather than temporary adjustments in behavior (Garbarino, Kostelny, & Dubrow, 1991). Therefore, based on the previous discussion of self-system processes, we would anticipate that children exposed to marital violence may have problems in the following domains: ways to attain socially valued outcomes; experiencing the self as initiator and regulator of one's behavior; and feeling loved and cared for by oneself and others.

A DEVELOPMENTAL NEEDS ANALYSIS

Competence

Research on children exposed to marital violence has identified some problems for these children in the domain of competence, although considerably more research needs to be conducted. For example, in contrast to children who have not been exposed, school-aged children who have been exposed to marital violence are reported by their mothers to have lower social skills (Moore & Pepler, 1989) and school competence (Pepler & Moore, 1989). However, other studies (e.g., Rosenberg, 1984; Rossman & Rosenberg, 1992) indicate higher social competence from mothers' reports, although it should be noted that neither research group used *in vivo* observations of children and relied instead on a Child Behavior Checklist (Achenbach & Edelbrock, 1983) completed by mothers or the primary caretaking figures. Because the social competence scale on the Child Behavior Checklist asks for participation in activities, hobbies, organizations, and groups, answers can vary depending on social class, access to community activities, and interviewing style of the data collector. Rosenberg (1984) also found that many of these children prefer to be away from the tense situation in the home if possible, and tend to play outside and participate in activities, but that does not necessarily indicate higher social competence in its truest sense.

In considering contradictory findings such as those just cited, it should be noted that most of the research on children exposed to marital violence has been accomplished with the aid of mothers and children from battered women's shelters or other community agencies. Thus, our current knowledge is based on the experience and perceptions of volunteer children and mothers who seek assistance from community agencies. We do not know how well these results would generalize to nonvolunteers within the same agencies or to violent families who might be identified in community samples. Our work with shelter children's coordinators suggests that volunteer families are some of the more well organized in the shelter and that non-volunteer families are more chaotic. Children in nonvolunteer families may experience a more negative childrearing environment which could exacerbate their difficulties. Our work with mothers and children who have contacted community agencies but returned home suggests that, based on maternal report, these families may experience somewhat less violent environments and the children may show fewer behavior problems (Rossman & Rosenberg, 1992). However, children in community samples of divorcing families do experience difficulties in competence and other domains (Hodges, 1991). Thus, there is a clear need for further research to examine the status of children exposed to marital violence who do not come into contact with community agencies.

Returning to the existing research, other findings that pertain to the competence domain indicate that children exposed to marital violence evidence lower levels of perceived competence, perceived control, and self-esteem (Moore & Pepler, 1989; Rawlins & Rossman, 1991; Rossman & Rosenberg, 1992). In addition, children exposed to marital violence have difficulties in their social problem-solving abilities (Rosenberg, 1987b). First, children who are exposed to relatively high levels of violence (i.e., many types and a high frequency of violent behavior) perform significantly less well on an index of interpersonal sensitivity that assesses the ability to understand social situations and the thoughts and feelings of persons involved in these situations. Perhaps conflictual situations have aroused so much anxiety in the past that these children have not developed appropriate skills in this domain, or alternatively, perhaps the anxiety aroused by interpersonal conflict may interfere with skill expression (Fischer & Pipp, 1984). Second, children from violent homes tend to choose either passive or aggressive strategies to resolve interpersonal conflict, depending on the level of violence in the home, and are less likely to choose assertive strategies. Moreover, children who choose nonconstructive problem-solving strategies (i.e., verbal or physical aggression, passive resolution by others' actions) show more behavioral problems and fewer social competencies as perceived by their mothers (Groisser, 1986).

A needs analysis of these children's psychological functioning suggests that their low perceived competence, control, self-esteem, social problem-solving and possibly social competence skills may indicate interference with the development of self-system processes that contribute to competence need-fulfillment. As stated earlier, the attainment of competence needs requires that children develop self-system processes that facilitate obtaining socially valued outcomes through experiencing oneself as having strategies to achieve these outcomes and the capacity to enact them. The environmental characteristics thought to foster these processes lie in the structure provided in the caretaking environment and later at school with peers. Consistency in parenting and predictable home routines allow the child to discern the contingencies between the child's actions and the parents' behavior, thus developing a sense of personal capability and strategies for how to achieve outcomes successfully and how to avoid failure.

Research on these children recently has begun to assess specific family and other environmental characteristics to determine their contribution to the child's psychological functioning. These families generally are characterized by lower parenting consistency (Holden & Ritchie, 1991), and significantly greater family (Rossman & Rosenberg, 1992) and maternal stress (Holden & Ritchie, 1991) that may increase the unpredictability of the family environment for the child and undermine the development of healthy competence self-system processes.

Although not all maritally violent couples experience a cycle of violence in exactly the same way as described by Walker (1984), many battered women and their children find some predictability to the violence in their family environment. Such predictability can serve as a basis for the development of unhealthy competence self-system processes. Because physical aggression is modeled as a problem-solving coping strategy that produces results, and physical power is highlighted as an important capacity, children may develop competence self-system processes from the actual violent events themselves. Other capabilities that are likely to become important competence self-system processes include the development of aggressive attribution biases (Reinhold & Lochman, 1991) and aggressive problem-solving strategies (Rosenberg, 1987b). Moreover, coping strategies that function to avoid violent encounters or even mild interpersonal conflict may become equally important capacities to develop, especially for younger or physically weaker children. In that case, strategies may be learned to detect impending violence, such as the hypervigilant or sharpening perceptual style around aggressive stimuli noted in abused preschoolers (Rieder & Cicchetti, 1989).

In addition to developing competence self-system processes from the violent events themselves, children may try to create structure that will help them understand their dangerous, inconsistent family environment. In our own research, we have studied beliefs about control that children hold for themselves and their parents during incidents of marital conflict and violence (Rossman & Rosenberg, 1992). We found that these children attempt to place structure on their parents' violent incidents by blaming their own behavior. We speculate that holding themselves responsible may help them experience greater predictability by developing strategies to modify their own behavior. In reality, these control beliefs do not work, which may leave these children with self-system processes that reflect uncertainty about how to regulate their anger in interpersonal relationships, and confusion or depression about their capacity to achieve valued goals at home, with peers, or in school. Dodge and Somberg (1987) have described the peer rejection that accompanies aggressive biases and approaches to peer interaction, which may begin a cycle of further aggression and rejection.

In sum, it should be emphasized that these children are trying to discern structure, contingencies, and means-end relationships from their environment, despite their difficulties with social problem-solving and lowered feelings about their competence across multiple domains of their lives. The issue is that the consistencies that do exist for these children at home may be negative and socially deviant, leaving children exposed to marital violence to develop self-system processes that can lead to experiences and feelings of lowered competence, powerlessness, rejection, and confusion about socially appropriate and constructive strategies to obtain their goals.

Autonomy

An increasing body of literature is converging to reveal that children exposed to marital violence show elevated levels of internalizing (e.g., anxiety, depression, somatic complaints) and externalizing (e.g., aggression, delinquency) problem behaviors (Holden & Ritchie, 1991; Hughes, 1988; Jaffe, Wolfe, & Wilson, 1990; Rawlins & Rossman, 1991; Rosenberg & Rossman, 1990) even after controlling for marital discord, covert marital tension, or parenting variables such as discrepancy in child-rearing strategies (Jenkins & Smith, 1991). Whereas most of these findings pertain to school-age children, there is some indication that toddler and preschool children in these situations also show heightened levels of symptom behaviors (Hughes, 1988; Jouriles, Pfiffner, & O'Leary, 1988), particularly behaviors indicative of post-traumatic stress disorder (PTSD) such as psychosomatic and anxiety-related symptomatology (Rossman, 1992). A PTSD subscale based on the Child Behavior Checklist was significantly elevated for preschool children in violent homes compared to other preschoolers (Wolfe, Gentile, & Wolfe, 1989). Terr (1988) has noted PTSD and some dissociative symptoms in her preschool trauma clients. In addition, Pynoos and colleagues (Nader, Pynoos, Fairbanks & Frederick, 1990; Pynoos et al., 1987) reported PTSD symptoms in children who witnessed a schoolyard sniper attack. The symptoms were more severe for the children in closer proximity to the killings (Pynoos & Nader, 1989). Terr (1991) believes that children who experience ongoing chronic trauma, such as abuse or family violence, are likely to show more severe symptoms of distress than are children exposed to acute, single traumata. Overall, the elevated levels of problem behaviors and PTSD symptoms may be best understood as signs of heightened and unregulated distress. As such, they indicate problems of behavior and affect regulation that suggest that children exposed to marital violence may have difficulties with the fulfillment of autonomy needs and the development of autonomy self-system processes.

Support for the development of autonomy-related self-system processes is thought to be provided by caretaking practices that allow the child to experience personal choice and the ability to initiate and regulate his/her behavior and emotional expression. In homes with marital violence, children may see themselves responsible for or as initiating the violence. It is not unusual for children of battered women to report attempts to modify their own behavior (e.g., "I try to be good") to circumvent parental violence (Rossman & Rosenberg, 1992). Marital violence may become the focus of children's behavioral regulatory attempts because a primary motivation to behave in a certain manner is to avoid fear or physical injury to oneself or others (i.e., mother, siblings). These children's sense of personal choice or self-regulation may be overshadowed by the external demand to regulate parental behavior. It is possible that some of these children would have difficulty developing an internal locus of control.

Furthermore, models for modulated behavior and affect regulation may not be available in violent families. The message about affect regulation to these children is that anger is not controllable and that control over others resides in the person with the greatest physical and psychological power. It is possible that these children's beliefs about their own control would tend to be based on wishes about or distortions of the family situation. These beliefs could fulfill the need to feel some sense of personal control or regulation but would be based on a defensive (i.e., ego protective) foundation (Skinner, Chapman, & Baltes, 1988), and thus, might endanger the healthy development of other elements of the self-system. Rossman and Rosenberg (1992) found that children in high conflict and stress families (which included marital violence) who held strong beliefs of control over their parents' conflict and violence also showed dramatic deficits in perceived competence. Although the children's attempts to control their parents' violence were rarely successful, we speculate that they needed to retain them for ego protective purposes, and may have needed to reconcile their failures at control by sacrificing their beliefs about their own competence (by telling themselves they would have been able to control their parents' conflict and violence if only they were competent enough).

Whereas authoritative parenting (Baumrind, 1971) tends to promote healthy autonomy and a sense of self-control, authoritarian (in the extreme, abusive) and/or disorganized (permissive) parenting encourages a child to develop a sense of external control or confusion about control. Although parenting styles have not been studied extensively in families with maritally violent couples, power-assertive and possessive parent-child relationship styles were associated significantly with spousal aggression (Rossman, Rosenberg, Rawlins, & Malik, 1991). Negative, overcontrolling, and unrealistic attitudes about children have been found to characterize abusive parents (Azar, 1991; Wolfe, 1987) and to moderate negative child behavior outcomes in families with marital violence (Rossman et al., 1991). Most importantly, these parenting characteristics clearly distort what children learn about self-regulation and personal choice, demonstrating only that power and external sources regulate the self and dictate choice.

Relatedness

There is relatively little research information about children exposed to marital violence in the domain of relatedness. Findings of lower self-worth and aggressive expectations of others, as indicated by these children's choice of social problem-solving strategies, may reflect problems in the attainment of relatedness needs and the development of relatedness self-system processes, but more research clearly is needed in this area. Additional research could augment the literature such as that conducted on children who also are abused or children who are exposed to parental discord but not violence. For example, Cummings, Pellegrini, Notarius, and Cummings (1989) found that as marital discord becomes higher in families with preschoolers, children become more negatively reactive to adult anger. Additionally, Cummings and El-Sheikh (1990) found that insecurely attached preschool children were those most negative in their behavioral and emotional reactions to adult anger (i.e., as opposed to those children who were prosocially reactive). These types of findings, including those that characterize abused children as insecurely attached to their primary caretakers (e.g., Crittenden & Ainsworth, 1989), suggest that emotional security of attachment may be tied closely to the level of anger and violence in the marital relationship (Cummings & Davies, 1994).

The distress represented by heightened problem behaviors and lowered self-worth in children exposed to marital violence may indicate not only self-regulation problems but also failures in perceived security. For children of violent couples, a strong message is that relationships can be dangerous and/or unpredictable. This message would make fulfillment of relatedness needs and healthy development of relatedness self-system process (i.e., a felt security of relationships as a haven during danger, felt self-worth as an organizing self-structure) difficult to achieve. The aspects of sensitive caretaking (i.e., available caretaker when needed, predominantly positive tone during interaction) that are thought to foster development of relatedness self-system processes may be absent or inconsistent in maritally violent families. Maternal availability is lower in violent families (Rawlins & Rossman, 1991), and the level of emotional negativity is higher, at least in terms of the sheer frequency of marital conflict (Rossman & Rosenberg, 1992). Therefore, self-system processes such as "I'm not valuable" or "Relationships are potentially dangerous" may underlie how these children approach the task of fulfilling relatedness needs. Moreover, opportunities may be limited for children exposed to violence to observe role models in their families who have a positive sense of self-worth. Battered women, male batterers (Aguilar & Nightingale, 1991; Jaffe et al., 1990), and abusive parents (Wolfe, 1987) have lower self-worth than their nonbattered or nonabusive counterparts. Thus, neither observational nor interactive experiences with caretakers may be likely to provide these children with sources of information about positive self-esteem or being valued, both important building blocks for the development of relatedness self-system processes for successful interpersonal relationships and social interactions.

In sum, it seems both possible and useful to interpret these children's cognitions and behaviors as adaptations of need-fulfillment strategies to a conflictual and violent parenting environment. This type of framework could be helpful in understanding the difficulties of children in divorcing families where conflict is high or other situations that may involve various forms of psychological maltreatment.

RESEARCH ISSUES AND FUTURE DIRECTIONS

The developmental needs analysis presented here for children who are exposed to their parents' violence offers a framework for defining psychological maltreatment and for viewing these children's cognitive, behavioral, and emotional difficulties as adaptations to a violent and dysfunctional family system. While this discussion has been speculative in its attempt to integrate child symptoms with child needs and coping strategies as they develop in a non-normative caretaking environment, it has highlighted specific areas for research. Future research areas to pursue include:

1. More research is needed on children exposed to marital violence that integrates developmental theory with clinical outcome measures. Until recently, the majority of research studies on these children have been atheoretical in nature, focusing on differences between children who have and who have not been exposed to marital violence (e.g., Holden & Ritchie, 1991), or in some cases, attempting to make distinctions between children who have been exposed to marital verbal aggression but not physical aggression (Rossman & Rosenberg, 1992). Such investigations are needed to document that children exposed to family violence were affected by violence, although they themselves were not the direct recipients of the abuse. Now we are at a point in the field where it is necessary to incorporate theory into our research conceptualizations. An example of this approach is found in the work of Cicchetti and colleagues (e.g., Cicchetti & Carlson, 1989) who utilize attachment theory as an explanatory and predictive tool in the area of child abuse. The adaptation of Connell's (1988) motivational needs analysis and development of processes reflecting the self is one way to interpret symptomatology of children in violent homes. Other developmental theories/models could be applied, including attachment, emotion regulation (Kopp, 1989), development of aggression (Emery, 1989), and newer models of trauma (Terr, 1991), social perception and cognition (Grych & Fincham, 1993).

2. More identification and elaboration is needed regarding environmental characteristics that contribute to the psychological development of these children. By environmental characteristics, we mean qualities in the family, school, peer, and neighborhood environments. Until very recently, background environmental characteristics represented only one variable (i.e., the presence or absence of violence in the marital relationship). Slowly, the research community is recognizing that there are differences in violent relationships that need to be assessed, and that there are differences in parenting strategies and the quality of parent-child relationships within violent families. Although violent incidents between the marital couple are the most obvious events to assess, they do not occur continuously, and we

know relatively little about the intervening times in these children's family lives. In addition, we know even less about other environmental characteristics that affect these children, such as school, peer groups, and the quality of neighborhood life.

3. In contrast to research conducted on preschool and school-age children in violent homes, we have very little empirical information on adolescents exposed to such violence, including those where the violence occurred since they were young and those where violence started or escalated during adolescence. Information about this age group typically comes from clinician reports, or most recently, from retrospective accounts from juvenile or criminal institutions where adolescents have been committed for serious violent crimes. One of the authors (M. R.), who consults with attorneys who represent extremely violent juvenile and adult offenders, has found that these individuals, typically males, were exposed to extreme marital violence as they were growing up and also experienced multiple and serious forms of physical and psychological abuse. This finding also has been documented by Lewis and colleagues who interviewed violent delinquents and prison inmates on death row (Lewis, Mallouh, & Webb, 1989). There continue to be many unanswered questions about the complicated relationship between exposure to violence, experiencing abuse, and later violent behavior. Recent reviews (DiLalla & Gottesman, 1991; Widom, 1991) provide a promising beginning to identifying environmental, biological, and genetic contributors to various kinds of violent and antisocial behavior. The field needs prospective longitudinal research that begins to identify adolescents at risk of committing violent crimes, and to determine what distinguishes them from adolescents from similar environmental circumstances who are at lower risk.

4. Connell's model (1988) and our adaptation to children exposed to marital violence can guide thinking and conceptualization regarding how developmental systems may be distorted for children in violent families. Specific information is needed to determine the salience of each fundamental need during different developmental periods (i.e., infancy, preschool, school-age, and adolescence). The relationship between specific self-system processes of these children and the key features of their environments also deserve further study. Rather than continuing the research focus on child outcome only, it would be important to think about the processes that contribute to outcome and attempt to identify and elaborate on those processes.

5. Research that informs intervention and evaluates interventions with children in violent families also is a high priority. Given empirical

information about these children's self-system processes and the relationship to environmental characteristics, it might be helpful to develop new assessment instruments. Such measures could assess aspects of the caretaking environment and children's understandings and strategies regarding need fulfillment. These types of instruments could be used to gather information for situations such as custody determinations where the children have not been physically abused but the wife has been battered. Recently, several states (e.g., California, Louisiana, and others) have endorsed the idea that exposure to marital violence must be a consideration when making custody and visitation rights decisions. This has also been supported by a recent task force of the American Psychological Association (1996).

Interventions need to get both appropriate environmental provisions in place and restructure distorted self-system processes. Once interventions are in place, good evaluation procedures will be crucial (Rosenberg & Rossman, 1990). Further progress requires major research and social service policy efforts to change the process of developmental distortion, aggression, and victimization that is likely to be the legacy of children who are exposed to marital violence.

REFERENCES

Achenbach, T. M., & Edelbrock, C. (1983). *Manual for the Child Behavior Checklist and Revised Child Behavior Profile.* Burlington, VT: Department of Psychiatry, University of Vermont.

Aguilar, R., & Nightingale, N. (1991). *Low self-esteem and the battered woman.* Paper presented at the annual meeting of the Rocky Mountain Psychological Association, Denver, CO.

American Psychological Association (1996). *Violence and the family: Report of the American Psychological Association Presidential Task Force on violence and the family.* Washington, DC: Author.

Azar, S. T. (1991). *The determinants of "maladaptive" parenting: Validation of a social cognitive model.* Paper presented at the "New directions in child and family research: Shaping Head Start in the 90's" conference, Arlington, VA.

Baumrind, D. (1971). Current patterns of parental authority. *Developmental Psychology Monograph, 4,* 887-896.

Child Abuse Prevention and Treatment Act of 1974 (1974). Public law 92-247. *U.S. Statutes at Large, 88,* 4-8.

Cicchetti, D., & Carlson, V. (Eds.). (1989). *Child maltreatment: Theory and research on the causes and consequences of child abuse and neglect.* New York: Cambridge University Press.

Claussen, A. H., & Crittenden, P. M. (1991). Physical and psychological maltreatment: Relationship among types of maltreatment. *Child Abuse and Neglect, 15,* 5-18.

Connell, J. P. (1988). Context, self and action: A motivational analysis of self-system processes across the life-span. In D. Cicchetti (Eds.), *The self in transition: Infancy to childhood* (pp. 119-137). Chicago: University of Chicago Press.

Crittenden, P. M., & Ainsworth, M. D. S. (1989). Child maltreatment and attachment theory. In D. Cicchetti & V. Carlson (Eds.), *Child maltreatment: Theory and research on the causes and consequences of child abuse and neglect* (pp. 183-199). New York: Cambridge University Press.

Cummings, E. M., & Davies, P. T. (1994). *Children and marital conflict: The impact of family dispute and resolution.* New York: Guilford.

Cummings, E. M., & El-Sheikh, M. (1990). Children's coping with angry environments: A process-oriented approach. In E. M. Cummings, A. L. Greene & K. H. Karrakee (Eds.), *Life-span developmental psychology: Perspectives on stress and coping* (pp. 131-150). Hillsdale, NJ: Erlbaum.

Cummings, J. S., Pellegrini, D., Notarius, C., & Cummings, E. M. (1989). Children's responses to angry adult behavior as a function of marital distress and history of interparent hostility. *Child Development, 60,* 1035-1043.

DiLalla, L. F., & Gottesman, I. I. (1991). Biological and genetic contributors to violence–Widom's untold tale. *Psychological Bulletin, 109,* 125-129.

Dodge, K. A., & Somberg, D. R. (1987). Hostile attributions among aggressive boys are exacerbated under conditions of threat to self. *Child Development, 58,* 213-224.

Emery, R. E. (1989). Family violence. *American Psychologist, 44,* 321-328.

Fischer, K. W., & Pipp, S. C. (1984). Development of the structures of unconscious thought. In K. S. Bowers & D. Meichenbaum (Eds.), *The unconscious reconsidered* (pp. 88-148). New York: Wiley.

Garbarino, J., Guttman, E., & Seeley, J. (1986). *The psychologically battered child: Strategies for identification, assessment and intervention.* San Francisco: Jossey-Bass.

Garbarino, J., Kostelny, K., & Dubrow, N. (1991). What children can tell us about living in danger. *American Psychologist, 46,* 376-383.

Groisser, D. (1986). *Child witness to interparental violence: Social problem solving skills and behavioral adjustment.* Unpublished Master's thesis. University of Denver, Denver, CO.

Grych, J. H., & Fincham, F. D. (1993). Children's appraisals of marital conflict: Initial investigations of the cognitive-contextual framework. *Child Development, 64,* 215-230.

Hart, S. N., & Brassard, M. R. (1990). Psychological maltreatment of children. In R. T. Ammerman & M. Hersen (Eds.), *Treatment of family violence: A sourcebook* (pp. 77-112). New York: Wiley.

Hodges, W. F. (1991). *Interventions for children of divorce: Custody, access, and psychopathology* (2nd edition). New York: Wiley.

Holden, G. W., & Ritchie, K. L. (1991). Linking extreme marital discord, child-rearing, and child behavior problems: Evidence from battered women. *Child Development, 62,* 311-327.

Hughes, H. M. (1988). Psychological and behavioral correlates of family violence in child witnesses and victims. *American Journal of Orthopsychiatry, 58,* 77-90.

Jaffe, P. G., Wolfe, D. A., & Wilson, S. K. (1990). *Children of battered women.* Newbury Park, CA: Sage.

Jenkins, J. M., & Smith, M. A. (1991). Marital disharmony and children's behavioral problems: Aspects of a poor marriage that affect children adversely. *Journal of Child Psychology and Psychiatry, 32,* 793-810.

Jouriles, E. M., Pfiffner, L. J., & O'Leary, S. G. (1988). Marital conflict, parenting, and toddler conduct problems. *Journal of Abnormal Child Psychology, 16,* 197-206.

Kopp, C. B. (1989). Regulation of distress and negative emotions: A developmental view. *Developmental Psychology, 25,* 343-354.

Lewis, D. O., Mallouh, C., & Webb, V. (1989). Child abuse, delinquency, and violent criminality. In D. Cicchetti & V. Carlson (Eds.), *Child maltreatment: Theory and research on the causes of child abuse and neglect* (pp. 707-721). New York: Cambridge University Press.

McGee, R. A., & Wolfe, D. A. (1991). Psychological maltreatment: Toward an operational definition. *Development and Psychopathology, 3,* 3-22.

Moore, T. E., & Peplar, D. (1989, August). *Domestic violence and children's psychosocial adjustment: Exploring the linkage.* Paper presented at the annual meeting of the American Psychological Association, New Orleans, LA.

Nader, K., Pynoos, R., Fairbanks, L., & Frederick, C. (1990). Children's PTSD reactions one year after a sniper attack at their school. *American Journal of Psychiatry, 147,* 1526-1530.

Office for the Study of the Psychological Rights of the Child (1983, October). *Proceedings of the International Conference on Psychological Abuse of Children and Youth.* Indiana University, Indianapolis, IN.

Peplar, D., & Moore, T. E. (1989). *Children exposed to family violence: Home environments and cognitive functioning.* Paper presented at the meeting of the Society for Research in Child Development, Kansas City, MO.

Pynoos, R., & Nader, K. (1989). Children's memory and proximity to violence. *Journal of the American Academy of Child and Adolescent Psychiatry, 28,* 236-241.

Pynoos, R. S., Frederick, C., Nader, K., Arroyo, W., Steinberg, A., Eth, S., Nunez, R., & Fairbanks, L. (1987). Life threat and posttraumatic stress in school-age children. *Archives of General Psychiatry, 44,* 1057-1063.

Rawlins, C., & Rossman, B. B. R. (1991). *Siblingship as a protective factor for children in violent families.* Paper presented at the meeting of the Society for Research in Child Development, Seattle, WA.

Reinhold, D. P., & Lochman, J. E. (1991). *Attributional and affect labeling biases in mothers and aggressive sons.* Paper presented at the meeting of the Society for Research in Child Development, Seattle, WA.

Rieder, C., & Cicchetti, D. (1989). Organizational perspective on cognitive control functioning and cognitive-affective balance in maltreated children. *Developmental Psychology, 25,* 382-393.

Rosenberg, M. S. (1984). *The impact of witnessing interparental violence on children's behavior, perceived competence and social problem solving abilities.* Unpublished Doctoral Dissertation: University of Virginia, Charlottesville, VA.

Rosenberg, M. S. (1987a). New directions for research on the psychological maltreatment of children. *American Psychologist, 42,* 166-171.

Rosenberg, M. S. (1987b). Children of battered women: The effects of witnessing violence on their social problem-solving abilities. *The Behavior Therapist, 4,* 85-89.

Rosenberg, M. S., & Rossman, B. B. R. (1990). The child witness to marital violence. In R. T. Ammerman & M. Hersen (Eds.), *Treatment of family violence: A sourcebook* (pp. 183-210). New York: Wiley.

Rossman, B. B. R. (1992, April). *Trauma symptoms in child witnesses to parental violence.* Paper presented in the workshop, Perceptual and Memory Aspects of Reactions to Trauma. The Children's Hospital Rosenberry Conference: Psychic Trauma in Childhood and Adolescence, Denver, CO.

Rossman, B. B. R., & Rosenberg, M.S. (1992). Family stress and functioning in children: The moderating effects of children's beliefs about their control over parental conflict. *Journal of Child Psychology and Psychiatry, 33,* 699-715.

Rossman, B. B. R., Rosenberg, M. S., Rawlins, C., & Malik, N. (1991, June). *A needs perspective on risk and protective factors for children in violent families.* Paper presented at the National Working Conference "New Directions in Child and Family Research: Shaping Head Start in the Nineties," Arlington, VA.

Shaver, P. R., Goodman, G. S., Rosenberg, M. S., & Orcutt, H. (1991). The search for a definition of psychological maltreatment. *Development and Psychopathology, 3,* 79-86.

Skinner, E. A., Chapman, M., & Baltes, P. B. (1988). Control, means-ends, and agency beliefs: A new conceptualization and its measurement during childhood. *Journal of Personality and Social Psychology, 54,* 117-133.

Terr, L. (1988). What happens to early memories of trauma? A study of twenty children under age five at the time of documented traumatic events. *Journal of the American Academy of Child and Adolescent Psychiatry, 27,* 96-104.

Terr, L. (1991). Child traumas: An outline and overview. *American Journal of Psychiatry, 148,* 10-20.

Walker, L. E. A. (1984). *The battered woman syndrome.* New York: Springer.

Widom, C. S. (1991). A tail on an untold tale: Response to "Biological and genetic contributors to violence–Widom's untold tale." *Psychological Bulletin, 109,* 130-132.

Willis, D., Holden, E. W., & Rosenberg, M. S. (Eds.). (1992). *Child abuse prevention: Developmental and ecological perspectives.* New York: Wiley.

Wolfe, D. A. (1987). *Child abuse: Implications for child development and psychopathology.* Newbury Park, CA: Sage.

Wolfe, V. V., Gentile, C., & Wolfe, D. A. (1989). The impact of sexual abuse on children: A PTSD formulation. *Behavior Therapy, 20,* 215-228.

SEXUALLY MALTREATED CHILDREN, INCEST SURVIVORS, AND INCEST OFFENDERS: ISSUES, INTERVENTIONS, AND RESEARCH

Sibling Child Sexual Abuse: Research Review and Clinical Implications

Judith L. Alpert

SUMMARY. Although sex play is a part of normal childhood development, some sexual activity may be coerced or forced and may have negative long-term consequences and, thus, be considered abusive. However, childhood sexual abuse perpetrated by siblings, cousins, or peers receives relatively little attention from either researchers or practitioners. In the present article, the literature on sibling child sexual abuse is critically reviewed, and particular attention is focused on defining sibling sexual abuse, and determining its scope

Address correspondence to: Judith L. Alpert, Department of Applied Psychology, New York University, 239 Greene Street, New York, NY 10003.

[Haworth co-indexing entry note]: "Sibling Child Sexual Abuse: Research Review and Clinical Implications." Alpert, Judith L. Co-published simultaneously in *Journal of Aggression, Maltreatment & Trauma* (Haworth Maltreatment & Trauma Press, an imprint of The Haworth Press, Inc.) Vol. 1, No. (#1), 1997, pp. 263-275; and: *Violence and Sexual Abuse at Home: Current Issues in Spousal Battering and Child Maltreatment* (ed: Robert Geffner, Susan B. Sorenson, and Paula K. Lundberg-Love) Haworth Maltreatment & Trauma Press, an imprint of The Haworth Press, Inc., 1997, pp. 263-275. Single or multiple copies of this article are available for a fee from The Haworth Document Delivery Service [1-800-342-9678, 9:00 a.m. - 5:00 p.m. (EST). E-mail address: getinfo@haworth.com].

and effects. Clinical implications are derived as well. Although the article focuses on sibling sexual abuse, the concepts considered here also apply to other forms of same-age (or near same-age) child sexual relationships. *[Article copies available for a fee from The Haworth Document Delivery Service: 1-800-342-9678. E-mail address: getinfo@ haworth.com]*

KEYWORDS. Domestic violence, child maltreatment, treatment, incest

The most frequently reported type of incest is father-daughter. However, the most frequent type of incest is believed to be brother-sister (Dixen & Jenkins, 1981; Finkelhor, 1980; Weeks, 1976). In his survey of 796 college undergraduates, Finkelhor (1979) found that 39% and 4% of the incest reported by girls was sibling incest and father-daughter incest respectively. Although sibling incest is believed to be the most common form of incest, there are relatively few references in the professional or popular literature. Even more sparse are references to peer or cousin sexual assault/abuse, despite evidence which indicates that most childhood sexual encounters occur with a friend (Haugaard & Tilly, 1988). The present article focuses on child sexual abuse by siblings rather than cousins or peers, as this is the emphasis in the literature. The concepts also, however, apply to other forms of same-age (or near same-age) relationships such as cousins or peers.

The intent of this article is to: (1) place into professional currency the topic of sibling sexual abuse, and (2) further research and professional practice in this area. This article is composed of two sections. The first section includes a literature review. While numerous topics could be reviewed (e.g., definition, scope, effects, family characteristics, the abuser, the abuse, clinical intervention), given space limitations, the literature relevant to three topics are considered: definition, scope, and effects. Questions related to these topics will be presented. This section provides some of the principal findings in the area of sibling child sexual abuse. The second section focuses on the clinical implications resulting from the selected literature review.

Prior to a consideration of the literature, some general comments are warranted. The sibling sexual abuse literature has many of the problems common to the sexual abuse literature in general (see Finkelhor, 1986, for a discussion of some of these problems). Some of these problems concern: defining abuse, specifically defining abusive relationships and acts; selecting samples, specifically selecting representative samples of the abuse cases; utilizing control groups with stratification for sex and race; and designing studies with respect to selecting instrumentation and utilizing a conceptual framework.

The sibling sexual abuse literature is problematic. A major problem is the collapsing across categories in studies. That is, some of the literature does not differentiate among the various types of abuse (sexual, physical, or emotional). Even when it is clear that sexual abuse is considered, some of the literature does not differentiate among sibling, cousin, or peer abuse. Furthermore, when it is clear that incest is the focus, some of the literature does not differentiate among the various types of incest (sibling-sibling, parent-child, etc.). In general, those studies which do not differentiate among the various types of abuse (sexual, physical, emotional) or the relationship between the abused and the abuser in incest cases (father-daughter, sibling-sibling, etc.) will not be considered.

SELECTIVE LITERATURE REVIEW

The literature relevant to three areas (definition, scope, and effects) is considered here. Each of these topics is discussed separately.

Definition

How does one distinguish natural curiosity and exploration from sexual abuse between siblings? Research demonstrates that preschool and school age children engage in a broad and divergent range of sexual behaviors relatively frequently (Friedrich, Grambsch, Broughton, Kuiper, & Beilke, 1991; Lamb & Coakley, 1993). Young children, for example, engage in such non-contact sexual behaviors as dressing and undressing in front of each other and voyeurism, and such contact sexual behaviors as kissing, hugging, and touching of sexual body parts (Friedrich et al., 1991; Gil, 1993). Finkelhor et al. (1986) indicate that the misdiagnosis of all sibling sexual behavior as normal may account for the inattention to sibling sexual abuse. That is, sibling sexual activity often is considered common ("everyone does it"), benign in its effects, exploratory, mutually agreed upon, and mutually enjoyed. For this reason, it has received scant attention. Sibling sexual abuse is often dismissed under the labels of "normal" or "experimentation."

Those who attempt to distinguish abusive sexual encounters from normal behavior most frequently point to two variables: (1) consent or, alternatively, coercion (intimidation, force, or violence) (e.g., Bank & Kahn,

1982; Finkelhor, 1979; O'Brien, 1991), and (2) age difference between sex partners (Finkelhor, 1979; O'Brien, 1991). In general, the use of coercion and the age difference between partners have been identified as exploitive or abusive behavior. For example, Finkelhor and Hotaling (1984) suggest that sexual contact is abusive: (1) if it occurs as the result of force, threat, deceit, or while unconscious, or through exploitation of an authority relationship, no matter what the age of the partner, and (2) with a child less than 13 years of age if the perpetrator is five or more years older than the victim, or with a child 13-16 years of age if the perpetrator is 10 years older than the victim. Both of these variables (coercion, age discrepancy) have received research attention.

Regarding consent and coercion, it is difficult to determine when or whether they are operative. An act that may appear to be based on consent may actually be based on fear. Although a sibling may not necessarily use intimidation (or force or violence), it may be operative nevertheless, and the victim may experience fear and, consequently, comply. Clearly the concept of "consent" is a complex one. To determine whether there is consent, there must be knowledge of the sexual activity, the age and sex of the individuals involved, the family situation, and the cultural context.

Finkelhor (1979) holds that both the age and the age difference of the children are significant in determining sexual abuse. He considered developmental differences, and noted that the best indicators of substantial age disparity should be different for each age group. Thus, he proposed a six-fold classification in which he distinguished among three age groups and two sex-partner-age-disparity groups. The three age groups are children (0-8), preadolescents (9-12), and adolescents (13+). The two sex-partner-age-disparity groups are peer and nonpeer. The age disparities identified by Finkelhor are: (1) more than two years for the child group, (2) more than three years for the preadolescent group, and (3) more than five years for the adolescent group. His basis for such differentiation, however, was not specified.

Also utilized to distinguish sexually abusive from normal behavior are the following variables: age appropriate behavior, frequency, duration, and purpose of behavior (Wiehe, 1990). Wiehe (1990) points out that frequency and duration should not be used as the only criteria in differentiating sexual abuse from sexual play, since one instance of sexual contact could constitute sexual abuse.

In sum, it is important to acknowledge that universally accepted criteria for distinguishing sexually abusive from normal behavior does not yet exist. De Jong (1989) offers six questions which may assist the clinician in distinguishing sexual experimentation from exploitation, and these questions concern age difference, developmental level, motivation, coercion, outside influence, and the individual's response to contact. The current perspective involves a recognition that sometimes it is difficult to distinguish sex play from sex abuse, that there is a continuum of sibling sexual contacts, and that a significant number of such contacts have an exploitive character to them. This exploitive character derives from the use of force or from the coercion inherent in the age disparity between partners. A definition which highlights age and the exploitative aspects of the sexual contact is recommended.

Finkelhor's (1979) six-fold classification could be particularly helpful in future research as it accounts for sexual abuse differentially affecting children based on their age as well as the dimension of power disparity. His use of the term "peer partner" in his discussion of sex activity between siblings close in age, however, could be confusing, as others use the term "peer" to refer to sex among peers who are not siblings. It would be helpful if future work used "close in age" or "dissimilar in age." Also, future work should document the various forms coercion may take. Qualitative research is indicated as well, as it could further our understanding of the consent-coercion continuum. The issues of definition are summarized in Table 1.

Scope of Problem

What is the scope of sibling sexual abuse? The prevalence rates vary widely. Some of these differences can be explained by differences in the studies on which the rates are based. The studies used different samples and methods, and different definitions of sexual abuse. For example, studies that report higher rates tend to occur in face-to-face interviews and when more specific questions are asked. Often the authors are referring to

TABLE 1. Definition Issues in Sibling Incest

- Universally-accepted criteria for distinguishing sexually abusive from normal behavior do not yet exist.

- It is difficult to distinguish sex play from sex abuse.

- There is a continuum of sibling sexual contacts.

- A significant number of sibling sexual contacts have an exploitive character to them.

- The exploitive character derives from the use of force or from the coercion inherent in the age disparity between partners.

---

different events (e.g., sibling incest versus sibling sexual contact). For example, the prevalence rates vary from 2.5% for sibling incest (Russell, 1986) to 15% for sibling sexual acts (Finkelhor, 1980).

There are many different prevalence estimates, including those that estimate prevalence in the general population. Finkelhor, for example, reported that 13% (15% of the girls and 10% of the boys) from a survey of 796 college undergraduates experienced sexual acts with siblings. The use of force or a large age disparity between partners existed in 25% of the cases. For these reasons, 3% could be described as exploitative. Russell (1986) estimated prevalence in the general population and reported that 2.5% of the 930 women she interviewed had experienced sibling incest. Similarly, Wyatt (1985) found that 3% of the adult women in a sample reported sibling abuse.

Also, there are studies which indicate prevalence in a clinical sample. These studies estimate sibling incest from reports of an abused sample. Wiehe (1990), for example, conducted a questionnaire study with 150 abused respondents, many who were in treatment or support groups. He found that 67% of the respondents indicated that they had been sexually abused by a sibling while growing up. Eighty-nine percent of the victims were females while 11% were male.

Estimates derived from other clinical samples have estimated the percent of sibling incest from a sample of incest victims. For example, sibling incest represented 39% and 21% of the incest reported by the girls and boys, respectively, while father-daughter incest represented 4% (Finkelhor, 1979). In contrast, Russell (1986) found that sibling incest represented 15% of the incest cases while father-daughter incest represented 23%. Wyatt's (1985) findings are similar to those of Russell's. She reports that 12% and 24% of all incest cases were sibling incest and father-daughter incest, respectively. Similarly, sibling incest comprised 11% of all incest cases in De Jong's (1989) study of 831 sexually abused children less than age 14 who were evaluated for sexual assault.

As is typical of all types of sexual assault, these estimates are probably underestimates. There are several reasons why these are, in all likelihood, underestimates. First, many victims and perpetrators do not report abuse. Factors such as shame, embarrassment, threat of force, repression, dissociation, and amnesia contribute to their silence. In fact, Finkelhor (1979) found that only 12% of his respondents told anyone about their sibling sexual experiences, and that the reluctance to report was greater among those who had experiences with much older siblings. Second, some professionals and parents do not recognize the problem. Thus, the results of those prevalence studies which rely on the reports of professionals or parents will be low. Third, brother-sister incest rates ideally should be calculated on the basis of women who have at least one older brother because incest almost always involves an abuse of power in which an older brother sexually abuses a younger sister. Most of the studies do not question whether the respondents have siblings.

There also is an indication that cousin incest is as common or more common than sibling incest (De Jong, 1989; Finkelhor, 1979; Russell, 1983; Wyatt, 1985). Cousin incest ranges from 18-28%; variation in definitions of abuse, samples and method can account for this range. Finkelhor found that cousin incest represented 28% of all incest reported by college student respondents. In surveys of adult women, the percentage of all incest which involved cousins was 18% (Russell, 1983) and 23% (Wyatt, 1985). Also, there are studies based on clinical samples. In De Jong's (1989) clinical study of 831 sexually abused children under age 14 who were evaluated for sexual assault complaints, 5.9% and 4.2% were victims of cousin and sibling incest, respectively.

In sum, prevalence rates of sibling sexual abuse vary widely, and very few victims disclose their abuse. There are many estimates, and all are believed to be underestimates. In addition, as indicated, there are other limitations to the estimates. Some of our "working underestimates," derived from data presented above, are that approximately 3% of the population has been sexually abused by a sibling, approximately 67% of sibling abuse is sibling sexual abuse, and approximately 12% of all incest is sibling incest. Incest by cousins is believed to be even more common than sibling incest, although less is written about it. In addition, although prevalence rates on sexual abuse between peers are minimal, evidence suggests that most childhood sexual encounters occur with a friend. The scope of sibling abuse is summarized in Table 2.

Effects

What are the effects of sibling sexual abuse? Most of the sibling sexual abuse literature concerns effects. Characteristic of this literature is a schism between those who purport that the effects are negative (e.g., Bank & Kahn, 1982; Russell, 1986) and those who purport that they are positive or neutral (e.g., Fox, 1980; Meiselman, 1978). As Herman (1981) points out, some of those studies which indicate that the sexual activity was perceived as beneficial focused on the perpetrator's perception. Some of the discrepancy in outcomes across studies can be accounted for by differences in the victims' ages, developmental stage, degree of coercion, and other variables. One relatively consistent finding is that, in general, negative effects

TABLE 2. Scope of Sibling Incest

- Prevalence rates of sibling sexual abuse vary widely.
- Very few victims disclose their abuse.
- Estimates of sibling sexual abuse are believed to be underestimates.
- Prevalence estimates include:

  a. 3% of the population has been sexually abused by a sibling,

  b. 67% of sibling abuse is sibling sexual abuse, and

  c. 12% of all incest is sibling incest.

---

result from *coercive* sexual contact between siblings, cousins, and peers (e.g., Kilpatrick, 1986).

The focus here is on long term effects as most of the research focuses on long- rather than short-term effects. Also, the review here focuses on effects for the victim only (see Daie, Witztum, & Eleff (1989) for a consideration of effects on the perpetrator). The review considers representative studies, which consist of single case reports and clinical vignettes, as well as more traditional research. Some of the problems, controversies, and issues within this developing literature are discussed below.

Finkelhor (1986) and Kilpatrick (1987) point out some of the methodological problems inherent in the effect literature. They include, for example: differences across studies in the definition of terms (e.g., sexual abuse, sexual experience, and coercion); sampling problems, small numbers of cases, and combining age and socioeconomic groups; research design limitations, such as lack of a control group, single interview post-abuse evaluation, lack of pre-abuse baseline, limited number of effects considered, lack of conceptual frameworks, and unreliable or invalid measures of consequences.

A major problem with the effects literature concerns the nonrepresentative samples and the resultant difficulty in making generalizations. For example, Finkelhor (1980) points out that his sample of college students was highly specialized as college attendance selects for people who are psychologically healthy. Thus, the sample may grossly under represent those whose sibling experiences led to a truly negative outcome. In contrast, Wiehe's (1990) sample consists of those who chose, for the most part, to respond to an advertisement calling for abused siblings. It is a highly specialized group as well. Wiehe's sample may be biased in the direction of individuals who were sharply aware of their abuse or more inclined to disclose it and discuss it.

Most of the effects literature concerns aspects of an adult's current sexual activity. Those aspects which have received most attention include: frequency of current heterosexual and homosexual activity, sexual adjustment, and level of sexual self-esteem.

Regarding frequency of sexual activity, Finkelhor (1979) found that women who had sibling sexual experiences were more likely to be sexually active than those who had not. In addition, later age sibling sexual experiences, both age similar and age discrepant, whether judged positively or negatively by the partners, were associated with increased current incidence of intercourse. Negative experiences at an early age had no such effect. Also, Finkelhor reported that respondents who had a homosexual sibling experience had a higher rate of adult homosexual activity, but that sibling sex, in general, was not associated with more adult homosexual activity.

Regarding sexual adjustment, some studies indicate no deleterious effects while others indicate the opposite. For example, Greenwald and Leitenberg (1989) concluded that adult sexual adjustment was not influenced by typical early childhood, noncoercive sexual experiences among similar-age children. Others, however, point to sexual dysfunction as an effect. For example, two types of dysfunction are reported by victims of sibling sexual abuse. These include: avoidance of sexual contact and sexual compulsivity or promiscuity (Wiehe, 1990). In addition, in a consideration of four clinical cases, Daie et al. (1989) report lasting difficulties in establishing and maintaining close sexual relationships. The discrepancy regarding effects on sexual adjustment across studies may be related to the use of coercion. The data seem to indicate that coercion is associated with adult sexual dysfunction.

Regarding sexual self esteem, Finkelhor (1979) found that the effect of sibling sex on self esteem depended on what happened and when it occurred. Those who had sexual activity with age discrepant siblings scored lower in sexual self esteem than those with no childhood sex experiences. In contrast, those who engaged sexually with a sibling of similar age and judged this experience positively, had higher levels of sexual self esteem.

In general, a narrow view of effects is indicated in the literature. There is little focus, for example, on the impact of abuse on raising children or performing at work. Some effects which have been considered include sexual revictimization, subsequent mental health, and relationships. With respect to revictimization, the literature supports the conclusion that incest victims tend to be revictimized later in life. Russell (1986), for example, found that victims of brother-sister incest, in contrast to women who were not incest victims, had a number of revictimization experiences, such as physical violence by a husband or ex-husband (50% brother-sister incest victims vs. 18% nonincest victims) and unwanted sexual experience with an authority figure (58% vs. 27%). Much of the research concerned with the outcomes of sexual abuse on mental health are comparison studies, in which the mental health status of those abused by siblings is compared with the status of those abused by fathers. This literature leads to inconsistent results. Weinberg (1955), for example, found that daughters who were incest victims were better adjusted as adults than were sisters who were abused by their brothers. The latter engaged in more promiscuous sexual relationships and were more likely to become prostitutes. Russell (1986) attempts to shed light on differences between incest by fathers and that by brothers. She points out that while the age difference in most cases of brother-sister incest is smaller, the sexual encounter may be less stressful and, in some cases, pleasurable. Furthermore, Russell suggests that when pleasure occurs in an abusive context, it may intensify the trauma and be associated with more self-blame, shame, and guilt.

Some of the studies relevant to mental health involve victim reports. There seems to be a wide range in the degree of trauma reported by victims of all kinds of incest, as Russell (1986) indicates. In in-depth interviews of 930 randomly selected women from various backgrounds, victims of brother-sister incest and other incest victims were compared on some variables. Victims of brother-sister incest often reported an ambivalent or positive response to the sexual activity, but that these feelings were almost always overwhelmed by more substantial negative reactions. Coercion was substantial in Haugaard and Tilly's (1988) retrospective study based on the reports of over 100 undergraduates who were victims of childhood sexual encounters (encounters occurring when one child is less than age 13 and the other child is age 15 or younger). They found similarly deleterious outcomes in two groups of children: those children coerced by another child and those children having a sexual encounter with an adult.

Difficulty in establishing and maintaining close relationships has been reported in several studies (e.g., Bank & Kahn, 1982; Daie et al., 1989). Russell's data suggest that brother-sister incest may have a considerable effect on a victim's marital history. Almost half (47%) of the victims of brother-sister abuse never married, the highest nonmarriage rate reported by any of the incest victims.

In summary, it appears that one can no longer assume that incestuous sibling activity is benign. In fact, when coercion is involved, it seems to impact adversely on functioning in such areas as adult sexual activity, mental health, and relationships. Moreover, the effects are more negative in female victims than in their male counterparts (Bank & Kahn, 1982; Finkelhor, 1980). Although there is less research on the effects of sexual activity among cousins and peers, the literature suggests that coercive sexual activity negatively impacts those victims as well.

CLINICAL IMPLICATIONS

Practitioners must consider the possibility that their patients have been sexually abused as children by siblings, cousins, and/or peers. This review suggests that children who are victims of sibling, cousin, and peer sexual abuse typically "don't tell." As indicated elsewhere (Alpert, 1991), a history of sexual abuse often remains undetected. We may not know that our patients are victims of sibling sexual abuse because we do not inquire about their sexual abuse history and because they may not identify themselves as abuse victims. In our practices, we must not assume that sexual behavior between siblings is without adverse effects. Although some sexual activity clearly can be classified as normal curiosity and exploration, other activity may be abusive. In general, the use of coercion and age differences between partners have been identified as factors underlying exploitation/abuse. Obviously, other variables also need to be considered. Determining "consent" is complex since sexual activity that may appear to be based on consent may actually be based on fear. To better determine whether there truly was consent, questioning should be detailed and should consider the relationship between the parties involved. Also the feelings before, during and after the event, and the events leading up to the sexual activity, as well as the sexual activity itself, require consideration by the clinician. Although some sexual activity between siblings may not result in deleterious effects, some of this activity is traumatic.

Practitioners need to begin to document this abuse as well. We need to consider the nature of abuse, ages of the children involved, developmental tasks which may be disrupted, the effects of early versus late abuse, and the effects of early versus late intervention. Practitioners are in a unique position to contribute to this developing body of literature.

Previously, some mental health professionals assumed that sexual activity between father and daughter was a function of the child's fantasy life. We now know that some fathers and, less frequently, mothers sexually abuse their daughters and sometimes their sons. Similarly, we can no longer assume that sexual activity between siblings is benign, exploratory, or the result of mutual consent. We now know that some of this sexual activity is exploitive and abusive.

REFERENCE LIST

Alpert, J. L. (1991). Retrospective treatment of incest victims: Suggested analytic attitudes. *Psychoanalytic Review, 78,* 425-435.

Bank, S. P., & Kahn, M. D. (1982). *The sibling bond.* New York: Basic Books.

Daie, N., Witztum, E., & Eleff, M. (1989). *Journal of Clinical Psychiatry, 50,* 428-431.

De Jong, A. R. (1989). Sexual interactions among siblings and cousins: Experimentation or exploitation? *Child Abuse and Neglect, 13,* 271-279.

Dixen, J., & Jenkins, J. C. (1981). Incestuous child sexual abuse: A review of treatment strategies. *Clinical Psychology Review, 1,* 211-222.

Finkelhor, D. H. (1979). *Sexually victimized children.* New York: Free Press.

Finkelhor, D. H. (1980). Sex among siblings: A survey on prevalence, variety, and effects. *Archives of Sexual Behavior, 9,* 171-195.

Finkelhor, D. et al. (1986). *A sourcebook on child sexual abuse.* Beverly Hills, CA: Sage.

Finkelhor, D. H., & Hotaling, G. T. (1984). Sexual abuse in the national incidence study of child abuse and neglect: An appraisal. *Child Abuse and Neglect, 8,* 23-33.

Fox, R. (1980). *The red lamp of incest.* New York: Dutton.

Friedrich, W. N., Grambsch, P., Broughton, D., Kuiper, J., & Beilke, R. L. (1991). Normative sexual behavior in children. *Pediatrics, 88,* 456-464.

Gil, E. (1993). Age-appropriate sex play versus problematic and sexual behaviors. In E. Gil, & T. C. Johnson (Eds.), *Sexualized children: Assessment and treatment of sexualized children and children who molest* (pp. 21-39). Baltimore: Launch Press.

Greenwald, E., & Leitenberg, H. (1989). Long-term effects of sexual experiences with siblings and nonsiblings during childhood. *Archives of Sexual Behavior, 18,* 389-399.

Haugaard, J. J., & Tilly, C. (1988). Characteristics predicting children's responses to sexual encounters with other children. *Child Abuse and Neglect, 12,* 209-218.

Herman, J. L. (1981). *Father-daughter incest.* Cambridge, MA: Harvard.

Kilpatrick, A. C. (1986). Some correlates of women's childhood sexual experiences: A retrospective study. *Journal of Sex Research, 22,* 221-242.

Kilpatrick, A. C. (1987). Childhood sexual experiences: Problems and issues in studying long-range effects. *The Journal of Sex Research, 23,* 173-196.

Lamb, S., & Coakley, M. (1993). "Normal" childhood sexual play and games: Differentiating play from abuse. *Child Abuse and Neglect, 17,* 515-526.

Meiselman, K. C. (1978). *Incest: A psychological study of causes and effects with treatment recommendations.* San Francisco: Jossey-Bass.

O'Brien, M. J. (1991). Taking sibling incest seriously. In M. Q. Patton (Ed.), *Family sexual abuse: Frontline research and evaluation* (pp. 75-92). Newbury Park, CA: Sage.

Russell, D. E. H. (1983). The incidence and prevalence of intrafamilial and extrafamilial sexual abuse of female children. *Child Abuse and Neglect, 7,* 133-146.

Russell, D. E. (1986). *The secret trauma: Incest in the lives of girls and women.* New York: Basic Books.

Weeks, R. B. (1976). The sexually exploited child. *Southern Medical Journal, 69,* 848-850.

Weinberg, S. K. (1955). *Incest behavior.* New York: Citadel Press.

Wiehe, V. R. (1990). *Sibling abuse: Hidden physical, emotional, and sexual trauma.* Lexintgon, MA: Lexington Books/D.C. Heath.

Wyatt, G. E. (1985). The sexual abuse of Afro-American and white-American women in childhood. *Child Abuse and Neglect, 9,* 507-519.

Current Treatment Strategies for Sexually Abused Children

Carolyn Ivens Tyndall

SUMMARY. Given the disturbingly high prevalence of child sexual abuse, the expertise of medical and mental health professionals in treating child sexual abuse victims is essential. Relevant issues in treating these children include the mindfulness of developmental considerations, incorporation of a multi-modal therapeutic evaluation approach, clarification of treatment goals, appropriate use of and integration of various treatment modalities, and effective treatment termination. This article provides an introduction and overview of treatment of sexually abused children of all ages, from preschoolers to adolescents, with special emphasis on the importance of developmentally linked evaluation and treatment strategies. Treatment is discussed in terms of goals, stages from evaluation to termination, and formats and modalities including individual psychotherapy, family psychotherapy, group psychotherapy and hypnotherapy, to provide a comprehensive overview of current treatment strategies for sexually abused children. *[Article copies available for a fee from The Haworth Document Delivery Service: 1-800-342-9678. E-mail address: getinfo@haworth.com]*

KEYWORDS. Incest, family violence, psychotherapy, child maltreatment, effects on children

---

Address correspondence to: Carolyn Ivens Tyndall, PhD, Resource Psychological Consultants, 4800 Sugar Grove Boulevard, Suite 315, Stafford, TX 77477.

[Haworth co-indexing entry note]: "Current Treatment Strategies for Sexually Abused Children." Tyndall, Carolyn Ivens. Co-published simultaneously in *Journal of Aggression, Maltreatment & Trauma* (Haworth Maltreatment & Trauma Press, an imprint of The Haworth Press, Inc.) Vol. 1, No. 1 (#1), 1997, pp. 277-291; and: *Violence and Sexual Abuse at Home: Current Issues in Spousal Battering and Child Maltreatment* (ed: Robert Geffner, Susan B. Sorenson, and Paula K. Lundberg-Love) Haworth Maltreatment & Trauma Press, an imprint of The Haworth Press, Inc., 1997, pp. 277-291. Single or multiple copies of this article are available for a fee from The Haworth Document Delivery Service [1-800-342-9678, 9:00 a.m. - 5:00 p.m. (EST). E-mail address: getinfo@haworth.com].

277

In contrast to a decade ago, today's professional and lay literatures are filled with reports of a disturbingly high prevalence of child sexual abuse, particularly incest. Due to the enormity of this problem in our society and the serious impact of abuse on victims and their families, it is important not only that preventive measures be developed, but that medical and mental health professionals acquire specific expertise in the treatment of victims of child sexual abuse.

Developmental considerations are of importance in discussing sexual abuse treatment. Relevant issues include age at the time of onset of the abuse, the developmental stages during which the abuse continued, and age at the time of disclosure and treatment. An introduction to and overview of the treatment of children through adolescence is provided herein with special emphasis on the importance of developmentally linked treatment strategies for sexually abused children.

This article provides an introduction and overview of treatment approaches and strategies for sexually abused children and adolescents. The models and techniques described apply most directly to children sexually abused by a parent or other adult family member but are generally relevant to cases of sibling abuse and, to some extent, extrafamilial abuse. Treatment is discussed in terms of goals, stages from evaluation to termination, formats and modalities, with an attempt to provide a comprehensive overview of current strategies.

EVALUATION OF TREATMENT NEEDS

The first task of treatment of a sexually abused child is a therapeutic evaluation. The evaluation is separate and different from a forensic assessment (e.g., conducted for legal purposes) or any other evaluation utilized to assess the validity of the abuse report. The therapeutic evaluation, an integral first stage of treatment, is used to identify problem areas, as well as the strengths and coping styles of the child. The evaluation should determine whether and how to provide treatment to the child.

Whereas the information obtained from the evaluation is important, the therapeutic nature and function of the evaluation is equally essential. In order to insure a therapeutic experience, adequate time (usually two or more sessions) must be allocated. During these sessions, the therapist must carefully establish rapport with the child and develop a sense of safety for the child in the treatment situation. These, of course, are no small tasks with a child who has been traumatized by sexual abuse. An important aspect of the development of safety and rapport is the avoidance of intrusion. For example, it is important to empower the child with some choice and sense of control regarding decisions about when and how to discuss the abuse with the therapist. The additional therapeutic tasks of the evaluation involve preparing the child for the treatment process. Thus, the caution to avoid intrusion must be balanced with the clear message that the sexual abuse can and should be talked about freely in therapy.

Several specific areas of information should be obtained from the therapeutic evaluation. Details regarding who perpetrated the abuse, when and where it occurred, how long it lasted, and what specific abusive behaviors occurred are critical. The child's reaction, including subjective experience and behavioral symptoms, to the abuse is assessed. Family support and reaction as well as broader social support are assessed to further understand the child's experience and to determine the most efficacious treatment modalities. Internal resources (e.g., intellectual functioning, previously developed self-esteem, interpersonal skills) and preferred coping styles or defenses (e.g., dissociation, intellectualization) are assessed to plan interventions which utilize and support already existing resources and tendencies. Specific questions which frequently are overlooked should be addressed. Were there additional abuse incidents or additional perpetrators which have never been disclosed? Is there any indication of sadistic abuse? Has the child perpetrated abuse against another child since the experience of abuse? These questions often are difficult to assess, and complete answers may not be revealed until later in the treatment process, but the therapist should attend to them in the evaluation phase with ongoing attention throughout treatment.

The therapeutic evaluation should be a multi-modal assessment, including child interview, observation, family evaluation, caretaker report, teacher report, and possibly psychological testing. The interview with and clinical observation of the child can reveal much information regarding the abuse, problems, and strengths. The interview may be supplemented by psychological tests to obtain information about symptoms, underlying dynamics, and coping styles. The family evaluation helps determine the extent to which the family will be an asset or a deterrent to the child's recovery. Most experts agree that the family evaluation should not include the victim and perpetrator in the same session at this phase of treatment. Gardner (1987) argues that victims and perpetrators must be evaluated together in order to validate reports, an approach from a forensic perspective with emphasis on ruling out "false allegations." This has been criticized from many perspectives, and is counter to a therapeutic approach.

The family's willingness and ability to support the treatment process is essential information that will affect not only the child's responsiveness to and progress in treatment, but practical aspects such as the length and regularity of therapy attendance. Regardless of a child's ability to benefit from any particular treatment modality, if the parent is not compliant, the treatment cannot proceed. Thus, planning short-term interventions which are likely to be completed may be more useful than initiating, for example, a long-term group treatment which will be aborted by the parent. Likewise, if the child is in the custody of a social service agency due to the abuse, similar practical issues must be considered in treatment planning. Finally, interview and written data from the child, caretaker and teacher provide additional information regarding the child's symptomatic reaction to the abuse, including general behavior problems as assessed by the Child Behavior Checklist (Achenbach & Edelbrock, 1983) or other comprehensive symptom checklists (e.g., sexual behavior problems as assessed by the Child Sexual Behavior Inventory) (Friedrich et al., 1992). Identification of specific behaviors not only helps to focus intervention, but also provides criteria by which to assess therapeutic progress.

GOALS OF TREATMENT

Several general treatment goals apply to almost all child victims of sexual abuse. The more specific aspects of each, as well as any additional goals, are determined on an individual basis during the evaluation phase of treatment. These goals, listed in Table 1, often are addressed simultaneously and through various treatment modalities (to be discussed below).

Alleviation of presenting symptoms is central to psychotherapy with all populations. In the case of child sexual abuse victims, these symptoms include general behavior problems and specific sexual behavior problems. Common presenting symptoms can be identified as immediate, short-term or long-term problems (see Table 2).

Many victims present with a distorted or confused understanding of the abusive experience due to a lack of information, the misinformation they received (directly or subtly) from the perpetrator, the reactions of family, friends or others, and/or the implementation of defense or coping mechanisms involving cognitive distortion (e.g., dissociation, magical thinking). The correction of distortions and clarification of reality is an important goal of treatment. However, in cases of long-term repeated abuse, total memory retrieval of each incident may not be necessary. Memories need only be recalled in a quantity and specificity enough to clarify reality, overcome denial, understand behavior, minimize risk of further abuse, and otherwise recover.

A serious consequence of child sexual abuse involves boundary problems due to the severe physical and psychological intrusion inherent in the

TABLE 1. Treatment Goals for Child Sexual Abuse Victims

- Ameliorate presenting symptoms
- Develop a realistic and factual understanding of the abusive experience
- Ventilation of feelings associated with the abuse
- Develop healthy physical, psychological and interpersonal boundaries
- Accomplish an appropriate balance between a sense of personal safety and a self protective awareness
- Increase self esteem
- Learn about healthy sexuality
- Prevent perpetration or sexual acting out

abusive act, as well as the more subtle but constant absence of appropriate boundaries in incestuous families. Thus, treatment must facilitate the development or re-establishment of healthy physical, psychological and interpersonal boundaries.

The development of a sense of physical and emotional safety is essential to the resolution of most presenting symptoms and the progress of healthy development. This safety is violated by the abusive experience, and must be reclaimed. However, encouraging a child to develop a nondiscriminating trust could predispose the child to further victimization in the future. Thus, a sensitive and difficult therapeutic task involves helping the child achieve a healthy balance between feeling safe and trusting and remaining aware of potential danger.

Most children experience an assault to their self esteem during sexual abuse, and treatment should address this problem, directly and indirectly, to increase self esteem and self efficacy. Therapeutic interactions, often nonverbal, in various modalities, are powerful in addressing this issue. For example, carefully attending to the child's verbalizations, reinforcing positive self-statements, providing positive feedback, and the timely challenging of irrational negative beliefs are interventions which may improve self esteem.

Accurate information about healthy sexuality should be provided during treatment. This can be accomplished directly with the child (usually the most effective approach) and/or indirectly through educating and coaching parents in providing sex education to their child.

TABLE 2. Consequences of Child Sexual Abuse

Short-term Consequences:
- sleeping difficulties, enuresis, nightmares, fear of the dark
- withdrawal from peers
- eating disorders
- running away
- learning difficulties, behavioral problems in school, truancy
- depression
- substance abuse
- anxiety and fears of being alone and/or unsafe
- guilt
- shame
- low self-esteem
- anger at the perpetrator, siblings, non-abusive parent
- promiscuity or aggressive sexual behavior

Long-term Consequences:
- poorly developed identity
- poor self image
- limited capacity for basic trust
- suppressed anger
- intense feeling of inferiority and low self-esteem
- difficulties with intimacy and sexual functioning
- vulnerability to subsequent exploitation and victimization
- impaired capacity for trust
- impaired body image
- social withdrawal and impaired peer relations
- flashbacks
- sleep disorder
- depression
- dissociative experiences

Although most victims of child sexual abuse do not become perpetrators, victims may be at higher risk than nonvictims to perpetrate abuse or act out sexually. Furthermore, many older children and adolescents are aware of this information, and experience anxiety about their risk for becoming a perpetrator (Ivens, 1989b). Thus, treatment should address directly the issue of sexualized behavior to prevent the perpetuation of abuse.

INDIVIDUAL PSYCHOTHERAPY

Most child sexual abuse victims will need treatment with individual psychotherapy, and for many this modality will constitute the primary or only treatment available or appropriate. Generally, the technique of individual psychotherapy with this population is the same as that with a general child population, but additional issues specific to the abuse experience need to be addressed. The format of individual treatment varies, primarily based on the developmental level of the child. Various theoretical perspectives can be applied, including behavioral approaches (which have been researched most often) as well as cognitive, interpersonal, and eclectic approaches. A traditional psychoanalytic approach is not recommended for the treatment of sexually abused children (Friedrich, 1990).

The first task of individual psychotherapy with sexually abused children is to establish a trusting therapeutic relationship, a task which can be slow and difficult due to the intrusion and violation of trust these children underwent during their abuse experience. This initial task is so important to the process that it should not be viewed as a prerequisite to the therapeutic work but as a primary, integral and ongoing part of the work. To facilitate progress in this area, consistency of the therapist is essential, and consistency of the therapeutic setting (e.g., time, room, furnishing) should be maximized. Small consistencies can be important such as a "ritual" of a particular statement or activity upon the initiation and ending of each session. Furthermore, the child should be given permission to "take his/ her time" to establish trust, a statement which inherently assumes that trust will develop but avoids intrusion and decreases anxiety. As noted in the above discussion of the therapeutic evaluation, a careful balance is necessary between avoiding intrusion and openly discussing the abuse.

In addition to establishing a trusting relationship, each of the goals of treatment listed in Table 1 can be addressed in individual psychotherapy. The presenting symptoms can be intervened upon directly in individual therapy whereas other modalities may impact this area less intensely. The educational component of individual psychotherapy addresses the goals of understanding the abuse, utilizing appropriate caution against potential future danger, and learning about healthy sexuality. The interactional and experiential aspects and, for older children, the verbal processing address boundary and self esteem issues as well as provide opportunities for the identification and ventilation of feelings. The safety of the therapeutic relationship serves as a foundation for a general sense of internal safety. Finally, potential or actual abuse of others by the victim is frequently and effectively addressed in the context of the safe therapeutic relationship of individual psychotherapy that enables the child to tolerate discussion of such a difficult issue.

The format for individual treatment of young children (preschool and primary grades) is play therapy. Equipment utilized in the therapy includes items such as a doll family, a baby doll, bottle, clothing, blanket, doll house, action figures, play dough, sand tray, paper, crayons, books, and household items. The interactional and active aspects of the treatment are primary; verbal aspects are secondary. Abuse issues must be acknowledged and addressed, but for this age group, specific verbal disclosure and discussion are not always essential nor advisable, especially for very young children and children whose abuse occurred at a preverbal stage of development. For these children, the abuse issues can be worked through symbolically via play activities. Specifically, the child can work through anxiety and fear through repetition and mastery, can express anger in nondestructive ways such as verbalization, drawing and safe appropriate physical activities, can develop interpersonal skills through practice and by observing the therapist's modeling and positive reinforcement, and can overcome feelings of shame through nonjudgmental interactions with the therapist.

Individual treatment of older children combines some of these play therapy techniques with more direct verbal interactions and always includes the discussion of the abuse experience. Utilization of art therapy techniques (e.g., drawing, painting, collages, clay modeling) is very effective with children in this age range, as is reading and discussing books about abuse and about sexuality (to be read and discussed in session to educate the child, validate the child's experience, and encourage more personal discussion).

Individual treatment of adolescents combines relationship-focused processes with direct problem solving and education. The adolescent must become able to verbalize the abusive experience if treatment is to be complete. Issues of psychological and interpersonal boundaries are of utmost importance, and feelings of anger and shame often are focal issues in the treatment.

GROUP PSYCHOTHERAPY

Many experts agree that group psychotherapy is frequently a treatment of choice for victims of sexual abuse, particularly for adolescent victims (Celano, 1990; Friedrich, 1990; Gagliano, 1987; Hazzard, King, & Webb, 1986; Ivens, 1989a; Nelki & Watters, 1989; Porter, Blick, & Sgroi, 1982; Silovsky & Hembree-Kigin, 1994). Group therapy typically is utilized in conjunction with other treatment modalities either following initial individual psychotherapy or simultaneously with other modalities. Specific determination, of course, is made on an individual basis and depends on the child's needs and his/her capacity to benefit from each treatment modality.

Effective screening and preparation of the child for group membership is essential to the success of the group and to the individual's progress. General group screening criteria (i.e., ruling out mental retardation and psychosis) are basic. Inclusion criteria specific to sexual abuse groups include the potential to talk about the molestation, the ability to control impulses and tolerate limit-setting, and sufficient ego strength for group process (Mandell & Damon, 1989). Additionally, Ivens (1989a) recommends that children whose report of abuse is questionable be excluded from group therapy until the allegations have been validated because, in the rare event that the child has fabricated the allegation, the social pressure of a victims' group would greatly increase the child's difficulty in retracting a false allegation.

Numerous formats or models for child therapy groups exist, and the particular format utilized typically is determined by the age of the child and practical considerations. Therapy groups may be time limited or ongoing, open or closed, structured or unstructured, and with various levels of homogeneity of members in terms of age, gender, and abuse experience (e.g, incest vs. extrafamilial abuse).

Most therapy groups described in the current literature, especially those including any empirical outcome data, are short-term and relatively structured. Some short-term groups are primarily educative (Berliner & Ernst, 1984; Friedrich, Berliner, Urquiza, & Beilke, 1988), and range from four to six highly structured sessions that focus primarily on the victimization experience, courtroom preparation, and prevention. Other structured models have been reported by Nelki and Watters (1989) and Sturkie (1983), each consisting of nine sessions, with a specified theme or aim for each session, such as believability, guilt and responsibility, body integrity, and other life crises.

Unstructured therapy groups, such as those conducted by Tyndall (1994), are typically ongoing with an expectation of moderate to long-term (4 to 18 months) participation of each member. The organization of each session alternates between active and quiet, between task-oriented and playful, and between therapist-focused and peer-focused interactions or activities. The therapist remains aware of specific goals for each child during each session and capitalizes on specific discussions and activities that develop spontaneously. The spontaneous ideas and reactions of the children are utilized and shaped into therapeutic activities. For example, the commonly arising topic of "boys" in adolescent and preadolescent girls' groups can be directed by the skilled therapist into a productive examination and discussion of the impact of the abuse upon heterosexual relationships. Examples of specific activities or techniques which can be incorporated into an unstructured format in groups of various developmental levels to achieve particular treatment goals are provided in Table 3.

FAMILY PSYCHOTHERAPY

Most experts in the field espouse a family psychotherapy component to treatment of child sexual abuse victims, emphasizing that family psychotherapy usually is appropriate only in the later phase of treatment after all family members, including the victim, perpetrator, non-offending parent(s), and siblings, have participated in individual or group psychotherapy and have demonstrated some degree of therapeutic progress (Friedrich, 1990; Furniss, 1983; Giarretto, 1976; Ivens, 1989a; Porter et al., 1982). Most models of treatment for incestuous families initiate family sessions with the victim and non-offending parent first, then, in intact marriages, marital sessions, and finally sessions including the victim and perpetrator. Family psychotherapy including the child incest victim is recommended only when the adults included in the family sessions take total responsibility for the abuse. This criterion, of course, requires significant therapeutic progress by the parents prior to the family sessions, and sometimes this is not achieved.

The primary tasks of family psychotherapy include an apology by the perpetrator to the victim, an explanation by the perpetrator which absolves the child victim of any responsibility for the abuse, clarification of physical and interpersonal boundaries in the family, and problem solving to assure physical and psychological protection of the child. Additional issues also involve the role of the non-offending parent, reactions of siblings, and issues of parental authority and control by the perpetrator.

The therapist's balanced approach in the family psychotherapy sessions is essential to treatment success. The victim must be actively supported and protected while the family system simultaneously is valued and respected. As Mrazek (1981) asserts, the therapist must achieve a balance of compassion and control. This includes compassion for each family member including the perpetrator, a task which can be difficult. Understanding the child victim's ambivalent feelings of loyalty and rage toward the perpetrator can help the therapist maintain a therapeutic balance.

It is important to note before concluding this section that the model recommended above is the ideal, and reality may create dilemmas for the therapist. For example, when courts have mandated contact between a victim and perpetrator despite the perpetrator's continued denial or other inability to meet the criteria described above, the therapist may be forced to choose between providing no potentially therapeutic contact between victim and perpetrator, and proceeding with family sessions despite obvious severe limitations in appropriateness and therapeutic effectiveness.

HYPNOSIS

Utilization of clinical hypnosis is well known and accepted as valuable in the treatment of many psychological and interpersonal problems, and has recently been discussed in regard to the treatment of problems specifically related to sexual abuse (e.g., Dolan, 1991; Spiegel, 1993). Due to the nature of the problems experienced by individuals involved in child sexual abuse, skillfully administered hypnotic interventions may be quite efficacious.

Carefully conceptualized, planned, and executed hypnotic techniques can result in very powerful and effective treatment for child and adolescent victims of sexual abuse (Friedrich, 1990; Ivens, 1989a; Rhue & Lynn, 1991). First, children typically are excellent hypnotic subjects (Gardner & Olness, 1981). Secondly, hypnosis is effective in facilitating the development and strengthening of the therapeutic relationship as well as the internal sense of safety that is necessary for the traumatized child to deal with the painful and sensitive issues of sexual victimization. The abuse experience itself often involves and/or results in many hypnotic phenomenon (e.g., dissociation, time distortion, age regression), so the teaching of self hypnosis can provide a sense of control and allow healthy, productive utilization of hypnotic phenomenon. Related to this issue, application of hypnotic methods is appropriate in treating complicated Post Traumatic Stress Disorder (Brown & Fromm, 1986; Spiegel, 1993), a common diagnosis in more severely disturbed abuse victims. Hypnosis is an effective tool for addressing many of the common presenting symptoms of sexually abused children such as insomnia, nightmares, enuresis, anxiety, fearfulness and somatic symptoms (Friedrich, 1990). Finally, in the treatment of children abused at a very young (preverbal) age, the symbolic aspects of hypnotic techniques are quite effective, particularly when integrated into a hypnotic play therapy approach that interweaves conversational induction, therapeutic metaphors (story telling), and indirect suggestion into the therapeutic play interactions. Therefore, the utilization of hypnotic techniques may facilitate the alleviation of behavioral symptoms, definition and stabilization of boundaries (physical and psychological), modulation of affect, capacity for self soothing, increased self control and mastery, and ego strengthening.

TABLE 3. Group Therapy Activities for Sexually Abused Children

Preschool and Primary Grade

Play Therapy Techniques	Utilize dolls, human or animal figures, or puppets to work through anxiety or fears through repetition and mastery, with support and validation by peers
Creative Arts Techniques	Utilize clay or drawing materials to express feelings or to demonstrate abusive experience, while also attending to boundary and intrusion issues in interactions during activity
Story Telling	Read or tell stories regarding recovery from abusive experiences (literal or metaphorical) to validate child's experience of victimization and provide models of healthy recovery

Latency Age

Warm-up Activities	Initiate games using nonthreatening information about self and others to break ice and begin disclosure and feedback process and to increase self confidence (e.g., touch-tag question game)
Psychodrama	Set up "TV Talk Show" drama with interviews regarding abuse and other relevant experience, or act out relevant family interactions (e.g., confrontation of perpetrator), to allow more free expression of experiences and feelings and to allow child to practice behavior in supportive, validating environment
Creative Arts Techniques	Utilize visual art, music or movement modalities to express feelings
Group Art Activities	Set up group drawing or other project to express common feelings, with attention to interactions during activity, and therapeutic interventions around issues of intrusion and cooperation, and impact of feelings about abusive experiences on interpersonal interactions
Tape Recording	Use audio or video tape to allow children to relate their experience, and then share it with the group. (Many children who are hesitant to disclose abuse or feelings directly in group will go to a private area of room and tape themselves, then return and eagerly play the tape for the group)
Affirmation Games	Initiate simple circle or touch-tag games requiring statements expressing positive observations about self or other members (e.g., "What I like about me today is _____"), to increase self esteem

Reading Activities	Utilize books about sexually abused children to provide validation of experience, model for recovery, and educational information about sexual abuse, and to decrease hesitation to discuss abuse
Writing Projects	Develop group project of writing about abuse, including individual description of experience, or letters to perpetrators (their own or unknown perpetrators in treatment), or writing to other victims
Anger Work	Utilize nerf balls, batakas, cushions, etc., to allow anger discharge, and follow with group processing
Adolescence	
Verbal Processing	Facilitate group process along with directed feedback regarding relevant problems/issues
Psychodrama	Use traditional psychodrama or revised dramatic and movement games such as charades to allow expression and lead into more direct examination of feelings and issues
Creative Arts Techniqus	Utilize visual art, music or movement modalities to express feelings
Group Art Activities	Group drawing or other project to express common feelings, with attention to interactions during activity, and therapeutic interventions around issues of intrusion and cooperation, and impact of feelings about abusive experiences on interpersonal interactions
Self Affirmation Games	Initiate games and activities requiring statements expressing positive observations about self to increase self esteem
Reading Activities	Utilize books about sexually abused adolescents to provide validation of experience, model for recovery, and educational information about sexual abuse, and to decrease hesitation to discuss abuse
Writing Projects	Supervise letter writing or other writing about abuse experience, or letters to perpetrators (their own or unknown perpetrators in treatment) or other victims
Anger Work	Utilize nerf balls, batakas, cushions, etc., to allow anger discharge, and follow with group processing
Group Hypnosis	Use to increase group cohesion, develop sense of safety, decrease anxiety, and address common problems

TERMINATING TREATMENT

Termination is the final, and perhaps the most important, phase of treatment. The criteria for termination are directly related to the treatment goals and the evaluation of the individual child's problems or symptoms. When treatment goals have been accomplished or when continued progress toward these goals can continue without further treatment, the child and the family should carefully be prepared for termination.

During the termination phase of treatment, it is essential that the child and the parents receive permission and encouragement to return for further treatment if or when needed. This recommendation should be very specific, explaining that whereas treatment has been successful, as the child reaches a higher developmental level (especially physically and psychologically significant phases such as puberty) he or she may need to return to treatment to rework the abuse and sexual issues at a deeper level. The need for further treatment should not be viewed as a failure. When premature termination is necessary due to variables beyond the therapist's, not to mention the child's, control every effort should be made to address termination issues. In cases of premature termination, the therapist needs to consolidate the progress that has been made to increase the likelihood that the child will be open to therapeutic experiences, should they arise in the future.

REFERENCES

Achenbach, T. M., & Edelbrock, C. (1983). *Manual for the child behavior checklist and revised child behavior profile*. Burlington, VT: University of Vermont Department of Psychiatry.

Berliner, L., & Ernst, E. (1984). Group work with preadolescent sexual assault victims. In I. Stuart & J. Greer (Eds.), *Victims of sexual aggression: Treatment of children, women, and men* (pp. 105-124). New York: Van Nostrand Reinhold.

Brown, D. P., & Fromm, E. (1986). *Hypnotherapy and hypnoanalysis*. Hillsdale, N.J.: Lawrence Erlbaum.

Celano, M. P. (1990). Activities and games for group psychotherapy with sexually abuse children. *International Journal of group Psychotherapy, 40,* 419-429.

Dolan, Y. M. (1991). *Resolving sexual abuse: Solution-focused therapy and Ericksonian hypnosis for adult survivors*. New York: W.W. Norton.

Friedrich, W. N. (1990). *Psychotherapy of sexually abused children and their families*. New York: W.W. Norton.

Friedrich, W. N., Berliner, L., Urquiza, A. J., & Beilke, R. L. (1988). Brief diagnostic group treatment of sexually abused boys. *Journal of Interpersonal Violence, 3,* 331-343.

Friedrich, W. N., Grambsch, P., Damon, L., Hewitt, S., Koverola, C., Lang, R. A.,

Wolfe, V., & Broughton, D. (1992). Child Sexual Behavior Inventory: Normative and clinical findings. *Psychological Assessment, 4,* 303-311.

Furniss, T. (1983). Family process in the treatment of intrafamilial child sexual abuse. *Journal of Family Therapy, 5,* 263-278.

Gagliano, C. K. (1987). Group treatment for sexually abused girls. *Social Casework, 68,* 102-108.

Gardner, G. G., & Olness, K. (1981). *Hypnosis and hypnotherapy with children.* Orlando: Grune & Stratton.

Gardner, R. A. (1987). *The parent alienation syndrome and the differentiation between fabricated and genuine child sex abuse.* Kresskil, New Jersey: Creative Therapeutics.

Giarretto, H. (1976). Humanistic treatment of father-daughter incest. In R. E. Helfer & C. H. Kempe (Eds.), *Child abuse and neglect: The family and the community* (pp. 263-278). Cambridge, MA: Ballinger.

Hazzard, A., King, H. E., & Webb, C. (1986). Group therapy with sexually abused adolescent girls. *American Journal of Psychotherapy, 40,* 213-223.

Ivens, C. (1989a, August). Hypnotherapy with child victims and with perpetrators of child sexual abuse. In M. R. Nash (Chair), *Hypnosis and sexual abuse: Clinical and research perspectives.* Symposium presented at the American Psychological Association Annual Convention. New Orleans, LA.

Ivens, C. (1989b, August). *Identification, evaluation and treatment of child sexual abuse: Victims, perpetrators and families.* Workshop presented at the American Psychological Association Annual Convention. New Orleans, LA.

Mandell, J. G., & Damon, L. (1989). *Group treatment for sexually abused children.* New York: Guilford Press.

Mrazek, P. B. (1981). Group psychotherapy with sexually abused children. In P. B. Mrazek & C. H. Kempe (Eds.), *Sexually abused children and their families* (pp. 199-210). New York: Pergamon Press.

Nelki, J. S., & Watters, J. (1989). A group for sexually abused young children: Unraveling the web. *Child Abuse and Neglect, 13,* 369-377.

Porter, F. S., Blick, L. C., & Sgroi, S. M. (1982). Treatment of the sexually abused child. In S. Sgroi (Ed.), *Handbook of clinical intervention in child sexual abuse* (pp. 109-145). Lexington, MA: Lexington Books.

Rhue, J. W., & Lynn, S. J. (1991). The use of hypnotic techniques with sexually abused children. In W. C. Wester & D. J. O'Grady (Eds.), *Clinical hypnosis with children* (pp. 69-84). New York, NY: Brunner/Mazel.

Silovsky, J. F., & Hembree-Kigin, T. L. (1994). Family and group treatment for sexually abused children: A review. *Journal of Child Sexual Abuse, 3(3),* 1-20.

Spiegel, D. (1993). Hypnosis in the treatment of post traumatic stress disorders. In J. W., S. J. Lynn, & I. Kirsh (Eds.), *Handbook of clinical hypnosis* (pp. 493-508). Washington, D.C.: American Psychological Association Press.

Sturkie, K. (1983). Structured group treatment for sexually abused children. *Health and Social Work, 8,* 299-308.

Tyndall, C. I. (1994). *Treatment strategies for sexually abused children.* Workshop presented for the University of Houston at Victoria, Victoria, TX.

Treating the Sexual Concerns
of Adult Incest Survivors
and Their Partners

Christine A. Courtois

SUMMARY. Negative attitudes about sex and sexuality and many types of sexual dysfunction are common aftereffects of sexual child abuse and incest. The traumatic sexualization and the aversive sexual conditioning resulting from childhood abuse have long gone unrecognized, however. This article presents research findings regarding the impact of incest on sexual attitudes and functioning along with treatment recommendations. *[Article copies available for a fee from The Haworth Document Delivery Service: 1-800-342-9678. E-mail address: getinfo@haworth.com]*

KEYWORDS. Child sexual abuse, psychotherapy, domestic violence, sexual trauma, sexual dysfunctions, recovery

Incest and other forms of sexual child abuse introduce a child to sexual functioning and sexuality in ways that are psychologically and physically overwhelming. The abusive behaviors are age-inappropriate and "out of synch" with the child's maturation, out of the child's control, and at the

Address correspondence to: Christine A. Courtois, PhD, 3 Washington Circle, Suite 206, Washington, DC 20037.

[Haworth co-indexing entry note]: "Treating the Sexual Concerns of Adult Incest Survivors and Their Partners." Courtois, Christine A. Co-published simultaneously in *Journal of Aggression, Maltreatment & Trauma* (Haworth Maltreatment & Trauma Press, an imprint of The Haworth Press, Inc.) Vol. 1, No. 1 (#1), 1997, pp. 293-310; and: *Violence and Sexual Abuse at Home: Current Issues in Spousal Battering and Child Maltreatment* (ed: Robert Geffner, Susan B. Sorenson, and Paula K. Lundberg-Love) Haworth Maltreatment & Trauma Press, an imprint of The Haworth Press, Inc., 1997, pp. 293-310. Single or multiple copies of this article are available for a fee from The Haworth Document Delivery Service [1-800-342-9678, 9:00 a.m. - 5:00 p.m. (EST). E-mail address: getinfo@haworth.com].

293

whim of someone else's needs and desires, usually someone older, more knowledgeable, and in a greater position of authority or strength. This type of abuse involves intimate violation and exploitation that can cause its victims serious consequences initially as well as in the long-term.

Finkelhor and Browne (1985) reviewed the available literature on sexual child abuse and its aftereffects. They arrived at four main trauma-inducing dimensions or "traumagenic dynamics" of such abuse, each with its own dynamics, psychological impact, and behavioral manifestations: (1) traumatic sexualization; (2) betrayal; (3) powerlessness; and, (4) stigmatization. In describing their conceptualization, they wrote:

> These traumagenic dynamics are generalized dynamics not necessar-
> ily unique to sexual abuse; they occur in other kinds of trauma. But
> the conjunction of these four dynamics in one set of circumstances is
> what makes the trauma of sexual abuse unique, different from such
> childhood traumas as the divorce of a child's parents or even being
> the victim of physical child abuse. These dynamics alter children's
> cognitive and emotional orientation to the world, and create trauma
> by distorting children's self-concept, world view, and affective capa-
> cities. (pp. 530-531)

Key concepts throughout this article include: *traumatic sexualization*, a "process in which a child's sexuality (including both sexual feelings and sexual attitudes) is shaped in a developmentally inappropriate and inter-personally dysfunctional fashion as a result of the sexual abuse"; *betrayal*, "the dynamic by which children discover that someone on whom they were vitally dependent has caused them harm" (or has failed to protect or believe them); *powerlessness*, "the process in which the child's will, desires, and sense of efficacy are continually contravened"; and, *stigmati-zation*, "the negative connotations (e.g., badness, shame, and guilt) that are communicated to the child around the experience and that then become incorporated into the child's self-image" (Finkelhor & Browne, 1985, pp. 531-532). Each abuse circumstance varies with the relative severity, intensity, and interplay of these dynamics along with the child's personal-ity and premorbid functioning, developmental stage, and coping and sup-port resources.

This article has as its primary focus the impact of child sexual abuse and incest upon adult sexuality. Each of the traumagenic dynamics con-tributes to the sexual consequences and their severity. *Traumatic sexual-ization*, the *modus operandi* of the abuse, results in particular dynamics and specific psychological and behavioral repercussions. Traumatic sexu-alization posits sexual contact that is non-consensual and used to meet the needs and desires of the abuser. The child's introduction to sexual activity is coerced and results in the association of sexuality with negative or ambivalent emotions and memories, or with overwhelming physical/ sexual sensation. The abuser misrepresents the sexual activity and often rewards it with positive attention and affection. The abuser ignores the child's needs and views the child's body as a sexual fetish.

The *psychological impact* of traumatic sexualization can be profound. Sexual issues often take on increased salience. These include: confusion about sexuality, sexual norms and sexual identity; sexual orientation; the identification of sex with love and care-getting or care-giving; negative associations to sexual activities and physical sensations; and, avoidance of and aversion to sex and intimacy. *Behavioral manifestations* include sexual preoccupations and compulsive sexual behaviors, sexual preco- ciousness, sexual aggression, promiscuity, prostitution, and inappropriate sexualization of parenting. Sexual dysfunctions of all sorts can result, including avoidance and phobias. Body hatred and alienation as well as ambivalence about reproduction can occur (Westerlund, 1992).

The traumatic impact of sexual abuse on interpersonal functioning in general, and sexual functioning in particular, has long been recognized by those involved in the study of adult incest survivors and their treatment (Carnes, 1991; Courtois, 1979, 1988; Jehu, 1988; Maltz, 1991; Maltz & Holman, 1987; Russell, 1986; Sprei & Courtois, 1988, Westerlund, 1992). It has been one of the most robust findings concerning the long-term aftereffects of sexual child abuse. Although the association is both logical and common, it has been long overlooked in the general therapeutic com- munity and, in particular, by therapists who specialize in the treatment of sexual concerns and dysfunctions. It also has been largely unrecognized by the medical community. The reasons for not seeing or neglecting the connection have to do with the societal denial of incest and other forms of sexual child abuse and family violence (Butler, 1985; Summit, 1983) to which sex therapists are not immune, and to the faction within the sex education/sex therapy field that has held incest to be non-hurtful and even beneficial to the child. (This group, known as the "pro-incest lobby," encompasses some sexologists as well as lay groups such as the Rene Guyon Society and the North American Man-Boy Love Association).

As the emphasis has shifted and long-term consequences of sexual abuse have been identified, treatment needs have been given greater con- sideration. The general course of treatment for adult survivors of sexual child abuse has been articulated to include sequencing and pacing (Briere, 1989, 1991; Courtois, 1988, 1991; Jehu, 1988; Kirschner, Kirschner, & Rappaport, 1993; Kluft, 1989; Lundberg-Love, 1990; Maltz, 1991;

McCann & Pearlman, 1990; Meiselman, 1990). These authors are in general agreement that sexual recovery, on average, occurs later in the therapy process, that is, after the trauma resolution phase of treatment. Lundberg-Love (1990) describes the process as one in which the therapy must recount, repair, and resolve: recount the abuse incident, repair the psychological aftereffects, and resolve behavioral and interpersonal issues, including sexual functioning. Maltz (1991) outlines a very similar process and underscores the fact the sexual aftereffects are not adequately addressed in available therapy resources and that effects must be identified, a process often impeded by the survivor's shame, guilt, and denial. Alternatively, other clinicians propose treatment models in which the trauma and relational/sexual difficulties are treated concurrently or in an alternating sequence to the primary therapy (Follette, 1991; Jehu, 1988; Johnson, 1989; Kirschner et al., 1993).

This article reviews the findings of recent research on the sexual aftereffects of incest. Treatment needs are discussed, as are general strategies that have been devised to treat the sexual consequences of sexual child abuse.

AFTEREFFECTS OF INCEST ARE OFTEN POST-TRAUMATIC AND DISSOCIATIVE

Substantial research and clinical data identify sexual child abuse as a major form of traumatic stress for the child, with high potential for traumatic consequences, including sexual effects. It should be noted however that not all abuse is traumatic nor are all consequences severe. This said, aftereffects and symptoms may be severe enough to meet the criteria for the diagnosis of Post-traumatic Stress Disorder (PTSD). This diagnosis is supraordinate in that it encompasses many of the predominant symptoms for which incest survivors seek treatment (Briere, 1989; Courtois, 1988; Donaldson & Gardner, 1985). PTSD is characterized by denial/numbing symptoms that function to blunt reactions to the trauma in alternation with intrusive/re-experiencing ones that cause them to return. This alternation or approach-avoidance process allows the gradual accommodation and resolution of the traumatic material that might otherwise overwhelm the psyche if faced directly and with full force (Horowitz, 1986). Post-traumatic reactions usually have three courses: acute, chronic, and/or delayed.

Clinical observations regarding trauma recently have returned to the early discovery by Pierre Janet that dissociation is a mental process that is often used defensively in response to trauma, especially trauma of a severe and chronic sort, such as child abuse and incest (van der Hart & Horst,

1989). Dissociation, when used defensively, interferes with the normally integrated psychological functions of consciousness, identity, and memory (American Psychiatric Association, 1994). A most common description of this process is that of the child leaving her body during the abuse, floating above and watching "it" happen to "her" (split consciousness and identity). When used repeatedly, dissociation becomes an adaptive response to the abuse and its use may extend to other stressors as well. Aspects of the trauma are thus encapsulated in the interest of psychological defense and survival. This can occur chronically or may resurface at a later time.

Post-traumatic stress reactions currently are conceptualized as inherently dissociative due to the alternation between numbing and reexperiencing symptoms. Trauma resolution involves the recollection and reworking of the traumatic material so that split-off dimensions are reconnected and then processed sufficiently to interrupt the alternating phases. It is basically the same process as the recount, repair, resolve model (Lundberg-Love, 1990), described earlier.

SEXUAL AND INTERPERSONAL CONSEQUENCES OF INCEST

Data identifying a connection between experiences of incest and sexual/interpersonal functioning have been available since some of the earliest studies of incest and its aftereffects (Kinsey, Pomeroy, Martin, & Gebhard, 1953). Some of the early literature emphasized the child's supposed enjoyment of the sexual activity, and labeled the child as the seducer due to having a "charming and pleasing personality" (Bender & Blau, 1937). Observations such as this have been debunked. Even if a child has a "charming and pleasing personality," it is the adult who is responsible for the behavior, not the child. Finkelhor and Browne (1985) concluded the following after a comprehensive review of the available literature on the effects of child sexual abuse:

> The sexual problems of adult victims of sexual abuse have been among the most researched and best established effects. Clinicians have reported that victimized clients often have an aversion to sex, flashbacks to the molestation experience, difficulty with arousal and orgasm, and vaginismus, as well as negative attitudes towards their sexuality and their bodies. The frequently demonstrated higher risk of sexual abuse victims to later sexual assault may also be related to traumatic sexualization, and some victims find themselves inappropriately sexualizing their children . . . Such problems and behavior, as well as victims' self-reports, suggest the various psychologi-

cal effects produced by traumatic sexualization. At its most basic level, sexual abuse heightens awareness of sexual issues . . . Confusion often arises, especially about sexual identity . . . Traumatic sexualization is also associated with confusion about sexual norms and standards . . . Another impact . . . is in the negative connotations that come to be associated with sex . . . revulsion, fear, anger, a sense of powerlessness, or other negative emotions can contaminate later sexual experiences. These feelings may become generalized as an aversion to all sex and intimacy, and very probably also account for the sexual dysfunctions reported by victims. (pp. 534-535)

Finkelhor and Browne's findings have been substantiated and extended by recent studies that are described in this section. Courtois (1979) found a "sleeper" effect (also noted by the other researchers) in which the sexual effects, although not present and/or disruptive at the time of the abuse, may emerge as the victim/survivor enters adolescence and adulthood and attempts sexual activity, a normal developmental task of these life stages.

Difficulty maintaining sexual functioning within an intimate relationship has been observed (Bass & Davis, 1988; Courtois, 1988; Kirschner et al., 1993; Maltz, 1991; Maltz & Holman, 1987; Westerlund, 1992). In a common scenario, a survivor is able to function well sexually until a relationship becomes serious and/or committed, at which time sexual feelings and functioning may deteriorate markedly. The pattern is paradoxical until understood within the context of sexual abuse. The lessons of the past, namely: love equals abuse; commitment equates with entrapment, loss of control, and powerlessness; and legal commitment (i.e., marriage that connotes sex with a related versus unrelated partner), all contribute to the inhibition of sexual feelings and functioning. Many survivors describe increased fears regarding vulnerability and control issues which lead to sexual aversion and/or the inability to be sexual.

Maltz and Holman (1987) report sexual effects within three main categories: (1) sexual development/emergence in adolescence at which time the victim is conscious of being at a different level of experience than peers. This typically leads to social and sexual withdrawal or patterns of compulsive and sometimes indiscriminate sexual activity, or alternation between the two; (2) sexual identity and gender preference issues, including difficulty identifying as a sexual being with sexual feelings and difficulty determining gender preference and reasons for it; and, (3) sexual dysfunction, ranging from total inability to be sexual at one extreme to patterns of compulsivity and hyperarousal at the other. Most types of sexual dysfunction may have had their origin in the abuse and any other exploitive sexual experiences.

Jehu (1988) and colleagues reported on a sample of 51 college women who had been sexually abused in childhood. Of this sample, 95% had sexual dysfunction, 92% had a mood disturbance encompassing emotions of shame, self-blame, guilt and depression; 90% had interpersonal problems with men, including discord, insecurity, mistrust, fear, and the splitting of sex and affection in relationships. Sexual stress, including recapitulations of features of the abuse (e.g., revictimization of some sort, prostitution), emotional reactions, cognitive reactions, physiological reactions to patterns of arousal, and behavioral reactions, including aversions and compulsive and/or ritualized sexual activity were observed. Frawley (1988) found incest to be correlated with 50% of the sexual dysfunction variables measured in 82 women abused by their fathers. Compared to controls, the women reported a lower capacity for sexual arousal and orgasm, less sexual satisfaction, more dysfunction with intimate partners than with casual lovers, and more sexual guilt. Frawley wrote, "These results support a view of father-daughter incest as a core, damaging experience in a child's life; an experience which fundamentally affects the survivor's ability to function sexually" (p. 44).

Sprei and Courtois (1988), in their review article on sexual dysfunction arising from sexual assault and abuse, have reported that childhood molestation, especially incest, is more indicative of later sexual dysfunction than is rape in adulthood, although rape can have a profound impact. These authors identified the following categories of sexual distress and dysfunction: (1) desire disorder–low desire due to fear and aversion to sex and phobias; (2) arousal disorder; (3) orgasmic disorder; (4) coital pain, including vaginismus, dyspareunia, and genital pain; (5) frequency dissatisfaction and/or general sexual dissatisfaction; (6) other problems, such as paraphilias, promiscuity and indiscriminate sexual activity, compulsive sex, ritualized sex, sexual abstinence, sadomasochistic practices, flashbacks, and chemical and/or relationship dependencies. These can occur alone or in combination.

Briere and Runtz (1991) found that child sexual abuse has a higher correlation with later sexual dysfunction than either emotional or physical abuse. Lundberg-Love (1988) reported that adult survivors exhibit difficulties in two main categories of sexual functioning: (1) arousal problems, including aversion to particular sex acts, flashbacks, dissociative symptoms, and the utilization of alcohol or drugs to reduce inhibition and to enable sexual arousal, and (2) orgasmic problems, including painful intercourse. The author notes that:

> Regardless of whether survivors felt pain, pleasure, or numbness during the incestuous abuse, the majority of them appear to associate

sexual arousal with the feelings they experienced during the abuse. Indeed, the salience of early sexual experience appears to be particularly robust, such that the biological response to sexual stimulation becomes conditioned to the negative feelings surrounding the abuse. Often these feelings include disgust, anger, fear, nausea, guilt, and powerlessness. (Lundberg-Love, 1988, pg. 4)

Several investigators (e.g., Frawley, 1988; Lundberg-Love, 1988; Maltz & Holman, 1987; Westerlund, 1992) suggest a higher degree of exploration or choice of a lesbian lifestyle among their survivor samples. They posit that incest sometimes disrupts gender preference through early conditioning or that the survivor later searches for pre-oedipal mothering. Loulan (1987) found the same percentage of lesbian women (38%) to have been sexually abused during childhood as Russell (1986) reported in a random community-based sample of women. Loulan concluded that lesbians are not more likely to have suffered sexual child abuse than the general population, an association sometimes projected onto lesbians to "explain" their sexual preference. Both gender of victim and gender of perpetrator and conditioning may serve to affect or disrupt a survivor's sexual preference in adulthood.

Westerlund (1992) studied 72 women volunteers via questionnaires and conducted follow-up interviews with 10 of these women who represented various sexual preferences (i.e., heterosexual, celibate, undecided, and bisexual) and sexual "lifestyles" (i.e., aversion, inhibition, celibacy, compulsion, "promiscuity," prostitution, and sadomasochism). Concerning body perception and reproduction, 74% of the respondents held negative and/or distorted body perceptions, including body hatred and estrangement (apparently related to anger and guilt about incest), non-"ownership" or alienation from their bodies, not feeling in control of their bodies, and not feeling attractive or making themselves unattractive through self-neglect, poor hygiene, poor posture, or other means. Reproductive capacity was an unwelcome developmental milestone for 58% of the sample, and included a concern about being able to bear a normal child and fear of not being a good parent. Pregnancy was problematic predominantly due to shame, confusion, and fear for 80% of the sample who had been pregnant. Birth experiences were difficult because "the body" was again "out of control and in pain."

Westerlund (1992) also reported on the sexual preference and lifestyle issues of a sample of abused women. Many respondents expressed concern that others might automatically attribute their sexual preference to the incest and some wondered about their "true" sexual identity in the absence of incest. The following sexual "lifestyles" and percentages were reported: sexual aversion characterized by reclusion, fear and avoidance, 14%; sexual inhibition characterized by shame, fear, anger, and mistrust, 63%; sexual compulsion characterized by sexual thought, feeling, behavior, and/or activity with a driven, unnatural quality or with power and anger, 23%; a period of celibacy associated with avoidance of or freedom from feelings of guilt, anger, and shame, 49%; a period of self-defined "promiscuity" and self-abuse as an expression of or illusion of control and anger, 21%; a period of prostitution, 12%; and "the split" or the non-integration of emotional intimacy and sexual intimacy, 28%. In addition, a small percentage of the respondents reported a masochistic or sadomasochistic orientation, and some past sexual activity with children or animals. All of Westerlund's respondents reported that their incest experience influenced adult sexual functioning in several discrete areas, including sexual fantasies, sexual desire, sexual arousal, inhibition, orgasm, and the "split" between intimacy and sexual functioning. Westerlund concluded that difficulties with arousal appeared to be most common, followed by desire and orgasmic problems. Responses were very individualized, and some respondents reported sexual satisfaction and/or no problems with sexual functioning. Maltz (1991) echoed the findings of each of these researchers in a list of the top 10 sexual symptoms of sexual abuse: (1) avoidance, fear or lack of interest in sex; (2) sex as an obligation; (3) negative feelings such as anger, disgust, or guilt associated with touch; (4) difficulty becoming aroused or feeling sensation; (5) feeling emotionally distant or not present during sex; (6) experiencing intrusive or disturbing sexual thoughts and images; (7) engaging in compulsive or inappropriate sexual behaviors; (8) having difficulty establishing or maintaining an intimate relationship; (9) experiencing vaginal pain or orgasmic difficulties; and (10) having erectile or ejaculatory difficulties.

A number of researchers and clinicians have noted the overlap between sexual child abuse and chemical, relational, and sexual addictions and/or co-addiction (Carnes, 1991; Kasl, 1989; Klausner & Hasselbring, 1990; Ogden, 1991). Sexual abuse in tandem with physical and emotional abuse can result in many dependent and addictive-type patterns of relating and being sexual. Emotions and conflict are best managed sexually in ways that avoid true intimacy or satisfaction. Many behaviors described as addictive, co-addictive, or co-dependent are frequently based upon the behaviors necessary to survive or accommodate abuse and/or which incorporate cognitions developed in response to abuse. Thus, they should be identified as coping mechanisms that have outlived their usefulness and become problematic.

The relationship between incest-related trauma and post-traumatic reactions and sexual functioning is increasingly understood. Ogden (1991) identified the following as post-traumatic origins of sexual distress: (1) they are learned; (2) they often begin early as survival mechanisms; (3) they may generate positive as well as negative patterns; (4) they invalidate the individual's sense of self; (5) they tend to remain long after the situation changes; (6) they may create phobic avoidance of stress; and (7) they may create compulsive dependencies or more stress (p. 12).

The traumatic reactions may be acute, chronic, and/or appear in delayed or alternating patterns. Triggers in the environment (such as smells, sounds, body sensations, specific emotions, events, and locations) may cause the individual to experience flashbacks during sexual activity or when sexual thoughts or feelings are evoked. Flashbacks can involve a complete re-experiencing of a traumatic event or partial, isolated sensory fragments (pain, smell, sound, emotion) reminiscent of the abuse. Triggers also may cause numbing or distancing responses, quite the opposite of flashback phenomena. Flashback and shutdown processes can occur in alternating patterns and thus fit the post-traumatic, dissociative process described at the beginning of this article. Understanding sexual reactions as post-traumatic adaptations provides the clinician with a specific conceptual model within which to conduct treatment.

One last sexual pattern deserves mention, that of revictimization. Many of the traumatic, emotional, cognitive, and sexual aftereffects of incest may put adult survivors at particular risk for additional sexual abuse and victimization throughout the lifespan (Courtois, 1988; Kluft, 1989; Mayall & Gold, 1995; Russell, 1986). This is not to imply that survivors wish to be revictimized, but rather that they are rendered vulnerable due to their past experiences and many of the negative cognitions and dysfunctional behaviors learned within the context of abuse.

In summary, although the research cited here has limitations concerning its generalizability, enough consistency among studies supports the conclusion that sexual child abuse adversely affects sexual development and sexuality for a sizeable proportion of adult survivors. According to Westerlund (1992): ". . . the majority of women in therapy with incest histories might experience difficulties with sexual functioning" (p. 86). Incest typically is traumatic psychologically and physically, and renders the victim vulnerable to traumatic consequences which, in turn, impact sexual functioning. Sexual aftereffects, like other effects, are inherently subjective and vary across the lifespan. Clinicians must appreciate the aggregate data while differentially assessing and treating the sexual effects experienced by each survivor.

TREATMENT OF SEXUAL AFTEREFFECTS

As discussed above, the course and sequencing of incest therapy have been devised and articulated by clinicians treating this population. In a review of incest treatment phases, Courtois (1991) found most conceptualizations to include three stages: (1) preparatory, alliance-building, ego-enhancing, and stabilizing; (2) traumatic resolution; and (3) treatment of interpersonal and behavioral difficulties. (For further details, the reader is referred to Courtois, 1991.) Of particular pertinence to the treatment of sexual aftereffects is the recommendation of many experienced clinicians that such treatment is most efficaciously undertaken later in treatment (Stage 3), or after the bulk of the trauma resolution work is completed. Clinicians must be aware that the depth and duration of each phase of treatment varies markedly by survivor and some may be able to approach sexual issues sooner than others. It also should be noted that the work of Stages 1 and 2 may disrupt sexual functioning that was previously adequate and/or satisfactory. Clinicians with such an awareness are better prepared for the intensive reactions and temporary regressions which frequently characterize trauma-based treatment.

Until recently, special treatment for the sexual concerns of survivors has not been available, and the sex therapy field has not adequately assessed or addressed the role of sexual abuse/trauma in causing sexual distress and dysfunction. Additionally, many survivors have not sought sex therapy for sexual problems. Reasons survivors do not seek therapy include an inability to trust the motivations of people who would enter the field of sex therapy, an expectation that sex therapy would feel coercive, a tendency to minimize or deny sexual problems, and a sense that the sexual problems in evidence were really not sexual problems *per se* but problems of trust and intimacy that could be worked out in individual or couples therapy (Westerlund, 1992). Westerlund recommends that treatment modifications and special strategies be developed for incest survivors seeking sex therapy, particularly in the areas of control, the pacing of exercises and behaviors, and the encouragement of the client to "take charge of things" after she has been assisted to resolve issues of self-blame and complicity. The survivor must be assisted in overcoming emotional roadblocks such as anger, guilt, and shame that can undermine treatment progress.

The treatment of the sexual concerns of survivors and their partners parallels general therapy processes and encompasses many of its most important philosophical underpinnings. Specifically, healing is for the survivor. His/her subjective experience and perspective are both respected and assessed. The readiness/motivation/ego strength of the survivor are important to assess, and the survivor must actively engage in the process and take responsibility for personal recovery and behavior. The post-traumatic orientation holds that symptoms that require treatment often prove to be adaptations or defenses to the early trauma that have outlasted their usefulness and have become problematic. They must be de-pathologized by clinician and survivor alike, their necessity understood in the context of the trauma (Summit, 1983), and as "functional dysfunctions" rather than as premorbid conditions (Sprei & Courtois, 1988).

The survivor may experience intense transference reactions toward the therapist and/or partner when engaged in sexual healing work, even when the survivor is highly motivated and committed to the treatment (Maltz, 1991). The survivor may experience the therapeutic attempts to resolve the sexuality issues as coercive and out of her control. The clinician, survivor, and partner must be prepared for traumatic transference responses and be clear that the pacing of the work needs to be in the survivor's control. Survivors must heal at their own pace so that the dynamic of powerlessness associated with the abuse does not continue.

Sexual healing takes time, effort, courage, and hard work. The survivor does healing work when ready and motivated to do so. Maltz (1991) has identified several main ways in which motivation develops, including awareness that a problem exists and that it is related to the abuse, relationship distress for self and partner, anger about the abuse, and the determination to reclaim one's birthright. Fears, misinformation, naivete, and negative attitudes and beliefs may impede the ability to address sexual concerns. These must be addressed directly before proceeding. Jehu (1988) and Maltz (1991), both experienced sex therapists, stress that attitude and belief change are crucial. Some of the most important work is educational and is geared towards the restructuring of whatever cognitive distortions underlie the sexual difficulties.

The sexual healing process involves developing awareness of the problem and challenging patterns of denial. Survivors need to make the decision to heal and work through the trauma and all of its sexual repercussions in order to reconstitute, heal, and grow. Like the process, healing goals are very individualized and should be delineated as such (Chu, 1988; Jehu, 1988). The damage of abuse may, at times, be so pervasive as to make complete healing impossible. The survivor may need to take "vacations" from healing to reach individual goals and to "re-charge" or re-channel motivation or energy for more healing work (Jehu, 1988; Maltz, 1991).

THE SPECIFICS OF SEXUAL HEALING

Much of this section is a synthesis of prior work (Jehu, 1988; Maltz, 1991; Sprei & Courtois, 1988; Westerlund, 1992). The preliminary issues for survivors involve their gaining awareness of sexual concerns, admitting pain and loss to self and others that stem from sexual concerns, and seeking outside help or specific help within the context of other therapy. A second consideration is to make the connection between the sexual abuse of the past and the sexual repercussions in the present (Maltz, 1991). Maltz discussed the "child abuse mind-set," a phrase describing a cognitive set that is familiar to clinicians treating survivors. The "mind-set" is derived from the abuse, and negatively conditions sexuality, sexual attitudes and behaviors. Both Jehu (1988) and Maltz (1991) offer dramatic clinical vignettes which convey the pervasive negative reactions that survivors attach to sexual feeling and functioning. At some time early in the sexual healing process, the survivor must make the decision to heal and to separate sexuality from sexual abuse. Many survivors describe the goal of taking back what was taken from them, and reclaiming themselves, their birthright, and their sexuality.

Education about abuse effects and the use of assessment instruments help the survivor understand the abuse repercussions. Jehu (1988) and Maltz (1991) developed specialized assessment instruments to identify beliefs, relationship variables, target goals, sexual fears, sexual effects, sexual behaviors, sexual dysfunctions, and triggers to various sexual responses. Standard, formal sexual dysfunction protocols can be used to further assess medical, psychological, biological, dyadic, and environmental/cultural/familial considerations in preparation for goal-setting and intervention.

Therapy goals should be determined with the survivor who is encouraged to take control, to pace his/her work, and to begin alone before engaging in couples work. Informed consent is especially important because the survivor must be willing to take the initiative on a problem area that is particularly sensitive due to its having been the focus of the abuse.

Whatever the ultimate goal(s), a common starting point is to challenge the "sexual abuse mind set" through education and cognitive techniques. Survivors identify beliefs they hold about themselves and sex to identify any cognitive distortions they might have. Common beliefs include statements such as "I am bad because I was abused," "I was abused because I am bad," "Sex is dirty," "Feeling sexual is bad," and "Sex equals abuse." Jehu (1988) documented the effect of belief change on both mood disturbances and sexual dysfunction in survivors. Westerlund (1992) emphasized the importance of cognitive techniques and "self-talk" to interrupt and correct problematic thoughts and beliefs.

The next stage involves determining conditioned or automatic cognitive, emotional, and somatic responses in order to develop some control over them. Many survivors detach or dissociate from their bodies in response to sexual interaction and/or sexual responsivity. They can identify triggers to their numbing responses and can then condition different responses to the triggers. Maltz (1991) designed exercises for the detailed identification of triggers and techniques that address them. She also developed exercises for survivors to learn positive associations to touch and to deal with flashbacks of the abuse. Survivors must be gently and persistently challenged to separate past from present. Westerlund (1992) described body and anger work as precursors to direct work on sexual functioning.

It is at this stage, according to Maltz (1991), that clients begin to explore their responses and sexual preferences (turn-offs as well as turn-ons), and to examine unhealthy sexual behaviors such as compulsions, promiscuity, unsafe sex, and any sadomasochistic practices. S/he must learn to set limits on these to gain perspective and develop alternative behaviors. Maltz describes the development of a safe time-out for healing. Westerlund suggests body techniques to offer alternative ways for fulfilling needs and reversing dysfunctions.

More specific sexual and body exploration occurs at the next stage which may be lengthy and must be under the survivor's control. Jehu (1988) offered a clinical vignette of a client who needed several months to desensitize herself from the belief that sexual arousal was bad, a necessary step before proceeding in therapy. Survivors work on healing the mind-body split caused by sexual trauma by first exploring their own bodies and responses and then by moving on to exploring with their partners. Sensate focus exercises (Masters & Johnson, 1970) can be modified for use with survivors. For example, survivors may begin by wearing clothes and achieving nudity gradually as comfort dictates.

The identified triggers are "de-fused" over time by conditioning them to pleasurable rather than hurtful/abusive activities and by reconditioning touch with positive, pleasurable sensation. Systematic desensitization (Lazarus, 1971) might be utilized repeatedly to decondition cues and sexual responses, and may therefore require a considerable amount of time, patience, and perseverance. Specific sexual concerns, such as aversions, dysfunctions, and compulsions, each need to be addressed so that cognitions and behaviors are modified over time. Techniques are geared to make change a gradual and emotionally manageable process which includes insight, re-learning and reconditioning to the positive and/or pleasurable.

Sexual healing often involves a partner. Westerlund (1992) notes that "The importance of a trustworthy and understanding partner should not be underestimated. . . . Increased and improved selectivity of partners may only develop, however, after substantial work on self-esteem and trust issues. To enter a sexual relationship with an appropriate, non-exploitive partner, a woman must both be able to believe that she deserves such a partner and be able to trust that the partner is real. The latter may prove more difficult with a male partner" (p. 153).

The partner often is a secondary victim of the abuse in that s/he may suffer from negative self-esteem, anger and resentment, mistrust, and ultimately, sexual and emotional withdrawal and sexual dysfunction as a result of the survivor's distress. Survivors should be encouraged to envision and utilize the partner as a healing resource, and whenever possible, to include him/her in the healing process. Potentially helpful partners have been underutilized as resources to the detriment of both the survivor and the partner (Davis, 1991; Maltz, 1991). A major benefit is derived in perceiving the present partner as an ally and differentiating him/her from the past abuser(s) (Westerlund, 1992).

Partners, like survivors, benefit from education about sexual abuse and its effects. They often are relieved to learn of the normalcy of the survivor's sexual restrictions and difficulties, given the past experiences of abuse. Partners often perceive sexual distress as personal rejection and may need direct assistance to separate the self from the effects (i.e., to de-personalize the survivor's reactions). Partners have self-esteem, sexual functioning, and other losses to confront as a result of the abuse. They should be encouraged to identify and to confront their feelings while allowing survivors the latitude to do the same. They must, however, be encouraged not to act for the survivor, especially without the survivor's specific consent. For example, the partner may become overwhelmed after learning that a relative s/he held in esteem is the abuser and may be tempted to lash out against that person to protect or speak for the survivor.

The same principle of permitting the survivor to be in control holds for sexual healing. Survivors and partners must agree on mutual goals and should be encouraged to reclaim sexual functioning by first increasing communication skills and non-sexual intimacy, and then by building on various gains to gradually achieve greater sexual satisfaction. In some cases, aversions and avoidance are not necessarily dysfunctional or subject to change. The couple's sexual repertoire can deliberately exclude certain activities which continue to be overly distressing to the survivor. On the other hand, some triggers can be minimized, extinguished, or changed to allow new meaning to be attached to them (Sprei & Courtois, 1988).

Sexual healing for survivors and partners often is slower than conventional sex therapy and more uneven in pace. The sexual conditioning of the abuse must be identified and unlearned for new learning regarding sexual feeling and functioning to take place. The reclamation of sexuality and the potential for sexual intimacy reward the efforts of both survivors and their partners.

CONCLUSION

The effects of incest trauma on sexuality and sexual functioning can be quite pronounced. Survivors may have distorted or negatively influenced body responses and perceptions such that they are literally alienated from themselves. The alienation may extend to reproductive issues, sexual preference, sexual response, and ability to function sexually. Helping professionals must become aware of the various ways sexuality can be impacted by incest experiences and must be prepared to treat sexual concerns as part of incest therapy. Standard sex therapy techniques need to be modified for survivors to include a heavy emphasis on education and cognitive mastery before moving on to sexual exercises. Survivors are encouraged to face the effects of abuse and to reclaim their sexual functioning at a pace that is comfortable and manageable for them. Partners are included whenever possible, with enhancement of sexual functioning and intimacy as the stated goals of treatment.

REFERENCES

American Psychiatric Association (1994). *Diagnostic and statistical manual of mental disorders* (4th ed.). Washington, DC: Author.

Bass, E., & Davis, L. (1988). *The courage to heal: A guide for women survivors of child sexual abuse.* New York: Harper & Row.

Bender, L., & Blau, A. (1937). A reaction of children to sexual relations with adults. *American Journal of Orthopsychiatry, 7,* 500-518.

Briere, J. (Ed.) (1991). *Treating victims of child sexual abuse.* San Francisco: Jossey-Bass.

Briere, J. (1989). *Therapy for adults molested as children: Beyond survival.* New York: Springer.

Briere, J., & Runtz, M. (1991). The long-term effects of sexual abuse: A review and synthesis. In J. Briere (Ed.), *Treating victims of child sexual abuse* (pp. 3-14). San Francisco: Jossey-Bass.

Butler, S. (1985). *Conspiracy of silence: The trauma of incest.* New York: Bantam Books.

Carnes, P. (1991). *Don't call it love: Recovery from sexual addiction.* New York: Bantam Books.

Chu, J. (1988). Ten traps for therapists in the treatment of trauma survivors. *Dissociation, 1,* 4, 24-32.

Courtois, C. A. (1991). Theory, sequencing, and strategy in treating adult survivors. In J. Briere (Ed.), *Treating victims of child sexual abuse* (pp. 47-60). San Francisco: Jossey-Bass.

Courtois, C. A. (1988). *Healing the incest wound: Adult survivors in therapy.* New York: W.W. Norton.

Courtois, C. A. (1979). *Characteristics of a volunteer sample of adult women who experienced incest in childhood and adolescence.* Unpublished doctoral dissertation, University of Maryland.

Davis, L. (1991). *Allies in healing.* New York: Harper Perennial.

Donaldson, M. A., & Gardner, R. (1985). Diagnosis and treatment of traumatic stress among women after childhood incest. In C. R. Figley (Ed.), *Trauma and its wake: The study and treatment of post-traumatic stress disorder* (pp. 356-377). New York: Brunner/Mazel.

Finkelhor, D., & Browne, A. (1985). The traumatic impact of child sexual abuse: A conceptualization. *American Journal of Orthopsychiatry, 55,* 530-541.

Follette, V. (1991). Marital therapy for sexual abuse survivors. In J. Briere (Ed.). *Treating victims of child sexual abuse* (pp. 61-72). San Francisco: Jossey-Bass.

Frawley, M. G. (1988). *The sexual lives of adult survivors of father-daughter incest.* Dissertation summary, unpublished manuscript.

Horowitz, M. J. (1986). *Stress response syndromes* (2nd Ed.). Northwale, NJ: Jason Aronson.

Jehu, D. (1988). *Beyond sexual abuse: Therapy with women who were childhood victims.* New York: John Wiley.

Johnson, S. (1989). Integrating marital and individual therapy for incest survivors: A case study. *Psychotherapy, 26,* 96-102.

Kasl, C. (1989). *Women, sex and addiction: A search for love and power.* New York: Harper & Row.

Kinsey, A., Pomeroy, W., Martin, C., & Gebhard, P. (1953). *Sexual behavior in the human female.* Philadelphia: Saunders.

Kirschner, S., Kirschner, D., & Rappaport, R. (1993). *Working with adult incest survivors.* New York: Brunner/Mazel.

Klausner, M. A., & Hasselbring, B. (1990). *Aching for love: The sexual drama of the adult child. Healing strategies for women.* San Francisco: Harper & Row.

R. P. Kluft (Ed.) (1989). Treatment of victims of sexual abuse. *The Psychiatric Clinics of North America, 12,* 295-305.

Lazarus, A. (1971). *Behavior therapy and beyond.* New York: McGraw-Hill.

Loulan, J. (1987). *Lesbian passion: Loving ourselves and each other.* San Francisco: Spinster/Aunt Lute.

Lundberg-Love, P. (1990). Adult survivors of incest. In R. A. Ammerman & M.

Hersen (Eds.). *Treatment of family violence: A source book* (pp. 169-184). New York: John Wiley.

Lundberg-Love, P. K. (1988, March). *Sexuality issues in the treatment of adult incest survivors*. In P. K. Lundberg-Love (Chair), The impact of incest upon the sexuality of adult women. Symposium presented at the Society for the Scientific Study of Sex Biennial Meeting, Dallas, TX.

Maltz, W. (1991). *The sexual healing journey: A guide for survivors of sexual abuse*. New York: HarperCollins.

Maltz, W., & Holman, B. (1987). *Incest and sexuality*. Lexington, MA: Lexington Books.

Masters, W., & Johnson, V. (1970). *Human sexual inadequacy*. Boston: Little, Brown.

Mayall, A., & Gold, S. (1995). Definitional issues and mediating variables in the sexual revictimization of women sexually abused as children. *Journal of Interpersonal Violence*, *10*, 26-42.

McCann, I., & Pearlman, L. (1990). *Psychological trauma and the adult survivor: Theory, therapy, and transformation*. New York: Brunner/Mazel.

Meiselman, K. C. (1990). *Resolving the trauma of incest: Reintegration therapy with survivors*. San Francisco: Jossey-Bass.

Ogden, G. (1991). *Sexual recovery: Everywoman's guide through sexual co-dependency*. Deerfield Beach, FL: Health Communications.

Russell, D. E. H. (1986). *The secret trauma: Incest in the lives of girls and women*. New York: Basic Books.

Sprei, J., & Courtois, C. (1988). The treatment of women's sexual dysfunctions arising from sexual assault. In J. R. Field & R. A. Brown (Eds.). *Treatment of sexual problems in individual and marital therapy* (pp. 267-300). New York: Spectrum.

Summit, R. (1983). The child sexual abuse accommodation syndrome. *Child Abuse and Neglect*, *7*, 177-193.

van der Hart, O., & Horst, R. (1989). The dissociation theory of Pierre Janet. *Journal of Traumatic Stress*, *2*, 397-412.

Westerlund, E. (1992). *Women's sexuality after childhood incest*. New York: W. W. Norton.

Current Treatment Strategies
for Dissociative Identity Disorders
in Adult Sexual Abuse Survivors

Paula K. Lundberg-Love

SUMMARY. During the past decade, increasing numbers of clinicians and researchers have suggested that the dissociative disorders, including dissociative identity disorder (DID), may be more prevalent than previously hypothesized. The "rediscovery" of DID is due, in part, to the recognition that early childhood trauma in conjunction with the propensity to dissociate, are etiologic factors for the development of DID. The purpose of this article is to raise clinical consciousness regarding DID, discuss the definition and etiology of the dissociative disorders, their assessment, and an approach to treatment of the sexual abuse survivor who has DID. This treatment program, while integrating some of the techniques recommended by others, is unique in its step-by-step flexible organization as well as its multifaceted format. The author's experience to date suggests that the sooner that a dissociative disorder can be identified in the adult sexual abuse survivor client, the more rapid the therapeutic progress. *[Article copies available for a fee from The Haworth Document Delivery Service: 1-800-342-9678. E-mail address: getinfo@haworth.com]*

KEYWORDS. Incest, sexual trauma, domestic violence, psychotherapy, recovery, dissociation

---

Address correspondence to: Paula K. Lundberg-Love, PhD, Department of Psychology, University of Texas-Tyler, 3900 University Boulevard, Tyler, TX 75799.

[Haworth co-indexing entry note]: "Current Treatment Strategies for Dissociative Identity Disorders in Adult Sexual Abuse Survivors." Lundberg-Love, Paula K. Co-published simultaneously in *Journal of Aggression, Maltreatment & Trauma* (Haworth Maltreatment & Trauma Press, an imprint of The Haworth Press, Inc.) Vol. 1, No. 1 (#1), 1997, pp. 311-333; and: *Violence and Sexual Abuse at Home: Current Issues in Spousal Battering and Child Maltreatment* (ed: Robert Geffner, Susan B. Sorenson, and Paula K. Lundberg-Love) Haworth Maltreatment & Trauma Press, an imprint of The Haworth Press, Inc., 1997, pp. 311-333. Single or multiple copies of this article are available for a fee from The Haworth Document Delivery Service [1-800-342-9678, 9:00 a.m. - 5:00 p.m. (EST). E-mail address: getinfo@haworth.com].

During the past decade there has been a renewed interest in the identification and treatment of dissociative disorders. This has occurred, in part, as a result of the burgeoning knowledge regarding the consequences of childhood sexual and physical abuse. As increasing numbers of clinicians have had the occasion to treat adult survivors of child abuse, they have observed that those who were abused physically and/or sexually before the age of six often are at greater risk for the development of a dissociative disorder. As a result, clinicians have suggested that the dissociative disorders, including dissociative identity disorder (DID), may be more prevalent than previously hypothesized.

Because the definitive North American psychiatric epidemiological studies used the Diagnostic Interview Schedule, an instrument that does not inquire about any of the dissociative disorders, prevalence data regarding these disorders were not obtained from the Epidemiological Catchment Area studies (Ross, 1991). To date, only Ross (1989) has sought to determine the prevalence of dissociative disorders in non-clinical samples. In a random sample of 1,055 respondents from the general population of Winnipeg, Canada, 5% of the individuals tested on the Dissociative Experiences Survey (DES) (Bernstein & Putnam, 1986) scored in the range considered diagnostic for a dissociative disorder. In the second phase of the study, Ross (1991) administered the Dissociative Disorders Interview Schedule (DDIS) to 454 of the respondents from the first prevalence study. Of these individuals, 11.2% reported some type of dissociative disorder and 3.1% were designated as having DID.

The author's experience suggests that the sooner that DID can be identified in the adult sexual abuse survivor client, the more rapid the therapeutic progress. Thus, this article discusses the definition and etiology of dissociative disorders, the assessment of dissociative disorders, and then an approach to their treatment in adult survivors of sexual trauma.

DIAGNOSTIC CRITERIA FOR AND ETIOLOGY OF DID

Dissociation is a psychological coping mechanism that involves the processes of separating, segregating and isolating various aspects of experience from one another. Typically dissociation compartmentalizes traumatic, destructive, or affectively negative material and keeps it from contaminating non-threatening material (Block, 1991). Braun (1990) defines dissociation as "the separation of an idea or thought process from the main stream of consciousness" (p. 972).

Recent studies suggest that there is a relationship between traumatization, one's dissociative proficiency, and one's hypnotic capacity (Bliss

1986; Carlson & Putnam, 1989). DID clients often display phenomena similar to that seen in research subjects without DID who are highly hypnotizable (Bliss, 1986). These include experiences of intense absorption, spontaneous trances, complex amnesias, hypermnesia, anesthesias, spontaneous negative hallucinations and age regressions, dissociated motor activities, complex multimodal imagery, out-of-body experiences, hidden observer-like phenomena and trance-logic (Bliss, 1986; Hilgard, 1986; Kluft, 1988; Loewenstein, 1991; Loewenstein, Hornstein, & Farber, 1988; Putnam, 1989).

Ross (1989) and Braun (1986) suggest that there is a continuum of dissociative phenomena. These can range from the "highway hypnosis" that occurs when one is driving and suddenly realizes that s/he missed the freeway exit because her/his mind was "elsewhere," to diagnostic entities such as dissociative fugue (DF), dissociative amnesia (DA), depersonalization disorder (DD) and dissociative identity disorder (DID) (Ross, 1989). According to the diagnostic criteria of the DSM-IV (American Psychiatric Association, 1994), dissociative fugue is sudden, unexpected travel from home or one's customary place of work with the inability to recall one's past. Confusion about an individual's personal identity or the assumption of a new identity may occur. Typically DF does not occur only within the context of DID and it is not secondary to ingestion of a substance (e.g., medication, drugs of abuse) or a general medical condition (e.g., temporal lobe epilepsy). Symptoms of DF usually cause clinically significant distress/impairment in social and occupational areas of functioning.

Dissociative amnesia consists of one or more episodes of the inability to recall important personal information, often of a traumatic or stressful nature, that is too extensive to be explained by ordinary forgetfulness. This disorder typically does not occur independently of DID, post-traumatic stress disorder (PTSD), acute stress disorder, or somatization disorder. Like DF, DA is not due to the psychological effects of drug ingestion, neurological conditions or other general medical conditions, and distress or impairment exists with respect to social and/or occupational functioning.

Persistent or recurrent episodes of feeling detached from one's mental processes or body (e.g., feeling as if one is an outside observer or feeling like one is in a dream) is a criterion of depersonalization disorder. During a depersonalization episode reality testing remains intact. Furthermore, DD is not diagnosed if it is due to certain other medical disorders or drug ingestion, or if it does not impair social and/or occupational functioning.

Finally, DID is characterized by the presence of two or more distinct identities or personality states, each of which possesses its own relatively enduring pattern of perceiving, relating to, and thinking about the environment and self. At least two of the identities recurrently take control of the individual's behavior and there is an inability to recall important personal information that is too extensive to be explained by ordinary forgetfulness. Similar to the other dissociative disorders listed above, DID does not result from the physiological effects of drugs, alcohol or general medical conditions. In children, such symptoms are not attributable to fantasy play or imaginary playmates. Thus, DID as well as other dissociative disorders result from problems regarding the integration of memory, affect and cognition. Braun (1988) suggests that DID potentially can impact four components of human behavior, including behavior, affect, sensation and knowledge (the BASK model), and that theoretically, memories consist of these components. Brickman (1992) proposes that consistent dissociation in the face of trauma becomes DID when the dissociated parts of the self become separate enough to form distinct personalities that alternately emerge and take control of behavior. Regardless, competing theories that seek to explain the genesis of DID along with compelling and clinically useful data suggest that repeated childhood trauma enhances dissociative capacities that, in turn, may provide the basis for the creation and elaboration of alternate personalities (i.e., "alters") over time (Putnam, 1989).

Indeed, many individuals who meet the criteria for DID have a history of early childhood trauma, particularly sexual abuse, physical abuse or both (Putnam, 1989). However, not all individuals who have DID are necessarily victims of abuse. Clinical researchers such as Putnam (1989) and Ross (1989) who have studied hundreds of cases of DID, indicate that 85% of clients with DID have a history of sexual abuse and 80% have a history of physical and sexual abuse. However, severe neglect and the witnessing of extreme violence and/or trauma also potentially can precipitate DID.

Another characteristic that distinguishes DID clients when they enter treatment is that they often have numerous prior diagnoses (Ross, 1989). For example, DID clients have often received a diagnosis of affective disorder (63.7%), personality disorder (57.4%), anxiety disorder (44.3%), schizophrenia (40.8%), substance abuse (31.4%), adjustment disorder (21.1%), somatization disorder (18.8%), eating disorder (16.3%), and organic mental disorder (12.8%) prior to being diagnosed as DID (Ross, 1989). Additionally, many clients have been involved with legal, welfare and other social services, and many have complicated nonpsychiatric medical histories. According to Ross (1989), 11.9% have been convicted of a crime and 12.3% have been in prison. Although the predominance of DID clients are female, it is hypothesized that the majority of male clients with

DID tend to end up in the criminal justice system. Therefore, the prevalence of males with DID may be significantly underestimated because many may be incarcerated. Ross suggests that the following features are common to many clients with DID: (a) history of childhood physical and/or sexual abuse, (b) headache, (c) "blank" spells, (d) voices inside the head, (e) the absence of formal thought disorder, (f) many features of the DSM-IV criteria for borderline personality disorder, (g) prior unsuccessful treatment and other psychiatric diagnoses, and (h) self-destructive behavior.

In spite of the recent media attention given to DID, the majority of clients do not present for treatment and announce that they have a dissociative disorder. In fact, most clients initially present with a wide array of clinical symptoms. During the course of treatment a therapist may realize that a client has a dissociative disorder instead of, or in addition to, the apparent presenting symptoms and the initial diagnosis. Thus, although it is imperative to emphasize the initial assessment phase of treatment, one must realize that the awareness of dissociative disorders, particularly DID, may emerge gradually over the course of therapy.

Clients with dissociative disorders may have a profusion of psychological, neurological and medical symptoms, some or many of which may have been refractory to treatment. The core dissociative symptoms include amnesia/time loss, fugue episodes, depersonalization, and sleepwalking (Putnam, 1989). Concurrent psychological symptoms include depression/suicide attempts, anxiety/phobias, substance abuse, transsexualism/transvestism, auditory hallucinations, self-mutilation, and catatonia. Clients often report specific or ill-defined medical symptoms, including headache (commonly migraine-like), seizures, syncope (fainting), sensory and visual disturbances, cardio-respiratory symptoms, gastrointestinal disorders, gynecological disorders, dermatological symptoms, unexplained fevers and idiosyncratic responses to pharmacological agents. Prior to the identification of DID, it is not uncommon for clients to have seen many physicians and received equivocal diagnoses because underlying physiological or pathophysiological mechanisms have not been identified. This is often due to the fact that when pathophysiological mechanisms have been identified to explain a client's medical disorders, the nature of DID is such that the symptoms frequently are transitory or sporadic, which is very confusing for physicians.

The antecedents of severe childhood physical and/or sexual trauma have been correlated with DID. Typically, the trauma has occurred prior to age six in a child who has the propensity, whether inherited or acquired, to dissociate. Children who have experienced extreme neglect, extreme poverty, other types of maltreatment or trauma, or those who have observed violent death, also may be at risk for DID.

ASSESSMENT OF DISSOCIATIVE DISORDERS

The first step in the assessment of dissociative disorders is a detailed clinical interview and a mental status exam. Specifically, a client needs to be asked about symptoms such as amnesias, fugue states, as well as experiences of hearing internal voices and feeling compelled from within the psyche to behave in an uncharacteristic way. Additionally, the literature includes diagnostic tools such as the Structured Clinical Interview for Dissociative Disorders (SCID-D) (Steinberg, 1993), the Dissociative Disorders Interview Schedule (DDIS) (Ross, 1989), a screening instrument, the Dissociative Experiences Scale (DES and DES-II) (Bernstein & Putnam, 1986; Carlson & Putnam, 1993), and a semi-structured mental status examination (MSE) devised by Loewenstein (1991).

Since the introduction of the original DES (Bernstein & Putnam, 1986), a modified instrument entitled the DES-II has been introduced and its use has been recommended by others (Carlson & Putnam, 1989). The DES-II consists of 28 scenarios about experiences that one may have experienced in daily life. On the DES-II, the individual is asked to determine to what degree the experience described in the questions applies to her/him, and to circle the number (0, 10, 20, 30 . . . 100) to show what percentage of time it occurs. The sum of the percentages associated with each question is determined and a mean score obtained; this is the overall DES-II score. Additional subscale scores can be obtained for Profound Amnesia, Derealization and Depersonalization, and Absorption and Imaginative Involvement. The first DES had a test-retest reliability of 0.84, and good clinical validity (Bernstein & Putnam, 1986). When an individual scores at or above 30, it is strongly suggestive that a dissociative disorder may be present. Scores in the range of the 40s or 50s are suggestive of DID. The majority of adults who complete this instrument obtain a score of less than 12. Some individuals with eating disorders or substance abuse disorders may score in the 20s.

When someone scores high on the DES, it is appropriate to follow up with a structured interview, such as the Dissociative Disorders Interview Schedule (DDIS) developed by Ross (1989). The DDIS is a 131-item structured interview with an overall inter-rater reliability of 0.68 (Ross et al., 1989). The utilization of these two instruments permits a practitioner to differentiate the diagnosis of a dissociative disorder from other diagnoses with a high degree of accuracy. The false-positive rate for a DDIS diagnosis of DID is less than 1% in clinical populations (Ross, 1991).

The SCID-D (Steinberg, 1993) can be used instead of or in addition to the DDIS. The SCID-D is a semistructured diagnostic interview for the systematic assessment of five dissociative symptoms: amnesia, depersonalization, derealization, identity confusion and identity alteration. It yields a total score and individual scores for each dissociative symptom. Severity rating definitions (1 = absent, 2 = mild, 3 = moderate, 4 = severe) are used to operationalize the assessment of the five dissociative symptom areas.

In summary, by using the DES-II and Loewenstein's MSE, a therapist can screen for a possible dissociative disorder during an initial session. Given a positive response on the DES-II, the DDIS and/or the SCID-D can be administered during subsequent sessions. This strategy potentially can identify the dissociative client early in the treatment process. However, it is important for the clinician to recognize that clients with dissociative disorders often carry a number of psychiatric diagnoses. Therefore, treatment for various disorders may need to be sequenced appropriately depending upon the nature and severity of the various concomitant diagnoses.

One of the most common concomitant diagnoses for an individual with DID may be post-traumatic stress disorder (PTSD). PTSD can occur when an individual has been exposed to a traumatic event wherein s/he experienced, observed, or was confronted with an event(s) that involve(s) actual or threatened death or serious injury, or a threat to the physical integrity of oneself or others. Additionally, the person's response to the traumatic event typically involved intense fear, helplessness or horror, and the trauma is re-experienced persistently in one or more of the following ways:

1. recurrent and intrusive recollections
2. recurrent distressing dreams of the event
3. acting or feeling as if the traumatic event were recurring (e.g., a sense of reliving the experience, illusions, hallucinations and dissociative flashback episodes that may occur on awakening or when intoxicated)
4. intense psychological distress when exposed to internal or external cues that symbolize or resemble an aspect of the traumatic event
5. physiological reactivity upon exposure to internal or external cues that symbolize or resemble an aspect of the traumatic event.

Also present is the persistent avoidance of stimuli associated with the trauma and a numbing of general responsiveness not present before the trauma, as indicated by three of the following symptoms:

1. efforts to avoid thoughts, feelings or conversations associated with the trauma
2. efforts to avoid activities, places or people that arouse recollections of the trauma
3. inability to recall an important aspect of the trauma
4. markedly diminished interest or participation in significant activities
5. feeling of detachment or estrangement from others
6. restricted range of affect
7. sense of a foreshortened future (e.g., does not expect to have a career, marriage, children or a normal life span).

Finally, there are persistent symptoms of increased arousal that were not present prior to the trauma as indicated by the presence of two or more of the following symptoms:

1. difficulty falling or staying asleep
2. irritability or outbursts of anger
3. difficulty concentrating
4. hypervigilance
5. exaggerated startle response.

The duration of the syndrome must have persisted for more than one month, and clinically significant impairment in social, occupational, or other areas of functioning must exist. Clearly, because both dissociative disorders and PTSD stem from traumatic experience, some similarities exist among them. Indeed, Ross (1989) has suggested that PTSD may exist along a continuum of the dissociative disorders.

THE TREATMENT PROCESS

Some resistance still exists among many mental health practitioners regarding the recognition and treatment of DID (Ross, 1990). Indeed, a book has recently been published that "delivers a blistering rebuttal to many long-held assumptions" about DID (Spanos, 1996). This is unfortunate because preliminary outcome data suggest that DID is a disorder that is quite treatable with psychotherapy. One of the fundamental errors therapists often make when they first encounter a client with DID is to believe that a wide array of new therapeutic techniques must be mastered in order to treat the client successfully. Kluft (1993) suggests that certain basic principles of psychotherapy need to be incorporated within the treatment process. These include: (a) a secure treatment framework with firm consistent boundaries implemented at a carefully executed pace, (b) the establishment and maintenance of a strong therapeutic alliance, (c) a focus on achieving mastery of various coping skills, (d) the identification and processing of buried traumata, (e) the facilitation of cooperation among and the evenhanded consistent interaction with all alter personalities, (f) the correction of cognitive errors, (g) the restoration of shattered basic assumptions, and (h) the teaching, modeling and reinforcement of responsibility.

One of the purposes of this article is to describe an approach to the treatment of the adult sexual abuse survivor who has DID. This treatment program is a derivative of the prototype program developed for recovery from childhood sexual abuse (Lundberg-Love, 1990). Although this treatment approach integrates some of the basic techniques described by Putnam (1989), Ross (1989), Kluft (1993), and Barach (1994), it is unique in its step-by-step organization and its multifaceted format. The initial phases of treatment include assessment, anxiety management training, and the identification of possible "alters," which are, as Ross (1990) has suggested, fragmented components of a single personality that are abnormally personified, dissociated one from another, and amnesic for each other. If and when alters are identified, the determination and disclosure of the tentative DID diagnosis can ensue. Once the preliminary diagnosis is made, the therapist should begin very carefully paced initial interventions. For the author, these include identifying the alternate personalities as they present themselves, obtaining information regarding the alters' respective histories and functions, and producing a pictorial or hand-crafted physical representation of the client's perception of her/his internal world (i.e., the "inner schema" or the "system"). This is an ongoing process.

Subsequent treatment issues involve the development of communication and cooperation among the alters, the development of co-consciousness across personalities (i.e., various personalities experiencing life's events simultaneously without amnesic barriers), the acquisition of knowledge regarding one's trauma history and the attendant processing of the associated issues and emotions. The term often used to describe this latter therapeutic technique is "abreaction" (i.e., a "re-expressing" of early trauma). As the trauma is processed over time, the integration of alters tends to occur. Some alters just fade away after the disclosure of the trauma they experienced. Others coalesce or fuse with one another until finally the client's experience of self is that of a unified entity. After integration is complete, the therapeutic focus centers upon the development of post-integration coping skills.

Depending upon individual circumstances, treatment teams may include a variety of professional disciplines. Treatment plans also may include psychoeducational interventions as well as bibliotherapy and expressive therapies. Additionally, clients may have multiple legal involvements that also may require supportive intervention; it is wise to try to avoid planned therapeutic interventions that may compromise the credibility of the clients in forensic proceedings at a later point (Barach, 1994).

Anxiety Management Training

Anxiety management is a critical initial intervention for all adult survivors of sexual abuse, regardless of whether they have a dissociative disorder. This is because during the course of the treatment process, survivors often will experience situations which will require the ability to diminish problematic feelings and sensations. As a result, it is incumbent upon the therapist to provide clients with a mechanism for soothing themselves during such difficult times when they experience strong and often painful emotions. Teaching clients a variety of anxiety management strategies is one means for doing this. Proficiency in such techniques is empowering and promotes affective and cognitive mastery and provides a therapeutic intervention that can be utilized outside of sessions whenever needed. Also, because most adult survivors of abuse struggle with control issues, especially those surrounding control over their bodies, the ability to perform relaxation exercises successfully can minimize a wide array of symptoms. Relaxation exercises are particularly useful during phases of therapy when memories return because they provide a mechanism for the titration of flashback experiences. Additionally, they provide a means for controlling pain whether physical or emotional. Thus, anxiety management techniques enable clients to regulate various aversive internal states.

Different clients prefer different types of anxiety management techniques ranging from progressive muscle relaxation, autogenic techniques, imagery, mediative approaches, to deep breathing and verbal cuing. The author provides an audiotape containing a wide array of relaxation exercises. It is the responsibility of the clients to practice with the tape and develop their own procedures for anxiety management. It is the responsibility of the therapist to make sure that the clients successfully master at least one of these procedures. The therapist can use biofeedback equipment to assess the clients' proficiency at their chosen techniques. This is particularly important during phases of therapy when recollections may return at inopportune times. Client education also is implemented to encourage the use of visual imagery and metaphor wherein the mind can be envisioned as a library with numerous volumes, or a clothing armoire with many drawers, or a filing cabinet with assorted drawers. Clients are taught that during stressful times, anxiety management techniques can be used in conjunction with the library, armoire, or filing cabinet imagery in order "to hold" or "to put away" difficult recollections until the issues can be examined and processed during the next therapy session. In this manner, clients learn how to handle flashbacks, recollections and the general discomfort of the therapeutic process.

However, some important caveats are in order. Therapists who treat DID agree that clients may frequently enter trance states both during and outside of treatment, even when a therapist has not performed any specific procedure. Indeed, many relaxation techniques tend to be considered a form of autohypnotic procedure. As such, in many states of the United States, any information or recollections that might emerge spontaneously during such an exercise may not be introduced in certain forensic situations. Thus, it is critical that clients be provided with and asked to sign an informed consent document that outlines this information. In some cases with substantial legal involvement, the utilization of autohypnotic relaxation exercises may be precluded. It is the responsibility of the therapist to disclose such information fully prior to the instruction of such techniques. Also, it is strongly recommended that all therapists who teach such techniques to clients complete formal continuing education and become certified to use hypnotherapy.

Identification of Alternate Personalities or States

Once clients have learned to manage their anxiety and some degree of therapeutic alliance has been forged, the therapist can begin to question a client to elicit a history of a subjective sense of various internal identities or parts. Loewenstein in his MSE (1991) asks various questions that seek to identify the possible presence of alternate personalities. However, if the DES-II, SCID-D and/or DDIS previously have been administered, then one would already have asked such questions. Clinicians have suggested a more indirect, possibly less suggestive method for the initial identification of alters (Putnam, 1989).

The author has adapted Putnam's method and has found it rather effective. Once a client is comfortable with and demonstrates a modicum of proficiency regarding a deep breathing relaxation technique, the therapist suggests that an exercise be conducted during the session. Typically, the client is told that this exercise may seem a bit strange but that it is merely an exercise. The client's task is simply to observe her/his own behavior and report the response to the therapist. The therapist explains that she would like the client to do a deep breathing relaxation exercise with her and that when the client feels relaxed, the therapist will ask some questions. If the client is comfortable with this exercise, the relaxation process ensues. When the client appears relaxed (e.g., decreased respiration rate, relaxed body posture), the therapist quietly inquires, "Is there anyone else inside?" Often a client may pause before responding, or a body movement may occur, or the facial expression may change. If the client answers affirmatively, the therapist then begins to ask questions regarding who else is inside, and attempts to elicit information regarding identities and their respective histories. Also, it is not uncommon for this exercise to facilitate a switch in personalities. Then the therapist can begin to meet and to develop a therapeutic alliance with whatever alter felt safe enough to emerge. At the cessation of this exercise, its possible diagnostic implications are discussed with the client. However, it is important to note that, more recently, when the author has elected not to utilize this exercise, eventually a given alter emerges unsolicited during a session and announces its existence. So, lest anyone conclude that asking such a question creates an alternate personality, this does not appear to be the case. In the author's experience, if one is dealing with a case involving DID, alternate personalities make themselves known in a variety of ways. All the aforementioned exercise does is hasten the process of disclosure *if* the collective consciousness of the client is ready to proceed in such a manner.

In general, an ongoing issue during therapy is the client's acceptance of the diagnosis of DID. Many clients are uncomfortable with or reluctant to accept the possibility of alternate personalities. Experience suggests that clients may need time and demonstrable evidence before they are comfortable acknowledging their DID diagnosis. The author tends to talk about therapeutic possibilities and what that means in terms of treatment options. Typically, this discussion involves client education regarding the coping mechanism of dissociation and its relationship to childhood trauma. The emphasis is on reducing the stigma of the disorder by reframing it as a quite understandable unconscious survival mechanism used in response to intolerable events and emotions. It is important that the therapist not pressure a client to entertain such a diagnosis. Rather, the rule for the therapist should be patience, and the client should be assured repeatedly that over time it will become apparent whether the diagnosis of DID is indicated. The diagnosis will be based upon systematic data collection regarding behavioral events that do or do not occur as client and therapist continue the therapeutic journey. Clients' fears regarding the possibility of DID often are related to a fear of being labeled "crazy." The thought of having internal "voices" tends to reinforce these fears. The author explains that such a fear is common to many survivors of sexual trauma and may suggest that a client may want to read a book that reframes DID in a more positive manner (e.g., Gil, 1990). Reading this book tends to facilitate more open discussion of the possibility of DID. The most important tenet to recall, however, is not to pressure the client into acceptance of DID. Rather, such a diagnosis merely provides the therapist additional therapeutic options.

Initial Intervention

Many initial therapeutic interventions involve the use of dissociation and the associated emergence of any alternate personalities (i.e., alters). Relaxation exercises can be utilized during therapy to facilitate "switching" from one personality to another. Although one initial goal of therapy is to identify the names, histories and functions of each alter, it is critical that the therapist do this in a carefully paced, prudent manner. The most important goal of treatment is to maintain, or hopefully to improve, clients' levels of functioning while therapy progresses. Decompensation of a client often is an indication that the therapeutic process is moving too fast.

It is important to recognize that there can be many types of alters. They can include children, adolescents, protectors, persecutors, internal self-helpers, individuals of the opposite sex and task-specific alters. One goal of therapy is to understand how each personality came to exist, what its functions are, the extent of the alter's knowledge regarding the internal personality structure/system and an alter's knowledge about others within the system.

As clients learn more about their internal system, the author may schedule a special videotaped session wherein "that alter who has the most information about the structure of the internal system" is invited to come out and diagram the system. A large newsprint, flip-chart pad and numerous colored markers (possibly those with fragrances) are provided for this purpose. This mapping process typically provides an initial representation of the internal schema.

Historically, mapping the personality system has been a fundamental treatment intervention, and one that the author and others (Putnam, 1989; Ross, 1989) find useful. During the early part of this century Morton Prince (1909) and Walter Franklin Prince (1917) published diagrams of the inter-relationships among the alter personalities of their patients. Mapping also can be an ongoing therapeutic process. Each diagram is an outline for the exploration of the internal world of the DID client. In fact, the pictorial representation of the system, its attendant colors, its symmetry or the lack thereof, and the symbolism embodied within the map can be as informative as the identities of and information regarding the various alters themselves. How alters are arranged in space and how they are connected within the arrangement often are related to the chronology of their traumata, their respective levels of responsibility within the system and their various sub-relationships, and even the location of empty spaces can be informative.

Individuals tend to diagram their systems in a variety of ways and the structure tends to evolve over time. Maps initially become more differentiated and then coalesce over time. Sometimes systems are represented as analogous to concentric solar systems, floor plans, landscapes, geometrical figures, or layered structures. One client seen by the author depicted her system as a Kachina doll-like figure whose quasi-anatomical parts and Native American detailed costume represented various alters. Interestingly, this young woman had no Native American genealogy nor any particular knowledge of that culture. She since has discovered some artistic abilities of which she was unaware prior to therapy, yet the symbolism of her internal schema remained enigmatic. However, as the client continued in therapy, aspects of the Kachina doll evolved into a corporate type of organizational flow chart, and finally a unified body structure. This client achieved final integration, and the changes in her "map" reflected ongoing integrative processes. Indeed, during the past year this former client, who has been symptom-free for over three years, sent the author a note saying that she finally understood the significance of the Kachina doll figure after attending a workshop on symbolism of expressive arts.

Another client opted to use modeling clay to construct a three-dimensional spherical model wherein different colors, different areas of color and a precise layering process depicted the client's understanding of the ages and affective qualities of her alters. She elected to put the "host" personality at the core of the sphere. Child alters were layered over the core with adolescent and adult alters layered over the children's layer. It was constructed such that each piece could be separated from the whole and reassembled much like a jigsaw puzzle. Sad, depressed and the most severely traumatized alters tended to be represented by dark colors. Affectively "brighter" and child alters were represented by light pink, yellow, and light blue pieces. Angry alters were red, orange and hot pink.

Overall, the process of mapping reveals various trends across time and the author repeats this exercise when therapeutic milestones or significant behavioral changes are noted by the clinician. These pictorial trends can include but are not limited to symbolic parallels among the images within the pictorial product and the progress of the therapeutic process, the conservation and continuity of color and form, and a visually metaphoric progression toward personality integration. In general, the mapping process provides a pictorial representation of the relationship among alters and can be a guide for the exploration of the interior world of clients. However, not all therapists choose to utilize a mapping process. This aspect of treatment reflects the therapist's training and orientation. Successful treatment can proceed even if a therapist elects not to utilize the mapping procedure. Again, this technique just seems to provide information in a more organized fashion and may accelerate the therapeutic process.

The Development of Co-Consciousness

A significant portion of the therapeutic process tends to be devoted to the development of communication and cooperation among personalities. This process is known as the development of co-consciousness. Co-consciousness, a term coined by Prince (1906), describes a state of awareness in which one personality is able to experience directly the thoughts, feelings, and actions of another alter (Kluft, 1984). Through various communication techniques, alters are able to learn about each other and eventually develop the ability to be present even though they may not be in executive control. Enhancement of co-consciousness is thought to be a necessary precondition for eventual successful fusion and/or integration. One technique to encourage interpersonality communication is the establishment of a bulletin board upon which any alter can leave a message, comment, draw or write a letter (Putnam, 1989). Typically, a notebook is carried that serves as the bulletin board. All alters are encouraged by the therapist to communicate via the bulletin board when they feel so inclined. Often the bulletin board can be the medium for internal dialogue. It is important to specify that pictorial messages are appropriate for the bulletin board because some alters cannot write or print or because some are more expressive in a pictorial modality. From time to time the therapist can review the bulletin board and associate the various handwritings with their respective alters.

Journaling and other expressive activities are strongly encouraged. The preponderance of clients with DID may have many talents and each should be encouraged to identify and to develop various modalities for emotional expression (e.g., writing, painting, drawing, sculpting, composing or performing various types of art, music, dance). Then, whenever clients require symbolic ventilation activities for the expression of any particular emotion, they have alternative behaviors to perform in an appropriate manner.

Another method for enhancing co-consciousness among alters involves the establishment of cooperation around common goals. Therapeutic techniques for facilitating cooperation include "talking through," the development of an internal decision-making process, and the development of a procedure for controlled or facilitated switching (Putnam, 1989). "Talking through" refers to the process whereby a therapist literally alerts the host personality that important information is about to be announced and that all alters are responsible for listening. For example, a therapist might say, "Okay, I want everyone inside to listen carefully. I am about to discuss some important information and your undivided attention is needed." Then the message is communicated. Although a therapist should assume that all personalities are listening at all times, such is not always the case. Thus, talking through is a technique for enhancing the possibility that the great majority of personalities will be listening to the therapist. Typically, it will be necessary for the therapist to repeat his/her phrases and suggestions a number of times and obtain feedback regarding "who" has heard "what." It is important that the system learn to assume responsibility for the dissemination of the information to all alters. Many therapeutic metaphors can be utilized. Older alters can help younger ones. Some alters can activate "speakers" within the system. Some alters can translate for others. Symbolic interventions that can enhance group participation serve to foster cooperation, and such cooperation gives rise to co-consciousness.

Obtaining feedback regarding "which" alters heard "what" cannot be stressed enough. Child alters tend to interpret the therapist's language in a very concrete manner. Just as no two people hear precisely the same message when exposed to the same phrase, alters also can exhibit selective perception and/or interpretation. Questions and comments from alters should be entertained and discussed. Thus, talking through is a fundamental, versatile technique that can be used in contract negotiations with alters, and that can convey important information, define boundaries, and establish fundamental principles.

The development of a decision-making process within the system is another technique for establishing cooperation around common goals. Typically, the system is asked to devise some type of metaphor for the decision-making process. Common examples include a board of directors meeting, a negotiation table, a summit meeting, the United Nations General Assembly, or a corporate managerial hierarchy. However, it is important to remember that the decision process cannot always be as simple as "one alter, one vote," especially when child and adolescent alters outnumber older alters. Internal self-helpers, alters who tend to be wise advisors possessing spiritual aspects, can be instrumental in the success of intrasystem negotiations. Points of disagreement for alters can be opportunities for the system to devise a consensus for decision making. Contracts among various alters with appropriate reinforcements for child alters often can be utilized.

The control of dissociation and the facilitation of switching is another fundamental skill to be honed by the system. Control over the process of switching tends to be developed gradually. As alters begin to recognize the existence of and develop communication with other alters, internal trust develops. There is a greater propensity to "share" the body. Alters learn to work as a team. They develop the ability to call upon one another, particularly the other self-helpers/protectors. A useful phrase that can be utilized by a client to facilitate switching when necessary is, "I would like for whomever can most appropriately handle this situation to please do so." The words "most appropriately" constitute the critical operative phrase within the suggestion and should be emphasized repeatedly. This approach has been successful when clients begin to experience flashbacks or abreactions at inopportune times.

Working Through the Trauma

Working through the trauma often involves abreaction, defined as the process or the experience of vividly reliving an event (Breuer & Freud, 1957). This phase of treatment involves recounting the abuse as well as identifying the feelings and salient issues associated with the early trauma. The abreactive debriefing process involves the integration of cognition, affect, sensation and behavior. At times, the utilization of age-appropriate techniques with child alters, the resolution of conflict with hostile alters, and the transformation of negative alters are required. Child alters often harbor the memories and the affect associated with early trauma. As a result, they may abreact the trauma when "out" or they may be Pollyana-like (Putnam, 1989).

When working with alters, it is critical for therapists to respect all alters, not make negative comments regarding any alters, and not develop any favorite alters. Before working with an authoritarian, negative alter, it is strongly recommended that substantial consultation with a more experienced therapist occur. Entire articles and chapters have been written about therapeutic techniques with "persecutor personalities" (e.g., Kluft, 1984; Putnam, 1989; Ross, 1989). When working with hostile, negative or persecutor alters, it is important for psychotherapists to retain their composure and to recall that within the majority of hostile alters there exist frightened, angry children. Interventions that reduce fear and promote appropriate emotional ventilation and conflict resolution tend to be successful. The fostering of empathy within other alters for the hostile alter, and vice-versa, can markedly reduce fear and distrust among personalities. Typically, this can be achieved by the therapist talking through and explaining to the negative alter that the therapist understands how difficult and painful it must have been for that alter to do what needed to be done in order to protect the other alters. Also, the therapist needs to understand that sometimes "protectors" behave in a manner similar to that of the perpetrators in order to ensure the survival of the individual. Although this message may need to be conveyed a number of times via "talking through" and direct discussion, the author has found that usually the negative alter will verbalize the wish that the other alters would understand that information. This then opens the door for therapist mediation between the negative alter and the other alters. When the negative alter's behavior can be reframed to a positive and often a "heroic" perspective, the isolation, fear and dislike of the negative alter by the other alters tends to diminish over time. Eventually, the other alters come to recognize the real contributions that negative alters have made and the negativity of those alters transform into positive, life affirming qualities.

Resolution and Integration

Most practitioners suggest that integration is the appropriate long-range therapeutic goal (Barach, 1994; Putnam, 1989; Ross, 1989). In the author's clinical experience, that is also the case. The terms "integration" and "fusion" are often used interchangeably. Many practitioners, however, distinguish between these processes. Integration tends to be understood as a "more pervasive and thorough psychic restructuring" while fusion is viewed as a preliminary "compacting" process that establishes the groundwork for integration (Kluft, 1984). From this vantage point, fusion comprises a process whereby some type of resolution has occurred and dissociative barriers have "dissolved." Integration is a cumulative process, whereby spontaneous and metaphorically-mediated fusions coalesce over periods of weeks to months to yield a synthesis of previously separate alters that become a more unified personality structure.

Kluft (1984) suggests an operational definition of integration that requires: (a) continuity of contemporary memory, (b) absence of overt signs of a dissociative identity, (c) a subjective sense of unity, (d) absence of alter personalities on hypnotic re-exploration, (e) modification of transference phenomena, and (f) clinical evidence that the unified client's self-representation includes acknowledgment of attitudes and awareness that previously were segregated in various alter personalities. These criteria need to be maintained consistently over at least a three-month period. Also, these criteria apply only to final integration. Many clients exhibit spontaneous partial fusions among alters in response to various stimuli both inside and outside the therapeutic setting. However, integration, as defined by Kluft (1993), is the maintenance of the previously enumerated criteria for at least 27 months. Moreover, integration is not the end point of therapy. Rather, it is more like the "two-thirds" point of the treatment process.

Although spontaneous partial fusions of alters can occur in the absence of treatment, spontaneous total integrations are rare in adult DID clients. Partial fusions occur over time as part of the therapeutic process. However, operational criteria have not been defined to assess the outcome of partial fusions. Even less is understood empirically about what occurs psychologically during the process of integration.

Typically, there is some degree of client resistance to the concept of integration because most alters define integration as extinction. In the author's clinical experience, consistent judicious demonstrations of concrete examples of integration across the course of treatment facilitate the process. For example, this practitioner tends to provide concrete metaphors for integration whenever the opportunity arises. These can include, but certainly are not limited to: (a) the mixing of paints (e.g., yellow and blue) to illustrate that no alter disappears, but instead "blends with" the attributes of other alters, (b) the weaving together of transparent plastic colored strips to demonstrate that pink strips woven with blue strips create a lavender colored mat that possesses greater cumulative strength and utility than any given individual strip, and (c) the braiding of material, ribbon or thread of various colors to demonstrate the enhanced strength of the braided (integrated), multicolored product. Typically, the client is encouraged to generate his or her own metaphors for integration. One client envisioned her alters as strands of DNA that would weave together in an alpha-helical pattern. Another perceived her solar system coalescing into one planet. Basically, metaphors for fusion and integration are limited only by the imaginations of the therapist and the client. Integration ceremonies can be created by the client. However, it is not uncommon to experience integration failures. Relapses of fusions and the discovery of additional layers of alters are to be expected (Kluft, 1993; Putnam, 1989), and then additional therapeutic work as enumerated above is conducted with the newly found alters. After integration is achieved, the next task of therapy requires that new coping skills for life's stresses be constructed in the wake of no longer having a variety of alters on whom to depend (Kluft, 1993; Putnam, 1989; Ross, 1989).

Development of Post-Resolution Coping Skills

Whereas a good prognosis appears to be associated with a commitment to therapy and change, a willingness to utilize nondissociative coping skills and a lack of investment in the uniqueness of alters are critical for recovery (Putnam, 1989). Successful resolution requires that an individual develop new coping skills to deal with life's stressors. In general, clients need to learn how to solve all of the problems that were handled previously by dissociation and switching without utilizing those mechanisms. Additionally, the integrated individual typically requires a period of grief resolution. Readjustments within important relationships have to be negotiated, and possible attempts to sabotage the integrated configuration need to be resolved. Finally, the integrated personality must learn to reduce its reliance upon dissociative mechanisms. Initially, reduced reliance upon dissociation can result in a concomitant increase in depression. As a result, cognitive re-structuring typically is required during this phase of therapy.

As clients resolve the therapeutic issues that stem from integration, they also have the opportunity to address any previously unresolved behavioral issues such as assertiveness problems, anxiety control, family-of-origin issues, substance abuse relapse, eating-disordered behavior and the prevention of potential victimization. As these residual difficulties are resolved, there can be a gradual reduction in therapeutic interaction. Over time, a consistent absence of alter behavior and a sustained remission of core symptomatology can be indicators for termination. Nevertheless, it is important to inform clients that temporary relapses or the need for additional "booster" therapeutic sessions approximates the norm, and that seeking early therapeutic intervention can preclude the subsequent development of more refractory symptomatology. Hence, clients should be encouraged to view such sessions as opportunities for therapeutic refinement, not as setbacks or failures. Clients may need to be reminded that therapy is a journey and in the words of Abraham Lincoln, "the best thing about the future is that it comes only one day at a time."

CONCLUSION AND FUTURE DIRECTIONS

The psychotherapy of the adult sexual abuse survivor who meets the diagnostic criteria for DID can be more effective when a dissociative identity disorder is diagnosed early in treatment. However, the dynamics of dissociative identity disorder are such that until the dissociation is evident, the diagnostic process is stymied. Therapy with clients who have a history of sexual abuse and a diagnosis of dissociative identity disorder is analogous to completing a jigsaw puzzle utilizing pieces of affect, cognition, behavior and time. Through the reconstitution of experience, clients are empowered to strive for highly productive and meaningful lives. Because individuals with DID often are bright, talented people, early identification and appropriate treatment can facilitate the therapeutic process. Hence, clinicians who treat adult survivors of sexual abuse need to be cognizant of the possibility of the presence of dissociative identity disorder in people who experienced severe early childhood trauma. This article has attempted to raise clinical consciousness regarding DID so that clients can receive expeditious, appropriate referral and treatment.

With respect to the future direction of the field, Ross (1992) proposed a trauma model of psychopathology suggesting that childhood trauma results in particular psychobiological dysregulations. According to this model, there exist traumatized subgroups of many DSM-IV diagnostic categories that, if studied with appropriate measures, may exhibit a distinctive phenomenology, natural history, response to psychopharmacology and psychotherapy, pattern of familial transmission, psychobiology and prognosis (Ross, 1992). In effect, Ross predicts that a paradigmatic shift in our conceptualization of psychopathology will occur when we view trauma as a primary etiological variable in many psychiatric disorders. Such a view, in turn, has the propensity to clarify our understanding of individual differences within various diagnostic categories and various responses to psychopharmacological agents. Indeed, this author's review of the Ross article (Lundberg-Love, 1992) led her to propose a three-dimensional model of psychopathology that would be determined by the intersection of the axes of genetic predisposition, biological perturbation and cumulative experience, particularly trauma history. These models (Lundberg-Love, 1992; Ross, 1992) underscore the need for systematic, empirical, and biological study of the phenomenon of childhood trauma and DID. Such research has the potential to stimulate a paradigmatic shift in the understanding of the etiology of psychiatric disorders as well as an improvement in the technique and delivery of treatment resources.

REFERENCES

American Psychiatric Association (1994). *Diagnostic and statistical manual of mental disorders* (4th ed., rev.) Washington, DC: APA.

Barach, P. M. (1994). *Guidelines for treating dissociative identity disorder (multiple personality disorder) in adults*. Skokie, IL: The International Society for the Study of Dissociation (ISSD).

Bernstein, E. M., & Putnam, F. W. (1986). Development reliability and validity of a dissociation scale. *Journal of Nervous and Mental Disease, 174*, 727-735.

Bliss, E. L. (1986). *Multiple personality. Allied disorders and hypnosis*. New York: Oxford University Press.

Block, J. P. (1991). *Assessment and treatment of multiple personality and dissociative disorders*. Sarasota, FL: Professional Resource Press.

Braun, B. G. (1986). *Treatment of multiple personality disorder*. Washington, DC: American Psychiatric Press.

Braun, B. G. (1988). The BASK (behavior, affect, sensation, knowledge) model of dissociation. *Dissociation, 1*, 4-23.

Braun, B. G. (1990). Multiple personality disorder: An overview. *The American Journal of Occupational Therapy, 44*, 971-977.

Breuer, J., & Freud, S. (1957). *Studies on hysteria.* New York: Basic. (Original work published 1895)

Brickman, J. (1992). Female lives, feminist deaths: The relationship of the Montreal massacre to dissociation, incest, and violence against women. *Canadian Psychology, 33*, 128-149.

Carlson, E. B., & Putnam, F. W. (1989). Integrating research in dissociation and hypnotic susceptibility: Are there two pathways to hypnotizability? *Dissociation, 2*, 32-38.

Carlson, E. B., & Putnam, F. W. (1993). An update on the Dissociative Experiences Scale. *Dissociation, 6*, 16-28.

Gil, E. (1990). *United we stand.* San Francisco: Launch Press.

Hilgard, E. R. (1986). *Divided consciousness: Multiple controls in human thought and action* (expanded ed.). New York: John Wiley.

Kluft, R. P. (1984). Treatment of multiple personality disorder. *Psychiatric clinics of North America, 7*, 9-29.

Kluft, R. P. (1988). The dissociative disorders. In J. A. Talbot, R. E. Hales & S. C. Yudovsky (Eds.), *American Psychiatric Press textbook of psychiatry* (pp. 237-259). Washington, D.C.: American Psychiatric Press.

Kluft, R. P. (1993). Basic principles in conducting the psychotherapy of multiple personality disorder. In R. P. Kluft & C. G. Fine (Eds.), *Clinical perspectives on multiple personality disorder* (pp. 19-50). Washington, DC: American Psychiatric Press.

Loewenstein, R. J. (1991). An office mental status examination for complex chronic dissociative symptoms and multiple personality disorder. *Psychiatric Clinics of North America, 14*, 567-604.

Loewenstein, R. J., Hornstein, N., & Farber, B. (1988). Open trial of clonazepam in the treatment of posttraumatic stress symptoms in MPD. *Dissociation, 1*, 3-12.

Lundberg-Love, P. K. (1990). Adult survivors of incest. In R. T. Ammerman & M. Hersen (Eds.), *Treatment of family violence: A sourcebook* (pp. 211-240). New York: John Wiley.

Lundberg-Love, P. K. (1992). Childhood sexual abuse and psychobiology: A commentary. *Journal of Child Sexual Abuse, 1*, 107-109.

Prince, M. (1906). *Dissociation of a personality.* New York: Longman, Green.

Prince, M. (1909). Experiments to determine co-conscious (subconscious) ideation. *Journal of Abnormal Psychology, 11*, 33-42.

Prince, W. F. (1917). The Doris case of quintuple personality. *Journal of Abnormal Psychology, 11*, 73-122.

Putnam, F. W. (1989). *Diagnosis and treatment of multiple personality disorder.* New York: Guilford.

Ross, C. A. (1989). *Multiple personality disorder: Diagnosis, clinical features, and treatment.* New York: John Wiley and Sons.

Ross, C. A. (1990). Twelve cognitive errors about multiple personality disorder. *American Journal of Psychotherapy, XLIV,* (3), 348-356.

Ross, C. A. (1991). Epidemiology of multiple personality and dissociation. *Psychiatric Clinics of North America, 14,* 503-517.

Ross, C. A. (1992) Childhood sexual abuse and psychobiology. *Journal of Child Sexual Abuse, 1,* 95-102.

Ross, C. A., Heber, S., Norton, G. R., Anderson, D., Anderson, G., & Burchet, P. (1989). The dissociative disorders interview schedule: A structured interview. *Dissociation, 2,* 169-189.

Spanos, N. (1996). *Multiple identities and false memories: A sociocultural perspective.* Washington, D.C.: American Psychological Association.

Steinberg, M. (1993). *Interviewer's guide to the structured clinical interview for DSM-IV dissociative disorders (SCID-D).* Washington, D.C.: American Psychiatric Press.

Characteristics and Treatment
of Incest Offenders:
A Review

Joanne L. Brown
George S. (Jeb) Brown

SUMMARY. Sexual abuse of children has emerged as a widespread, multifaceted social problem. This article presents a summary of the professional literature on one aspect of sexual abuse, namely incest offenders. It begins with a description of the characteristics of incest offenders, including gender, personality, sexual orientation, number of victims, patterns of sexual arousal, and neurological anomalies. A discussion then follows of treatment options for incest offenders, including individual, group, and family therapy, psychoeducational skills training, behavioral treatments, chemical castration, and relapse prevention. The article concludes with a review of available data on recidivism. *[Article copies available for a fee from The Haworth Document Delivery Service: 1-800-342-9678. E-mail address: getinfo@ haworth.com]*

KEYWORDS. Child abuse, child molester, sex offender, sexual abuse, pedophilia, sexual orientation

Address correspondence to: Joanne L. Brown, PhD, University of Utah Neuropsychiatric Institute Professional Offices, 546 Chipeta Way, Suite 2242, Salt Lake City, UT 84108.

[Haworth co-indexing entry note]: "Characteristics and Treatment of Incest Offenders: A Review." Brown, Joanne L., and George S. (Jeb) Brown. Co-published simultaneously in *Journal of Aggression, Maltreatment & Trauma* (Haworth Maltreatment & Trauma Press, an imprint of The Haworth Press, Inc.) Vol. 1, No. 1 (#1), 1997, pp. 335-354; and: *Violence and Sexual Abuse at Home: Current Issues in Spousal Battering and Child Maltreatment* (ed: Robert Geffner, Susan B. Sorenson, and Paula K. Lundberg-Love) Haworth Maltreatment & Trauma Press, an imprint of The Haworth Press, Inc., 1997, pp. 335-354. Single or multiple copies of this article are available for a fee from The Haworth Document Delivery Service [1-800-342-9678, 9:00 a.m. - 5:00 p.m. (EST). E-mail address: getinfo@ haworth.com].

Sexual abuse of children has emerged as a widespread, multifaceted social problem. This article focuses on one aspect of this problem, incest offenders. One class of such offenders is the pedophile. Pedophilia refers to sexual desires and responses directed towards a prepubescent child, whereas hebephilia refers to attraction to a pubescent child. In common usage, however, pedophilia or its noun form, pedophile, is generally applied to all child molestation, and the term hebephilia is rarely encountered. This article focuses on incest offenders, one class of pedophiles. Over the last decade, a significant amount of literature on incest offenders has emerged. Generally, the literature attempts to describe offenders and explain their behavior. More recently, characteristics of offenders have been used to guide treatment and to assess its effects on reducing recidivism rates. The purpose of this article is to present an overview of the professional literature on incest offenders.

CHARACTERISTICS OF INCEST OFFENDERS

Gender

The literature on incest offenders almost exclusively describes male offenders. Only a few descriptions of female offenders exist (Elliott, 1994; Matthews, Matthews & Speltz, 1991; McCarty, 1986) even though 24% of abused males and 13% of abused females report being abused by females (Finkelhor & Hotaling, 1984). McCarty (1986) reviewed the case records of 26 mother-child sexual abuse cases. The majority of these mothers described their childhoods negatively and reported that they had experienced traumatic events (e.g., sexual and physical abuse, multiple caretakers, breakup of parents' marriage, alcoholic parents). This article focuses on male offenders since they comprise most of the perpetrators, but it is important to keep in mind that women also commit sexual offenses towards children.

For the remainder of this article, the term incest offender will be used to refer to a male offender who has committed an intergenerational offense, that is, an adult male who has sexually abused a child family member. Incest between siblings also occurs, often in families where intergenerational incest also has been present (Mayer, 1988), but issues related to intragenerational incest are beyond the scope of this article (see Alpert, 1997, in this volume).

Personality of Offenders

Incest has been attributed to numerous factors, including dysfunctional relationships, chemical abuse, sexual problems, and social isolation. Likewise, it has been hypothesized that men commit incestuous acts because they find sexual contact with a child emotionally gratifying, because they are capable of being sexually aroused by a child, because they are unable to receive sexual and emotional gratification from an adult, and because they are not deterred by the social conventions and inhibitions against having a sexual relationship with a child (Cole, 1992; Finkelhor, 1986; Hanson, Lipovsky, & Saunders, 1994; Pawlak, Boulet, & Bradford, 1991). Character disordered men with low impulse control, low frustration tolerance, low self-esteem, and a high need for immediate gratification are believed to be at risk for the molestation of children (Mayer, 1988).

Incest offenders have been described as individuals with repressed anger that is denied on a conscious level and that is expressed through the incestuous act. They do not easily learn from past experience. They often sexualize relationships, tend toward addictions, are self-centered, lack empathy, and project blame for their behavior onto others. They lack self-control, have poor communication skills, don't experience guilt for antisocial acts, lack meaningful social relationships, and may lie, deny, and manipulate (Mayer, 1988). They report the lack of a satisfying emotional relationship with their wives or adult partners, marital mistrustfulness, and the lack of mutual friends and common interests (Lang, Langevin, Van Santen, & Billingsley, 1990).

Incest offenders have been found to share deviant attitudes in three domains. They tend to believe in the concept of male sexual entitlement, perceive children as sexually attractive and motivated to experience sex, and minimize harm caused by sexual abuse (Hanson, Gizzarelli, & Scott, 1994). This supports the view of offenders as uninhibited men who believe that their own sexual needs must be satisfied. Such a belief could prevent offenders from developing appropriate self-control when presented with opportunities to offend.

Research utilizing the Minnesota Multiphasic Personality Inventory (MMPI) with incest offenders generally has found that they do not exhibit severe psychopathology as measured by this instrument (Erickson, Luxenberg, Walbek, & Seely, 1987; Groff & Hubble, 1984; Marshall & Hall, 1995; Scott & Stone, 1986). Likewise, the MMPI has not been able to differentiate among different sex offender populations (Goeke & Boyer, 1993; Vaupel & Goeke, 1994). It is clear that there is no personality profile that represents an incest offender.

Sexual Orientation

Groth (1978) has suggested differentiating between fixated and regressed pedophiles. Fixated pedophiles have a strong and enduring sexual interest in children that emerges in adolescence and continues throughout life. Although the fixated pedophile may be capable of sexual relations with adult females, it is not his primary sexual preference. Contrary to popular myth, men who molest male children are not homosexual in the traditional sense, and are rarely attracted to adult males. In differentiating pedophiles, it is useful to describe them in terms of sexual arousal/ sexual preference (i.e., attracted to males, females, or both), age preference (exclusive type who is attracted only to children, or nonexclusive type who is attracted to children and adults), and sexual behaviors (limited to incest, limited to children, limited to adults, or combinations).

The fixated offender primarily has sexual fantasies directed towards children. He often will perceive his behavior as not being harmful to the child, and in the authors' experience, will frequently describe as positive a sexual relationship he had as a child with an adult male. In general, the fixated offender will experience less psychological conflict regarding his behavior, will be less likely to have been under the influence of alcohol or other drugs when committing the offense, and more likely to have had multiple victims.

The regressed pedophile is one who has achieved a more "mature" level of psychosexual functioning and has a primary sexual orientation to age appropriate females but who, during a period of stress, regresses to a less mature pattern of behavior. The regressed offender also may exhibit a pattern of compulsive behavior (Carnes, 1990), wherein he goes through periods of time where he attempts to resist impulses, yields to temptations, experiences guilt and self-loathing, and then repeats this pattern. Alcohol is likely to play a role in the initiation and continuation of the incest. The regressed offender is considered to be a better candidate for treatment and at lower risk for recidivism. It is important to realize, however, that these categories of regressed versus fixated offenders represent extremes of a continuum, and many offenders will not fit neatly into either category.

In fact, various typologies have been presented for incest offenders, but the research suggests that none fit very well (Marshall, 1996). In fact, Abel and Rouleau (1990) reported remarkably high levels of multiple paraphilias among outpatient sex offenders. Using diagnostic criteria, 61.4% of heterosexual pedophiles and 55.5% of rapists reported three or more paraphilias. More recent research (Marshall, Barbaree, & Eccles, 1991) found far less evidence of multiple paraphilias. It is not clear what produced these different results, perhaps criteria used or sampling bias.

Number of Victims

Incest offenders are thought to differ from other child molesters in that they are less likely to molest children not in their immediate family and are likely to have fewer victims. Abel, Becker, Murphy, and Flanagan (1981) reported the results of a confidential survey conducted with offenders referred to an outpatient assessment and treatment program. Heterosexual incest offenders reported an average of 2.1 victims, compared to 62.4 victims for heterosexual non-incestuous pedophiles.

Owen and Steele (1991) described a sample of incarcerated incest offenders. Twenty-five percent of the sample had one known victim, 45% had two or three victims, and 30% had more than four victims, with a maximum of 12 victims. Similarly, Abel, Becker, Cunningham-Rathner, Mittleman and Rouleau (1988) reported that 49% of incest offenders referred to an outpatient program acknowledged abusing children outside of the family at the time they were abusing their own.

Sexual Arousal

Direct measurement of physiological arousal to sexual stimuli usually is done by means of a plethysmograph, a device for measuring penile erection. The offender is systematically exposed to various visual and/or auditory erotic stimuli, and his degree of physical response is quantified via a metal strain gauge.

A series of investigations using plethysmography have compared incest to non-incest offenders. The research was prompted by Quinsey's (1977) speculation that incest offenders differ from non-incest child molesters in their motivation to molest. He hypothesized that whereas non-incest pedophiles are motivated by sexual interest in children, incest offenders are more likely to molest because of faulty family dynamics.

Abel et al. (1981), for example, exposed both incest and non-incest pedophiles to audio taped presentations of sexual acts while wearing a penile plethysmograph. The audiotaped descriptions of various sexual acts included one in which a child initiated sex, one of a "mutually consenting child" and adult, and others depicting nonphysical coercion, physical coercion, sadism, physical assault, and mutual adult sex. Some of the scenes described an incestuous relationship, whereas others described sex with a stranger. While listening to the scenes, offenders' erections were measured using plethysmography. Offenders also were asked to self-report on their degree of arousal. The results of the investigation showed very similar arousal patterns between incest and non-incest child molesters. Also, what incest offenders reported as their patterns of arousal differed from their actual patterns of arousal. Incest offenders reported high rates of arousal for socially appropriate sexual acts and low rates of arousal for deviant scenes. The psychophysiologic results, however, contradicted these self-reports. Incest offenders, like other pedophiles, were more aroused by scenes of sex with children than they were by those with consenting adults. Also, they were aroused by scenes of sex with an unknown child as well as those involving an incestuous act.

These results indicate that incest offenders' self-reports about their arousal patterns are unreliable and that their patterns of sexual arousal may not differ from those of other pedophiles. Furthermore, the results do not support Quinsey's (1977) hypothesis that incest is a result of problematic family dynamics. Instead, the data suggest that incest offenders, like other child molesters, may have a sexual preference for young children.

In a more recent study, however, incest offenders displayed either a nondiscriminating profile or an adult-preference profile (Barbaree & Marshall, 1989). Similarly, Marshall (1996) found that only 28% of father-daughter incest offenders showed equal or greater arousal to children compared with their responses to adults. The results of these studies need to be considered along with those of Hall, Proctor, and Nelson (1988), who found that 80% of the offenders who exhibited sexual arousal to deviant stimuli were able to inhibit sexual arousal voluntarily and completely. Other studies have demonstrated that men can inhibit penile volume response to erotic films when instructed to do so (e.g., Hensen & Rubin, 1971; Marshall, 1996). Abel et al. (1981), on other hand, found that instructions to become aroused or to suppress arousal had little effect on the size of penile erections. Finally, Marshall and Barbaree (1988) found that more than 20% of men who admit to child molesting display arousal that is too low to permit interpretation.

The results of these psychophysiological investigations appear to be confusing and contradictory. Problems with design of samples used in some of the studies may account for part of the differences found. Many studies, for example, included natural fathers, stepfathers, and adoptive fathers in a sample of incest offenders without clearly differentiating them. It may be that the level of sexual arousal to children varies across these groups. The extent to which offenders can inhibit their arousal to deviant stimuli and, thereby, falsify a socially appropriate response also remains unknown. It, therefore, is still unclear as to whether incest offenders can be distinguished from other child molesters solely on the basis of psychophysiological assessment.

Rapist versus Molester

Groth (1978) proposed a distinction between sex offenders based on motivational intent. Is the offender seeking sexual and emotional contact, or is he motivated also by the need for power or to derive sadistic pleasure from inflicting pain? This distinction can be thought of as the molester-versus-rapist continuum.

The molester uses seduction, enticement or entrapment to gain access to the child sexually. He is likely to fantasize that there is a loving relationship with the child and consciously wish to avoid harming the child. The rapist, in contrast, resorts to the use of threat or violence. Anger and the need to dominate are motivators and, in extreme cases, inflicting pain and fear in the child contribute to the rapist's sexual arousal. Understandably, the latter group are at lower likelihood for successful treatment.

Incest offenders typically present with mixed qualities of both the molester and the rapist. They may also progress along the continuum from molester to rapist as they become more involved with abuse, when they fear exposure, or when they encounter resistance from the child. Groth (1983) has estimated that about 10-15% of incest offenders manifest rapist qualities exclusively.

Neurological/Neuropsychological Anomalies

Researchers recently have investigated the neurological functioning of sex offenders. Langevin, Wortzman, Dickey, and Wright (1988), for example, used a battery of tests to compare 91 male incest offenders with 36 male nonviolent non-sex offenders for the presence of neurological impairment. Although incest offenders had intelligence scores within normal limits, their scores were significantly lower than the nonviolent non-sex offenders. Neuropsychological impairment among incest offenders was associated with violence and a non-biological relationship to the victim, but not with substance abuse.

In an attempt to identify the area of the brain responsible for the neuropsychological impairment, a group of pedophiles, incest offenders, sexual aggressors against adult females and nonviolent non-sex offenders were examined using computerized tomography (CT) scans. Heterosexual and homosexual pedophiles showed verbal deficits and left-hemispheric brain dysfunction, whereas bisexual pedophiles showed right-hemispheric visual-spatial deficits (Langevin, Wortzman, Wright, & Handy, 1989).

Another study (Wright, Nobrega, Langevin, & Wortzman, 1990) computed brain area and optical density for each hemisphere of the brain and for four sections within hemispheres for groups of pedophiles, incest offenders, sexually aggressive offenders of adult women, and a control group. Brains of sex offenders were relatively smaller in the left hemisphere compared to controls. Likewise, brain area segments corresponding to left frontal and temporal areas were smaller in sex offenders than in controls. The data from these studies suggest a possible link between neuropsychological anomalies and the commission of deviant sex acts. However, additional research is needed before we fully understand this potentially critical relationship, and the role of biological factors.

TREATMENT

During the 1930s and 1940s, sex offenders were believed to be victims of hereditary defects that resulted in permanent psychiatric disorders. Incarceration was the norm and treatment was almost nonexistent. During the 1960s a shift occurred and a number of rehabilitation programs emerged (Brecker, 1978).

The type of treatment designed for incest offenders depends upon a therapist's particular theoretical orientation regarding the reasons for incestuous behavior. Clinicians who believe offenders misinterpret the reactions of victims of abuse set treatment goals to increase the offender's cognitive and affective awareness of the harmful effects of incest on victims. Clinicians who believe that incest results from faulty family dynamics design programs that help offenders develop awareness and insight into the personal and family dynamics that contributed to incest. Those who see incest as a result of skill deficits teach offenders communication, parenting, and social skills, as well as stress and anger management (Freeman-Longo & Wall, 1986; Mayer, 1988). If one believes that incest is primarily a result of sexual deviancy, then treatment aims to reduce offenders' deviant levels of arousal.

The following sections describe treatment methods, modalities, and techniques used to treat incest offenders. It concludes with a description of a few multifaceted treatment programs for incest offenders.

Insight-Oriented Individual Psychotherapy

Intrapsychic approaches traditionally have conceptualized individual psychotherapy as a process in which a trained therapist assists a client to gain insight into childhood experiences that influence current emotions, motives, and interpersonal relationships. With incest offenders, this form of therapy is directed toward having offenders understand the antecedents of sexual abuse and examine conscious and unconscious impulses, urges, and fears, in order to facilitate healthy choices in the present. Although such therapy can be useful, it appears necessary for the therapist to alter the traditional emphasis on neutrality in order to impact offenders' denial and their difficulty experiencing empathy towards others.

Group Psychotherapy

The literature on the treatment of incest offenders supports the use of group psychotherapy (Groth, 1983; Marshall, 1994, 1996; Mayer, 1988). Groups provide an opportunity for offenders to deal with concerns and problems they experience in relationship to both men and women. Attitudes toward role expectations in the family can be explored. Issues pertinent to forming and maintaining relationships based on trust, intimacy, and reciprocity can be addressed. In a group setting, offenders can explore how relationships with important adults during their formative years influenced later relationships and how current life events triggered offending. It also is a place where they can explore more satisfying styles of relating to others. Offenders can work together to discover why they found relating sexually to a child emotionally satisfying, why they are capable of being aroused by a child, why they have been unable to receive sufficient sexual and emotional gratification from adults, and why they could not inhibit their impulses to molest. Some groups described in the literature (Brown & Brown, 1990) require offenders to write an autobiography, sexual history, a detailed description of the molestation, and to keep a journal of current sexual fantasies. They are further required to read portions of these written assignments in group therapy.

Homogenous open-ended groups of incest perpetrators which allow for the development of cohesion are recommended (Peters & Roether, 1972). Core group members will tend to draw new members into an open discussion of their sexual behaviors, while modeling appropriate attitudes and behavior. Peer acceptance and peer rivalry often rapidly initiate the new members into group participation and discussion. Group members seem to reduce their own social isolation by adding "another member to the club," and to relieve their shame through universalizing the deviant act by acknowledgment that "everyone here does it." Furthermore, core group members can deal with the denial or resistance of a new member more effectively than can the therapist. If the therapist challenges a new member, the others will likely come to their peer's defense. If a peer confronts the new member, however, the group can more easily accept or reject it rather than automatically react against the authority of the therapist.

As the group matures, the expectations and attitudes of the therapist can be transmitted to some group members. These experienced members will, in turn, impart these attitudes to new members. Thus, identification with the therapist and altered social behavior can be produced through the action of peers who are in various stages of growth and development. At this point in the history of a group, the therapist can become more active and make observations about members, who are now less sensitive to criticism than when they entered treatment (Mayer, 1988).

Family Therapy

Families in which incest occurs often exhibit marked dysfunction. As discussed previously, incest often is viewed in part as being a result of family dysfunction. For this reason, family therapy is crucial if the offender is to remain a part of the family.

In the authors' experience, however, it is important to modify traditional family therapy techniques to suit the unique demands of treating the incestuous family. Insisting that the entire family meet together early in treatment, for example, may further traumatize the victim. The child often feels intimidated in the presence of the offender and may feel pressure to deny his or her own needs and feelings in the interest of maintaining family stability. Likewise, reframing techniques or others that explain behavior in terms of the function served in the family system may reduce an offender's responsibility for his behavior and may lead the child or spouse to feel somehow to blame.

Giarretto, Giarretto, and Sgroi (1985) recommend a sequence of steps in working with the family which are designed initially to strengthen the bond between a nonabusing mother and victim(s) as well as other children. The father is involved only after this foundation has been established and when he has accepted full responsibility for his behavior, apologized to the victim, and acknowledged the wrong he has done. Likewise, Trepper and Barrett (1989) describe family therapy interventions designed to be implemented with incestuous families.

Psychoeducational Skills Training

Incest offenders have demonstrated a lower percentage of appropriate social skills than non-offenders in the form of conversation, affect and voice quality. Behavior modification, rehearsal, social reinforcement and videotape feedback have been successful treatment techniques (Hopkins, 1993; Valliant & Antonowicz, 1992). Because incest offenders also tend to be uninformed or misinformed about human sexuality, sex education classes are typically utilized to alleviate this deficit (Groth, 1983).

Most offenders typically do not express their feelings (Overholser & Beck, 1986). Additionally, they often harbor anger and displace it onto their victims. Skills training groups focus on multiple aspects of assertiveness skills, including making eye contact, duration of reply, latency of response, loudness of speech, and quality of affect (Becker, Blanchard, Murphy, & Coleman, 1978).

Rosen and Fracher (1983) classified incest offenders into three groups. According to their system, aggressive offenders experience anger as an antecedent to molestation, whereas nonviolent offenders experience anxiety prior to sexual abuse, and sociopathic offenders engage in incest to experience affective arousal. Tension reduction and anger management training are recommended for the first two groups of offenders. The goal of tension reduction training is to teach offenders to reduce negative arousal states that stem from anxiety or anger. Training addresses cognitive, somatic, and behavioral manifestations of anxiety and anger. Progressive muscle relaxation, biofeedback training and imagery are used to reduce these negative arousal states. Anger management classes teach offenders to be assertive without transgressing against someone else and to deal with adversity in ways other than retaliation or withdrawal.

The majority of incest offenders have little realization of the short- or long-term consequences of their offenses against the victim. Empathy skills training involves teaching offenders to explore and verbalize their victims' feelings (Groth, 1983).

Behavioral Treatments

Behavioral therapy is based on the assumption that behavior is learned and can be unlearned and changed. Behavioral techniques have been used to decrease incest offenders' excessive arousal to deviant stimuli and to increase their arousal to non-deviant sexual stimuli. In an effort to extinguish arousal to children, a variety of aversion-suppression methods have been employed. They include covert sensitization, electrical aversion, odor aversion, chemical aversion, suppression, and satiation techniques (Holmes, 1991; Quinsey, 1973).

Covert sensitization is a procedure in which all stimuli are presented through the imagination. The therapist verbally describes a deviant sexual scene and then an aversive scene. The client is asked to imagine these scenes and to place himself in the scenes as they are described. The nature of the aversive scene is determined by interviewing the client and may include socially aversive stimuli (such as going to jail) or physically aversive stimuli (such as vomitus or blood). Usually a scene lasts about 10 minutes and two scenes are presented within each session (Mayer, 1988; Quinsey, 1977)

The authors have found a variant of this technique particularly useful in the treatment of incest offenders. The technique involves instructing the offender to pair sexual abuse fantasies with heightened awareness of the victim's facial expressions and emotional state. It is based on the observation that offenders frequently depersonalize their victims by imagining them as faceless or without emotion. Asking the offender to imagine his victim frightened, crying or experiencing some other emotion appropriate to trauma can provoke or heighten anxiety in the offender. If the offender experiences the anxiety as aversive, his deviant sexual fantasies are likely to diminish over time. This technique has the virtue of reflecting real life events and can be used to heighten the offender's capacity for awareness and empathy. Primarily, it is useful in the treatment of offenders who already possess some capacity for caring and empathy. It is contraindicated for individuals whose motivation for sexual offenses is of a more sadistic nature.

Other aversion techniques involve pairing a noxious stimulus (such as electric shock, an odor, or a chemical) with a sexually deviant scene. The scenes usually last for approximately two minutes (Quinsey, 1977).

In a satiation procedure, the client is first asked to masturbate to non-deviant fantasies until ejaculation. The client is then instructed to continue to masturbate for 30-45 minutes to deviant fantasies. Throughout this process, the client is required to verbalize his fantasies, which are recorded and monitored for client compliance (Johnston, Hudson, & Marshall, 1992; Marshall & Barbaree, 1978). Satiation appears to destroy the erotic nature of deviant urges by boring the offender with his own fantasies. Sexual arousal requires newness and variety to sustain itself. Boredom, on the other hand, is believed to destroy specific sexual arousal patterns. Other advantages of satiation procedures are that they do not require extensive therapist time, and they capitalize on a naturally-occurring phenomenon (Marshall & Barbaree, 1988).

Treatment methods employed to counteract deficient arousal to nondeviant sexual stimuli include masturbatory conditioning, exposure, fading and systematic desensitization to adult women. Procedures such as these typically involve paring deviant with appropriate masturbatory fantasies, and fading in appropriate sexual visual stimuli while fading out inappropriate stimuli.

Chemical Castration

The purpose of psychopharmacological approaches to the treatment of incest perpetrators is to decrease their libido, thereby facilitating self-control of sexual behaviors. Medroxyprogesterone acetate (Depo-Provera), a testosterone-suppressing agent, is the most widely administered drug. It decreases libido, erotic fantasies that often precede abuse, erections and ejaculations (Berlin & Meinecke, 1981; Bradford, 1983). Side effects include weight gain, lethargy, cold sweats, nightmares, hot flashes, hypertension, elevated blood glucose, dyspnea (shortness of breath) and hypogonadism. Depo-Provera has been shown to be 85% effective in eliminating deviant sexual behaviors as long as it is taken on a regular basis (Berlin, 1982). It is not a cure, however, and relapse often follows the discontinuation of medication. It is, therefore, not recommended as an exclusive treatment modality.

Sexual Addiction and Twelve Step Recovery Programs

Carnes (1990) noted that for many offenders, the cycle of compulsive sexual acting out followed by intense shame and guilt is similar to that found in other addictive disorders. The sexual activity is sought compulsively as a way to escape negative feelings, while the resulting shame further drives the individual into a state of isolation and despair. Carnes proposed the concept of the sexual addict and articulated principles of recovery based on the Twelve Step process as practiced by Alcoholics Anonymous.

Relapse Prevention

Relapse prevention is a maintenance model that provides clients with the tools required to sustain changes achieved in therapy. The goal of the program is to teach offenders sexual control over time and across situations (Nelson, Miner, Marques, & Russell, 1988).

During the first phase of this program, the offender's assumption that treatment will alleviate his desire for atypical sex preference is broken down. The offender is taught to recognize high risk situations which pose a threat to self-control and increase the probability of a relapse. Relapse fantasies are reviewed and the offender's repertoire of coping behaviors are assessed. Treatment involves teaching the offender adaptive coping strategies to deal with high risk situations. The client begins by brainstorming possible alternatives to abuse. Each alternative is then examined in terms of its positive and negative consequences. The offender is assisted in assessing which alternative will have a desired effect and in choosing the best possible option (Nelson et al., 1988).

Parents United

Incest offenders and their families tend to be isolated and have poor external supports. The disclosure of abuse tends to increase isolation, as the family attempts to cope with their own shame and the reactions of others. For this reason, the use of a mixed self-help group psychotherapy program, such as Parents United, can be helpful. Parents United chapters exist across the country and are based on the model Child Sexual Abuse Treatment Program in San Jose, California (Giarretto, Giarretto, & Sgroi, 1985). Although this program insists on the importance of an appropriately trained therapist in conducting groups, it also encourages offenders and families to support one another, and allows advanced clients to assist new clients entering treatment.

Model Programs

Oregon State Hospital has a correctional treatment program for chronic sex offenders, including incest perpetrators. The program uses both psychological and physiological data to change the attitudes and behavior of offenders. Perpetrators are required to write detailed descriptions of past sexual offenses and have their physiological responses to sexual stimuli measured by a penile plethysmograph. Treatment involves group psychotherapy, social skills training, and aspects of behavioral and chemical treatments. The relapse prevention model is used to sustain changes made in treatment.

The Fremont Community Correctional Center is a halfway house located in Salt Lake City operated by the Utah Department of Corrections, with specialized treatment services for incest offenders. The Center for Family Development, a non-profit comprehensive sexual abuse treatment program, provides the treatment services under a contractual arrangement with the Department of Corrections. Forty beds are allocated to incest offenders (Brown & Brown, 1990). The Fremont program utilizes individual, group and family psychotherapy, as well as specific psychoeducational groups addressing human sexuality, communication skills, parenting and child development, and stress management. Families also are encouraged to become involved in the Parents United program offered through the Center for Family Development.

The program opened in 1983. At that time there was less use of behavioral techniques to assess and alter deviant sexual responses. Treatment focused on identifying personal and family dynamics contributing to abuse, and enhancing offenders' capacity for empathy and intimate adult relationships. Over time, the program has increased its utilization of behavioral techniques. Plethysmographic assessment and ongoing reassessment have become a standard part of treatment. These changes were made in response to increasing awareness that many offenders exhibit more sexual deviance than was initially recognized. Also, the program increasingly was referred more disturbed offenders due to overcrowding in the prison system. The use of a halfway house offers several advantages. The offender can be removed from his home but continue to work because comprehensive treatment is provided in the evening. Treatment, provided to other family members on an outpatient basis, can be coordinated and family members can be involved in their appropriate regimens.

TREATMENT EFFICACY

In the treatment of incest offenders, the primary goal is to prevent the subsequent occurrence of sexual abuse. Ultimately, treatment is judged effective only if it reduces recidivism more than would have occurred without intervention. Recidivism data, however, must be interpreted with extreme caution. Under-reporting of sexual crimes by victims is well established (Furby, Weinrott, & Blackshaw, 1989), so generally it is believed that reported recidivism rates are an underestimate of the true rate of re-offenses.

Quinsey (1977) cited factors considered predictive of recidivism. Behaviors exhibited in childhood include experiences of brutality, bed wetting, fire setting, cruelty to animals, and delinquent acts between the ages of 8 and 13. Relapse predictors from adult life include: (a) escalation of seriousness of offenses over time, (b) interrelated criminality with sex offenses, (c) sustained sexual excitement prior to the offenses, (d) lack of concern for the victim, (e) bizarre fantasies with minor offenses, (f) explosive outbursts, (g) the absence of psychosis, (h) the absence of alcohol consumption related to the offense, (i) low intelligence, (j) lack of warmth, and (k) the lack of social skills.

Although the factors described above are believed to predict recidivism, the published literature contains few references to studies that actually estimate recidivism rates. Furthermore, the studies that measure recidivism usually have followed molesters for brief periods of time and have included more than one type of sex offender in their samples.

Owen and Williams (1989) found that during the first year after completing treatment, 18% of 110 incest offenders were convicted of a felony offense. They did not indicate, however, what percentage of these re-offenses were for sex-related crimes. Freeman-Longo and Wall (1986) discussed a treatment program designed for chronic sex offenders. Results from the program indicate that fewer than 10% of the men who completed all phases of the program were convicted of subsequent sexual offenses. In other research, 51 convicted adult male incest and heterosexual pedophilic offenders participated in a therapeutic outcome study (Lang, Pugh, &

Langevin, 1988). Non-incest offenders showed more resistance in treatment to addressing their disturbed family relationships, their verbal hostility, irritability, and anger. Incest offenders changed the most in treatment and showed the lowest recidivism rates. Likewise, Hanson, Steffy, and Gauthier (1993) showed that incest offenders were reconvicted at a lower rate than other child molesters. Factors associated with increased recidivism were never being married and previous sexual offenses outside the family.

Long-term follow-ups are rare but noteworthy. Marshall and Barbaree (1988) collected recidivism data in Canada for a period of over 10 years to evaluate the effectiveness of a cognitive-behavioral treatment program. Police and children's aid society records provided data on 126 adult pedophiles. Findings indicate that recidivism increased over time and that there were lower rates of recidivism for treated adults. Contrary to expectations, non-incest pedophiles demonstrated the clearest treatment benefits, and indices of deviant sexual preferences did not predict treatment outcome. At the Oregon State Hospital the rate of recidivism for sex offenders over a six-year period was 10-14% (Holmes, 1991). The Fremont Community Correctional Center reported that 3 out of 250 men who completed the program were confirmed to have re-offended.

Finally, many treatment techniques suggested in the literature are based on single case studies and do not have empirical data to support them. Treatment is difficult to evaluate and more information is needed about the type of offenders who benefit from different techniques or a combination of techniques and under what conditions treatment is most effective.

Marshall (1996) has developed strategies to achieve the goal of assigning offenders to appropriate treatment programs. Based upon offender's criminal history, level of substance abuse, employment history, and pretreatment phallometric results, offenders are assigned to one of five levels of risk. Treatment is then tailored to offenders in each category of risk. It may include intensive outpatient treatment, inpatient treatment, and extensive post release supervision. Offenders whose needs are extensive and whose risk is above the moderate level would enter a comprehensive program. Other, low risk offenders would receive a more circumscribed program. Current research is under way to determine the validity of this system.

CONCLUSION

Until recently, there was a dearth of research on the characteristics and treatment needs of incest offenders. This is due, in part, to the prevailing societal view that incest offenders were incapable of change, a view which held that sexual abuse was ingrained in the personality of the offender and efforts to change would prove futile. However, mental health professionals are, with increasing frequency, viewing many offenders as capable of change. With a larger number of offenders being prosecuted and mandated into treatment, practitioners have begun to search for the most appropriate intervention strategies for these clients. Since the idea of treating incest offenders is relatively new, it is an evolving field.

All programs share the common goal of eliminating further sexual abuse. They also agree that the offender needs to take responsibility for his actions. Although all of the programs strive to help the men gain control of their behavior, they utilize different approaches to treatment. To date, no one approach has been found to be more effective than the others. Thus, consideration should be given to all of the basic approaches in the development of standards for this newly emerging service.

It is difficult to predict long-term success when treating incest offenders. A few programs have begun to publish evaluation data. Future research will build upon these preliminary findings and will improve the organization of services for offenders. Further research can help answer a crucial question: Which treatment methods are most effective in eliminating sexual abuse behaviors among which types of offenders?

REFERENCES

Abel, G., Becker, J., Cunningham-Rathner, J., Mittleman, M., & Rouleau, J. L. (1988). Multiple paraphiliac diagnoses among sex offenders. *Bulletin of the American Academy of Psychiatry and the Law, 16*, 153-168.

Abel, G., Becker, J., Murphy, W., & Flanagan, B. (1981). Identifying dangerous child molesters. In R. Stuart (Ed.), *Violent behavior: Social learning approaches to prediction, management, and treatment* (pp. 116-137). New York: Brunner/Mazel.

Abel, G., & Rouleau, J. (1990). The nature and extent of sexual assault. In W. Marshall, D. Laws, & H. Barbaree (Eds.), *Handbook of sexual assault: Issues, theories and treatment of the offender* (pp. 9-21). New York: Plenum.

Alpert, J. L. (1997). Sibling child sexual abuse: Research review and clinical implications. In R. Geffner, S. B. Sorenson, & P. K. Lundberg-Love (Eds.), *Violence and sexual abuse at home: Current issues in spousal battering and child maltreatment.* Binghamton, NY: The Haworth Press, Inc.

Barbaree, H. E., & Marshall, W. L. (1989). Erectile responses among heterosexual child molesters, father-daughter incest offenders, and matched non-offenders: Five Distinct age-preference profiles. *Canadian Journal of Behavioral Science, 21*, 70-82.

Becker, J. V., Blanchard, E. B., Murphy, W. D., & Coleman, E. (1978). Evaluating social skills of sexual aggressors. *Criminal Justice and Behavior, 514,* 357-367.

Berlin, F. S. (1982). Sex offenders: A biomedical perspective. In J. Greer & I. Stuart (Eds.), *The sexual aggressor: Current perspectives on treatment* (Vol. 1, pp. 83-126). New York: Van Nostrand Reinhold.

Berlin, F. S., & Meinecke, C. F. (1981). Treatment of sex offenders with antiandrogen medication: Conceptualization, review of treatment modalities, and preliminary findings. *American Journal of Psychiatry, 138,* 601-607.

Bradford, J. (1983). The hormonal treatment of sex offenders. *Bulletin of American Academy of Psychiatry and Law, 11,* 159-166.

Brecker, E. M. (1978). *Treatment programs for sex offenders.* Washington, DC: U.S. Dept. of Justice.

Brown, J. L., & Brown, G. S. (1990). The treatment of incest offenders in a community correctional facility. *Family Violence Bulletin, 6,* 12-16.

Carnes, P. (1990). Sexual addiction. In A. Horton, B. Johnson, L. Roundy & D. Williams (Eds.), *The incest perpetrator: A family no one wants to treat* (pp. 126-146). Newbury Park, CA: Sage.

Cole, W. (1992). Incest perpetrators, their assessment and treatment. *Clinical Forensic Psychiatry, 15,* 689-700.

Elliott, M. (1994). *Female sexual abuse of children.* New York, NY: Guilford Publications.

Erickson, W. D., Luxenberg, M. G., Walbek, N. H., & Seely, R. K. (1987). Frequency of MMPI two-point code types among sex offenders. *Journal of Consulting and Clinical Psychology, 55,* 566-570.

Finkelhor, D. (1986). Abusers: Special topics. In D. Finkelhor (Ed.), *A sourcebook on child sexual abuse* (pp. 555-584). Newbury Park, CA: Sage.

Finkelhor, D., & Hotaling, G. (1984). Sexual abuse in the national incidence study of child abuse and neglect. *Child Abuse and Neglect, 8,* 22-32.

Freeman-Longo, R. E., & Wall, R. V. (1986). Changing a lifetime of sexual crime. *Psychology Today, Mar. 20,* 58-64.

Furby, L., Weinrott, M. R., & Blackshaw, L. (1989). Sex offender recidivism: A review. *Psychological Bulletin, 105,* 3-30.

Giarretto, H., Giarretto, M., & Sgroi, S. M. (1985). Coordinated community treatment of incest. In A. W. Burgess, N. A. Groth, L. L. Holmstrom & S. M. Sgroi (Eds.), *Sexual abuse of children and adolescents* (pp. 231-240). Lexington, MA: Lexington Books.

Goeke, J. M. & Boyer, M. C. (1993). The failure to construct an MMPI-based incest perpetrator scale. *International Journal of Offender Therapy & Comparative Criminology, 37,* 271-277.

Groff, M. G., & Hubble, L. M. (1984). A comparison of father-daughter and stepfather-stepdaughter incest. *Criminal Justice and Behavior, 11,* 461-475.

Groth, N. A. (1978). Patterns of sexual assault against children and adolescents. In A. Burgess, A. Groth, L. Holmstrom & S. Sgroi (Eds.), *Sexual assault of children and adolescents* (pp. 3-24). Lexington, MA: D.C. Heath and Company.

Groth, N. A. (1983). Treatment of the sexual offender in a correctional institution. In J. Greer & I. Stuart (Eds.), *The sexual aggressor: Current perspectives on treatment* (pp. 160-176). New York: Van Nostrand Reinhold.

Hall, G. C., Proctor, W. C., & Nelson, G. M. (1988). Validity of physiological measures of pedophilic sexual arousal in a sexual offender population. *Journal of Consulting and Clinical Psychology, 56*, 118-122.

Hanson, R. F., Lipovsky, J. A., & Saunders, B. E. (1994). Characteristics of fathers in incest families. *Journal of Interpersonal Violence, 9*, 155-169.

Hanson, R. K., Gizzarelli, R., & Scott, H. (1994). The attitudes of incest offenders: Sexual entitlement and acceptance of sex with children. *Criminal Justice and Behavior, 21*, 187-202.

Hanson, R. K., Steffy, R. A., & Gauthier, R. (1993). Long-term recidivism of child molesters. *Journal of Consulting and Clinical Psychology, 61*, 646-652.

Hensen, D. C., & Rubin, H. B. (1971). Voluntary control of eroticism. *Journal of Applied Behavior Analysis, 4*, 37-44.

Holmes, R. M. (1991). *Sex crimes*. Newbury Park, CA: Sage.

Hopkins, R. E. (1993). An evaluation of social skills groups for sex offenders. *Issues in Criminology & Legal Psychology, 19*, 52-59.

Johnston, P., Hudson, S. M., & Marshall, W. L. (1992). The effects of masturbatory reconditioning with nonfamilial child molesters. *Behavior Research and Therapy, 30*, 559-561.

Lang, R. A., Langevin, R., Van Santen, V., & Billingsley, D. (1990). Marital relations in incest offenders. *Journal of Sex and Marital Therapy, 16*, 214-229.

Lang, R. A., Pugh, G. M., & Langevin, R. (1988). Treatment of incest and pedophilic offenders: A pilot study. *Behavioral Sciences and the Law, 6*, 239-255.

Langevin, R., Wortzman, G., Dickey, R., & Wright, P. (1988). Neuropsychological impairment in incest offenders. *Annals of Sex Research, 1*, 401-415.

Langevin, R., Wortzman, G., Wright, P., & Handy, L. (1989). Studies of brain damaged dysfunction in sex offenders. *Annals of Sex Research, 2*, 163-179.

Marshall, W. L. (1996). Assessment, treatment, and theorizing about sex offenders. *Criminal Justice and Behavior, 23*(1), 162-199.

Marshall, W. L. (1994). Treatment effects on denial and minimization in incarcerated sex offenders. *Behaviour Research & Therapy, 32*, 559-564.

Marshall, W. L., & Barbaree, H. E. (1988). The reduction of deviant arousal: Satiation treatment for sexual aggressors. *Criminal Justice and Behavior, 15*, 499-511.

Marshall, W. L., Barbaree, H. E., & Eccles, A. (1991). Early onset and deviant sexuality in child molesters. *Journal of Interpersonal Violence, 6*, 323-336.

Marshall, W. L., & Hall, G. N. (1995). The value of the MMPI in deciding forensic issues in accused sexual offenders. *Sexual Abuse: A Journal of Research and Treatment, 7*, 205-219.

Matthews, J. K., Matthews, R., & Speltz, K. (1991). Female sexual offenders: A typology. In M. J. Patton (Ed.), *Family sexual abuse, frontline research and evaluation* (pp. 225-243). Newbury Park, CA: Sage.

Mayer, A. (1988). *Sex offenders: Approaches to understanding and management*, Holmes Beach, FL: Learning Publications.

McCarty, L. (1986). Mother-child incest: Characteristics of the offender. *Child Welfare, 65*, 447-458.

Nelson, C., Miner, M., Marques, J., & Russell, K. (1988). Relapse prevention: A cognitive-behavioral model for treatment of the rapist and child molester. *Journal of Social Work and Human Sexuality, 7*, 125-143.

Overholser, J. C., & Beck, S. (1986). Multimethod assessment of rapists, child molesters, and three control groups on behavioral and psychological measures. *Journal of Consulting and Clinical Psychology, 54*, 682-687.

Owen, G., & Steele, N. (1991). Incest offenders after treatment. In M. Q. Patton (Ed.), *Family sexual abuse* (pp. 115-136). Newbury Park, CA: Sage.

Owen, G., & Williams, J. (1989). *Incest offenders after treatment: A follow-up study of men released from the Transitional Sex Offenders Program at Lino Lakes Correctional Facility.* Saint Paul, MN: Wilder Foundation.

Pawlak, A. E., Boulet, J. R., & Bradford, J. M. (1991). Discriminant analysis of a sexual-functioning inventory with intrafamilial and extrafamilial child molesters. *Archives of Sexual Behavior, 20*, 27-34.

Peters, J. J., & Roether, H. A. (1972). Group psychotherapy for probationed sex offenders. In H. L. P. Resnik & M. E. Wolfgang (Eds.), *Sexual behaviors* (pp. 255-266). Boston: Little, Brown.

Quinsey, V. L. (1973). Methodological issues in evaluating the effectiveness of aversion therapies for institutionalized child molesters. *The Canadian Psychologist, 14*, 350-361.

Quinsey, V. L. (1977). The assessment and treatment of child molesters: A review. *Canadian Psychological Review, 18*, 204-220.

Rosen, R. C., & Fracher, J. C. (1983). Tension-reduction training in the treatment of compulsive sex offenders. In J. G. Greer & I. R. Stuart (Eds.), *The sexual aggressors* (pp. 144-159). New York: Van Nostrand Reinhold.

Scott, R. L., & Stone, D. A. (1986). MMPI profile constellations in incest families. *Journal of Consulting and Clinical Psychology, 54*, 364-368.

Trepper, T., & Barrett, M. J. (1989). *Systemic treatment of incest: A therapeutic handbook.* New York: Brunner/Mazel.

Valliant, P. M., & Antonowicz, D. H. (1992). Rapists, incest offenders, and child molesters in treatment: cognitive and social skills training. *International Journal of Offender Therapy and Comparative Criminology, 36*, 221-230.

Vaupel, S. C., & Goeke, J. M. (1994). Incest perpetrator MMPI profiles and the variable of offense admission status. *International Journal of Offender Therapy & Comparative Criminology, 38*, 69-77.

Wright, P., Nobrega, J., Langevin, R., & Wortzman, G. (1990). Brain density and symmetry in pedophilic and sexually aggressive offenders. *Annals of Sex Research, 3*, 319-328.

Index

Page numbers in italics indicate figures; page numbers followed by t indicate tables.

Abel, G., 339
Abreaction, 319,327
Abuse, terminology, 2-3
Accidental deaths, 201
Addictive behaviors, 301,347
Adolescents
  risk factors for abuse, 165,172
  sexually maltreated
    impact, 298
    treatment, 10-11,284-286,289t
  in violent families, 258
Adult sexual abuse survivors. *See*
    also Child sexual
    maltreatment
  dissociative identity disorders in,
    311-331
    assessment, 316-318
    diagnosis and etiology,
      312-316
    treatment, 12-13,318-330
  partners of, 307-308
  post-traumatic effects, 296-297
  sexual and interpersonal issues
    impact of incest, 293-302
    treatment, 303-308
  of sibling incest, 271-273
Affirmation games, 288t,289t
Age
  of children
    homicide victims, 193t,194,
      200,202
    as risk factor for abuse,
      161-168,*169,170,*175,
      182t-187t

  in sibling sexual maltreatment,
    266-267
Aggressiveness
  in children of battered women,
    252-253
  interventions, 234-236
  modeling by parents, 231-232
Alcohol abuse. *See* Substance abuse
Alpert, J. L., 10,263
Alternate personalities. *See*
    Dissociative identity
    disorder
American Association for Marriage
    and Family Therapy, 29
American Association for Protecting
    Children, 152-153
American Psychological Association,
    32
American Psychological Association
    Ethical Standards, 46
Ammerman, R. T., 8,207,214
Amnesia, dissociative, 313
Analogue study, of therapist response
    to spouse/partner
    maltreatment, 27-39
Anatomically detailed dolls, 10
Anger control, 218-219,254-255,
    344-345
Anwar, R. A. H., 82
Anxiety, in children of battered
    women, 232
Anxiety management training, 220,
    320-321
Arousal-aggression theory, 68-73

characteristics, 336-342
treatment, 342-352
risk factors for, 155,161,
162t-163t,165,168,183t
sibling, 10,263-273
clinical implications, 273
effects, 269-273
literature review, 264-273
scope of problem, 267-269
statistics, 264
terminology, 265-267
suggestibility, 10
treatment, 10-11,277-290
assessment, 278-280
family, 286-287
goals, 280-282
group, 284-286,288t-289t
hypnosis, 287
individual, 283-284
women offenders with history of,
121,122
Child witnesses. *See* Child observers
Cicchetti, D., 210t,211
Co-consciousness, 325-327
Co-dependent behavior, 301
Cognition, in arousal-aggression
theory, 68-73
Cognitive-behavioral therapy
for children of battered women,
236,238
for incest offenders, 345-346,350
Collmer, C. W., 209,210t
Colorado, 133
Competence
in child observers, 250-253
defined, 248-249
Comprehensive Behavioral
Treatment, 216-221
Confidentiality, 51-52
Conflict, coping strategies in child
observers, 251-253
Conflict Tactics Scale, 60,85
Connell, J. P., 248-250
Contracts, in spouse/partner
maltreatment, 137

Control beliefs, in child observers,
253,254-255
Cook, A. R., 28,29
Cook, D. R., 28,29
Copeland, A. R., 192
Counseling. *See*
Intervention/treatment
County metropolitan status, as risk
factor for child abuse, 163t,
*164,167,170,*171,176
Couples/family therapy
for incest offenders, 344
for sexually maltreated children,
286-287
shared responsibility perspective,
28-29,46
for spouse/partner maltreatment
as appropriate option, 144-146
controversy, 7,135
solution-focused, 135-144
Courtois, C. A., 13,293,298,299,303
Courts. *See* Custody; Divorce; Legal
issues
Cousin incest, 269
Covert sensitization, 345-346
Cultural factors, 15,72-73. *See also*
Race/ethnicity
Custody
current issues, 9-10
joint, 107
spouse/partner maltreatment and,
106-109

Death. *See* Homicide
Decision making in
co-consciousness, 326
De Jong, A. R., 265,266
Denial, in spouse/partner
maltreatment, 136-137
Depersonalization disorder, 313
Depo-Provera (medroxyprogesterone
acetate), 346-347
Depression
in battered women, 236-237
in children of battered women,
232

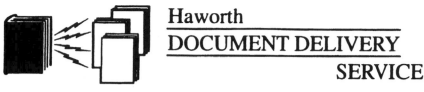

Haworth
DOCUMENT DELIVERY
SERVICE

This valuable service provides a single-article order form for any article from a Haworth journal.

- *Time Saving:* No running around from library to library to find a specific article.
- *Cost Effective:* All costs are kept down to a minimum.
- *Fast Delivery:* Choose from several options, including same-day FAX.
- *No Copyright Hassles:* You will be supplied by the original publisher.
- *Easy Payment:* Choose from several easy payment methods.

Open Accounts Welcome for ...
- Library Interlibrary Loan Departments
- Library Network/Consortia Wishing to Provide Single-Article Services
- Indexing/Abstracting Services with Single Article Provision Services
- Document Provision Brokers and Freelance Information Service Providers

---

MAIL or *FAX* THIS ENTIRE ORDER FORM TO:

Haworth Document Delivery Service
The Haworth Press, Inc.
10 Alice Street
Binghamton, NY 13904-1580

or FAX: 1-800-895-0582
or CALL: 1-800-342-9678
9am-5pm EST

PLEASE SEND ME PHOTOCOPIES OF THE FOLLOWING SINGLE ARTICLES:

1) Journal Title: _____

    Vol/Issue/Year: _____ Starting & Ending Pages: _____

    Article Title: _____

2) Journal Title: _____

    Vol/Issue/Year: _____ Starting & Ending Pages: _____

    Article Title: _____

3) Journal Title: _____

    Vol/Issue/Year: _____ Starting & Ending Pages: _____

    Article Title: _____

4) Journal Title: _____

    Vol/Issue/Year: _____ Starting & Ending Pages: _____

    Article Title: _____

(See other side for Costs and Payment Information)

COSTS: Please figure your cost to order quality copies of an article.

1. Set-up charge per article: $8.00
   ($8.00 × number of separate articles) _____

2. Photocopying charge for each article:

   1-10 pages: $1.00 _____

   11-19 pages: $3.00 _____

   20-29 pages: $5.00 _____

   30+ pages: $2.00/10 pages _____

3. Flexicover (optional): $2.00/article _____

4. Postage & Handling: US: $1.00 for the first article/
   $.50 each additional article _____

   Federal Express: $25.00 _____

   Outside US: $2.00 for first article/
   $.50 each additional article _____

5. Same-day FAX service: $.35 per page _____

                              GRAND TOTAL: _____

METHOD OF PAYMENT: (please check one)

❑ Check enclosed   ❑ Please ship and bill. PO # _____
                   (sorry we can ship and bill to bookstores only! All others must pre-pay)

❑ Charge to my credit card: ❑ Visa; ❑ MasterCard; ❑ Discover;
                             ❑ American Express;

Account Number: _____ Expiration date: _____

Signature: X_____

Name: _____ Institution: _____

Address: _____

_____

City: _____ State: _____ Zip: _____

Phone Number: _____ FAX Number: _____

MAIL or *FAX* THIS ENTIRE ORDER FORM TO:

Haworth Document Delivery Service	**or FAX:** 1-800-895-0582
The Haworth Press, Inc.	**or CALL:** 1-800-342-9678
10 Alice Street	9am-5pm EST)
Binghamton, NY 13904-1580	